To: Art and Trudi
with regard and affection
Q. Meeh...
7/13/09

FAITH, FORTITUDE, AND FEAR

A Rational Approach to the Jewish History

FAITH, FORTITUDE, AND FEAR

A Rational Approach to the Jewish History

HOOSHANG MESHKINPOUR, M.D.

University of California, Irvine

ISBN: 1-4196-1138-0
Library of Congress Control Number: 2005907432

Cover photo used with permission by photographer
Copyright© 2005 Joseph Fung www.valerieandjoe.com

To order additional copies of this book, please contact.
Publisher: BookSurge, LLC
North Charleston, South Carolina
www.booksurge.com
1-866-308-6235
orders@booksurge.com

To the memory of my father
Habibolah Meshkinpour, 1911-1991
From whom I received the inspiration of this
undertaking

Genuine tragedy is a case not of right against wrong but of right against right.

— Hegel

ACKNOWLEDGMENTS

I am grateful to my wife, who patiently dealt with me for almost a decade while I buried myself in books, periodicals, and volumes of encyclopedia or spent long hours searching the cyber media. Without her encouragement it would have been a more distressing task. I am also indebted to all those friends who caringly reviewed these pages and provided me with their valuable and constructive comments.

Contents

FAITH, FORTITUDE, AND FEAR

PREFACE

The history of the Jews, like the history of other people, is cloaked in the guise of metaphors, legends, and myths. Indeed, in many instances the mythological encounters have replaced the historic events. It is quite conceivable that the mythical tales might have been life giving to a powerful collective unconscious, born of social necessity, by which humans have tried to achieve in mind what is unachievable in the real world. However, the distinction of this early *subjective* thinking from the modern, rational, and *objective* analysis of historical events is of prime importance. Therefore, the purpose of writing this book was to learn which parts of the Jewish history are based on the documented historical and anthropological evidence and which portions are derived from myth.

   Faith, Fortitude, and Fear looks upon the Jewish history through three principal premises. First, the Jewish history, like the history of others, is deeply influenced by the ever-changing social forces and indeed is not a predetermined divine drama. Second, in spite of their higher rate of inbreeding, Jews do not represent a homogeneous ethnic group with common physical and biological characteristics. In fact, the similarity between Jews and the gentiles they live among is more pronounced than between Jews living in different geographic locations. *For instance, there are vast differences between Yemenis and German Jews.* Hence, in my walk through Jewish history, I have set aside the myth of Jews as a distinct race. Third, except for a limited period in their history, Jews neither lived within sovereign borders nor spoke a common language through most of their history, and therefore they do not represent a nation. I have diligently distinguished between the "nation of Israel" and the mythical encounter of "nation of Jews" through these pages.

The prominent characteristic of this book is its balanced, objective, and impartial analysis of the Jewish history. The principal theme of the book is not a lachrymose presentation of the Jewish history, nor does it underscore unnecessarily the negative events. The book circumvents the glorification of any aspect of the Jewish history. Above all, it avoids repeating comments or statements with anti-Semitic connotations. On the matters of controversy, I painfully tried to avoid any one-sidedness and expressed both sides of the issue, leaving the conclusion to the reader. *Faith, Fortitude, and Fear* is not a comprehensive history of the Jews, but the structure of the book is chronological and highlights most of the important events. It was written to attract both Jewish and non-Jewish readers. It is valuable to Jewish readers who are interested in learning their true history without going through the inconvenience of unraveling historiography and mythology. The book is also aimed at non-Jewish readers who are interested in knowing the small group of people who have had an important impact on other civilizations. Particularly at this historic juncture, knowing about the Jews and their history is instrumental in understanding the centuries-old conflict in the Middle East.

The book begins with the Hebrews' simple nomadic life, the story of the patriarchs, the slavery of the tribes in Egypt, their exodus, the conquest of the Promised Land, and finally the rise and fall of ancient Israel. Although recent studies, archaeological and textual, have questioned the historicity of the patriarchal accounts, and some biblical scholars have viewed the reign of Saul as the first reference of historical relevance to the "people of Israel," these accounts have not been widely endorsed by most scholars. Nonetheless, these narratives, even though they were mere mythology, are considered the fundamental myths of origin for the Jews. Therefore, I abridged this part as it appears in the Old Testament of the Bible at the beginning of chapter 1. After reviewing the religion of the Israelites, which to a great extent reflects the harsh living conditions of these people and was instrumental in helping them cope with their struggle for survival, I present a brief insight into the origin of the Hebrew Bible. A critical appraisal of the recent archaeological studies and their impact on the controversy over the Bible as a historical document versus a literary masterpiece is the next topic presented in this chapter. The chapter concludes with an analysis of the Hebrew culture and the Mosaic Ten Commandments.

The second chapter commences with the fall of Jerusalem, Babylonian exile, and the return. This chapter focuses on a major crisis in the religion that is characterized by the rise of many religious-political sects, such as the Qumran, Pharisees, and Sadducees, and the many bloody struggles among them. We learn that the concepts of heaven and hell were not originally in the religion of the Hebrews but were adopted from Persian and Greek cultures during this period. Paradise was then promised to those who participated in these struggles and were killed. Similarly, festivals like Pesach, Rosh-Ha-Shanah and Hanukah, which were initially celebrated to highlight certain important natural events, evolved into important religious holidays. The struggle among rival sects eventually ended with the rise of Christianity, the destruction of the Second Temple of Jerusalem, and the beginning of a long period of exile for the Jews. It was during this period that the Talmud, the interpretations of the written codes in the Old Testament and one of the most complex productions of the human mind, was written and then served as the fundamental principles for life in the Diaspora.

Chapter 3 reviews the life of the Jews in the East and the land of Christianity through the Middle Ages. We learn how the ongoing war between religion and philosophy in the land of Islam reached a turning point, and faith was looked upon through reason. Therefore, influenced by the rationalist school of Islamic theology, the Mu`tazilites, Maimonides, and others exercised the reason and logic to defend the faith. We also learn that the Jewish life of Christendom was quite unpredictable, and social calm was periodically interrupted by unpleasant events. The impact of the Crusades and Inquisition, expulsion of Jews from Spain and other countries, and life in the ghettos are among the most prominent events in the Jewish history of the Middle Ages. The Jewish lack of interest in agriculture and the Jews' interest in trade were both molded through the Middle Ages. A

detailed discussion of the economic and social factors that forced the
Jews of the medieval European communities out of agriculture and
into trade and usury brings the chapter to its close.

Chapter 4 describes the Jews at the dawn of modernity. The
seventeenth century was a turning point in the Jewish history that was
signified by three prominent social upheavals. Renewed interest in
messianic movements, the Hasidic movement promoting theology
without rabbis, and the tide of heresy challenging the religious
tradition were indeed instrumental in disrupting the conventional
Jewish establishment of the Middle Ages and paved the road to
modernity. These three social events, despite their characteristic
differences, all had one thing in common: they aimed at the
traditional Jewish establishment of the Middle Ages. Before the
seventeenth century, Jewish communities were homogenous, the
Jewish identity was well defined, and in the eyes of Jews the Jewish
history was a predetermined divine setting. After this turning point
and under the influence of these three major social upheavals, the
Jewish communities lost their homogeneity, the Jewish identity
became a subject of interpretation, and the Jewish history was viewed
as a dynamic process that was deeply influenced by social, political,
and economic forces.

The Age of Enlightenment in Europe and its expression in
Jewish communities, known as the Haskalah movement, and the great
French Revolution, as a prominent manifestation of this intellectual
progress, had a significant impact on the liberation of Jews from life
in the ghettos, and granted them their civil rights. Concurrently, the
liberation of Jews from the yoke of Talmudic teachings, the only
educational system that had governed Jewish communities for more
than fourteen centuries, drastically reduced the traditional
homogeneity of Jewish thinking. The rise of reform in Judaism and
the evolution of Jewish thought in the eighteenth and nineteenth
centuries introduced different denominations among Jews. These
factors, which are highlighted in chapter 5, were instrumental in the
emancipation of the Jews. These were among the principal dynamics
that brought the Jews into the mainstream of the gentile society and
consequently introduced hundreds and thousands of Jewish original
thinkers to the arts, science, and literature over the next three
centuries.

Chapter 6 focuses on the fundamental and yet complicated issue of hatred toward Jews. The many facets of anti-Semitism and its effect on world Jewry are the main themes of this chapter. The chapter commences with a review of the historic roots of hatred in the pagan period and the rationale for hating Jews in early Christianity, through the Middle Ages and during the Protestant Reformation period. The anti-Jewish sentiment in the land of Islam and its origin, which is substantially different from the anti-Semitism of Christendom, is the next subject in this chapter. The ethnic character of the Jews that historically has made them an attractive prey for anti-Semitism is another focus of the chapter. Here I have elaborated on the contradiction within the core of the Jewish ethnic character in which Jews have set a high goal for mankind on earth, yet they have avoided almost all the political events of the past twenty centuries. Anti-Semitism as a political instrument, state anti-Semitism and its impact on the persecution of the Eastern European Jews, and white supremacy are among the other fascinating subjects of discussion in this chapter. The chapter ends with a discussion of subtle anti-Semitism, another facet of anti-Jewish hatred.

Chapter 7 is devoted to major social issues of world Jewry in the modern era. We learn that in the early twentieth century, Jews, for the first time, initiated and became responsible for arranging for a homeland, rather than expecting the arrival of the Messiah to achieve the task, as they had done in the past. This resulted in the rise of political Zionism as a presumptive remedy to anti-Semitism. The position of the social democracy movement of the nineteenth century on the "Jewish issue," with a particular emphasis on the differences between the viewpoints of Karl Marx and those of other pioneers of the left movement on this matter, is the next topic in this chapter. The philosophical doctrine of National Socialism and the Holocaust and its aftermath that eventually resulted in the establishment of the State of Israel brings this chapter to its end.

Finally, chapter 8 explores the Jews in the postmodern era with an in-depth discussion on the crisis of the Jewish identity. The chapter begins with the over half a century old complicated and sensitive Arab-Israel issue. I have presented the key interactive players of the conflict and have painfully tried to provide a fair and balanced picture of the entire tragedy. Here I explain why this subject has become so complicated and why a simpler resolution of the conflict is not yet on the horizon. The relations of the State of Israel with that of world Jewry and the conflicting issues among them are then presented. This subject is followed by a discussion of Jewish fundamentalism and its relation to the rest of Jewry, a topic of interest and concern. The changing pattern of Jewish demography in America is yet another topic that has attracted the attention of many modern thinkers. Here the plausible factors that shrank the Jewish population of the postmodern era are reviewed and their conceivable impacts on the Jewish societies of the future are analyzed. The crisis of the Jewish identity with the controversy over the definition of "who is a Jew?" at its core and its ramifications for the future of the Jewish communities and world Jewry in general brings the book to its close.

Chapter One

THE ORIGIN OF A PEOPLE

The great saga of the Bible is a family drama that transforms itself into a historic spectacle. The story begins in the Garden of Eden and, after going through several generations and the account of Noah's flood, focuses on the fate of a single family, that of Abraham, the first patriarch. God makes a covenant with Abraham and promises him the land: "To your seed have I given this land, from the river of Egypt to the great river, the river Euphrates."[1] Abraham marries Sarah, who at age ninety gives birth to Isaac. Jacob, Isaac's son, the third-generation patriarch, wrestles with God or an angel and receives the name Israel, meaning "he who struggled with God." The divine promise of land once again is reiterated to Jacob: "I am the Lord, the God of Abraham and the God of Isaac, your father; the land on which you lie I will give to you and to your descendants; and your descendants shall be like the dust of the earth, and you shall spread abroad to the west and to the east and to the north and to the south; and by you and your descendants shall all the families of the earth bless themselves. Behold, I am with you and will keep you wherever you go, and will bring you back to this land; for I will not leave you until I have done that of which I have spoken to you."[2]

---

[1] Genesis 15:18.
[2] Genesis 28:13–15.

The Story of the Hebrew Tribes and the Exodus

Jacob marries two daughters of Laban and fathers twelve sons from his wives and two of their maidservants. In the biblical narratives, the twelve Hebrew[3] tribes are presented as the descendents of the twelve sons of Jacob: Asher, Benjamin, Dan, Gad, Issachar, Joseph, Judah, Levi, Naphtali, Reuben, Simeon, and Zebulun. Among them, Joseph, Jacob's favorite, dreams he would reign over the entire family, thereby provoking his brothers' resentment. Reuben and Judah dissuaded their brothers, who were determined to murder Joseph, to not do so. Nonetheless, the brothers sell Joseph to a caravan of Ishmaelites, who in turn take him to Egypt and sell him as a slave. Joseph, the fourth patriarch, achieves a position of eminence in Egypt and reunites the children of Israel. Nonetheless, Patriarch Jacob, while on his deathbed, confers the royal birthright to Judah and not to his favorite son, Joseph: "Judah, you are he whom your brothers shall praise; your hand shall be in the neck of your enemies; your father's children shall bow down in your presence."[4] According to the biblical accounts, time changes and a new pharaoh comes to power who does not know Joseph and fears that the Hebrews may betray Egypt to one of her enemies. Therefore, the Israelites endured 430 years of slavery in the land of Egypt. Eventually, Moses and Aaron, the fourth-generation descendants of Jacob's son Levi, lead the exodus of Israelites out of slavery in Egypt. The biblical narrative of the patriarchs is in essence a magnificent story of both a family and a nation.[5]

Although historic and archaeological investigations support some of the biblical accounts about the ancestors of the Hebrews, the main intention of scribers who compiled these scriptures centuries later was indeed the theology rather than the ancient history.[6]

---

[3] The term "Hebrew" originates from *Ivrim*, referring to "people from the other side of the river." Some have considered *Habiru* or *Habiri* as the origin of this term. In Genesis 40:15, Joseph explains to the Egyptians that he was kidnapped in the "land of Hebrew," and in Exodus 2:6, Pharaoh's sister introduces Moses as a "Hebrew boy."

[4] Genesis 49:8.

[5] I. Finkelstein and N. A. Silberman, *The Bible Unearthed: Archeology's New Vision of Ancient Israel and the Origin of its Sacred Texts* (New York: Free Press, 2001), 27.

[6] J.C.H. Laughlin, *Archeology and the Bible* (London: Routledge, 2000), 76.

Therefore, from a historical point of view, these encounters should be interpreted cautiously. For instance, Moses, in a gathering of Hebrews, says, "My father was a wandering Aramaic." This statement obviously refers to the nomadic background of the Hebrews and their Aramaic origin. However, historical evidence indicates that their background was not exclusively Aramaic.[7] In addition to the Aramaeans, who were a group of Semitic tribes that had invaded the eastern coast of the Mediterranean Sea around the second millennium BCE, the ancestry of the Israelites was also comprised of Amorites and Hittites.[8]

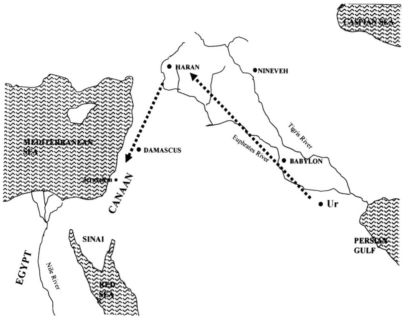

The Hebrew Migrations According to the Biblical Narratives

According to the biblical narratives, the ancestors of the Israelites were initially living in the Ur region of Sumer, around the

---

[7] W. G. Dever, *What Did the Biblical Writers Know, and When Did They Know It?* (Grand Rapids, MI: Eerdmans, 2001), 122.
[8] The Hittites were among the most powerful and civilized of the early Indo-European peoples inhabiting Asia Minor and north Syria. The Bible connects them with the Canaanites.

southern bank of the Euphrates River.[9] They then migrated north and west and settled in Carrahe or Haran, a colony of the Babylonian Empire over a thousand years BCE and from there later migrated to the south and west eventually inhabited in Canaan, the area west of the Jordan River.[10] The social and economical structure expressed in Genesis nonetheless corresponds to the Middle Bronze Age, or the period between 2000 and 1550 BCE.[11]

Contemporary archeological studies, however, suggest that the Israelites were native Canaanites.[12] They probably represent the modern humans who had migrated from East Africa into these regions as early as 100,000 years ago.[13] Alternatively, they were an extension of the Stone Age Europeans who had migrated south during the last glacial period, about ten thousand years ago.[14,15] Indeed, Neanderthal remains discovered near Haifa and around the Sea of Galilee strongly suggest the area was inhabited as early as forty thousand years ago.[16] It is conceivable that a class within the Canaanite society, the Yahweh worshippers among them, became known as the Hebrews or the Israelites. It is also plausible that some Hebrews escaped forced labor in Egypt and joined the Canaanite settlers. Eventually, the religion and mythology of the foreigners from Egypt became the religion of Israel.[17]

The history of the tribes, as the descendants of Jacob, must also be viewed with great caution.[18] In order to tell a continuous story of the tribes, Jewish scribes who compiled and edited the Old Testament in the sixth and fifth centuries BCE often substituted the historic events with those of legends.

---

[9] Genesis 11:31.

[10] Genesis 12:5.

[11] J.C.H. Laughlin, *Archeology and the Bible* (London: Routledge, 2000), 73.

[12] K. Armstrong, *Jerusalem: One City, Three Faiths* (New York: Ballantine Books, 1997), 24.

[13] L. L. Cavalli-Sforza, *Genes, Peoples and Languages* (New York, North Point Press, 2000), 61

[14] Ibid., 75

[15] W. Durant, *The Story of Civilization: Our Oriental Heritage* (New York: Simon & Schuster, 1963), 300.

[16] Ibid.

[17] K. Armstrong, *Jerusalem: One City, Three Faiths* (New York: Ballantine Books, 1997), 24.

[18] *Encyclopedia Encarta*, "Jews," CD-ROM, 1994, Microsoft Corporation.

According to Naomi Glatzer, late professor of religion, the story of the tribes is buried under the ashes of the biblical scribes' emotional sentiments.[19] For instance, Reuben, Simeon, Levi, and Judah are from the same mother, and the tribes they represent have a friendlier relationship in comparison with the other tribes.

Israelites and the Neighboring People

On the other hand, since Asher and Gad were the children of a maidservant, they represented the tribes that were always subordinate. In another example, the first contract between Hebrew tribes and

---

[19]Ibid.

Syrians, through which the borders of their pastures north to Gilead[20] were eliminated, has been described as a contract between two individuals, Jacob and Laban: "These women are my daughters, and these children are mine and these flocks and all that you have, all are mine. So how could I harm my own daughters and grandchildren? Come now and we will sign a peace pact, you and I, and will live by its terms.[21] And Jacob said to his brothers, gather stones; and they took stones, and made a heap; and they ate there upon the heap.[22] This heap shall be witness, and this pillar shall be witness, that I will not pass over this heap to you, and that you shall not pass over this heap and this pillar to me, for harm."[23]

Chronology is yet another major problem in the core of the biblical narratives. Patriarchal figures have unusually long life spans, and there are contradictions in their sequence. For instance, Abraham lives 175 years,[24] Isaac 180,[25] Jacob 147,[26] and Joseph 110 years.[27] Moses and Aaron are introduced as the fourth-generation descendant of Jacob's son Levi,[28] while Joshua, a contemporary of Moses and Aaron, is presented as the twelfth-generation descendant of Jacob's son Joseph.[29]

A number of recent archaeological studies have, however, raised questions about the historicity of patriarchal accounts. In the opinion of many biblical scholars, the story of the patriarchs represents a mythology rather than a true historic event. Nonetheless, the mythological nature of the story of patriarchs has not been widely endorsed by most scholars.[30] Unless a new body of information, archaeological and textual, becomes available, the debate over historicity versus the mythological nature of biblical narratives of the patriarchs shall continue.

---

[20] Gilead was the region east of the Jordan River, north of the Moab plains, and south of Bashan.
[21] Genesis 31:42–44.
[22] Genesis 31:46.
[23] Genesis 31:52.
[24] Genesis 25:7.
[25] Genesis 35:27.
[26] Genesis 47:28.
[27] Genesis 50:26.
[28] Exodus 6:16–20.
[29] Chronicles I 7:24–27.
[30] J.C.H. Laughlin, *Archeology and the Bible* (London: Routledge, 2000), 73, 75.

Some of the Hebrew tribes, probably those who belonged to the house of Joseph or the tribe of Levi,[31] wandered in search of green land toward Egypt between 1694 and 1600 BCE. This migration probably occurred during the reign of the Hyksos dynasty, the Canaanites who had conquered Egypt.[32] Migrations from Canaan, with its unpredictable climate, to the fertile land of Egypt and the Nile, as a reliable source of fresh water, were not unusual and took place many times in the past.[33] Indeed, archaeological sources substantiate the migrations from Canaan to Egypt as described in the book of Exodus.[34] In fact, these journeys were the characteristic feature of the nomadic life of the Hebrew tribes. The kingdom of Hyksos was eventually brought to an end around 1570 BCE, when the Hebrew were persecuted and forced into slavery. According to the Bible, the Hebrew were in bondage from 1650 to 1220 BCE, 430 years altogether, a number that has been supported by the account of British archaeologist Sir William Petrie.[35] According to the biblical narratives, Moses, the first great prophet who had entered into a covenant with Yahweh[36] on Sinai, led the exodus of Hebrews from the land of Egypt.

The Exodus as a historical event, the way it appears in the biblical narratives, has been a subject of intense debate. There are controversies on a number of questions. Did Exodus really happen? What was the magnitude of this migration? What was the timing of Exodus? Where was the exact location of "crossing the sea"? What was the true motivation behind the Exodus of Hebrew slaves from the land of Egypt? Did they truly wander in the wilderness? And finally,

---

[31] R. E. Friedman, *Who Wrote the Bible?* (New York: HarperSanFrancisco, 1987), 82.

[32] I. Finkelstein and N. A. Silberman, *The Bible Unearthed: Archeology's New Vision of Ancient Israel and the Origin of Its Sacred Texts* (New York: Free Press, 2001), 55.

[33] Ibid.

[34] Ibid., 56.

[35] W. Petrie and M. Flinders, *Egypt and Israel* (London: 1925), quoted in W. Durant, *The Story of Civilization: Our Oriental Heritage* (New York: Simon & Schuster, 1963), 301.

[36] The origin of the term *Yahweh*, the God of the Hebrews, is not clear. Moses speaks of Yahweh for the first time in Exodus 3:14. Yahweh has been mentioned about seven thousand times in the Old Testament of the Bible. In addition, terms such as "Adonai" and "Elohim" have been used interchangeably with Yahweh. However, all three terms have been translated as "Lord" in the English version of the Bible.

in the aftermath of Exodus, was the Promised Land conquered by force?

Indeed, recent archaeological investigations have failed to substantiate the occurrence and the magnitude of the Exodus as it appears in the Bible.[37-38] Archaeological records neither found any reference to Exodus in the Egyptian monuments[39] nor on the Sinai Peninsula, where the presumptive passage into Canaan occurred.[40] Numerous archaeological excavations in this region have failed to yield any evidence of the migration of Hebrews,[41] yet pastoral activities belonging to the third millennium BCE have been disclosed in the same areas.[42] Other scholars have pointed out that migration of a large number of Hebrew slaves, six hundred thousand men on foot with their women and children,[43] against the will of their Egyptian masters did not seem possible in the thirteenth century BCE when Egyptians had numerous strongholds on the passage to Canaan that they were defending militarily.[44] Some historians, however, believe that the lack of findings in these passages was due to the fact that the number of Hebrew slaves in Egypt did not exceed over a few thousand,[45,46] and therefore their departure did not make a substantial impact on the economy and social life of the Egyptians. Indeed, William G. Dever, in contrast to the school of *revisionists* in biblical studies who view the Hebrew Bible exclusively as literature,[47] prefers

---

[37] J.C.H. Laughlin, *Archeology and the Bible* (London: Routledge, 2000), 87.

[38] W. G. Dever, *What Did the Biblical Writers Know, and When Did They Know It?* (Grand Rapids, MI: Eerdmans, 2001), 99.

[39] W. Durant, *The Story of Civilization: Our Oriental Heritage* (New York: Simon & Schuster, 1935), 301.

[40] I. Finkelstein and N. A. Silberman, *The Bible Unearthed: Archeology's New Vision of Ancient Israel and the Origin of Its Sacred Texts* (New York: Free Press, 2001), 62.

[41] J.C.H. Laughlin, *Archeology and the Bible* (London: Routledge, 2000), 91.

[42] Ibid., 63.

[43] Exodus 12:37; Numbers 1:45–46.

[44] I. Finkelstein and N. A. Silberman, *The Bible Unearthed: Archeology's New Vision of Ancient Israel and the Origin of Its Sacred Texts* (New York: Free Press, 2001), 60.

[45] R. E. Friedman, *Who Wrote the Bible?* (New York: HarperSanFrancisco, 1987), 82.

[46] C. J. Humphreys, "How Many People Were in the Exodus from Egypt?" *Science and Christian Belief* 12:1 (2000): 17–34.

[47] W. G. Dever, *What Did the Biblical Writers Know, and When Did They Know It?* (Grand Rapids, MI: Eerdmans, 2001), 10.

the notion of a smaller-scale migration. He argues vigorously in favor of some historical truth to the biblical narratives. Dever believes that many in the tribe of Joseph indeed originated from Egypt. In his opinion, scribers who later wrote about Exodus exaggerated its dimensions and presented the migration of the house of Joseph as the exodus of all the Israelites, thus staging it as the chronicle of Israel's origin.[48] The biblical insistence upon the foreign origin of Israelites, as people who migrated from Egypt in search of their homeland, is not widely supported; rather it is more plausible that they were the native Canaanites who were joined by a trivial group from Egypt.[49]

The other debatable issue is about the timing of Exodus. In contrast to what has been documented in the book of Exodus, it is not conceivable that the migration of Hebrew slaves of that magnitude could have happened during the reign of Ramses II (1279–1212 BCE), when Egypt was at its peak of authority and in fact was the leading power of the world.[50] More likely, the Exodus must have taken place at the time of his descendant, Pharaoh Merneptah (1212–1202 BCE), who was ill and reigned over a very unstable government.[51]

In spite of extensive investigations, the exact location of the "crossing the sea" is also not known. Some, however, have tried to reconcile this biblical encounter and what might have been a plausible explanation by suggesting that possible crossing sites were the Gulf of Aqaba, the Lake of Serbonis in the north of the Sinai Peninsula, Lake Manzala west of Port Said, the Bitter Lakes between the Gulf of Suez in the south and the Delta estuary in the north, the Gulf of Suez, and even the salt lakes.[52, 53] There are many spots of shallow water in the Lake of Serbonis, adjacent to the Mediterranean Sea, that meet the characteristics of the crossing site[54] as they have been described in the

---

[48] Ibid., 121.

[49] K. Armstrong, *Jerusalem: One City, Three Faiths* (New York: Ballantine Books, 1996), 24.

[50] P. A. Johnson, *A History of the Jews* (New York: HarperPerennial, 1987), 25.

[51] I. Finkelstein and N. A. Silberman, *The Bible Unearthed: Archeology's New Vision of Ancient Israel and the Origin of Its Sacred Texts* (New York: Free Press, 2001), 59.

[52] P. A. Johnson, *A History of the Jews* (New York: HarperPerennial, 1987), 26.

[53] *Encyclopedia Judaica*, "Exodus," CD-ROM, 1997, Judaica Multimedia.

[54] Exodus 14:21.

Bible.[55] Others have held the view that crossing the sea must have been the mythological reconstruction of a natural event.[56]

Two hypotheses have been advanced to explain the motivation behind the Exodus of Hebrews from the land of Egypt. The first is that the Exodus was the effort of Hebrews in bondage to join other Hebrew tribes with which they retained a sense of kinship. The second hypothesis is that of Manetho, the Egyptian historian of the third century BCE.[57] He believed Egyptian authorities encouraged the Exodus of Hebrew slaves as a measure to protect Egyptian population against the spread of the plague that was endemic in the Hebrew camp. He claimed that they sent Moses, an Egyptian priest, into the slave community to teach them hygiene, a form of health maintenance that priests were trained to do. Others, however, have been reluctant to endorse this theory because of the perceived anti-Jewish sentiments.

The wandering of Israelites for forty years in the desert may at first sound hard to believe, but it is quite understandable within the context of their nomadic life style. According to biblical narratives, Israelites camped in Kadesh-Barnea, in the northern part of the Sinai Peninsula, more than any other localities during their migration to Canaan.[58] In spite of their prolonged stay in this area, Israel Finkelstein insists, archaeological studies have not produced even a single trace of their presence in this region.[59] In other words, having several million people wandering for forty years, as it appears in the biblical narratives,[60] must have left some archaeological footprints in the Sinai Peninsula, whereas excavations have not recovered any trace of them predating the tenth and ninth centuries BCE at this site.[61]

---

[55] H. H. Ben-Sassoon, *A History of Jewish People* (Cambridge, MA: Harvard University Press, 1976), 43–44.

[56] *Jewishencyclopedia.com*, "Exodus."

[57] W. Durant, *The Story of Civilization: Our Oriental Heritage* (New York: Simon & Schuster, 1963), 301.

[58] I. Finkelstein and N. A. Silberman, *The Bible Unearthed: Archeology's New Vision of Ancient Israel and the Origin of Its Sacred Texts* (New York: Free Press, 2001), 63.

[59] Ibid.

[60] Exodus 12:37; Numbers 1:45–46.

[61] J.C.H. Laughlin, *Archeology and the Bible* (London: Routledge, 2000), 91.

Finally, there remain debates over the means by which the Promised Land was captured. According to the biblical accounts, the Hebrews conquered Canaan, Jericho, and Palestine by force during this period. In more contemporary writings, the conquest of Canaan has been characterized as the story of hungry nomadic people who had arrived in a fertile land and engaged in a bitter fight with the local inhabitants. In these wars, like others, large-scale massacres occurred, and the conquerors killed as many people as they could and forced women into marriage.[62] It has been said that Gideon,[63] the commander who defeated the Medianites, killed more than 120,000 people in order to conquer two cities.[64] When Eleazar the Priest visited the Hebrew army that had defeated the Medianites, he blamed them for keeping women alive: "[A]nd they are the cause of the plague that destroyed us."[65] They were instructed, "Only little girls may live: you may keep them for yourselves."[66] Similarly, according to biblical narratives, the Yahweh worshipper tribes, under the leadership of Joshua, Moses's successor, crossed the Jordan River, conquered Jericho in a fierce battle in 1250 BCE, and settled in the western part of Palestine. Joshua was a warrior who believed in violence as a means of survival:[67] "And the Lord said to Joshua, Fear not, nor be dismayed; take all the people of war with you, and arise, go up to Ai; see, I have given to your hand the king of Ai, and his people, and his city, and his land. And you shall do to Ai and to her king as you did to Jericho and her king."[68] "For Joshua kept his spear pointed toward Ai until the last person was dead."[69] "So Joshua struck all the country of the hills, and the Negev, and of the valley and of the springs, and all their kings; he left none remaining, but completely destroyed all who breathed, as the Lord God of Israel commanded."[70]

---

[62] Numbers 31:1–18; Deuteronomy 7:16; Joshua 8:26, 10:24.

[63] According to the biblical narratives, Gideon or Jerubaal was offered the position of king of Israel. However, he rejected the offer on the ground that only the Lord may serve as a king.

[64] W. Durant, *The Story of Civilization: Our Oriental Heritage* (New York: Simon & Schuster, 1963), 302.

[65] Numbers 31:15–16.

[66] Numbers 31:18.

[67] W. Durant, *The Story of Civilization: Our Oriental Heritage* (New York: Simon & Schuster, 1963), 302.

[68] Joshua 8:1–2.

[69] Joshua 8:26.

[70] Joshua 10:40.

In contrast to these biblical accounts that describe the conquest of the Promised Land through intense force and violence, archaeological evidence suggests that the capture of the Promised Land must have occurred in the late Bronze Age and early Iron Age I,[71] between the fifteenth and eleventh centuries BCE, when this region was devoid of a substantial group of inhabitants and therefore the Hebrews did not meet a significant resistance.[72] These and other archaeological findings have led many scholars to conclude that the capture of the Promised Land did not occur through a full-scale military invasion.[73-74] Similarly, William Dever suggests that the whole scenario of the "Exodus-Conquest" cycle must be set aside as largely mythical.[75] The secular vision herein expressed is accepted by almost all archaeologists and by most biblical scholars today.[76]

Kingship of Israel

According to the biblical narratives, the tribes of the Hebrew eventually achieved a political unity in 1020 BCE, and Saul (1025–1005 BCE), a prominent landowner and the leader of the tribe of Benjamin, became the first king.

In the eyes of most biblical scholars, the reign of Saul[77] or his successors David and Solomon[78] are indeed the first references of historical relevance to the "people of Israel." After the death of Saul, one of his commanders, David (1005–970 BCE), from the tribe of Judah, took over the power. David promoted the Sinai covenant between God and Moses and enforced the substance of the covenant as the official religion in Palestine. He conquered Jerusalem, the strong Palestinian fortress, about 1000 BCE and named it the capital

---

[71] J.C.H. Laughlin, *Archeology and the Bible* (London: Routledge, 2000), 91.

[72] Ibid., 118.

[73] I. Finkelstein and N. A. Silberman, *The Bible Unearthed: Archeology's New Vision of Ancient Israel and the Origin of Its Sacred Texts* (New York: Free Press, 2001), 76.

[74] K. Armstrong, *Jerusalem: One City, Three Faiths* (New York: Ballantine Books, 1996), 23.

[75] W. G. Dever, *What Did the Biblical Writers Know, and When Did They Know It?* (Grand Rapids, MI: Eerdmans, 2001), 121.

[76] Ibid., 282

[77] Ibid., 267.

[78] B. Russell, *A History of Western Civilization* (New York: Touchstone, 1972), 309.

city for the newly established state.[79] There are indications that the conquest of Jerusalem was achieved mercifully, and David treated the inhabitants with respect.[80] However, under his leadership, the ancient Israeli army smashed all other small non-Israeli tribes and incorporated them into his kingdom, and in this manner he solidified his government.

David died around the beginning of the tenth century BCE. At the time of his death, neighboring countries either had a friendly relationship with Israel or they were subjugated to the state. Solomon (970–931 BCE), David's son, symbolized the glory and magnificence of the ancient Israel. He succeeded David and built for Yahweh a temple in Jerusalem and for himself a splendid palace. Over 150,000 slave workers and a number of engineers from Sidon and Tyre participated in the construction of the Temple of Jerusalem.

Solomon was a strong king who utilized his father's wealth in promoting trade and industry. He opened avenues of commerce with Africa, Asia, Arabia, and Asia Minor. He also spent freely to satisfy his personal desires. Although there have been many discussions about his seven hundred wives and three hundred concubines,[81] historians believe in sixty and eighty, respectively, as more realistic figures.[82]

According to some historians, Solomon's intention to marry influential women was to establish and improve his relationship with the strong powers of his time.

To improve the institution of his government, Solomon divided the country into twelve districts, of which only five corresponded to the original tribal classification. By doing so, he tried to reduce the conflicts among the tribes and at the same time increase the central power. However, toil work, heavy taxes, and general public dissatisfaction weakened the central power, and the government eventually collapsed in 922 BCE.

---

[79] K. Armstrong, *Jerusalem: One City, Three Faiths* (New York: Ballantine Books, 1996), 38.

[80] Ibid.

[81] Samuel 11:2.

[82] I. Finkelstein and N. A. Silberman, *The Bible Unearthed: Archeology's New Vision of Ancient Israel and the Origin of Its Sacred Texts* (New York: Free Press, 2001), 128.

Consequently, the monarchy was divided into two independent states. The kingdom of Israel[83] (925–721 BCE) in the north was comprised of the remaining tribes under the leadership of the dominant tribe of Ephraim. Because of access to the sea, the northern kingdom was involved more actively in trade and hence was economically superior. Nonetheless, its wealth and political importance made the northern kingdom more vulnerable to violence and instability. Indeed, during its existence for 210 years, nineteen kings from nine dynasties ruled in Israel, ten of whom died by violence and seven ruled for less than two years. To the south was the kingdom of Judah[84] (925–586 BCE), which consisted of two tribes of

[83] Kings of Israel in the North:

King	Dates	Comments
Jeroboam I	931–909 BCE	Revolted against Solomon's taxation and declared the northern tribes independence
Nadab	909–908	Assassinated by Baasha
Baasha	908–885	
Elah	885–884	Murdered by Zimri
Zimri	884	Committed suicide
Omri	884–873	Foundation of Samaria
Ahab	873–852	First king described in Old Testament with the independent historical reference; killed in war with Damascus
Ahaziah	852–851	Killed by Jehu
Jehoram	851–842	Killed by Jehu
Jehu	842–814	
Jehoahaz	817–800	
Joash	800–784	
Jeroboam II	788–747	
Zechariah	747	Killed in a coup
Shallum	747	Killed in a coup by Menahem
Menahem	747–737	
Pekahiah	735	Killed in a coup
Pekah	735–732	
Hoshea	732–724	Last king of Israel

[84] Kings of Judah in the South:

King	Dates	Comments
Rehoboam	931–914 BCE	Son of Solomon
Abijam	914–911	
Asa	911–870	
Jehoshaphat	870–846	First king of Judah to make a treaty with Israel
Jehoram	851–843	Died after prolonged illness

Judah and Benjamin. The territories of Judah were about one-third the size of the kingdom of Israel in the north with no access to the sea. Compared with the kingdom of Israel, Judah enjoyed a lower economic status. In the center of the kingdom were Jerusalem and the Temple and the monarchy that generally passed from father to son in the house of David. Probably for these reasons, the kingdom of Judah was more committed to the Mosaic Law and monotheism than its rival in the north.

The history of the Israelites for the next two centuries is in fact the story of struggles between the two kingdoms and the small local powers. It is noteworthy that the monotheism of Israelites was tenuous during this period, and many tried to reintroduce idolatry into Yahweh's religion, hence disrupting the homogeneity among these people. Under these circumstances, the religious leaders preached strongly against the idolatry, condemned the lavish lifestyle, and saw a return to the simple nomadic lifestyle of the past as the only remedy.

While archaeological studies have supported the historicity of the house of David,[85] the magnificence of the kingdom of David and Solomon in the tenth century BCE has been frequently questioned.[86] On the basis of recent archaeological data, it has been argued that the

Ahazia	843–842	
Athaliah	842–836	Introduced Baal cult into Judah; murdered all members of the house of David; was killed in an uprising
Jehoash	836–798	Killed by conspirators
Amaziah	798–769	Killed in a palace revolution
Azariah	785–753	Died of leprosy
Jotham	753–743	
Ahaz	743–727	Introduced Assyrian idolatry
Hezekiah	727–698	Purged the Assyrian influence from Temple
Manasseh	698–642	Reintroduced pagan practices
Amon	641–640	Killed in a coup
Josiah	639–609	Killed in a war, religious reform
Jehoahaz	609	Killed in a war with Egyptians
Jehoiakim	608–598	
Jehoiachin	597	Ruled for three months before being exiled to Babylonia
Zedekiah	597–586	Last king of Judah

[85] J.C.H. Laughlin, *Archeology and the Bible* (London: Routledge, 2000), 134.
[86] Kings I 9:17–19, 10:1–11.

population of Israelite settlements was about forty-five thousand during this period of history, most of them scattered among villages in the north, and only about five thousand of them had settled in Jerusalem and Hebron, the two major centers of the kingdom of Judah.[87] With sparse settlements and the paucity of widespread literacy in these communities, one can hardly envision the splendor of the monarchy of David and Solomon as it appears in the biblical narratives.[88] On the contrary, William Dever argues that while no one can claim that Solomon was ruling over a vast empire stretching from the Mediterranean Sea to the Euphrates River, no one can also deny the existence of a small statehood in this region during the tenth century BCE.[89]

The Israelites' Religion and the Hebrew Bible

Human existence, because of natural disasters, death, cruelty, and injustice, has been a painful experience. Mankind historically perceived these painful encounters as a weakness or wrongdoing on its part. Under these circumstances, among other functions religion has served as an effective instrument to alleviate humanity's internal suffering and pain. The religion of the Israelites was therefore, to a great extent, a reflection of the harsh reality of the life of these people who had to struggle for survival.

In the beginning, the Israelites, like other primitive people, worshipped numerous gods. Some of these gods were small idols called teraphim that people usually kept at their homes. In addition, according to the teachings of some priests, the practice of sorcery and witchcraft had a common place up to the time of Moses. Gradually, belief in sacrifice, prayer, and charity as measures to protect them against natural calamities became popular, and Yahweh was accepted as a national god for everyone, promoting a sense of unity among the tribes of Israel.

According to Will Durant, the conquerors of Canaan adopted the name of Yahweh from Yahu, one of the local gods, and attributed

---

[87] I. Finkelstein and N. A. Silberman, *The Bible Unearthed: Archeology's New Vision of Ancient Israel and the Origin of Its Sacred Texts* (New York: Free Press, 2001), 143.
[88] Ibid., 142
[89] W. G. Dever, *What Did the Biblical Writers Know, and When Did They Know It?* (Grand Rapids, MI: Eerdmans, 2001), 271.

their own nomadic character of strength and resilience to him.[90] In fact, the discovery of artifacts named Yah or Yahu in 1931 in the ruins of Canaan, dating back three thousand years BCE, supports this notion.

On the basis of the biblical narratives, it seemed that Yahweh was the god of thunder and storm who was living in mountains.[91] Herein, the capable writers of the Pentateuch,[92] who looked upon religion as an instrument of government as well, created a strong almighty god, a deity who, similar to the Iliad of Greek mythology, fought vigorously for his people. In this regard, Moses says, "The Lord is a warrior,"[93] and David indicates that "He gives me skill in war. And strength to bend a bow of bronze."[94] Yahweh, who has been portrayed exclusively as a male deity,[95] promised the Israelites the destruction of their enemies and the expansion of their territories. Considering the harsh living circumstances of the Hebrews, Yahweh's teaching was often at odds with the peace-seeking god of Hillel[96] and Christ. Yahweh was not confused with reconciliation, since he believed the Promised Land could only be conquered and maintained by the force of the sword. In fact, considering the circumstances, he did not have any other choice. Yahweh's teachings evolved into the peace-seeking wisdom expressed by the god of Hillel and Christ only after centuries of political subjugation, military defeats, and the advancement of new moral values.

The writers of the Pentateuch were also keen about maintaining the monarchy within the realm of religion.[97] They not

---

[90] W. Durant, *The History of Civilization: Our Oriental Heritage* (New York: Simon & Schuster, 1963), 1:310.

[91] Kings I 20:23.

[92] Pentateuch is the first five books of the Old Testament: Genesis, Exodus, Leviticus, Numbers, and Deuteronomy.

[93] Exodus 15:3.

[94] Samuel II 22:35.

[95] W. G. Dever, *What Did the Biblical Writers Know, and When Did They Know It?* (Grand Rapids, MI: Eerdmans, 2001), 193.

[96] Hillel the Elder was a philosopher and teacher of the first century BCE who founded the Hillel school of thought that had many followers up to the fifth century CE. He was known for his modesty and peace-seeking behavior very similar to Christ's. His famous advice indeed summarized his teachings: "What is hateful to you do not do to your neighbor; that is the whole of Torah; the rest is commentary; go study."

[97] Deuteronomy 17:14-18.

only recognized the monarchy but also attached a divine attribute to
it. Therefore, the rise of the monarchy is presented as Yahweh's
power on the earth; hence, what a king does is praised not as his own
rulings but rather as divine exercises.[98]

On the basis of the biblical narratives, many human
characteristics have been attributed to Yahweh. Like human beings,
Yahweh makes mistakes and is unhappy for making Saul a king of
Israel. He often gets upset and is easily annoyed when he says, for
example, "I forgive whom I like to forgive and I bless whom I like to
bless."[99] In the story of Jacob and Laban, he approves of the trick that
Jacob, as an act of revenge, played on Laban in order to inflict a big
loss upon him. In short, Jacob was interested in Laban's younger
daughter, Rachel. Laban promised Rachel to Jacob in exchange for
seven years of hard labor. However, at the end of this period, Laban
sent Leah, the older daughter, as the bride to Jacob's tent. In the
morning, when Jacob learned about the trick his father-in-law had
played on him, he confronted him. Laban convinced Jacob to work
seven more years in order to marry Rachel. As an act of revenge,
Jacob justified his behavior by saying, "Then, in my dream, the Angel
of God called to me that I should mate the white female goats with
streaked, speckled and mottled male goats. I am the God you met in
Bethel, the place where you anointed the pillar and made a vow to
serve me."[100] For instance, Yahweh does not claim that he has
knowledge of everything. In order to distinguish the Israelites from
their enemies, he instructs the Israelites to paint their houses with the
ram's blood: "And the blood shall to you for a token upon the houses
where ye are; and when I see the blood, I will pass over you, and the
plague shall not be upon you to destroy you, when I smite the land of
Egypt."[101]

Sometimes Yahweh passes harsh and cruel judgments,
rulings that were not unusual for the time. He punished people for the
wrongdoing of a few Israelites in connection with the girls from
Moab's tribe.[102] He suggested that Moses hang the head of the Israel

---

[98] Psalms 45.

[99] Exodus 33:19.

[100] Genesis 31:11–13.

[101] Exodus 12:7, 12:13.

[102] The daughters of Moab seduced young men of Israel into adultery, and they
invited the Israelites to the sacrifices of their gods. The people of Israel, by attending
the feast and worshipping the gods of Moab, triggered the anger of Yahweh.

tribal leaders in the midday sun before his eyes.[103] He also punished children for the sins their fathers or grandfathers had committed.[104] At times Yahweh was so furious that he wanted to destroy the Israelites altogether for worshipping the golden calf, and Moses had to mediate and seek his affection.[105] On another occasion, when Yahweh decided to ruin the Israelites for their disapproval of Moses, once again Moses asked for Yahweh's patience.[106] Nonetheless, Yahweh liked the people who worshipped him and followed his commands.[107]

In addition to Moses, Abraham also counseled Yahweh to be patient in handling the Israelites. In fact, Abraham was the one who encouraged Yahweh not to get upset with the people, and asked him to save Sodom and Gomorrah in case fifty, forty, thirty, twenty, or even ten decent people might have been residing there.[108]

The early religion of the Israelites had an abundance of Pagan borrowings.[109] In the beginning, Yahweh was not the only god recognized by the Israelites.[110] In fact, in the First Commandment, all Yahweh asked from the Israelites was to be placed above other gods. He confessed, "Thou shall not bow down thyself unto them nor serve them; for I the Lord thy God am a jealous God, visiting the iniquity of the fathers upon the children unto the third and fourth generations of them that hate me"[111]; "utterly overthrow" my rivals; "quite break down their images."[112] Moses also did not deny the existence of other gods among Israelites when he said, "Who else is like the Lord among the gods? Who is glorious in holiness like him?"[113] And "I know now that the Lord is greater than any other god because he delivered his people from the proud and cruel Egyptians."[114] The existence of gods other than Yahweh was also acknowledged by King Solomon when he said, "It is going to be a wonderful temple because

---

[103] Numbers 25:4.

[104] Deuteronomy 5:9–10.

[105] Exodus 30:11–14.

[106] Numbers 14:14–18.

[107] Exodus 20:5–6.

[108] Genesis 18:20–33.

[109] J. Kirsch, *King David: The Real Life of the Man Who Ruled Israel* (New York: Ballantine Books, 2000), 179.

[110] B. Russell, *A History of Western Philosophy* (New York: Touchstone, 1972), 310.

[111] Deuteronomy 5:9–10; Exodus 20:5.

[112] Exodus 23:24.

[113] Exodus 15:11.

[114] Exodus 18:11.

he is a great god, greater than any other."[115] In spite of the efforts of religious leaders to promote Yahweh as the most prominent god, at times each of the Israelite tribes independently arranged to worship other gods in hiding. These transient episodes of separation between Israelites and Yahweh continued well into Solomon's time, until the time when the tribes achieved a relative political and economical unity. It was only after this unity and the centralization of the religion and worship in the Temple of Jerusalem that Yahweh was considered the sole god among the Israelites. Indeed, Yahweh as the sole god appeared in Isaiah for the first time[116] when he said, "I am the Lord, and there is none else, there is no God beside me."[117]

Like Christianity and Islam, Jewish theology was based upon the fear of committing sins and its consequences.[118] For every sin there was a distinct punishment. Since humans had endless desires, there were naturally innumerable sins and corresponding punishments. In the Israelites' religion, there was initially no hell for the punishment of sinners. Instead, there was Sheol, "the land of darkness," that was equally horrifying. Except for the divine favorites such as Moses, Elijah,[119] and Enoch,[120] Sheol received all the dead. Israelites initially did not believe in the immortality of the soul and in life after death.[121] In fact, they expected the promised rewards and punishments in this life. Sinners suffered premature deaths, while believers enjoyed long and prosperous lives.[122] However, since justice often was not served in this life, they later adopted concepts such as heaven and hell similar to the Persians, Egyptians, and Greeks.

---

[115] Chronicles II 2:5.
[116] B. Russell, *A History of Western Philosophy* (New York, Touchstone, 1972), 312.
[117] Isaiah 45:5.
[118] B. Russell, *A History of Western Philosophy* (New York: Touchstone, 1972), 319.
[119] According to the biblical account, Elijah ascended to heaven in a fiery chariot.
[120] According to Genesis 4:17–18, Enoch was the son of Cain and the father of Irad. However, on the basis of Genesis 5:18–21, he was the son of Jared and father of Methuselah. Nonetheless, we learn from the verses that Enoch was always present before god. In contrast to his father, who lived 962 years, he disappeared at age 365 years. The fact that his age was the exact number of days in the solar calendar has raised the possibility that this mythological figure was actually adapted from Mehr teachings. Enoch is the symbol of immortality in Judaism. The resemblance between the story of Enoch and Idris, as it appears in verses 55 to 56 of Mariam in the Qur'an, is also interesting.
[121] J. Ashtiani, *Tahghighi dar Dinhe Yahood* (Teheran: Negaresh, 1989), 253.
[122] Exodus 20:12.

Prayer or sacrifice could absolve certain sins. At first, the Israelites, like the Aryans, offered human sacrifices,[123, 124] but gradually animal sacrifice and charity were substituted for this ritual. Priests usually blessed animals, typically calves, lambs, and kids,[125] before they were sacrificed, and after temporarily offering the animals to God, the priests ate the meat. Indeed, God's suggestion of a ram instead of Isaac, the son of Abraham, for sacrifice is a symbol of the substitution of animals in place of human sacrifice.[126] Circumcision was also considered a form of sacrifice[127] in which God accepted "part of body" instead of the "whole."[128] The Israelites were among the first people to learn how to circumcise. This was done not only as a sacrifice but also as a measure to promote individual hygiene. Circumcision became a symbol of distinguishing those who belonged to the Israeli community from idolaters.[129]

Restrictions for consuming certain food items, known as dietary laws, were frequently encountered in the biblical narratives. The meat of animals that were biblically considered unclean, or those that were not ritually slaughtered—fishes without scales and, above all, a mixture of a dairy product with meat—were strictly prohibited. The latter has been cited in three occasions in the Old Testament: "As you reap each of your crops, bring me the choicest sample of the first harvest, it shall be offered to the Lord your God. Do not boil a young goat in its mother's milk";[130] "And you must bring the best of the first of each year's crop to the house of the Lord your god. You must not cook a young goat in its mother's milk";[131] "Don't eat anything that has died a natural death. However, a foreigner among you may eat it. You may give it or sell it to him, but don't eat it yourself, for you are holy to the Lord your god. You must not boil a young goat in its

---

[123] W. G. Sumner, *Folkways* 6 (1906): 554, quoted in W. Durant, *The Story of Civilization: Our Oriental Heritage* (New York: Simon & Schuster, 1963), 1:313.

[124] Samuel II 21:8–9, 21:14.

[125] K. Crim, *The Perennial Dictionary of World Religions* (New York: HarperSanFrancisco, 1981), 638.

[126] Genesis 22:2–13.

[127] Genesis 17:10–12.

[128] W. Durant, *The Story of Civilization: Our Oriental Heritage* (New York: Simon & Schuster, 1963), 1:313.

[129] G. Wigoder, *The New Standard Jewish Encyclopedia* (New York: Facts on File, 1992), 216.

[130] Exodus 23:19.

[131] Exodus 34:26.

mother's milk."[132] Nonetheless, no explanation has been provided for any of these restrictions.[133] With regard to consumption of pork, there are, however, controversial viewpoints.[134] Some believe that the historical interest of the Israelites to worship this animal was the main reason to forbid eating pork. Others, in contrast, believed pork was forbidden merely as a public health issue.

Yahweh had offered the following provisions with regard to the priests' wages: "The offerings which you burn on the altar for me are my food, and are a pleasure to me; so see to it that they are brought regularly and are offered as I have instructed you.[135] On the Sabbath day two lambs of first year without spot, and two tenth deals of flour for a meat offering, mingled with oil, and the drink offering thereof."[136]

In the ancient times, the firstborn son of the family was in charge of religious services and rituals. Later, the members of the Levi tribe were charged with these responsibilities according to the covenant between God and Aaron, the elder brother of Moses, and as a reward for not participating in the worshipping of the golden calf: "But you and your sons, the priests, shall personally handle all the sacred service, including the altar and all that is within the veil, for the priesthood is your special gift of service. Anyone else who attempts to perform these duties shall die."[137] However, because of Aaron's role in the construction of the golden calf, "And I said unto them, whosoever hath any gold, let them break it off. So they gave it me: then I cast it into the fire, and there came out this calf,"[138] he was forbidden to enter the Promised Land.[139] In this manner, a circle of priests appeared that only members of the Levi tribe could enter. This circle neither owned or inherited land nor paid taxes. They generally earned a living through the charity people offered to the Temple of Jerusalem.[140] God promised Aaron's descendants, "Yours also are the

---

[132] Deuteronomy 14:21.
[133] G. Wigoder, *The New Standard Jewish Encyclopedia* (New York: Facts on File, 1992), 272.
[134] Leviticus 11:7; Deuteronomy 14:8.
[135] Numbers 28:1–2.
[136] Numbers 28:9–10.
[137] Numbers 18:7.
[138] Exodus 32:24.
[139] Numbers 20:12.
[140] Ezra 7:24.

first of the harvest gifts the people bring as offerings to the Lord—the best of the olive oil, wine, grain, and every other crop.[141] Your families may eat these unless they are ceremonially defiled at the time. So everything that is dedicated to the Lord shall be yours, including the firstborn sons of the people of Israel, and the firstborn of their animals."[142] During the Second Temple of Jerusalem, these priests accumulated a remarkable wealth, and some of them, like the priests in Babylon and Thebes, were wealthier than kings.

In 445 BCE, Ezra the Scribe, a renowned figure, along with the other Levite priests, read the Book of Law (also known as the Torah or Pentateuch) to those Israelites who were in Babylonian exile and asked them to accept the teachings as their conscience and obey it forever: "And whosoever will not do the law of thy God, and the law of the king, let judgment be executed speedily upon him, whether it be unto death, or to banishment, or to confiscation of good, or to imprisonment."[143] The Book of Law consists of the five books of Genesis, Exodus, Leviticus, Numbers, and Deuteronomy. Moses is the principal character in all five books, and according to the traditional teachings, he is considered the author of all volumes. In spite of this widely held assumption, no mention that Moses is indeed the author is found in these five volumes.[144]

In summary, there were Pagan borrowings in the early religion of Israelites, and Yahweh was not recognized as the sole God of Israel until the tribes achieved their national unity. Yahweh typically had many human attributes. The principles of the Jewish theology, like Christianity and Islam, were based upon the fear of committing sins and their consequences. Since there were endless human desires, so was there an infinite number of sins, which prayer, charity, and the offering of sacrifices could be used to absolve.

The Origin of the Hebrew Bible

The Bible is a prominent icon of Western civilization, and interest in the real authorship of this magnificent library is extremely

---

[141] Numbers 18:12.
[142] Numbers 18:14–15.
[143] Ezra 7:26.
[144] R. E. Friedman, *Who Wrote the Bible?* (New York: HarperSanFrancisco, 1987), 17.

deep seated. Throughout history, people have been curious about this library, its true origin, and how it attained its present configuration. Isaac ibn Yashush, a Jewish physician of the eleventh century CE, was the first to point out that some of the kings, whose names were mentioned in the Book of Law, in fact lived after Moses. Therefore, he concluded that at least certain parts of the Book of Law must have been written after Moses. Abraham ibn Ezra, a twelfth-century rabbi in Spain, criticized Yashush: "He who understands it must keep it quiet."[145]

Following numerous investigations, Thomas Hobbes, the British philosopher and a modern thinker, concluded that authors other than Moses wrote significant portions of the Pentateuch.[146] Later, Andrew van Maes, another investigator, claimed that although Moses is the author of the Pentateuch, others had edited the books and had modified its contents. It is noteworthy that because of this comment, the Catholic Church classified van Maes's manuscript as forbidden literature.

Baruch Spinoza, the seventeenth-century philosopher, pointed to the following verses in the Bible: "*And there has not arisen since in Israel a prophet like Moses, whom the Lord knew face to face*"[147] and "*In all the signs and the wonders, which the Lord sent him to do in the land of Egypt to Pharaoh, and to all his servants, and to all his land. And in all that mighty hand, and in all the great and awesome deeds which Moses performed in the sight of all Israel*"[148] (my emphasis). He claimed that these were the words of the people who had a chance to compare Moses with other prophets before passing judgment; hence, they must have been written after Moses. According to Spinoza, verses like these are often found in the Bible. He wrote, "It is . . . clearer than the sun at noon that the Pentateuch was not written by Moses, but by someone who lived long after Moses."[149] In this manner, Spinoza questioned the supernatural status of the Bible and reduced it to a human document. He was excommunicated by the Jewish community of Amsterdam and was condemned by Catholics

---

[145] Ibid., 19.
[146] Ibid., 20.
[147] Deuteronomy 34:10.
[148] Deuteronomy 34:11–12.
[149] R. E. Friedman, *Who Wrote the Bible?* (New York: HarperSanFrancisco, 1987), 21.

and Protestants as well. Later, Richard Simon, a French Catholic priest of the seventeenth century, indicated that Moses was the author of the "core" of the Pentateuch and others later added enormously to it.[150] According to Simon and other investigators, the Pentateuch or Book of Law is not the work of a single author, but in fact several authors had contributed to the volumes. Of the thirteen hundred copies of Simon's printed works, all but six were burned.

Richard Elliot Friedman, a Bible scholar and professor of Hebrew and comparative literature at the University of California at San Diego, recapitulated that the Book of Law is not the work of a single author. The following is a synopsis of the state of the investigations on this subject.

In the opinion of biblical investigators, the Book of Law is the product of the combination of four source documents, not unlike the New Testament, which begins with the four gospels of Matthew, Mark, Luke, and John. In the case of the New Testament, each gospel tells the story in its own way, and from the beginning, there was no question that the New Testament was written by four authors. However, in the case of the Old Testament, the four sources were interwoven delicately, so Moses was accepted as the author from the beginning to the end. Nonetheless, the idea that Moses may not be the single author of the Old Testament has often produced a harsh public reaction.

The principal element in the Book of Law is God the Creator, who is also a lawgiver and a king. This idea was introduced in the book of Genesis. The source document in which the creator is called Yahweh was written during the reign of Solomon or David in Judah between 848 and 722 BCE.[151] In contrast, the family of priests of Shiloh[152] in the northern part of Israel, between 922 and 722 BCE,[153]

---

[150] Ibid.

[151] R. E. Friedman, *Who Wrote the Bible?* (New York: HarperSanFrancisco, 1987), 61.

[152] The city of Shiloh was in the northern part, where the Tabernacle had been built. The Tabernacle was indeed known as the Tent of Meeting and had been constructed to house the ark or the Ten Commandments. According to the biblical accounts, this was the primary location of the nation's worship before Solomon built the Temple of Jerusalem. The city was also home to a large community of priests who considered themselves the descendants of Moses. Before the establishment of the monarchy, the priests not only functioned as judges and prophets, but they were handling the

wrote chapters in which the creator is called Elohim. According to Friedman, these two source documents are distinguished from each other not only by the style of writing but also by their contents. The third part, or the priestly codes, is the largest source document, which includes thirty chapters of Exodus and Numbers and the entire book of Leviticus. This part is principally the work of Aaron's family of priests that was probably put together during construction of the Second Temple of Jerusalem.[154] He further asserted that Moses's personality was less developed in the priestly code section when compared to two previously described source documents of the Pentateuch.[155] The book of Deuteronomy had yet a different author. This book carries a theme with a great emphasis on centralization of religion and the eternal and unconditional continuation of the kingdom of the house of David. Other scholars are of the opinion that Deuteronomy was probably put together around 622 BCE, during the reign of King Josiah (639–609 BCE).[156,157] Indeed, some biblical scholars have long maintained the position that seven of the books, Deuteronomy, Joshua, Judges, Ruth, Samuel I and II, and the book of Kings, or what is known as the Deuteronomic History, were compiled during the age of King Josiah.[158] In these volumes, King Josiah has been characteristically pictured as the champion of a great religious reformation modeled after Moses, Joshua, and David, and he was considered the rightful patron of the Temple.[159] "And the king commanded all the people, saying, keep the Passover to the Lord your God, as it is written in the book of this covenant. Surely there was not celebrated such a Passover from the days of the judges that judged Israel, nor in all the days of the kings of Israel, nor of the kings of

government as well. When the monarchy was established, the priests did not leave the scene, and in fact the king's power was always checked and balanced by them.

[153] R. E. Friedman, *Who Wrote the Bible?* (New York: HarperSanFrancisco, 1987), 24.

[154] Ibid., 162.

[155] Ibid., 198.

[156] King Josiah reigned from 648 to 609 BCE. He was the father of Jehoiakim and the grandfather of Jehoiachin, the last king of Judah.

[157] I. Finkelstein and N. A. Silberman, *The Bible Unearthed: Archeology's New Vision of Ancient Israel and the Origin of Its Sacred Texts* (New York: Free Press, 2001), 280.

[158] Ibid., 92.

[159] Ibid., 279.

Judah. But in the eighteenth year of King Josiah, when this Passover was celebrated to the Lord in Jerusalem."[160]

Finally, it is believed that another author, probably Ezra,[161] later gathered these four source documents and edited them.[162] The Book of Law achieved its present-day configuration about 300 BCE.[163] Some scholars of the *revisionist* school of thought, however, have viewed the Hebrew Bible as exclusively a product of the Persian-Hellenic period.[164]

The fascinating stories of creation and the flood, with their deep spiritual content, have probably been adapted from Mesopotamian mythology. It is quite possible that the Jews,[165] while in exile, learned them from the Babylonians. Similarly, the impact of Persian and Sumerian cultures in this regard cannot be excluded. The biblical story of the flood is remarkably similar to the story of a great flood detailed in the epic of Gilgamesh,[166] which was written in cuneiform about 2000 BCE.

The story of paradise is found in the folkloric literature of many nationalities such as the Egyptians, Hindus, Persians, Greeks, and Mexicans. In all of these cultures, paradise is characteristically very green, with trees that bear fruits that are forbidden to humans. Serpents and dragons in paradise symbolize the immortality that has

---

[160] Kings II 23:21–23.

[161] Ezra was a scribe who was employed by the Persian government. When he learned that the religion was in trouble after returning from his Babylonian exile, he led a group of Jews to Judah. He encouraged the people to observe the rules and regulations related to Sabbath, to pay their dues to the Temple of Jerusalem, and refuse mixed marriages.

[162] W. Durant, *The Story of Civilization: Our Oriental Heritage* (New York: Simon & Schuster, 1963), 329.

[163] Ibid.

[164] W. G. Dever, *What Did the Biblical Writers Know, and When Did They Know It?* (Grand Rapids, MI: Eerdmans, 2001), 274.

[165] The English term "Jew" stems from the Latin word *Judaeus*, referring to a citizen of Judah. The Hebrew equivalent of this word is *Yehudi*.

[166] Gilgamesh, the hero in the epic, is a tyrannical Babylonian king who ruled the city of Uruk. According to this story, the gods responded to the prayers of oppressed citizens and sent a wild man, Enkidu, to challenge Gilgamesh. The two men participated in a wrestling game that had no winner. The gods doomed Enkidu to die. Following this, Gilgamesh sought the secret of immortality from the wise man Utnapishtim. He described the secret to Gilgamesh as the story of a great flood.

been taken away from humans.[167] In folkloric literature, the snake and fig represent wisdom, curiosity, eternality, and masculinity. Behind these myths there was also the message that sex and knowledge were both enemies of the innocence and happiness of mankind, and the future of them would be more painful and devastating than the immediate and temporary pleasure they provided. Therefore, they were considered evil. In most of these stories, women were portrayed as attractive and lovable representations of the devil and men as providers of the family.

The Book of Law that Ezra and other priests preached to the Israelites was the basis upon which the social life of the Jews was leaning. This collection was a detailed and complex document that looked upon religion not only as a way of life but also as a governing instrument. In addition, many issues in human life such as nutrition, dietary codes, personal hygiene, public health, and sexual relations were discussed in that collection.[168] The Book of Law indeed goes into painful details of prescribing a blueprint of day-to-day life. It is within this context that Ernest Renan, a French philosopher, once described this document as "the tightest garment into which life was ever laced."[169]

The Ten Commandments

Most of the Mosaic teachings are contained in the Ten Commandments.[170] These commandments, which are in essence a reflection of the simple nomadic life of Hebrews, must be analyzed and interpreted only within the context of the time in which they were prepared.

A new form of theology is introduced in the First Commandment. In contrast to the past, this commandment is based upon the principal understanding that God is an invisible force and a

---

[167] T. W. Doane, *Bible Myths and Their Parallels in Other Religions* (New York: 1882, ch. 1), quoted in W. Durant, *The Story of Civilization: Our Oriental Heritage* (New York: Simon & Schuster, 1963), 329.
[168] Leviticus 13, 14, 15.
[169] E. Renan, *History of the People of Israel* (New York: 1888, 4:163), quoted in W. Durant, *The Story of Civilization: Our Oriental Heritage* (New York: Simon & Schuster, 1963), 330.
[170] Exodus 20:1–17; Deuteronomy 5:6–18

legislator,[171] who has determined a proper punishment for every sin his people may commit: "I am the Lord thy God, which have brought thee out of the land of Egypt, out of the house of bondage. Thou shalt have no other gods before me."[172] Clearly and repeatedly it has been emphasized in the Old Testament and elsewhere that refusing to follow his rules is interpreted as heresy and results in capital punishment. The scribes of the First Commandment, like the leaders of other religions, believed that the foundation of the Israelites' society must be based upon unity and strict enforcement of the religious codes.

The Second Commandment discouraged any representation of God: "Thou shalt not make unto thee any graven image, or any likeness of any thing that is in heaven above, or that is in the earth beneath, or that is in the water under the earth."[173] Creating his image, in any form or shape, was forbidden. God was conceived as beyond every form and image. Therefore, art was essentially forbidden because it was perceived as a false image of God.

The Third Commandment strongly advised against using God's name in vain. "Thou shalt not take the name of the Lord thy God in vain; for the Lord will not hold him guiltless that takes his name in vain."[174]

The Fourth Commandment sanctified the Sabbath of each week as the strongest institution of Judaism: "But the seventh day is the Sabbath of the Lord thy God; in it thou shalt not do any work, thou, nor thy son, nor thy daughter, thy manservant, nor thy maidservant, nor thy cattle, nor thy stranger that is within thy gates."[175] The term *Sabbath* originates from the Babylonian days of rest and seclusion called *sabbatu*. On this basis, the concept of

---

[171] In the ancient period, codes and commandments were often divinely wrapped and presented in a sacred parcel. In Egypt, codes were offered by Thoth, "the god," and codes of Hammurabi were sent by Shamash, god of the sun. Dionysus, one of the gods of Greece, presented the commandments in two stone tablets, and Ahurmazda appeared at Zoroaster in the midst of thunder and lightning and offered him the Book of Laws. Governing bodies believed that since these codes were serving everyone, they were sacred. Moreover, a sacred and divine wrapping probably impressed the masses more and encouraged them to abide by the laws.

[172] Exodus 20:2–3.

[173] Exodus 20:4; Deuteronomy 5:8.

[174] Deuteronomy 5:11; Exodus 20:7.

[175] Exodus 20:10.

Sabbath probably had been adopted from the Babylonians, perhaps during the time that the Israelites were exiled.

The Bible refers to three forbidden items on the Sabbath. First, "Don't even light the fires in your homes that day."[176] Second, "Even during plowing and harvest times, work only six days and rest on the seventh."[177] And third, "Because the Lord has appointed tomorrow as a day of seriousness and rest, a holy Sabbath to the Lord when we must refrain from doing our daily tasks. So cook as much as you want today, and keep what is left for tomorrow."[178] However, the Talmudic rabbis have elaborated extensively on this issue, and they have expanded the forbidden items to thirty-nine items, instead of three.

In addition to the Sabbath, the weekly holiday, Israelites celebrated other feasts as the primary life rhythms in their liturgy.[179] *Mazzoth* was celebrated at the harvest of barley, *Shavuoth* or *Pentecost* at the harvest of wheat, *Sukkoth* at the harvest of vintage, and *Pesach* or *Passover* to commemorate the birth of the first flock. *Rosh-Ha-Shanah*[180] was celebrated as the agricultural harvesting[181] and also as the New Year.

Later, religious attributes were added to these feasts, which were initially celebrated in connection with events in nature. Pesach originally consisted of two events: *Shag Ha Matzoth*, or the festival of unleavened bread, and *Shag Ha Pesach*, the festival of the Peschal lamb. Traditionally, they sacrificed a lamb or a goat on the first day of the festival and painted the blood on their homes, symbolizing they have offered the share of God. When the priests established their power, they added religious attributes to both festivals. Shag Ha Matzoth was identified by the hasty departure of the Israelites from Egypt,[182] and Shag Ha Pesach by the tenth plague, the death of the

---

[176] Exodus 35:3.

[177] Exodus 34:21.

[178] Exodus 16:23.

[179] K. Crim, *The Perennial Dictionary of World Religions* (New York, HarperSanFrancisco, 1981), 390.

[180] Rosh-Ha-Shanah, or New Year, is on the first day of the seventh month in the Hebrew calendar. Rabbis of the Talmudic period believed everyone's fate was determined on this day. Some, however, considered Rosh-Ha-Shanah as the day of creation.

[181] A. J. Kolatch, *The Jewish Book of Why* (New York: Jonathan David, 1981), 226.

[182] Exodus 23:15, 34:18.

firstborn Egyptians.[183] Similarly, Sukkoth was originally an agricultural celebration that was later attributed to Exodus and the Israelites' life in the desert.[184] We may read in the book of Leviticus that "Ye shall dwell in booths seven days; all that are Israelites born shall dwell in booths. That your generations may know that I made the children of Israel to dwell in booths, when I brought them out of the land of Egypt. I am the Lord your God."[185]

The Fifth Commandment sanctified the family, which, next to the Temple of Jerusalem, had the most impact in Jewish society. "Honor thy father and thy mother; that thy days may be long upon the land which the Lord thy God giventh thee."[186] The patriarchal family of Hebrew was a politico-economical unit, which usually consisted of the father of the family, his wives, his unmarried children, wives and children of his married sons and their slaves. The father enjoyed an irrefutable power in the family; wives and children could only survive by being subjugated to his power. If the father was a poor man, he could force his daughters into marriage or even sell them before they reached puberty.[187] In Hebrew society, as in other patriarchal societies, little attention was paid to the rights of women. In general, they were always subjugated to the men's power. In the book of Genesis, God says to the serpent, "From now on you and the woman will be enemies, as will your offspring and hers."[188] The religion of the Hebrews insisted upon husbands making decisions for their wives and stressed that the wives always follow their husbands: "You shall bear children in intense pain and suffering; yet even so, you shall welcome your husband's affections, and he shall be your master."[189]

Under these same decrees, however, the wives who produced many children deserved more respect and security. Marriage after age twenty was obligatory, and single life was usually considered a sin. Yahweh did not approve of abortion or other measures aimed at controlling the population. In this regard, we may read in Genesis that "Rachel, realizing she was barren, became envious of her sister and

---

[183] Exodus 12: 6–7, 13.
[184] K. Armstrong, *Jerusalem: One City, Three Faiths* (New York: Ballantine Books, 1996), 49.
[185] Leviticus 23:42–43.
[186] Exodus 20:12.
[187] Genesis 24:58; Judges 1:12–13.
[188] Genesis 3:15.
[189] Genesis 3:16.

exclaimed to Jacob, give me children or I will die."[190] Also when Lot, Abraham's nephew, went to live in a cave in the mountains with his two daughters, we read, "And the firstborn said unto the younger, our father is old, and there is not a man in the earth to come in unto us after the manner of all the earth. Come, let us make our father drink wine, and we will lie within him, that we may preserve seed of our father. And they made their father drink wine that night, and the firstborn went in, and lay with her father; and he perceived not when she lay down, nor when she arose. And it came to pass on the morrow, that the firstborn said unto the younger, behold, I lay yester night with my father; let us make him drink wine this night also, and go thou in, and lie with him, that we may preserve seed of our father. And they made their father drink wine that night also; and the younger arose, and lay with him, and he perceived not when she lay down, nor when she arose. Thus were both the daughters of Lot with child by their father."[191] In general, women's responsibility was to deliver plenty of children and provide for the husbands' needs.

The Sixth Commandment condemned violence: "Thou shalt not kill."[192] In spite of this commandment, there are numerous examples of slaughter and violent revenge in the Bible. Tribal fights and conspiracies that had been planned in previous generations often disrupted the peace and tranquility of these communities. According to Will Durant, if we pass judgment on the basis of the declarations that the priests had attributed to Yahweh, their own desire for war was no less than their interest in preaching.[193] As an example, one may point out that out of nineteen kings of Israel, eight were assassinated[194] and seven ruled less than two years. Large-scale killing of their enemies was viewed as an admirable achievement. This is mentioned in connection with one of King David's mighty men, Adino the Eznite: "He lift up his spear against eight hundred, whom he slew at one time."[195] Next in rank was Eleazar, the son of Dodo: "He arose, and smote the Philistines until his hand was weary, and his hand clave unto the sword, and the Lord wrought a great

---

[190] Genesis 30:1.
[191] Genesis 19:30–36.
[192] Deuteronomy 5:17; Exodus 20:13.
[193] W. Durant, *The Story of Civilization: Our Oriental Heritage* (New York: Simon & Schuster, 1963), 335.
[194] Ibid.
[195] Samuel II 23:8.

victory that day; and the people returned after him only to spoil."[196] In spite of this commandment, it was customary to destroy the cities that had been conquered at the time of war[197] and put men to the swords.

The Seventh Commandment acknowledged marriage as the basis of the family, similar to the Fifth Commandment, which made family the principal unit of society. In this manner, the vow of matrimony enjoyed the undeniable support of the religion, and a relation outside marriage was strongly condemned: "Thou shalt not commit adultery."[198] Parents used to arrange the marriage of their children.[199] Before the Babylonian exile, priests usually were not involved with this process. While there is no mention in this commandment about sex before marriage, it was the bride's obligation to prove her virginity or face the pain of death by stoning.[200] Prostitution was a common practice, particularly among other nations. Since trade with others had not been condemned in the Bible, non-Jewish women used to set up their booths along the roads, and in addition to trade, they engaged in prostitution. During the reign of King Solomon, the restrictions on this issue were relaxed, and therefore many of these prostitutes entered into Jerusalem and their numbers significantly increased. It is said that during the reign of Maccabees, prostitutes were even encountered in the Temple of Jerusalem.[201] In this period of Jewish history, as also among other cultures, love played a small role in the relationship between men and women. During peacetime, marriage was more or less a business transaction. In other words, men purchased their future wives: Jacob paid for Rachel and Leah with many years of hard work.[202] In wartime, it was acceptable for victors to forcefully marry the women of the victims.

Wealthy men used to have multiple wives. Barren women like Sarah, the wife of Abraham, often encouraged their husbands to have concubines. Similarly, Rachel and Leah had many children for

---

[196] Samuel II 23:10.
[197] Kings II 3:25.
[198] Exodus 20:14.
[199] Genesis 21:21, 28:2.
[200] Deuteronomy 22:21.
[201] W. W. Sanger, *The History of Prostitution: Its Extent, Causes and Effects Throughout the World* (1910), 37: 9, quoted in W. Durant, *The Story of Civilization: Our Oriental Heritage* (New York: Simon & Schuster, 1963), 335.
[202] Genesis 31:15.

Jacob, but when they were not able to bear any more children, they encouraged Jacob to sleep with a maid so he could have more children.[203] The duty of producing more children was an endless responsibility. Undoubtedly, reproduction was the main motivation in these endeavors under the harsh living conditions that produced a high rate of child mortality. Along the same lines, if the husband died, his brother was required to marry his brother's widow, and if the husband had no brother, then the closest man of the family would fulfill this duty. The Levirate law of marriage clearly states: "If a man's brother dies without a son, his widow must not marry outside the family; instead, her husband's brother must marry her and sleep with her. The first son she bears to him shall be counted as the son of the dead brother, so that his name will not be forgotten. But if the dead man's brother refuses to do his duty in this matter, then she shall go to the city elders and say to them, 'My husband's brother refuses to let his brother's name continue—he refuses to marry me.' The elders of the city will then summon him and talk it over with him, and if he still refuses, the widow shall walk over to him in the presence of the elders, pull his sandal from his foot and spit in his face. She shall then say, 'This is what happens to a man who refuses to build his brother's house.' And ever afterwards his house shall be referred to as 'the home of the man who had his sandal pulled off.'"[204]

Adultery with a man's wife was illegal and usually carried capital punishment for both parties.[205] Sex was prohibited for single women but was a forgivable sin for single men.[206] Divorce was feasible for men and, according to the biblical narratives, was a simple procedure: "When a man hath taken a wife, and married her, and it come to pass that he find no favour in her; because he hath found some uncleanness in her; then let him write her a bill of divorcement, and give it in her hand, and send her out of his house."[207] In contrast, divorce was impossible for women prior to the Talmudic domination. The husband was usually presented as a man

---

[203] Genesis 30:9.
[204] Deuteronomy 25:5–10.
[205] Leviticus 20:10; Deuteronomy 22:22.
[206] E. Westermarck, *Short History of Marriage* (New York: 1926), 1: 427, quoted in W. Durant, *The Story of Civilization: Our Oriental Heritage* (New York: Simon & Schuster, 1963), 336.
[207] Deuteronomy 24:1.

who was constantly sweating to provide for his wives and children. Before public opinion, the husband never abused his power.[208]

The Eighth Commandment sanctified private property. Respect for property along with respect for family and religion constituted the three principles of Hebrew societies. Prior to the reign of King Solomon, Hebrew people lived in tents and were constantly traveling from one place to another looking for green pastures. Later, when most people began cultivating olive, fig, and grape trees and the economic condition improved, they had surplus; hence they participated in trade and then owned land. Prior to the Babylonian exile, coins and money were not popular, and gold and silver were used as the instruments of exchange. Lending to others was encouraged, while borrowing was discouraged: "The Lord shall open unto thee his good treasure, the heaven to give the rain unto thy land in his season and to bless all the work of thine hand; and thou shalt lend unto many nations, and thou shalt not borrow"[209]

Hebrew people, like other nations, used to enslave war captives and convicts. In fact, thousands of slaves participated in the construction of the first Temple of Jerusalem. Slaves were considered the private property of the slave owners. However, slave owners did not have power over the life and death of their slaves. Often, slaves could pay for their freedom and even become landowners.[210] If a man became a slave before he married, his entire family were freed; but he married after he became a slave, then his wife and children remained slaves upon his freedom.[211] One could inherit the slaves of his father.[212] Creditors could sell the debtors or the debtor's children to recover delinquent loans. Later, due to the influence of the priests and the charity of people, these harsh rules gradually faded away.

Initially, Yahweh insisted upon freeing slaves after seven years and their debts to be absorbed by the community: "If you buy a Hebrew slave, he shall serve only six years and be freed in the

---

[208] W. Durant, *The Story of Civilization: Our Oriental Heritage* (New York: Simon & Schuster, 1963), 336.

[209] Deuteronomy 15:6, 28:12.

[210] W. G. Sumner, *Folkways* (Boston: 1906), 276, quoted in W. Durant, *The Story of Civilization: Our Oriental Heritage* (New York: Simon & Schuster, 1963), 337.

[211] Exodus 21:3,4

[212] Leviticus 25:46

seventh year, and need pay nothing to regain his freedom."[213]
However, when it became clear that this law was not enforceable,
Yahweh advised that the slaves be free on the fiftieth instead of
seventh year of service: "And ye shall hallow the fiftieth year, and
proclaim liberty throughout all the land unto all the inhabitants
thereof; it shall be a jubilee unto you; and ye shall return every man
unto his possession, and ye shall return every man unto his family."[214]
It is noteworthy to mention that a Hebrew could become a slave only
through the order of a court or because of a criminal act. Ironically,
Yahweh demanded that no one should exploit others: "Ye shall not
therefore oppress one another; but thou shalt fear thy God, for I am
the Lord your God.[215]

The Ninth Commandment demanded honesty from a witness.
According to this commandment, an oath was considered a religious
obligation. From this point on, they could not, as in the past, put their
hands on their testes and swear.[216] Lying was strongly prohibited:
"Thou shalt not bear false witness against thy neighbor."[217] In fact,
false witnesses were expected to receive the same punishment that the
victims had suffered.[218] Religion was the sole law of Israel, and in
fact a crime was considered a sin. Minor crimes could be dismissed
by offering a charity to the priests. Capital punishment was
recommended for idolatry, adultery, striking or cursing a parent, and
kidnapping or lying with a beast.[219]

Yahweh did not mind if people took the law in their own
hands in the case of murder. The family of the murdered used to take
its revenge on the murderer: "The avenger of his death shall
personally kill the murderer when he meets him."[220] The principle of
punishment was enunciated as "Eye for eye, hand for hand, foot for
foot. Burning for burning, wound for wound, stripe for stripe."[221]

---

[213] Exodus 21:2; Deuteronomy 15:12.
[214] Leviticus 25:10.
[215] Leviticus 25:17.
[216] Genesis 24:2–3.
[217] Exodus 20:16.
[218] H. Graetz, *Popular History of the Jews* (New York: 1919), 1:173, quoted in W. Durant, *The Story of Civilization: Our Oriental Heritage* (New York: Simon & Schuster, 1963), 338.
[219] Exodus 21:15–21, 22:19.
[220] Numbers 35:19.
[221] Exodus 21:24–25.

"And if a man caused a blemish in his neighbor; as he has done, so shall it be done to him. Breach for breach, eye for eye, tooth for tooth; as he has caused a blemish in a man, so shall it be done to him again."[222]

For certain crimes such as heresy and cursing God, death by stoning was suggested: "And the Lord said to Moses, take him outside the camp and tell all who heard him to lay their hands upon his head, then all the people are to execute him by stoning."[223]

In the final analysis, the Mosaic penile code proposed a system of equitable revenge regardless of the class status of the murderer or the murdered. In spite of the fact that the Mosaic penile code was written fifteen hundred years later than the code of Hammurabi,[224] there are many resemblances between the two.[225]

Finally, the Tenth Commandment aimed at a form of social order: "Thou shalt not covet thy neighbor's house, thou shalt not covet thy neighbor's wife, or his manservant, or his maidservant, or his ox, or his ass, or anything that is thy neighbor's."[226] Strangely, the greatest commandment is not among the ten[227] and appears elsewhere, when God says to Israel: "Don't seek vengeance. Don't bear a grudge; but love your neighbor as yourself, for I am Jehovah."[228]

The Book of Law in essence was a necessity to a people with harsh and cruel living conditions. But because the Book of Law represented the ideals of the priests, it was highly honored. If someone ignored a small part of these codes and experienced hardship in life, he or she would have simply perceived his or her difficult time as the direct consequence of ignoring the codes. Consequently, the Book of Law was greatly admired by the public. These codes and regulations also provided strength, perseverance, and

---

[222] Leviticus 24:19–20.

[223] Leviticus 24:13,14.

[224] The code of Hammurabi is the earliest known collection of the laws and edicts of the Babylonian king. The code has nothing to do with religion but is a criminal law of equal retaliation, similar to the Semitic law of "an eye for an eye." The law seeks to protect the weak and poor, women, children, and slaves against injustice at the hands of the rich and powerful.

[225] I. Wigoder, *The New Standard Jewish Encyclopedia* (New York: Facts on File, 1992), 408.

[226] Exodus 20:17.

[227] W. Durant, *The Story of Civilization: Our Oriental Heritage* (New York: Simon & Schuster, 1963), 339.

[228] Leviticus 19:18.

a sense of pride and unity to the Israelites, and became a heritage that the Jews carried on their shoulders, from one place to another, throughout their turbulent history.

Chronology:

100,000-12,000 years ago	The Canaanites, the ancestors of Israelites, settled in the region according to the contemporary archeological studies
3000 BCE	Migration of Israelite's ancestors from Sumer to Haran in Babylonian Empire according to the biblical narratives
2000–1550 BCE	Settlement of Hebrew tribes in Jordan Valley in the Middle Bronze Age
1694–1600 BCE	House of Joseph/Tribe of Levi wandered toward Egypt in search of green land
1570 BCE	The fall of the kingdom of Hyksos in Egypt and the forcing of Hebrews into slavery
1650–1220 BCE	Hebrew bondage in Egypt according to the biblical narratives
1020 BCE	National unity of the tribes of Israel
1004–928 BCE	Reigns of David and Solomon
922 BCE	The fall of ancient Israel and the establishment of the kingdom of Judah in the south and the kingdom of Israel in the north
873-852 BCE	The reign of King Ahab, the first king described in Old Testament with independent historical reference

Chapter Two

THE FALL AND RISE OF JERUSALEM

The Fall of Jerusalem, Exile, and Return

The kingdom of Israel in the north fell to the hands of the Assyrians in 734–721 BCE. From this point on, there is no historical reference to the ten tribes of Israel residing in this region. There are numerous predictions about the outcome of the lost tribes, none of which have been substantiated by historic evidence. Some believe the lost tribes migrated to the east and eventually in the fifth century CE joined the Nestorians, the followers of Nestorius, the Priest of Constantinople. Others insist that some of these tribes migrated further east and comprise the present-day Jews in Iran and Afghanistan. Modern historians, however, believe that as the two tribes of Judah and Benjamin grew stronger, the other ten weaker tribes of the north were incorporated into them. In support of this viewpoint, Israeli archaeologist Magen Broshi suggested a rather sudden and exceptional population growth in the southern kingdom of Judah and Jerusalem toward the end of the eighth century BCE, coinciding with the migration of the northern tribes to the south.[1]

---

[1] I. Finkelstein and N. A. Silberman, *The Bible Unearthed: Archeology's New Vision of Ancient Israel and the Origin of Its Sacred Texts* (New York: Free Press, 2001), 243.

The scribes of Deuteronomy viewed the fall of Samaria and the survival of Judah as God's retribution for Israel's sins in the days of King Ahab or Jeroboam II: "For so it was, that the people of Israel had sinned against the Lord their God, who had brought them up from the land of Egypt,. . . and the people of Israel did secretly those things that were not right against the Lord their God. . . . And they set up for themselves pillars and Asherim in every high hill. . . and did wicked things to provoke the Lord to anger; For they served idols. . . . Then the Lord warned Israel, and Judah, by all the prophets, and by all the seers, saying, Turn from your evil ways, and keep my commandments and my statutes, according to all the Torah which I commanded your fathers. . . . And they rejected his statutes, and his covenant that he made with their fathers. . . and sold themselves to do evil in the sight of the Lord, to provoke him to anger. Therefore the Lord was very angry with Israel, and removed them from his sight; there was none left but the tribe of Judah only."[2] However, the modern archaeological studies have substantiated the viewpoint that the Assyrians captured Samaria and the northern kingdom of Israel merely because of the rich resources and productive population, and ignored Judah altogether because of a lack of these attributes.[3]

The kingdom of Judah in the south, with a history that was robustly favored by biblical scribes,[4] maintained its identity for another century but always remained under the influence of the Assyrians. Before long, the center of power gradually shifted from the Assyrians to the Babylonians. Consequently, the Babylon's strongman, Nebuchadnezzar II, conquered Assyria and Egypt in 605 BCE and attacked the kingdom of Judah in 597 BCE. He overthrew King Jehoiachin and forced the artisans and professionals of Judah to move to Babylon. He selected Matenia, a prince of the house of David, as the new proxy governor of Judah and called him Zedekiah. King Zedekiah was soon pulled into controversial and divisive decision making. For a while, he vacillated between the reconciliatory policies toward Nebuchadnezzar that were advanced by the prophet

---

[2] Kings II 17:7–18.

[3] I. Finkelstein and N. A. Silberman, *The Bible Unearthed: Archeology's New Vision of Ancient Israel and the Origin of Its Sacred Texts* (New York: Free Press, 2001), 224.

[4] W. G. Dever, *What Did the Biblical Writers Know and When Did They Know It?* (Grand Rapids, MI: Eerdmans, 2001), 159.

Jeremiah[5] and the hard-line policies that were dictated by Judean patriots. Eventually, in 588 BCE, Zedekiah sided with the patriots and rejected the Babylonian dominance that triggered Nebuchadnezzar to attack Judah two years later. Nebuchadnezzar ruined Jerusalem and arrested the leaders of the insurgency movement. He also executed Zedekiah's children before Zedekiah's eyes and then blinded him and took him, along with other leaders of the insurgency, artisans, and distinguished people, to Babylon.[6] According to the biblical narratives, the exile was comprised of eighteen thousand people altogether: ten thousand of the best soldiers and craftsmen and, on other occasions, seven thousand mighty men and one thousand artisans.[7] Many of the Judean population escaped to Egypt and took the prophet Jeremiah along by force and against his will, while the poor peasants remained in Judah. After the fall of Judah, Jews were therefore scattered in three parts of the world: Babylon, Egypt, and Palestine.

Many, like the prophet Jeremiah, blamed the strongman and the patriots of Judah for the defeat. They claimed that in order to prevent the disaster, Zedekiah would have had to accept the yoke of Nebuchadnezzar. Jeremiah's writings sometimes imply that he himself might have been a pawn of Nebuchadnezzar. In this regard, Jeremiah, citing the words of God, said: "I created earth, man and animals and left them in the hand of Nebuchadnezzar II, the Babylonian King who is my servant. . . . I conferred the cattle and herds to him. . . . It is very important that all people accept his yoke. He who does not submit to him, I will revenge by sword, illness and famine until they are all destroyed in his hand."[8]

In contrast to Jeremiah, Ezekiel, whose prophecy lasted from 592 to 570 BCE, was more optimistic about the future of the Israelites. Ezekiel, who migrated to Babylon, was not as unhappy as Jeremiah with the statesmen of Judah. He believed the disaster would not last long and that Yahweh would free the Israelites again and live

---

[5] Jeremiah announced his prophecy in 625 BCE and preached against idolatry. He was one of the wise men who predicted the defeat of Judah in the hands of Babylonians. Since Jehoiakim was distressed by his pessimism, he arrested him and he remained in seclusion up to the fall of Judah.

[6] R. E. Friedman, *Who Wrote the Bible?* (New York: HarperSanFrancisco, 1987), 98.

[7] Kings II 24:14, 24:16.

[8] Jeremiah 37:6–8.

among them forever.[9] Ezekiel's book is in fact a reflection of the Israelites' life in exile. The fall of Jerusalem and the loss of the Temple nonetheless enhanced the status of priests in the eyes of the people. Indeed, the priests filled the vacuum that had been created by the loss of the Temple in the hearts of the masses.

The Persian Empire conquered Babylon in 539 BCE and expanded its territories westbound all the way to Asia Minor and Egypt. Cyrus the Great passed a royal decree a year later according to which all the Jews in exile were freed. Subsequently, a small proportion of Jews under the leadership of Zerubbabel and Sheshbazzar, both men from the house of David, migrated to Jerusalem. "The whole congregation together was forty and two thousand three hundred and three score."[10] This group, in addition to their own belongings, took with them the donations from those Jews who were determined to stay in Babylon. They also took gifts from Cyrus: "King Cyrus himself donated the gold bowls and other valuable items which King Nebuchadnezzar had taken from the Temple at Jerusalem and had placed in the temple of his own gods."[11] Richard Friedman, however, points out that the Ark of the Covenant that contained the Ten Commandments mysteriously was not among the items the Jews carried with them to Jerusalem,[12] and no trace of the Ark was ever found again.[13] In spite of the relatively short stay, exile had a significant cultural impact upon Jews. Jews adapted very well to the new circumstances in exile, and in fact the majority felt at home in Babylon; only a minority showed interest in a return to Jerusalem.[14]

The migrants found Jerusalem in ruins. The major task of reconstruction and development of the ruined homeland disappointed many of the Jews. Under these circumstances, the religious leaders, like Zechariah and Haggai, made every effort to improve the people's morale by leading them toward a spiritual life. The first endeavor was

---

[9] Ezekiel: 31:34–36.
[10] Ezra 2:64.
[11] Ezra 1:7.
[12] R. E. Friedman, *Who Wrote the Bible?* (New York: HarperSanFrancisco, 1987), 155.
[13] K. Armstrong, *Jerusalem: One City, Three Faiths* (New York: Ballantine Books, 1996), 95.
[14] K. Kautsky, *Foundation of Christianity* (New York: Monthly Review Press, 1925), 228–229.

the reconstruction of the Temple that was completed in 516 BCE. Jews celebrated this year to commemorate the end of the Babylonian exile that had lasted seventy years, from 586 to 516 BCE.

In contrast to the Temple, the rehabilitation of Jerusalem dragged on until 445 BCE. It was in this year that Nehemiah, the special envoy of King Artaxerxes I and then the governor of Judah, supervised the reconstruction of the city. He was a very rich and influential man and tried hard to attract the wandering Jews back to Jerusalem.[15] Besides their humanitarian sentiments, the Achameans dynasty of Persia viewed a stable Judah in the proximity of Egypt as a strong security measure for the empire, justifying their keen interest in and support for the Jews.[16]

In the same period, Ezra, who was a priest, a scriber, and perhaps the minister for Jewish affairs at the Persian court,[17] along with a group of his supporters, arrived in Jerusalem to enforce the religion that had suffered a tremendous decline. Under the leadership of Ezra, the observation of Sabbath, maintenance of the Temple, collection of dues to the Temple, and strong measures against mixed marriages were enforced.[18] Moreover, he selected a priest as the governor of Judah to pursue his policies, combining state and religion. Around the fourth century BCE, Judah was a country that was administered according to the priests' opinions and taste, and the Book of Law governed every aspect of the people's lives. It was at about this time that, mainly due to the efforts of scribes and probably under the leadership of Ezra, the Moses Book of Law achieved its present-day configuration.

The Greek Civilization and the Hasmonaean Uprising

Alexander the Great was the irrefutable power of the ancient world toward the end of the fourth century BCE who defeated the Persian Empire. The Achamean Empire fell in 331 BCE, and Judah, considered a satellite of the Persian dynasty for almost two centuries, slipped under the yoke of the Greeks.[19] From this point on, the Jews

---

[15] H. Fast, *The Jews: Story of a People* (New York: Dell, 1968), 79.

[16] K. Armstrong, *Jerusalem: One City, Three Faiths* (New York: Ballantine Books, 1996), 97.

[17] Ibid., 100.

[18] Ibid., 101.

[19] Ibid., 103.

migrated to other parts of the Greek Empire such as the coasts of the Black Sea, the Greek islands, and around the Mediterranean Sea. Alexander also moved a portion of the Jewish population of Palestine to Alexandria in northern Egypt. There they participated in the development of this port. These large-scale migrations became known as the Greek Diaspora. Being separated from the Jewish cultural centers, Jews gradually were attracted to the Greek culture. Many learned the Greek language and substituted it for Hebrew. The Greek traditions and manners also influenced them significantly. It is said that some of the Jews were so fascinated by the Greek way of life that they underwent operations to obliterate the sign of their circumcisions.[20] According to Kautsky, "So evil were these wicked persons, who made themselves artificial foreskins, that they even denied their Jewish names, replacing them by Greek names. A high Priest named Jesus called himself Jason, another high Priest named Eliochim called himself Alkimos, and a Menassah renamed himself Menelaus."[21] Many learned the Greek language and substituted it for Hebrew, a phenomenon that supposedly prompted the translation of the Pentateuch.[22] The Five Books of Moses were translated into Greek about the third century BCE and were called the Septuagint,[23] the version that later was used as a base for the present-day Hebrew edition of the Old Testament. The fascination of the Jews for the Greek culture, or Hellenism, is a characteristic of the Greek Diaspora.

The premature death of Alexander in 323 BCE produced a political and cultural uneasiness for the Jews. The entire empire was divided between Alexander's commanders, and Ptolemy I Soter took charge of Egypt, Judea, and Samaria. Located in the middle of the Arabian Peninsula trade routes, Judea as a part of Palestine achieved a strategic importance. Therefore, it was not surprising that Judea was the subject of numerous fierce arguments and struggles among the Egyptians, Syrians, and Phoenicians. Eventually, Antiochus III, the Syrian ruler, defeated the Egyptians in 198 BCE and Judea officially

---

[20] I. Wigoder, *The New Standard Jewish Encyclopedia* (New York: Facts on File, 1992), 216.

[21] K. Kautsky, *Foundation of Christianity* (New York: Monthly Review Press, 1925), 279.

[22] B. Russell, *A History of Western Philosophy* (New York: Touchstone, 1972), 321.

[23] The term "Septuagint" originates from the Greek meaning "the Seventy." According to legend, the Pentateuch was translated at the command of Ptolemy II (285–246 BCE) by seventy Jewish scholars.

came under the control of the Seleucids, who were ruling over Asia Minor, Mesopotamia, and Syria, or almost all of the Greek Empire by now.

With the further consolidation of power in the hands of the Seleucids, they tried very hard to substitute the Greek culture and their way of life for Judaism. However, these efforts had support only among a certain segment of the Jewish community known as the Hellenizers; otherwise, they met significant resistance from ordinary Jews. The conflict, however, reached its peak in 168 BCE, when Antiochus IV Epiphanes outlawed Judaism as an illegal practice and replaced the altar of Yahweh with that of Zeus in the Temple of Jerusalem.[24] Sabbath rituals, circumcision, and other Jewish liturgics were abandoned, and those who did not follow his edict were sentenced to death.

Under the leadership of Mattathias, the great priest, and his five sons, Judah Maccabee, Jonathan, Simon, John, and Eleazar, the Jews revolted against the Seleucid King Antiochus IV Epiphanes in 168 BCE. They defeated the Seleucid forces in a fierce battle, recaptured the Temple, and established the Hasmonaean or Maccabees dynasty. In 143 BCE, Simon, the last of the Maccabees brothers, took advantage of the struggles between the Egyptians, Romans, and Seleucids and secured the independence of Judea. A popular assembly named him the general and high priest of the second Jewish Commonwealth and made the latter office hereditary in the Hasmonaeans family.[25] In 125 BCE, during the reign of John Hyrcanus, the son of Simon, the Hasmonaeans recaptured Samaria and Edom and forced their inhabitants to accept Judaism. The independent Jewish state that was herein created focused its efforts in strengthening the institution of religion, promoting a fundamentalist interpretation of the religious codes, and purging the alien elements within the society. Moreover, the Hasmonaeans founded the Sanhedrin, an assembly of seventy-one theologians and legislators that functioned as a supreme court, in charge of all legislative and religious decisions in the country. During the reign of the Hasmonaeans, many natural events received religious and liturgical

---

[24] B. Russell, *A History of Western Philosophy* (New York: Touchstone, 1972), 315.
[25] W. Durant, *The Story of Civilization: Caesar and Christ* (New York: Simon & Schuster, 1963), 530.

attributes. For instance, the festival of Chanukah is celebrated as a dedication to the Maccabees' victory over the Seleucids.[26] About six hundred years after the Maccabees' victory, rabbis seeking to claim Chanukah as their own added the legend of the single flask of oil that miraculously burned for eight days. In fact, the historic background of Chanukah dates back many centuries before the Maccabees' victory and was related to the winter festival of Nayrot,[27] when, as the days grew shorter during wintertime, people feared that the sun might die and the world sink into an eternal darkness. In an effort to coax the sun back to life, they kindled a fire at the time of the solstice. When the solstice passed and daylight increased, the people celebrated the triumph of light over darkness. [28]

Hasmonaean governments gradually accumulated wealth, power, and influence and concurrently indulged in corruption. Although the Hasmonaeans came to power as a popular, grassroots rebellion against the Greek influence and tyranny, they soon declined into corruption and viciousness, which offended many Jews and generated numerous internal conflicts. While there were Jews who viewed the Hasmonaean kingdom as a continuation of King David's monarchy, a wide range of Jews resented them and felt that the Hasmonaeans had ruined the integrity of the Temple of Jerusalem. John Hyrcanus, the grandson of Mattathias, the Great Priest, mercilessly suppressed a mass uprising against the Hasmonaeans in his time. Another rebellion took place at Sukkoth during the officiating ceremony of Alexander Janaeus, the son of John Hyrcanus. This uprising was also brutally suppressed. Alexander executed six thousand people and in another occasion crucified eight hundred rebels and butchered their wives and children before their eyes.[29] The power struggle between Hyrcanus II and his brother Aristobulus II eventually evolved into a civil war where over twelve thousand Jews killed each other. In order to resolve their conflict, the two brothers appeared before the Roman general Pompey at Damascus in 63 BCE. Pompey ordered Aristobulus II to return control of the Temple of

---

[26] K. Armstrong, *Jerusalem: One City, Three Faiths* (New York: Ballantine Books, 1996), 117.

[27] S. T. Wine, "The Real History of Hannukah," *Humanistic Judaism* 21:3 (1993): 4.

[28] R. Wolfe, "A New view of the Maccabees," *Humanistic Judaism* 27:4 (1999): 35.

[29] K. Armstrong, *Jerusalem: One City, Three Faiths* (New York: Ballantine Books, 1996), 121.

Jerusalem to Hyrcanus II. Since the followers of Aristobulus II ignored Pompey's order, Pompey captured the Temple and took Aristobulus and his son to Rome.

Meanwhile, Antipater, who at one time was the governor of Judea, took the side of Hyrcanus in this conflict, and they both invited the Roman army to be their allies. Soon after the victory of Julius Caesar over Pompey, Antipater joined the circle of Caesar and in 47 BCE officially invited the governance of Rome in Judea. Thus Judea lost its independence and was officially incorporated into Roman territories, with Antipater as its governor. Finally, the Hasmonaeans achieved independence from the Greek domination to later become subservient to Rome.

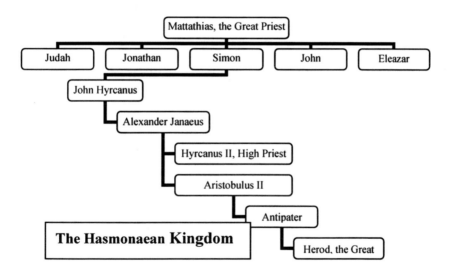

Herod, the son of Antipater, was an energetic ruler who came to power in 37 BCE. He, like his predecessors, suppressed opposition mercilessly, and murdered all possible rivals to his power, including his brother-in-law, Aristobulus III, the last Hasmonaean high priest. As a result of palace intrigues, he put to death his wife Mariamne and their two sons.[30] He also executed his father, Antipater, five days before his own death. In the aftermath of Herod's death, an uprising broke out in which Jews, the followers and the enemies of Herod, killed a few thousand of each other, and Romans crucified more than one thousand Jews.[31] Reconstruction of the Temple of Jerusalem was completed in 19 CE, a year after Herod's death. The same year, the high priest Joseph Caiaphas and the Roman commander Pontius Pilate took charge of Judea.

Alexander's victories and the influence of Greek culture, on the one hand, and the Hasmonaean brutal kingdom and their lust for Rome, on the other hand, advanced more conflicts among the Jews. In fact, the Hasmonaean kingdom was the product of the triumph of a Jewish fundamentalist movement that defeated Greek despotism and the Jewish supporters of the Greek culture. The triumph of the fundamentalist Jews, in spite of advancing eighty years of political independence, promoted a cultural setback of a different sort. In light of this new wave of fundamentalism, war for the first time was defined as the struggle between divine and evil forces. Moreover, redemption and paradise were promised only to those who had participated in these wars and were martyred.[32] Finally, the belief in the immortality of the soul and life after death, which did not exist in the traditional culture of Jews, began to emerge.[33]

The Religious Sects and the Rise of Christianity

The Hasmonaean kings increasingly slipped into the extravagant lifestyle characteristic of the Greeks. Since this lavishness and excess contradicted the simple nomadic life of the Hebrews, it naturally triggered enormous resentment among the people. Consequently, opposition groups and parties surfaced against a regime that became more and more brutal and eventually fell into the Roman sphere of power. Despite the Hasmonaeans' concerted efforts

---

[30] H. Fast, *The Jews: Story of a People* (New York: Dell, 1968), 104.
[31] K. Armstrong, *Jerusalem: One City, Three Faiths* (New York: Ballantine Books, 1996), 140.
[32] B. Russell, *A History of Western Philosophy* (New York: Touchstone, 1972), 316.
[33] Ibid., 315.

to keep it pure and free of foreign influence, the religion slowly but surely plummeted into a crisis.

Among the opposition was a group called the Qumran that was led by a circle of priests. The followers of this movement believed that the Hasmonaean rulers had disrespected the Temple of Jerusalem, and therefore the real sacred Temple was the spiritual circle they had established in exile. Therefore, the group openly encouraged people not to make contributions to the Temple of Jerusalem. According to the Jewish historian Josephus Flavius, the Qumran and the Essenes,[34] or Essaeans, both were the same group that began its political life about 150 BCE and continued up to the time of the destruction of the Temple by the Romans in 70 CE. They were against private property and slavery and opposed offering sacrifices to the Temple. They strongly believed that contributions to the Temple should be confined to food. Aside from their religious viewpoints, the Essenes' doctrine supported a form of social equity and justice:[35] "For none of them wishes to have any property of his own, either a house, or a slave, or land, or herds, or anything else productive of wealth. But rather, by joining together everything without exception, they all have a common profit from it."[36] Josephus Flavius also wrote: "They take no wives and keep no slaves. They imagine that the latter is not just, and the former gives rise to discord."[37] "They despised marriage, but adopted strange children, if they were still young and might still be taught, keeping them as their own, and instructing them in their customs and manners. They do not wish to abolish or prohibit marriage and the propagation of man. But they say that one must be on one's guard because of the unchastity of women, as no woman is satisfied with one man alone."[38] The Essenes ascribed everything to fate. They held the view that what humans do is what destiny has been prepared for them. They also believed in the immortality of the soul and punishment and reward after death. On the other hand, they refuted life after death and maintained that the body was corrupted after death. They used a solar instead of lunar

---

[34] The term has an Aramaic origin, meaning "the forgivers."
[35] K. Kautsky, *Foundation of Christianity* (New York: Monthly Review Press, 1925), 308.
[36] Ibid.
[37] Ibid., 311
[38] Ibid., 310

calendar and they believed in the Messiah.[39] It is said that early Christianity was indeed influenced by the Essenes' doctrine. The Dead Sea Scrolls, the historic document also known as Qumran's archives, was a collection of laws, stories, and poetry by this group. The scrolls were recovered by the archeologist Yigael Yadin in 1977.[40]

In addition to the Essenes, Josephus Flavius described two other opposition groups, the *Pharisees* and the *Sadducees*. In fact, these two groups were the prominent political parties of their time, expressing different social viewpoints and diverse religious doctrines.

The term *Pharisees* originates from the Hebrew word *Perushim*, meaning "separation" and "isolation." The Pharisees, like the Qumran, opposed those in control of the Temple, and both used to cite the Bible to justify their animosity. Josephus described them thus: "As for the two other sects, it is believed that the Pharisees interpret the law the more severely. They were the first who formed a sect that believed that everything is determined by fate and by god. In their opinion it may indeed depend on man whether he performs good or evil, but fate has its influence on man's actions. They believe, concerning the soul of man, that it is immortal, and that the souls of the good will enter into new bodies, while those of the wicked will be tormented by eternal suffering.[41] . . . The Pharisees are charitable and try to live in concord with the masses of the people." Flavius reported later, from the time of Herod: "There then existed people among the Jews who were proud of their strict observance of the law of their fathers, and who believed that god had a special affection for them. These people were called Pharisees. They had great power and were best able to oppose the king, but they were wise enough to wait for an opportunity, which would seem favorable for such an insurrection. When the Jews took an oath to be faithful to the Emperor Augustus and to obey the King Herod, these men refused to take the oath, and there were more than 6,000 of them."[42]

---

[39] K. Crim, *The Perennial Dictionary of World Religions* (New York: HarperSanFrancisco, 1981), 239.
[40] R. E. Friedman, *Who Wrote the Bible?* (New York: HarperSanFrancisco 1987), 129.
[41] K. Kautsky, *Foundation of Christianity* (New York: Monthly Review Press, 1925), 273.
[42] Ibid., 285.

The Pharisees appeared in the social scene during the reign of John Hyrcanus (135–104 BCE), and they turned into sworn enemies of early Christianity in the first century CE. In contrast to the Sadducees, they believed not only in the written law but also in the oral interpretation of the Bible. As we shall see later, the Pharisees were instrumental in the creation of the Talmud.[43]

The Sadducees were the sects of the Second Temple whose name probably is derived from the high priest Zadok, after whom the priesthood was called the race of Zadokides. For them, religion was primarily the Temple cult. Josephus Flavius wrote about them as such: "The other sect is that of Sadducees. They deny that fate has any influence at all and declare that god may not be blamed for the good or evil actions of the individual; man alone is responsible for these, in accordance with his own free will. They also deny that souls are immortal and that there is to be any reward or punishment after death."[44] In contrast to the Pharisees, the Sadducees only believed in the written law that accepted the Sadducees literally, and opposed the Pharisees' interpretation of the codes. The Sadducees generally represented the noble traditional priesthood and aristocrats. Historically, they had participated in the government of Judea and were among the supporters of Persian domination after returning from the Babylonian exile. After the fall of the Persian Empire, they shifted and were dedicated to the rule of Seleucid commanders.
The Sadducees suffered a significant blow during the reign of Herod and lost many of their followers. Flavius reports, "The rich were on the side of Sadducees but the mass of people clung to the Pharisees. . . . The sect of the Sadducees has but few adherents, but they are the most distinguished people of the country. However, affairs of state are not conducted according to their view."[45] Since their existence was bound to the Temple cult, the destruction of the Temple in 70 CE also led to their disappearance from the social arena.

The Sadducees, Pharisees, and Essenes were the prominent religious sects of Judea in the generation before Christ.[46] Roman

---

[43] B. Muraskin, "Hillel as a Jewish Humanist," *Humanistic Judaism*, 26:4 (1998): 31.
[44] K. Kautsky, *Foundation of Christianity* (New York: Monthly Review Press, 1925), 273.
[45] Ibid., 284.
[46] The term "Christ" originates from *Christos,* meaning "anointed" or "messiah."

domination, the struggle among the sects, and suffering under the Hasmonaeans had created an atmosphere of hope for the Jews that Yahweh would not let them down and they wouldn't remain under pagan domination for long.

Under such circumstances, the rise of *John the Baptist*, who was deeply sympathetic to the doctrine of the Essenes, was well received by many. So also was the reaction to Jesus when he came to Jordan to be baptized by John and proclaimed the early coming of the Kingdom of God.[47] In his preaching, Christ often referred to verses from Isaiah: "For unto us a child is born; unto us a Son is given; and the government shall be upon his shoulder. These will be his royal titles: Wonderful, Counselor, The Mighty God, The Everlasting Father, the Prince of Peace.[48] . . . His ever expanding, peaceful government will never end. He will rule with perfect fairness and justice from the throne of his father David."[49]

When the news came that John[50] was beheaded, the followers sought a subsequent leader, and Jesus assumed the burden and the risk. He returned to Galilee "and taught in the synagogues."[51] According to the Gospel of Luke, he read the following passage from Isaiah in Nazareth: "The spirit of the Lord God is upon me, because the Lord has anointed me to bring good news to the suffering and afflicted. He has sent me to comfort the broken-hearted, to announce liberty to captives and to open the eyes of the blind."[52] His religious sentiment was so strong that he could forgive any fault but disbelief.[53]

The first historic reference to Christ belongs to the historian Josephus Flavius in 93 CE[54] Josephus wrote, "At that time lived Jesus, a holy man, if man he may be called, for he performed wonderful works, and taught men, and joyfully received the truth. And many Jews and many Greeks followed him. He was the

---

[47] Matthew 3:11–12.

[48] Isaiah 9:6.

[49] Isaiah 9:7.

[50] John was arrested for criticizing King Herod's behavior of divorcing his wife and marrying the woman who was still married to his half-brother.

[51] Luke 4:14.

[52] Isaiah 61:1.

[53] W. Durant, *The Story of Civilization: Caesar and Christ* (New York: Simon & Schuster, 1963), 561.

[54] Ibid., 554.

Messiah."[55] Aside from the issue of whether he proclaimed to be the Messiah,[56] for which some have condemned him, it seems that Christ had serious difficulties with the Jewish religious leaders of his time. This difficulty is most visible in passages in the Gospels of John and Matthew that are, in general, less sympathetic to Jews and Jerusalem.[57] He said to the crowds and to his disciples, "You would think these Jewish leaders and these Pharisees were Moses, the way they keep making up so many laws! And of course you should obey their every whim! It may be all right to do what they say, but above anything else, do not follow their example. For they do not do what they tell you to do. They load you with impossible demands that they themselves do not even try to keep."[58]

Jesus, like Hillel, did not think that he was overthrowing the Judaic Law: "I came not to destroy the Law of Moses, but to fulfill it."[59] Jews of all sects, except for the Essenes, resented Christ because he assumed the authority to forgive sins and he spoke in the name of God.[60] Evidently, the priests of the Temple and the members of the Sanhedrin were most concerned that Christ's teachings might spark a political revolt. They feared that the Roman procurator would conceivably accuse them of neglecting their responsibility to maintain social order and may use that as an excuse to provoke a brutal repression.[61,62] The following statement in the Gospel of John supports this line of thinking: "And one of them, Caiaphas, who was high priest that year said, you stupid idiots—let this one man die for the people, why should the whole nation perish?"[63]

---

[55] Ibid.

[56] J. A. Garraty and P. Gay, *The Columbia History of the World* (New York: Harper and Row, 1972), 218.

[57] K. Armstrong, *Jerusalem: One City, Three Faiths* (New York: Ballantine Books, 1996), 160.

[58] Matthew 23:1–5.

[59] Matthew 5:17.

[60] W. Durant, *The Story of Civilization: Caesar and Christ* (New York: Simon & Schuster, 1963), 568.

[61] K. Armstrong, *Jerusalem: One City, Three Faiths* (New York: Ballantine Books, 1996), 143.

[62] T. Bokenkotter, *A Concise History of Catholic Church* (New York, Doubleday Publishing, 2004), 14

[63] John 11:49–50.

The four gospels present somewhat different stories of the trial of Christ, the charges against him, and his crucifixion.[64] In John's narrative, Christ and the high priest do not face each other; while Christ is inside and the high priest is among the crowd outside, the Roman procurator, Pontius Pilate, shuttles back and forth between them.[65] The high priest and the crowd eventually manage to obtain the conviction of Christ through Pontius Pilate.[66] According to the Gospels of Matthew and Mark, those who arrested Christ extradited him to Pontius Pilate, who proceeded with crucifixion the following day.[67] The Gospel of Luke, however, claims that the high priest did not face Christ alone; he was accompanied by scribes and elders, and there was no condemnation of Christ at that session.[68] According to Luke, Pontius Pilate was the one who finally sentenced Jesus.[69]

While the roles of the Roman procurator and the high priest during these proceedings have been the subject of controversy among historians, early Christianity and the Church have always blamed the Jews for the death of Christ and have considered the role of Pontius Pilate less important.[70] Others, however, have challenged this conclusion on several grounds. Ellis Rivkin of the Hebrew Union College in Cincinnati, Ohio, believes that the real religious court was separate from the Sanhedrin. He depicts the Sanhedrin as a political body that collaborated with the Roman occupation forces and lacked any religious legitimacy. In his opinion, Jesus was neither tried for his religious teachings nor for his beliefs. On the contrary, only the political consequences of his teachings were on trial.[71] Some Jewish writers doubt whether the Sanhedrin trial occurred at all. They believe that the nighttime hearing and the rushed verdict as described in the gospels is in violation of the Jewish religious law.[72] Finally, others

---

[64] R. E. Brown, *A Crucified Christ in Holy Week* (Collegeville, MN: Liturgical Press, 1986), 68.

[65] Ibid., 60.

[66] John 18:36–40.

[67] Matthew 27:24–30.

[68] R. E. Brown, *A Crucified Christ in Holy Week* (Collegeville, MN: Liturgical Press, 1986), 51.

[69] Luke 23:24–25.

[70] E. Abrams, *Faith or Fear* (New York: Free Press, 1997), 88.

[71] R. N. Ostling, "Why Was Christ Crucified?" *Time*, April 4, 1994.

[72] R. E. Brown, *A Crucified Christ in Holy Week* (Collegeville, MN: Liturgical Press, 1986), 13.

have insisted that neither the high priest nor the Sanhedrin were in a position to crucify Jesus.[73] Raymond Brown offers a rebuttal by arguing that the Sanhedrin were the single Jewish council that handled both religious and political matters. He further claims that there is no reason to believe that the Jews of 30 CE would have strictly observed the Jewish religious law that was codified two centuries later in the Mishnah, the classification of the oral Judaic codes.[74] He believes that many Jews sympathized with Christ, and Jesus was merely tried because of his anti-Temple pronouncements.[75] This view is supported in the following passage where Jesus bitterly denounced the Pharisees and the religious leaders: "You would think that these Jewish leaders and these Pharisees were Moses, the way they keep making up so many laws! . . . Everything they do is done for show. They act holy by wearing on their arms little prayer boxes with Scripture verses inside, and by lengthening the memorial fringes of their robes. And how they love to sit at the head table at banquets, and in the reserved pews in the synagogue! . . . Woe to you, Pharisees, and you other religious leaders. Hypocrites! For you won't let others enter the Kingdom of Heaven, and won't go in yourselves. And you pretend to be holy, with all your long, public prayers in the streets, while you are evicting widows from their homes. . . . You are so careful to polish the outside of the cup, but the inside is foul with extortion and greed. Blind Pharisees! First cleanse the inside of the cup, and then the whole cup will be clean. . . . For you build monuments to the prophets killed by your fathers and lay flowers on the graves of the godly men they destroyed, and say, we certainly would never have acted as our fathers did. . . . O Jerusalem, Jerusalem, the city that kills the prophets, and stones those god sends to her! How often I have wanted to gather your children together as a hen gathers her chicks under her wings, but you wouldn't let me. And now your house is left to you, desolate. For I tell you this, you will never see me again until you are ready to welcome the one sent to you from god."[76] Finally, others have expressed the opinion that Joseph

---

[73] K. Armstrong, *Jerusalem: One City, Three Faiths* (New York: Ballantine Books, 1996), 143.

[74] R. E. Brown, *A Crucified Christ in Holy Week* (Collegeville, MN: Liturgical Press, 1986), 13.

[75] Ibid.

[76] Matthew 23:1–39.

Caiaphas was indeed a pawn in the hands of the Roman procurator Pontius Pilate and he convicted Jesus because of fear for his own life.

Nevertheless, the Pharisees viewed Christ's teachings as heresy and blasphemous and often persecuted his followers. Therefore, his followers left Jerusalem and focused their activities outside the city. His disciples traveled widely, insisted upon the true observance of Judaism, and attracted many non-Jews. For instance, they preached that "Thou shalt not kill" means not only that one should not kill but should not even get angry, and "Thou shall not do adultery" includes any lustful feeling toward women as well. In addition to the non-Jews, Christ's teachings fascinated two groups of Jews: those who conceived him as the Messiah, and those who preferred the newer version of the religion of Christianity to the traditional Judaism.[77] The response of the ordinary Jews to the rise of these religious sects was a stricter observance of the codes, intolerance for those who dared to ignore them, and impatience for regaining their political independence. Therefore, the first century CE is signified by bloody struggles among the sects and courageous revolts against Rome.

The Romans' treatment of the Jews was harsh. As a Roman admirer once said, they behaved "like executioners rather than governor."[78] The uprising of the Zealots, a group of fanatical Jews who believed in God as the sole ruler of the Jewish nation, was a protest against this harsh and cruel behavior of the Romans in Judea. In 66 CE, when the Roman procurator took a large sum of money from the Temple treasury, the Zealots poured before the shrine and asked for his dismissal. In response, the Roman legions ravaged homes and slew thousands of Jews. In the aftermath of this event, the old and well-to-do Jews proposed peace and patience, whereas the poor and the young were in favor of an armed struggle against the Romans. The latter succeeded, and the fight between the Zealots and

---

[77] In the traditional Jewish literature, the Messiah has been described as an earthy man from the house of David (Isaiah 11:1) who, in contrast to Christ, does not suffer for the sins of his people. According to the Jewish tradition, the moment a Jew looks upon Christ as the Messiah, he is no longer a Jew. (R. R. Gorelik, *Messiah: Another Jewish View* [Irvine, CA: Eshav Books, 1993], 6; R. E. Brown, *A Crucified Christ in Holy Week* [Collegeville, MN: Liturgical Press, 1986], 63.

[78] W. Durant, *The Story of Civilization: Caesar and Christ* (New York: Simon & Schuster, 1963), 543.

the Romans lasted and gradually spread to the other cities. Although over twelve thousand Jews were killed, the radicals won.[79] The rebels surrounded the Roman garrison in Masada, persuaded them to disarm, and then slaughtered every one of them. Meanwhile, non-Jews in a number of cities were engaged in attacking Jews. According to Josephus Flavius, in one day, gentiles cut the throats of ten thousand Jews in Damascus.[80] By the end of 68 CE, the Romans had destroyed the strongholds of resistance in Judea, thus isolating Jerusalem, which was still under rebel control. In 69 CE, the Roman commanders Vespasian and his son Titus were dispatched to put down the revolt. One year later, they lay siege to and conquered Jerusalem and destroyed the Second Temple of Jerusalem. The Jews courageously defended the Temple, considering it an honor to defend the building, before it was set on fire.[81] The Western Wall was the only section of the Temple that was not demolished. Josephus Flavius estimated the number of dead to be about 1,197,000, while according to Tacitus, the Roman historian, this estimate is about 600,000.[82] Regardless of which figure is correct, the toll that the Jews paid in this uprising was significant, considering that the world Jewish population of the first century was around ten million, of which only half were inhabitants of Judea.[83] The remaining half were scattered in Alexandria, North Africa, Babylon, Antioch, and Rome. As the result of this defeat, the positions of high priest and the Sanhedrin were abolished, the properties of those who had participated in the revolt were confiscated and sold, the remaining Jews were forced to pay the pagan temple of Jupiter the same amount they formerly offered to the Temple of Jerusalem, and the Roman emperor took possession of all Jewish land.[84] It was then that the Sadducees disappeared from the social arena and the Pharisees became the leaders of a homeless people. In the aftermath of the Zealots defeat, Jerusalem for all practical purposes was a military base for the Tenth Roman Legion,

---

[79] Ibid., 544.

[80] Ibid.

[81] K. Armstrong, *Jerusalem: One City, Three Faiths* (New York: Ballantine Books, 1996), 152.

[82] W. Durant, *The Story of Civilization: Caesar and Christ* (New York: Simon & Schuster, 1963), 545.

[83] H. Fast, *The Jews: Story of a People* (New York: Dell, 1968), 113.

[84] K. Armstrong, *Jerusalem: One City, Three Faiths* (New York: Ballantine Books, 1996), 153.

with some Greek and Syrian civilian population and small communities of Jewish Christians and Jews.[85]

In 132 CE, under the leadership of Simon bar Kokhba, the Jews made a last effort for their independence and allegedly against Emperor Hadrian's plan to build a new city in Jerusalem. Simon claimed to be the Messiah, and Rabbi Akiba ben Joseph, a great scholar of the time who had preached peace all his life, blessed him as the redeemer and in this manner endorsed the uprising. This revolt was also fiercely put down by the Romans and resulted in over half a million dead.[86] In addition, once the unrest was crushed, a larger number of Jews were sold as slaves in the market.

Subsequently, Emperor Hadrian passed a decree that forbade the observance of the Sabbath and public performance of any Jewish religious rituals, including circumcision. Moreover, the name of Judea was changed to Palestina in an attempt to wipe out the connection between the land and the Jewish people. Jews were also prohibited from entering Jerusalem. From this date, probably until the conquest of Jerusalem by the Arabs in 637 CE, Jews were not allowed to live within the city borders.[87] It was not until the middle of the third century CE that Jews were permitted to visit and mourn the Temple from a distance.[88] The defeat of Simon bar Kokhba's revolt was a prominent turning point the in Jewish history. From this point on, Jews lost their status as a 'nation', dispersed all over the world, and lived as a minority. Hebrew, the national language, gave way to the spoken languages of other peoples. Jews then spoke and wrote in Aramaic, Arabic, and later in Spanish, German, Polish, Russian, English and so forth and so on.

The fall of Judea enhanced the conflicts between Jews and Christians. While Jews looked upon the fall of Judea and the destruction of the Temple as a disaster, Christians, on the other hand, perceived it as an indication that God had swayed his attention from

---

[85] Ibid., 154.
[86] Ibid., 163.
[87] E. Barnavi, *A Historical Atlas of the Jewish People* (New York: Schocken Books, 1992), 49.
[88] K. Armstrong, *Jerusalem: One City, Three Faiths* (New York: Ballantine Books, 1996), 169.

the Jews toward them. Therefore, the conflicts between Jews and Christians achieved new dimensions.

During the next three centuries, Christianity prospered and became a prominent religion in terms of its number of adherents. In 313 CE, Emperor Constantine I subscribed to Christianity and made it the official religion of the Roman Empire. Indeed, he viewed Christianity as a force that could bring about cohesion in his vast territories.

As Christianity achieved political power, new restrictions were imposed upon the Jews.[89] Christians were banned from trading with Jews, intermarriage between them was disciplined with capital punishment,[90] heavier taxes were forced upon them, and above all they were prohibited from owning slaves.[91] It is said that Gallus, the Roman emperor, imposed such heavy taxes on the Jews that some of them had no choice other than to sell their children in order to pay.[92] In contrast to Christ's teachings of love and forgiveness, the Christians in power had every intention of ostracizing the Jews as enemies of society.[93] Once again, in 352 CE, the Jews revolted against the Romans but again were defeated. Thousands of Jews were killed and many more thousands were sold into slavery.

During the reign of Emperor Julian (361–363 CE), however, the persecutions of the Jews were curtailed and some of the restrictions were removed. Under Julian, the tax system was revised, and many discriminatory laws against the Jews were abolished. In spite of the fact that Julian was raised in a Christian family, he lost his faith in Christianity and tried to restore paganism in Rome. His opposition to Christianity led him to regard the Jews favorably. He recognized Yahweh as a great god, and in 362 CE he ordered the reconstruction of the Temple of Jerusalem at the expense of the

---

[89] B. Russell, *A History of Western Philosophy* (New York: Touchstone, 1972), 326.
[90] S. W. Baron, *Social and Religious History of the Jews* (New York: Columbia University Press, 1937), 1: 266.
[91] K. Armstrong, *Jerusalem: One City, Three Faiths* (New York: Ballantine Books, 1996), 192.
[92] W. Durant, *The Story of Civilization: The Age of Faith* (New York: Simon & Schuster, 1950), 347.
[93] K. Armstrong, *Jerusalem: One City, Three Faiths* (New York: Ballantine Books, 1996), 193.

empire.[94] Jewish men, women, and children rushed to participate in the reconstruction of the Temple, an event for which they had impatiently waited for almost three centuries. Unfortunately, several explosions, probably due to underground gas collections, occurred in the process of laying the new foundation, and many of the workers were killed. Jews mourned this event while Christians celebrated and attributed this to the will of God. Nevertheless, because of the premature death of Emperor Julian in 363 CE, construction of the Temple was abandoned in the same year. The Jews returned to their hometowns in disappointment, and therefore the construction of the Third Temple of Jerusalem was never realized.

In light of what has just been described, Jews could not be blamed for not being fond of the Christian lands. Some of them moved to Mesopotamia and from there to Persia. In Persia, the Jews enjoyed tranquility. The state apparatus of the Sassanid dynasty in Persia solely included the nobles and did not allow the participation of average citizens. Therefore, in this setting, the differences between the average Jews and non-Jews were not that prominent. Although the persecution of the Jews continued in the Persian territories, the restrictions were more tolerable.

Others migrated to Babylon, Constantinople, North Africa, and the Arabian Peninsula. In Babylon, the Jews joined the communities that were among the oldest, dating back to 597 BCE, when Judea fell. Those who migrated to North Africa established Jewish communities that enjoyed relative freedom under the non-Christian emperors. Some settled in Egypt and Alexandria and learned shipping and navigation.

Those who moved to the Arabian Peninsula lived peacefully next to the Arabs of Medina and Khyber and introduced Judaism to the local residents. In fact, some Arabs converted to Judaism, and many more were influenced by the Jewish concept of revelation and Messianism,[95] which in turn prepared their subjective background for the acceptance of the Qur'an.

---

[94] G. Wigoder, *The New Standard Jewish Encyclopedia* (New York: Facts on File, 1992), 533.
[95] W. Durant, *The Story of Civilization: The Age of Faith* (New York: Simon & Schuster, 1950), 163.

The strong monotheism and the biblical encounters in the Qur'an suggest the Jewish influence. However, the variation between the stories in the Bible and the Qur'an imply that they were acquired through indirect sources, probably Jewish and Christian traders and travelers.[96]

Unlike the Jews within the Roman Empire, those Jews who were residing outside Rome were only occasionally persecuted, and they enjoyed longer periods of peace and tranquility. In these communities, Hebrew was the language of worship, but the Jews also used Aramaic in the day-to-day communication in the east and used Greek in Europe and Egypt. Religion was the core of education. In the absence of the Temple, the synagogue was the prime institution within the Jewish communities. The more they were persecuted, the more they became fascinated by their religion. The very survival of these communities was indeed dependent upon an ongoing hope and desire to believe in God.

The Talmud

Neither following the destruction of the Second Temple and the fall of Judah, nor throughout the period that Christianity rose to power and the animosities against the Jews achieved new dimensions, did Jews sit idle. Instead, they became more attached to their religion and compiled new liturgies and rituals. They also began to interpret their religion in a manner that more than ever promoted unity among them and reinforced the promise of the return of a savior or the Messiah alive. In fact, the bulk of what we know as Judaism today was formulated during this period.

Therefore, the scholars in two prominent Jewish communities of the world, Palestine and Babylon, gathered the oral interpretations of the written codes of the Old Testament and called them the Palestinian and Babylonian Talmud,[97] respectively. If the Old Testament was considered the religion of the ancient Hebrews, then

---

[96] J. A. Garraty and P. Gay, *The Columbia History of the World* (New York: Harper and Row, 1972), 259.

[97] "Talmud" is a Hebrew term meaning "study and search." Its Aramaic synonym is *Gemara*.

the Talmud must be viewed as the religion of Jews through the Diaspora and the Middle Ages.

After the destruction of the Second Temple, the Sadducees or the Temple Sect lost their support and disappeared from the political arena. Therefore, the Pharisees, who were more fundamentalist in their viewpoints, achieved the role of leadership. The Pharisees, in contrast to the Sadducees, believed that Moses had left numerous oral codes for the Israelites in addition to the written law that had been presented in the Torah or Pentateuch. These oral codes that had been conveyed from teacher to student and from one generation to another were gathered by the Pharisees' priests and were added to the religion.

The oral interpretations were indeed a response to the new necessities of their life. The written law that was crystallized in the Pentateuch no longer met the needs of the Jews under their new circumstances. Numerous drastic changes had occurred; for instance, Jerusalem was gone and the Jews had lost their independence. It was now the responsibility of the rabbis and at times the assembly of the Sanhedrin to interpret the written law and apply it to the new state of affairs.

The number of oral codes, the interpretations of the rabbis, and the conflicting opinions and commentaries that they had advanced about them were increasing each day. Therefore, memorizing the codes and their interpretations seemed unrealistic, prompting the need for a classification and organization of this body of literature. In addition, many of the teachers and priests, who had been the carriers of oral codes, were dispersed, and access to them seemed not feasible. Many teachers of the Sanhedrin and prominent rabbis such as Hillel, Akiva Ben Joseph, and Meir[98] submitted their own classifications of the oral laws that were not generally accepted. It was not until 189 CE that Rabbi Jehuda Hanasi[99] transformed the work of Akiva, Meir, and others, rearranged the entire oral law or interpretations of scriptures, and added his personal commentaries,

---

[98] Meir was a student of Rabbi Akiva Ben Joseph and an assembly member of the Sanhedrin in the first century CE.
[99] Jehuda Hanasi (135–220 CE) was a religious and political leader in the Jewish community of Palestine. He was recognized as "the sacred teacher" among the Jews of his time. Hanasi believed "ignorance" was at the core of Jewish suffering.

introducing a more plausible version that was named the Mishnah of Rabbi Jehuda, or the Mishnah ("oral teaching").

Since Rabbi Jehuda's days, the Mishnah has undergone numerous transformations. Scholars in Babylon, Palestine, and later in Europe debated, amended, analyzed, and illustrated the text to apply it to the new circumstances of their place and time. The authorities that contributed to the Babylonian version all lived before 499 CE, and those in the Palestinian or Jerusalem Talmud all lived before 399 CE. Therefore, it has been assumed that the work of the Babylonian version of the Talmud was completed before the end of the fifth century and the task of the Palestinian version by the fourth century CE. The Babylonian Talmud contains over two and one-half million words and is about three times as long and detailed as the Palestinian version.[100]

Commentaries, supplements, and discussions around Mishnah are called the Gemara. The sections that discuss the legal codes of Jewish law are named the Halakhah. The credit for the compilation and inscription of both versions of the Talmud goes to the poor scribes of the Babylonian and Palestinian synagogues and schools. These clerks, who generally belonged to the lowest stratum of the Jewish communities, were usually not paid for these services. Rather, they lived with and were supported by the more affluent members of the Jewish communities.

The Talmud has been organized into 6 orders, 63 tractates, and 523 chapters as follows:

Order	Tractate	Comment
Zeraim	11	On agriculture and charity
Moed	12	On feasts
Nashim	7	On marriage, pregnancy, and sexual relations
Nezikin	10	On the civil and penile codes
Kodashim	11	On saints
Tohorot	12	On cleanliness and hygiene

---

[100] G. Wigoder, *The New Standard Jewish Encyclopedia* (New York: Facts on File, 1992), 901.

The Talmud is not to be considered a masterpiece in literature. In it we find legends, astrology, superstition, magic, miracles, numerology, and the interpretation of dreams. The order in which this body of information is presented also has many shortcomings. Indeed, several tractates have been listed under the wrong orders, and many chapters are in incorrect tractates. At times, a subject starts in one tractate and then is left out and resumed in a different tractate. Many topics are discussed in these volumes, but many contradictions are often left unresolved.

In the Talmud, as in the Old Testament of the Bible, God is intelligent and omnipotent. The God of the Talmud also has many human qualities: he loves, hates, gets angry,[101] laughs,[102] cries,[103] feels remorse,[104] prays three times a day,[105] and even wears phylacteries[106] on his arm.[107] Some rabbis admit that the attribution of human characteristics to God was merely for a better understanding of the subject.

Jews of the rabbinical period believed in God not only as the creator but also as a father figure, a father who would not break the covenant with Israel and would always look upon them as the "chosen people." According to Will Durant, in the most desperate and hopeless circumstances, Jews mounted to such compensatory pride that God handed the Holy Scriptures first to them, and later the Christians and Muslims adopted them.[108]

There is nothing more sinful in Judaism than the belief in the plurality of God. Therefore, the Talmud defends monotheism against the polytheism of the pagans and the tritheism[109] of Christianity. It is no surprise that this has been emphasized in the principal Jewish

---

[101] Talmud, Berachoth, 6-b.
[102] Talmud, Aboda Zara, 3-b.
[103] Talmud, Chagiga, 3-b.
[104] Talmud, Sukkah, 52-b.
[105] Talmud, Aboda Zara, 3-b.
[106] Phylacteries or Tephillin are two black boxes fastened to leather straps. They are bounded on the arm and on the head usually during the Morning Prayer. The boxes contain four portions of the Pentateuch written on parchment.
[107] Talmud, Berachoth, 6-a.
[108] W. Durant, *The Story of Civilization: The Age of Faith* (New York: Simon & Schuster, 1963), 355.
[109] *Encyclopedia Encarta*, "Nominalism," CD-ROM, 2000.

prayer, "Shema Yisrael adonai elohenu, adonai ehad," meaning, "Hear, O Israel, the Lord is our God, the Lord is one." The Talmud also takes the position that there is no law but the will of God, and everything was created for a purpose.[110] "God created the snail as a cure for the scab, the fly as a cure for the sting of wasp, and the gnat as a cure for the bite of the serpent, and the serpent as a cure for a sore."[111] A human is described as being composed of body and soul, the former belonging to earth and the latter to God. The souls of human beings entice them to virtue and their bodies to sin.[112] Nevertheless, the Talmud trusts that human beings without their earthly desires may not toil or breed; we must be thankful to our ancestors, for if they had not committed sin, we would not have come into this world.[113] Rabbis believed that human beings are suffering because of their sin. If some people suffer more than they deserve, it is because they have not accepted the seriousness of their sins and their consequences. In other words, in the eyes of the Talmud, "There is no death without sin, and there is no suffering without iniquity."[114]

We rarely encounter a discussion on heaven and hell in the traditional Hebrew Scriptures. In contrast, the subject of heaven and hell has been illustrated in the Talmud in detail. It is understood that Jews adopted these two concepts from the Greeks and Persians during Hellenism and when they were exposed to the Persian culture in the preceding period.[115] In the Talmud, Ge Hinnom or hell, like heaven, is structured into seven levels, and only the wicked circumcised men enter it, but even then they would not be punished forever.[116] "All who descend into Ge Hinnom subsequently reascend, excepting three, who descend but do not reascend. He who commits adultery with a married woman publicly shames his neighbor, or fastens an evil epithet upon his neighbor."[117] On the other hand, heaven or Gan Eden is illustrated as a garden of physical and spiritual pleasures, where the

---

[110] W. Durant, *The Story of Civilization: The Age of Faith* (New York: Simon & Schuster, 1963), 354.
[111] Talmud, Shabbath 77-b.
[112] Talmud, Berachoth 6-a.
[113] Talmud, Avoda Zarah 5-a.
[114] Talmud, Shabbath 55-a.
[115] B. Russell, *A History of Western Philosophy* (New York: Touchstone, 1972), 331.
[116] Genesis Rabbah, xlviii-8.
[117] Talmud, Baba Metzia 58-b.

wine from the vintage of the first six days of creation will be served and God shall dine with the saved in a banquet. Many rabbis, however, confessed that no one could say what lies beyond the grave.[118]

The Talmud and Ethics

The Talmud is not only an encyclopedia of Jewish history and theology but also a compilation of medicine, culture, and art, a guide to industry, agriculture, gardening, commerce, tax, property, slavery, inheritance, law and penile code, government, and above all, ethics.

Ethics in Judaism, Christianity, and Islam is based upon a common understanding. All three religions strongly believe that the control of human behavior can be achieved only through the fear of God, a promise of happiness in heaven for the faithful and punishment for sinners in hell. In Judaism, as in Islam, ethics, law, and religion are indistinguishable. In other words, there is no difference between crime and sin. In these religions, what is legally considered a crime is religiously interpreted as hostility to God.

All three religions place primary importance on the sanctity of family, respect for parents and elders, care of children, and charity. In Judaism, as in Islam, voluntarily not wanting to have children was a major sin,[119] and in contrast, making a home and family was a religious edict. In this regard, the Talmud is of the same opinion as the Bible. We read in the Old Testament, "And god blessed them and told them multiply and fill the earth and subdue it; you are masters of the fish and birds and all the animals."[120] In the Talmud we encounter the idea that a childless man was accounted as dead.[121] The emphasis on this issue among these religions was probably a reflection of their desire to increase the number of their followers and to compensate for a high mortality rate in those communities. Contraception was condemned; however, under certain circumstances, rabbis allowed the

---

[118] Talmud, Berachoth 34-a.
[119] Talmud, Berachoth, 10-a.
[120] Genesis 1:28.
[121] Genesis Rabbah, lxxi-6.

use of this measure. "Three categories of women may use an absorbent in their marital intercourse: A minor, a pregnant woman and a nursing woman. The minor, because otherwise she might become pregnant, and as a result might die. A pregnant woman, because otherwise she might cause her fetus to degenerate into a sandal. A nursing woman, because otherwise she might have to wean her child prematurely and this would result in his death."[122]

Jews, like most other people of their time, were not happy to have daughters, but they welcomed and celebrated the birth of a son. They believed that a son carried the father's family name and protected his property and wealth. On the other hand, a daughter would marry another family and be lost to her parents. As a result, Jews would make every effort to educate their sons because they are the ones who would support the parents under any circumstances to the end. In spite of this distinction, when children were born, regardless of their gender, they were cared for.

The Talmud did not condemn sexual desire, but rabbis feared its attraction and made every effort to tame it. Some advised eating bread and salt to reduce the semen. Others suggested strenuous physical activity and the study of the Torah to tame sexual temptation. Rabbis believed that men must avoid any circumstances that might excite their passion: "A man should not walk behind a woman on the road, and even if his wife happens to be in front of him on a bridge, he should let her pass on one side, and whoever crosses a river behind a woman will have no portion in the future world.[123] Better go behind a lion than behind a woman."[124] In fact, even conversation with women was frowned upon. Finally, a few believed that "if a man sees that his evil inclination is prevailing upon him, let him go to a place where he is not known, and put on black garments, and wrap himself up in black garments, and let him do what his heart desires; but let him not profane the Name of Heaven publicly."[125]

Marriage was strongly encouraged. Fathers were urged to save for their daughters' dowries and for their sons' marriage expenses. This measure was emphasized so that the children's

---

[122] Talmud, Yevamoth, 12-b.
[123] Talmud, Berachoth, 61-a.
[124] Ibid.
[125] Talmud, Chagiga, 16-a.

marriages would not be delayed. Girls could legally marry at the age of twelve and one-half and boys at thirteen years of age. But in reality, girls used to marry at the age of fourteen and boys at the age of eighteen. The postponement of marriage was only justified in the case of Torah students. Jews strongly believed that "a man should build a house, plant a vineyard and then marry a wife."[126] In spite of that belief, this was not always easily achieved. Young men were advised to choose their wives not for their beauty but for their motherhood qualities: "Do not set your eyes on beauty but set your eyes on good family."[127] In spite of such advice, a prominent rabbi like Akiba ben Joseph believed that a man may divorce his wife if he finds a woman more beautiful than she is, for "it comes to pass, if she find no favor in his eyes."[128]

The details of conjugal relations have been legislated in the Talmud. It recommends once-a-week intercourse between husband and wife, preferably on Friday nights.[129] Women were expected to provide joy and satisfaction to their husbands and husbands to perform their conjugal duties; the failure by both was considered a serious matter.[130]

Virginity was important, and its value was emphasized in the Talmud,[131] as much as in the Old Testament.[132] Rabbis obviously had a lot of misunderstanding about this subject, yet they viewed it as the sole representation of a woman's supreme perfection and purity.

The Talmud, like the Qur'an, approves of polygamy: "A man may marry wives in addition to his first wife; provided only that he possesses the means to maintain them."[133] Under certain circumstances, however, the number of legal wives was restricted to four.[134] This restriction was based on the rabbis' recommendation that

---

[126] Talmud, Sotah 44-a.
[127] Talmud, Taanith 26-b.
[128] Talmud, Gittin 90-a.
[129] Talmud, Kethuboth 5-a.
[130] S. D. Goitein, *A Mediterranean Society* (Berkeley: University of California Press, 1999), 389.
[131] Talmud, Yebamoth 59-a, Ketuboth 6-b and 9-a.
[132] Deuteronomy 22:17.
[133] Talmud, Yebamoth 65-a.
[134] Talmud, Yebamoth 44-a.

a healthy individual must pay his marital visits on Friday evenings.[135] Having more than four wives then would reduce each wife's visit to less than one per month, which was not acceptable. According to the institution of Levirate, a Jewish man is obligated to marry his brother's childless widow. The position of the Old Testament is indeed very similar to that of the Talmud on this subject: "Wife of the dead shall not marry outside to a stranger; her husband's brother shall go in to her, and take her to him for a wife, and perform the duty of a husband's brother to her."[136]

Although the motivation behind this proposal was to promote higher birthrates in the communities that were suffering from high mortality, it was nevertheless an endorsement of polygamy. If the man did not wish to take his brother's wife, the widow could not marry another man until she performed the Halizah ceremony. The ceremony, as it appears in the book of Deuteronomy, is as follows: the widow goes up to the elders and says that her husband's brother refuses to let his brother's name to continue and refuses to marry her. Then the elders call him and speak to him. If he persists that he does not wish to take her, then the widow comes to him in the presence of the elders, pulls his shoe off his foot, spits in his face, and says, "So shall it be done to that man who will not build up his brother's house."[137] A special problem usually arises when the brother is younger than age thirteen and can neither legally marry the brother's widow nor can release her.[138] In contrast to a Levirate marriage, which was highly legislated, there was no law for a Sororate marriage where the sister took the place of a dead wife, yet it often did occur.[139] In general, polygamy was more frequently encountered among the rich Jewish men in Islamic countries than in the Christian lands.[140]

---

[135] Talmud, Kethuboth 62-b.

[136] Deuteronomy 25:5.

[137] Deuteronomy 25:9.

[138] According to the state of Israel's legislation of 1973, a Jewish man who refuses to participate in the Halizah ceremony is subject to imprisonment.

[139] S. D. Goitein, *A Mediterranean Society* (Berkeley: University of California Press, 1999), 401.

[140] G. F. Moore, *Judaism in the First Centuries of the Christian Era* (Massachusetts: 1932), 2: 22, quoted in W. Durant, *The Story of Civilization: The Age of Faith* (New York: Simon & Schuster, 1950), 380.

Some rabbis allowed the pleasure of watching: "A man will have a demerit in his record on Judgment Day for everything he beheld with his eyes and declined to enjoy."[141] On the other hand, others considered it a serious sin: "If one gazes at the little finger of a woman, it is as if he gazed at her secret place!"[142]

They believed "God hates divorce."[143] Yet, divorce by mutual consent of the husband and wife was allowed, but the husband could divorce his wife even without her permission. According to the prominent rabbi Hillel, a man can divorce his wife with no explanation.[144] In Hillel's opinion, appearing in public without a hair cover or speaking with strangers was sufficient grounds for divorce.[145] On the other hand, the wife could never divorce her husband without his permission. Divorce of an adulterous wife was a religious obligation,[146] and the divorce of a childless wife after ten years of marriage was highly recommended.[147] Even though adultery by the husband was condemned, it was not sufficient grounds for divorce.[148] Some rabbis allowed women to request divorce on the grounds of cruelty, impotence, and lack of support.[149] In general, however, many legal barriers were imposed in order to discourage divorce, as is still the case in many traditional Jewish communities today.

Sexual intercourse between a man and a married woman other than his wife was among the great sins like idolatry and murder, and carried a sentence of capital punishment: "If a heathen committed adultery with a Jewish betrothed maiden, he is stoned; with a fully married woman, he is strangled."[150] However, if sexual intercourse occurred between a Jewish man and a married non-Jewish woman, it was handled differently.[151] The man would be punished by whipping,

---

[141] Talmud, Kiddushin 4.
[142] Talmud, Berachoth 24-a and Shabbath 64-b.
[143] Malachi 2:16.
[144] Talmud, Yebamoth 29-a.
[145] Talmud, Nedarim 30-b.
[146] Talmud, Yebamoth 31-b.
[147] Talmud, Yebamoth 64-a.
[148] Talmud, Menachoth 2-a.
[149] Talmud, Ketuboth 77-a.
[150] Talmud, Sanhedrin 57-b.
[151] Ibid.

and if he was a Levite, then he would receive twice as many lashes.[152] This is not to indicate that a relation of this kind was approved by the Talmud. Instead, the Talmud placed a greater blame on the non-Jewish woman for being the reason the Jewish man got into trouble.

The Talmud, like the Islamic codes, was invented by men. The irrefutable support of men's rights in these volumes could scare every woman. Indeed, women's rights to a great extent have been ignored by these sages. While there are numerous references to the high moral standing of the Jewish women, they enjoy a low legal status. The economic security of women to a great extent depended on their dowries or what they had brought from their fathers' homes.[153] The Talmud, like Islam and Christianity, views women as a light-minded,[154] talkative[155] creature who extinguished the "soul of the world" through Eve's intelligent curiosity. As girls, they were not sent to school because it was believed that their capacity for learning was limited, and a little knowledge could be harmful. As women, they were not allowed to appear without a head cover in public, and a disregard for this rule could end up in divorce. Jews were prohibited from praying before women without a head cover.[156]

The Talmud exempts women from learning the Torah and active participation in the religious ceremonies.[157] Should a woman decide to learn the Torah or engage in ceremonies, she will receive a smaller reward than a man, since she was not obliged to do so to begin with. Maimonides expanded on this Talmudic edict, suggesting, "Everyone who teaches her daughter Torah can be compared to one who teaches her insipid matters."[158]

Women, however, were obliged to keep the Sabbath and the holidays. Jewish men were generally happy that God did not create

---

[152] I. Shahak, *Jewish History, Jewish Religion* (London: Pluto Press, 1997), 87.

[153] S. D. Goitein, *A Mediterranean Society* (Berkeley: University of California Press, 1999), 333.

[154] Talmud, Kiddushin 80-b.

[155] Talmud, Kiddushin 49-b.

[156] I. Abrahams, *Jewish Life in the Middle Ages* (Philadelphia: 1896), 277, quoted in W. Durant, *The Story of Civilization: The Age of Faith* (New York: Simon & Schuster, 1950), 379.

[157] Talmud, Kiddushin 34-a.

[158] Maimonides, *Talmud Torah Law*, rule 13, ch. 1.

them as women,[159] and Jewish women were thankful that they were created according to God's will.[160]

The Jewish law of inheritance, which had originated in the Israelite's agricultural economy, deemed it necessary to promote the accumulation of wealth in the hand of the firstborn son for the protection of the entire family. Therefore, the firstborn son received two shares of the father's wealth, while other male children each received one share.[161] After her husband died, a Jewish woman only inherited the equivalent of her dowry, even though she had no children. Daughters inherited only in the absence of sons; otherwise, they had to look to the generous hands of their older brothers.[162, 163]

Offensive commentaries about women are also encountered among these volumes.[164] For instance, "One hundred women equal one witness."[165] A woman has no right to own property, and whatever she produces belongs to her husband.[166] While there are numerous references to a "bad wife" in these volumes, rarely is a reference made to a "bad husband." It is stated: "Three kinds of persons do not see the face of Hell: one who suffers from oppressive poverty, one who is afflicted with bowel diseases, one who is in the hands of the Roman government; and some say: Also he who has a bad wife."[167] In fact, the Talmud is similar to the Old Testament in usually depicting the husband as a man who is constantly sweating for the well-being of his wife and children.

In contrast to the Qur'an,[168] there is no reference to wife beating in the Talmud. Here and there, however, men of religion have

---

[159] Talmud, Menachoth 43-b.

[160] Talmud, Berakhot 60-b.

[161] S. D. Goitein, *A Mediterranean Society* (Berkeley: University of California Press, 1999), 190.

[162] A. A. Neuman, *The Jews in Spain* (Philadelphia: 1942), 2: 63.

[163] Islamic laws of inheritance, whose origin was in the early trade society of Bedouin Arabs, in contrast to the Jewish code of inheritance, prompted splitting of the wealth among all children. Female heirs, however, received half of what male children received.

[164] Talmud, Sabbath 152-a.

[165] Talmud, Sotah 31-b and 47-b.

[166] Talmud, Ketuboth 47-b.

[167] Talmud, Eirubin, 41-b.

[168] Qur'an, 5:33.

justified this form of punishment. For instance, Yehudai Gaon, the reputable Talmudist of the eighth century, writes, "A wife should never raise her voice against her husband, but should remain silent even he beats her—as chastised women do." Moses Maimonides reiterates, "A woman who refuses to do her required work may be forced to do so, even with a stick."[169]

The Talmud and the Rituals

Religious rituals and ceremonies presented in the Talmud are indeed the interpretations of what is described in the Old Testament. Rabbis, young and old, liberal and conservative, have often interpreted and modified these statements from the Bible without any explanations. They have frequently added their own understandings of the subject and have tailored them for the new circumstances. Therefore, the characteristic feature of the Talmudic period was an overemphasis on the execution of perplexing and detailed religious rituals and ceremonies that only a proud and faithful people had the patience to follow.

After the destruction of the Temple of Jerusalem, prayer in a synagogue and an offering of charity replaced animal sacrifices at the Temple. According to the Talmud, although prayer at home had its own value, praying in the synagogue was something else. Rabbis insisted, "A man's prayer is heard by God only in the Synagogue"[170] and "God stands in the congregation of God."[171] And according to the Talmud, a congregation consists of no less than ten men.[172]

Circumcision was one form of offering and indeed an icon of reaffirming the covenant between Jews and Yahweh as appeared in the Old Testament. "And God said to Abraham, You shall keep my covenant therefore. ... Every male child among you shall be circumcised. And you shall circumcise the flesh of your foreskin; and it shall be a sign of the covenant between you and me. And he who is eight days old shall be circumcised among you, every male child in

---

[169] S. D. Goitein, *A Mediterranean Society* (Berkeley: University of California Press, 1999), 394.
[170] Talmud, Berachoth 6-a.
[171] Ibid.
[172] Talmud, Sanhedrin 2-a.

your generations, he who is born in the house, or foreign born slave.
. . . And the uncircumcised male child whose flesh of his foreskin is
not circumcised, that soul shall be cut off from his people; he has
broken my covenant."[173] Since other peoples like the Egyptians,
Ethiopians, Phoenicians, Syrians, and Arabs also practiced
circumcision, a hygienic reason might have existed for it. In the
Talmudic narratives, circumcision not only was a ceremony that Jews
were expected to go through but also included the slaves that served
Jews as well. A Jew was not allowed to keep an uncircumcised slave
more than twelve months. "If the slave refused to be circumcised. . .
he may bear with him for twelve months, then he must be sold to
idolaters."[174]

Physical cleanliness was considered the prerequisite of
mental health. Therefore, upon rising in the morning, before each
meal, and at the time of ritual ceremonies, Jews washed their hands.
Corpses, pregnancy, insects, pork, leprosy, menstruation, and sexual
intercourse were considered dirty, and contact with these required a
special prayer in the synagogue. When the position of the Old
Testament on these issues is compared with those of the Talmud, one
finds the former often having a more simple and liberal view. For
instance, we read about menstruation in the Old Testament: "There
must be no sexual relationship with a woman who is menstruating."[175]
This same issue has been illustrated in a remarkably more stringent
way in the Talmud: "And thou shalt not approach unto a woman as
long as she is impure by her uncleanness."[176] And "My daughter!
How was he to thee in thy days of menstruation? 'God forbid!' she
rejoined; 'he did not touch me even with his little finger.'"[177]
Therefore, the issue was no longer just "sexual intercourse" but had
been expanded to any kind of contact between a man and a
menstruating woman. In addition, a woman was considered unclean
up to forty days after the birth of a boy and eighty days after the birth
of a girl.

---

[173] Genesis 17:9–14.
[174] Talmud, Yebamoth 48-b.
[175] Leviticus 18:19.
[176] Talmud, Shabbath 13-a.
[177] Talmud, Shabbath 13-b.

Boys achieved the state of manhood at the age of thirteen, when they were obliged to observe the Law and perform all religious ceremonies and rituals. The ceremony of bar mitzvah cannot be traced earlier than the fifteenth century, and the girl's counterpart of the ceremony, bat mitzvah, not until the nineteenth century.[178]

Sometimes the Talmud gives medical instructions. The Jews of the fourth and fifth centuries, like other people living around the Mediterranean Sea, strongly believed in medical superstitions. Therefore, it is not surprising that many of these superstitions spilled over into the Talmud. In spite of this, an anatomical description of the larynx, esophagus, trachea, lungs, brain membranes, and sexual organs are found there. In addition, there are detailed descriptions of tuberculosis, lung tumors, liver cirrhosis, and other illnesses. For example, rabbis knew that flies near the drinking cups might carry sickness.[179] They recognized hemophilia as a hereditary illness and did not recommend circumcision in those cases. Moreover, the practice of exorcism and magic in the management of illnesses was a way of life.

Rabbis considered themselves as nutrition experts and often preached upon this subject. First of all, there was a blessing for everything: "A man is forbidden to taste anything before saying a blessing over it."[180] Good teeth were considered a prerequisite for good nutrition. For that reason, they did not recommend tooth extraction under any circumstances.[181] They also believed that good chewing strengthened the man's feet: "Chew well with your teeth, and you will find it in your steps."[182] Meat was a luxury item, but the consumption of vegetables and fruits was highly encouraged. Eating meat that contained blood was forbidden. Therefore, animals were killed in a way that most of their blood was drained. Consequently, rabbis became the most qualified to perform this task, and in preparation for a sacrifice, they usually examined the viscera to ensure that the animal was not sick.

---

[178] K. Crim, *The Perennial Dictionary of World Religions* (New York, HarperSanFrancisco, 1981), 91.
[179] Talmud, Ketuboth 27-a.
[180] Talmud, Berachoth 35-a.
[181] Talmud, Pesachim 113-a.
[182] Talmud, Shabbath 152-a.

According to the rabbis, the consumption of meat and dairy products together was not allowed. The issue has been raised in three different places in the Old Testament: "As you reap each of your crops, bring me the choicest sample of the first harvest, it shall be offered to the Lord your God. *Do not boil a young goat in its mother's milk*";[183] "And you must bring the best of the first of each year's crop to the house of the Lord your god. *You must not cook a young goat in its mother's milk*";[184] "Don't eat anything that has died a natural death. However, a foreigner among you may eat it. You may give it or sell it to him, but don't eat it yourself, for you are holy to the Lord your god. *You must not boil a young goat in its mother's milk*"[185] (my emphasis). However, throughout history, under the pretense of creating "a fence around Torah,"[186] rabbis have greatly expanded on this proscription. Hence, the interpretation of this biblical rule has been stretched to include not only young goat but all flesh, not only goat milk but also all dairy products, not only cooking together but also eating together or even storing together. They have furthered this argument to suggest separate cooking utensils and plates for meat and milk products as well as separate storing and washing areas. Nowhere in the Old Testament is there an explanation for this biblical dietary law. However, it has been suggested that cooking a kid in its mother's milk is a symbol of utmost cruelty, and the prohibition might have had an ethical origin.[187]

Sabbath, the greatest Jewish phenomenon, was apparently a complicated issue of this period, since a large section of the Talmud has been devoted to it. This subject has been presented again and again in detail, and rabbis with a hairsplitting curiosity have determined what Jews may do and what they cannot do on this day. In the opinion of rabbis, the desecration of Sabbath was an offense with a consequence as grave as practicing idolatry.[188] Even though the Old Testament only considers working, cooking, and setting a fire as the only cases for the desecration of Sabbath, rabbis of the Talmudic

---

[183] Exodus 23:19.
[184] Exodus 34:26.
[185] Deuteronomy 14:21.
[186] E. Barnavi, *A History Atlas of Jewish People* (New York: Schocken Books, 1992), 6.
[187] Ibid.
[188] Talmud, Eiruvin 69-b.

period expanded these restrictions to thirty-nine cases. Among them is the care of patients by Jewish physicians and midwives on Sabbath. A Jewish midwife was not obliged to attend the labor of a gentile woman on Sabbath. She was only obligated to a woman who observed the Sabbath: "An Israelite woman should not act as midwife to a heathen woman. . . . A Jewish woman may act as midwife to a heathen woman for payments but not gratuitously!"[189] The same recommendation has been advanced for the care of a gentile patient by Jewish physicians.[190] Today, Jewish physicians, even the religious ones, prefer the Hippocratic Oath over the rabbis' recommendations. Nonetheless, throughout history these recommendations have often provoked hatred and animosity of other peoples against Jews.

The Talmud often became an economic and financial adviser to the traditional Jewish communities. Rabbis considered forestalling a sin,[191] and shopkeepers were encouraged to take no more than one-sixth of the wholesale price as profit.[192] In fact, rabbis were responsible for overseeing the minimum wages and the maximum prices.[193] It is noteworthy that most often these regulations were doomed for failure, since rabbis were unable to separate the economic life of Jews from those of Muslims and Christians, and the law of supply and demand always superseded.

Life and the Talmud

According to Will Durant, "The Talmud was not a code of laws requiring strict obedience; it was a record of rabbinical opinion, gathered for the guidance of leisurely piety. The untutored masses obeyed only a choice few of the precepts of Law."[194] In other words, most Jews were not observing every detail, and the rabbis were not disappointed when parts of those laws were overlooked.

---

[189] Talmud, Avodah Zarah 26-a.
[190] Op. cit., on Shulhan Arukh, "Hoshen Mishpat," 194, quoted in I. Shahak, *Jewish History, Jewish Religion* (London: Pluto Press, 1997), 84.
[191] Talmud, Baba Bathra, 90-a.
[192] Talmud, Menachoth, 77-a.
[193] S. W. Baron, *Social and Religious History of the Jews* (New York: Columbia University Press, 1941), 1: 277, 2: 108.
[194] W. Durant, *The Story of Civilization: The Age of Faith* (New York: Simon & Schuster, 1963), 364.

The rabbis' insistence upon following the Talmud was to a great extent a reaction of the Jews against Christian states and the Church's effort to abandon them. Dispersed within these twenty volumes are various statements reflecting the hatred of the Talmud for Christianity. However, according to Will Durant, this hatred was mainly aimed at those Christians who had forgotten Christ's compassion. In support of this opinion, we can find many sages among the pages of the Talmud where the New Testament has indeed been glorified.

The Talmud was the core of Jewish education for over fourteen centuries. Young Jews studied the Talmud seven hours a day for seven years. They read and thought it over repeatedly until it was memorized. The method of learning was not confined to reading alone; it included discussions and disputations among students and between teachers and students where old codes were applied to new circumstances. These disputations usually resulted in a strong intellect and retentiveness, while they simultaneously narrowed the freedom of the Jewish mind.

This method of learning allowed them to indulge in the details of the Law and assume a dogmatic view of religion. Obviously, sinking into the Talmud left less time for learning other disciplines. In fact, according to Talmudic encounters, there was no need to learn anything else in any way: "Go then and find a time that is neither day nor night and learn then Greek wisdom."[195]

The Talmud cannot be assessed outside the historical settings in which it was created. We must always keep in mind that the Talmud was the instrument of living for a people who were forced out of their homeland, were repeatedly persecuted, and from time to time experienced the danger of complete disintegration. The role that the prophets played during and after the Babylonian exile in lifting the spirits of masses was similar to the role the Talmud played for the Diaspora throughout the Middle Ages. According to Will Durant, the Talmud was indeed a portable fatherland that Jews carried on their shoulders from one place to the next. When Jews were aliens in strange lands, by sinking their minds and hearts into the Talmud, they felt at home.

---

[195] Talmud, Menachoth 99-b.

Chronology:

721 BCE	Destruction of the northern kingdom of Israel by Assyrians
597 BCE	The first attack of Nebuchadnezzar; King Zedekia, the last king of Judah, replaced King Jehoiachin
586 BCE	Destruction of the Temple of Jerusalem
539 BCE	Persian Empire conquered Babylonia
516 BCE	Construction of the Second Temple of Jerusalem was completed, and this year was commemorated as the end of Babylonian exile
331 BCE	The fall of the Achamean Empire and the beginning of Greek influence in Judea
323 BCE	The death of Alexander the Great
198 BCE	Seleucids take control of Judea
168 BCE	Antiochus IV Epiphanes outlawed Judaism
168 BCE	The Maccabees' uprising and the establishment of the Hasmonaean kingdom
164 BCE	Judah Maccabee captured Jerusalem
63 BCE	Pompey's invasion of the Temple of Jerusalem
47 BCE	Antipater joined the circle of Caesar and officially invited the governance of Rome in Judea
37 BCE	Herod, the son of Antipater, came to power
66 CE	The uprising of the Zealots
70 CE	Destruction of the Second Temple of Jerusalem by Romans
73 CE	The fall of Masada
93 CE	The first historic reference to Christ by the historian Josephus Flavius
132 CE	The revolt of Simon bar Kokhba against Rome
313 CE	Inscription of Emperor Constantine I to Christianity
352 CE	The last revolt of Jews against Rome
363 CE	Emperor Julian died; construction of the Third Temple of Jerusalem was abandoned
399 CE	The Babylonian version of the Talmud completed
499 CE	Completion of the Palestinian version of the Talmud

Chapter Three

THE MEDIEVAL JEWS

By the early sixth century, the majority of Jews were scattered throughout Europe, North Africa, and the Middle East. Jerusalem, the emotionally charged Promised Land, was now under the Christian Rome. Jews had failed to regain the fatherland, and in the eyes of the Christians, their failure to rebuild the Temple was an indication that God had turned away from them. Christians, on the other hand, had appropriated their scriptures and considered themselves the new Israel.[1] Despite the fact that Jews had lost their homeland, the Temple and the priesthood, they still had their Bible, their rabbis and synagogues and by now they had compiled the Talmud. Jews were carrying these vastly detailed legal and moral systems on their shoulders from one place to another, and by immersing themselves in them they felt at home. Throughout the Middle Ages, wherever Jews were alienated, they were more absorbed in their religion and into these two documents.

Jews in the East

The story of the Eastern Jews can be separated into two distinct periods. Prior to the seventh century CE, the story is mainly

---

[1] K. Armstrong, *Jerusalem: One City, Three Faiths* (New York: Ballantine Books, 1996), 193.

about the Jewish communities of the Persian and Byzantine Empires, while after the rise of Islam our focus is on the Jews in the land of Islam.[2]

The history of the Jews in Persia dates back to the conquest of the Babylonian Empire by the Achaemenid king Cyrus in 538 BCE, even though many have claimed that Jews were living in Persia as early as 734 BCE, since the fall of Samaria, the ancient capital of Israel.[3] In their view, Persian Jews represented the lost tribes of Israel who migrated to eastern territories, and many resided in Iran almost two centuries before the conquest of Babylon. Nonetheless, a group of them received the support of the Achaemenids to rebuild the Temple of Jerusalem. For two centuries after the fall of the Babylonian Empire, the Jews were under Persian rule. In this manner, a satellite Jewish government was established that was directly accountable to the Persian Empire.

Very little is known about the history of the Persian Jews after the fall of the Achaemenids. However, the Persian Empire resumed its existence under the Sassanid dynasty in 226 CE, which extended its authority over the highly populated Jewish communities of Mesopotamia. Moreover, in the mid-fourth century, when Christianity achieved state power in Rome, the persecution of Jews also reached a new height. Therefore, many Jewish inhabitants of Rome migrated for their safety to the areas outside the empire during this period. Some of these communities moved east to Constantinople, and from Asia Minor they entered into Persian territories.

During the reign of the Sassanid dynasty, as early as the second century CE, Jews enjoyed self-government under one or several leaders, called exilarch, or head of the exile.[4] The office of the exilarch was hereditary, with their lineage linking to the house of David.[5] The exilarch was recognized by the court and held an honored

---

[2] S. D. Goitein, *A Mediterranean Society* (Berkeley: University of California Press, 1999), 28.
[3] *JewishEncyclopedia.com*, "Persia."
[4] G. Wigoder, *The New Standard Jewish Encyclopedia* (New York: Facts on File, 1992), 319.
[5] S. D. Goitein, *A Mediterranean Society* (Berkeley: University of California Press, 1999), 82.

seat in the king's council. He appointed judges and exercised criminal jurisdiction among the people in the Jewish community. It was during this period that the Babylonian Talmud, the commentaries on the Old Testament, was put together.

Because of the Zoroastrian influence in the Sassanid governments, occasional persecutions of Jews also transpired in Iran. The two most devastating of them were during the reign of Yazdegerd II (438–457) and again under Firuz (459–486), in which the murder of two Zoroastrian magi in the capital city of Isphahan was alleged.[6] In 513 CE, when the Sassanid king Kavadh II adopted the Mazdakism,[7] the Persian Jews (evidently on the premise that Mazdak's teachings were against Mosaic Law) took sides with the Zoroastrians. In the same year, Mar Zutra II, the young exilarch of the Persian Jewish community, revolted against the Mazdakites and Kavadh in the district of Mahoza. Eventually, after seven years of struggle, Mar Zutra was defeated in 520 CE, and he along with his grandfather and a group of Jewish religious leaders were executed.[8] Another, and probably less realistic, description of the Mar Zutra encounter is as follows: "The new exilarch took up arms against the Persians, perhaps because of Persian oppression of the Jewish religion. Marching at the head of 400 Jewish warriors, Mar Zutra succeeded in defeating the Persians and setting up an independent Jewish state, with Mahoza as his residence. The new state survived for seven years, but immorality spread among his followers and they were finally defeated by Persians in a battle."[9] The episode of Mar Zutra is based upon combined historical and legendary narratives.[10]

The Arabs conquered Mesopotamia in 637 CE and then Iran in 641. In order to restore normal conditions as quickly as possible, once they established their power they reinstated the self-

---

[6] G. Wigoder, *The New Standard Jewish Encyclopedia* (New York: Facts on File, 1992), 746.

[7] A social movement led by Mazdak in the late fifth and early sixth centuries against the Sassanid cast system and Zoroastrian religion in power. The movement was eventually defeated after the massacre of thousands of Mazdakites during the reign of Khosrow Anushirvan, the son of Kavadh, in 524 CE.

[8] G. Wigoder, *The New Standard Jewish Encyclopedia* (New York: Facts on File, 1992), 746.

[9] *Encyclopedia Judaica*, "Zutra Mar," CD-ROM, 1997, Judaica Multimedia.

[10] *Jewishencyclopedia.com* "Zutra Mar II."

government arrangements of the Sassanid dynasty's with the religious minorities. However, following the declaration of the Codes of Omar, restrictions and persecutions of the Jews every so often were revived. Jews were forbidden to carry arms and participate in the central government. They were not allowed to employ Muslim workers, and they could not build new synagogues or repair the old ones. Their survival in the Islamic countries was only possible at the cost of subordination to Muslims.[11] In order to be distinguished from Muslims, Jews were periodically forced to wear a yellow patch (called a *ghiyar*) on their sleeves. This ruling later achieved a remarkable historical significance, when the Christians reinstated it against the Jews. Otherwise, the Caliphs in Baghdad often did not take the yellow patch seriously, and in fact many of them even took advantage of the Jewish talents in their governments. As a result of this, the Jews of North Africa, Mesopotamia, Asia Minor, and later Spain enjoyed a relative tranquility for several centuries. In other words, the rise of Islam, beyond subordination to Muslims, did not cause a special hardship for the Jews residing within Islamic territories. This does not mean that Muslims demonstrated an extraordinary open-mindedness toward Jews. In contrast, other factors helped the Jews in this part of the world. First, in the sphere of Islamic influence and in contrast to Christian lands, Jews were not the only religious minority. Therefore, their presence was not as visible as in Europe. Second, Jews in the Islamic territories enjoyed consolidated and populated communities with their own established

---

[11] The commitments that dhimmis (non-Muslim people of the Book) reluctantly gave to Omar, the second Caliph, consisted of the following: "We shall not built synagogues. . . in towns and their surroundings and we shall not repair the old ones, and . . . we promise to serve generously any Muslim who may enter in our house for three nights. . . . We do not reveal our religion to him and we shall never try to convert him to our religion and . . . if any of our relatives accepted Islam, we shall not discourage him and we promise to respect Muslims and we rise as a gesture of respect before them and . . . do not speak about them and . . . do not imitate their names and . . . we promise not to ride on a horse, do not carry sword or other arms and . . . not to sell wine or encourage Muslims to drink and we shall shave the hair of forehead and do not carry cross around the neck and . . . not to sound loud in our churches and not to sing in front of Muslims and not to mourning loud for our dead and . . . we shall not bury our dead near to those of Muslims and we shall not accept the ownership of the slaves owned by Muslims and we shall not look at the Muslim homes." R. Reisnia, *Az Mazdak ta baad* (Teheran: Payam, 1979), 58.

institutions, and Muslims preferred working with these institutions instead of destroying them. In fact, the historic and economic roots of anti-Semitism in the way that occurred in Europe, as will be elaborated in chapter 6, did not develop in the Islamic countries.

In the aftermath of the assassination of Ali, the fourth caliph of Islam in 661 CE, Mu'awiya proclaimed himself the sole caliph of the empire in Jerusalem. Under him, the capital was moved from Kufa to Damascus, and the new era of Umayyads was established.

After the defeat of the Umayyads in 750 CE, the Abbasid caliphs took power. Abbasid dynasties of caliphs transferred the government from Damascus to Baghdad, enforced the centralized authority, and ruled until 1258 CE, coinciding with the rise of the Mongol Empire. The central power in Baghdad gradually drove the Jewish communities to the periphery and concurrently increased the authority of the rabbis in the Jewish communities. It was indeed during this period that because of the enhancement of rabbinical authority, the Talmud was recognized as the supreme legal document.

Meanwhile, Muslims invaded Spain in 711, and the Umayyads, in the aftermath of their defeat in Damascus, moved west to establish the independent Emirate of Cordova in 756. The Shiite Fatimids conquered Egypt in 969, and at one point in the history their empire stretched from Syria to the border of Morocco.[12] Saladin deposed the Fatimids in 1171 and founded the Ayyubid dynasty. The Almohade (the true believers) Berber kingdom of North Africa, an extreme puritanical Muslim group conquered Morocco, Algeria, Tunisia, and Libya and established their hegemony over southern Spain in 1148. The Almohade Muslims revoked the traditional contract of Islamic states with the *dhimmis* (non-Muslim people of the Book) and engaged in the forced conversion of the Jews and Christians within these territories. The reign of Almohade was signified by widespread killing of Jews and Christians.[13] The choice between the sword and Islam that was imposed by the Almohade kingdom was almost unheard of in other periods of Islamic rule. Eventually, in 1229, Christian Spain defeated the Almohade kingdom

---

[12] S. D. Goitein, *A Mediterranean Society* (Berkeley: University of California Press, 1999), 37.
[13] Ibid., 301.

and Muslims migrated to the south. Overall, the Emirate of Cordova in Spain, the Fatimids of Egypt, and later the Ayyubid dynasty were remarkably more tolerant of Jews than the Almohade dynasty and their Muslim counterpart in Baghdad.[14]

During this period, a great majority of over one million of the Jewish populations of the Islamic territories were farmers, although some engaged in trade around the cities. In Mediterranean communities, Jews were highly visible in growing olive trees for oil and grapes for wine production.[15] Jewish communities enjoyed a form of self-government, more or less according to the Sassanid period, headed by an exilarch who was independent when it came to the internal affairs of the Jewish communities. The system of the exilarch was in a way a state within a state[16] that lasted up to the thirteenth century CE.[17] Yet there were circumstances, among them the inheritance law, where the government imposed its authority over the Jewish communities.[18] Under the Jewish laws of inheritance, daughters were not entitled to any of their father's wealth beyond their dowries, whereas in Islam, a female heir was worth half of a male. When there was no son in the Jewish family, the daughter was entitled to the entire wealth, but in a Muslim family she would have received one-third, and the remaining two-thirds was confiscated by government. In circumstances like this, the government insisted that the Islamic code of inheritance must prevail.[19] Similarly, Shiites provided special rights to individuals who had converted to Islam over the estates of their Jewish relatives. In general, Muslims could inherit from infidels, but the reverse was not possible.[20]

In the fabric of the Jewish communities, in addition to the exilarch, there were intellectual leaders, or geonim, who headed three academies or yeshivas, one in Palestine and two in the cities of Sura and Pumbedita in Babylonia. However, the two latter academies

---

[14] Ibid., 30.
[15] Ibid., 235.
[16] Ibid., 290.
[17] G. Wigoder, *The New Standard Jewish Encyclopedia* (New York: Facts on File, 1992), 319.
[18] S. D. Goitein, *A Mediterranean Society* (Berkeley: University of California Press, 1999), 189, 190.
[19] Ibid.
[20] Ibid., 427.

moved to Baghdad toward the end of the ninth century while retaining their original names. The Jewish communities of the Byzantine Empire followed the academy in Palestine, while the communities in the Persian territories subscribed to the Babylonian academies.[21] The academies were in existence from the sixth to the eleventh centuries; their leaders enjoyed a considerable power and performed a prominent role in Jewish communities all over the world.

The geonim and the academies they led had a number of responsibilities in addition to the selection of the exilarch for the Jewish communities. First, the geonim and the academy members were responsible for preparing proper responses to all questions raised about the Bible and the Talmud. Second, they were charged to face the written or oral challenges, often submitted against Judaism by the Islamic religious leaders. Third, the academies were obligated to suppress and eliminate any doubt or hesitation expressed about the religion and faith by members of the Jewish communities. Indeed, the academies and the geonim were instrumental in eradicating any intellectual challenge against the authority of the rabbis. Under the leadership of Yehudai Gaon[22] of the Sura academy, who was a blind old man, the Babylonian Talmud was enforced as "the religious legal document" in 760 CE, and any departure from its content was considered heresy. Yehudai was a rabbi and a Gaon. In this manner, the Talmud was promoted to the level of the Bible. From this point on, Halakhah, the legal codes of the Talmud were observed as the Judaic legal document not only in the Jewish communities in the lands of Islam but also in the European communities under Christian rule.

The ambitious agenda of rabbis and geonim, as presented in the platform of the Sura and Pumbedita academies, were not always achieved peacefully and were indeed disputed here and there. As an example, in the eighth century the intellectual anti-Talmudic movement of the Qaraites[23] challenged the academies and undermined the authority of the rabbis; the movement spread throughout the Persian Empire, North Africa, and Spain and lasted for over four centuries.

---

[21] Ibid., 76.

[22] *Gaon* is the singular of *Geonim.*

[23] "Qaraites" is an Aramaic term and originates from *Qar,* meaning "reading."

In 762 CE, when Exilarch Solomon died, the academy of Sura refused to appoint Anan ben David, his nephew, who was in line as the successor. Anan denounced the decision of the geonim, left for Palestine, and proclaimed himself the exilarch. Anan established his own synagogue and invited Jews to set aside the Talmud. In his book *Sepher Ha-Mitzvoth* or *Book of Precepts*, he considered the Pentateuch, the five books of Moses, as the only valid religious document. This was exactly the doctrine that the Sadducees had initiated many centuries ago. Contrary to the Pharisees' viewpoint, Anan believed Christ did not intend to found a new religion, but instead, like himself, to get rid of oral law and its rabbinical interpretations represented in the Talmud.

Under the influence of the Mu`tazilites,[24] the early rationalist Islamic school of theology, the Qaraites later set aside some of Anan's teachings, namely the concepts of God and resurrection and the way they had been presented in the Bible. Some of the more open-minded of the sect, like Chivi al-Balchi, even questioned the entire Pentateuch as the binding law.[25] The Qaraites, by dropping the idea of a Messiah, convinced the Abbasids caliphs to approve their migration to Palestine and other Islamic territories.[26] Therefore, their followers built large communities in Palestine, Egypt, Byzantium, Morocco, and Spain, usually separate from the Jewish communities.[27] In spite of the fact that many well-to-do and rich Jews belonged to this movement, the Qaraites preached a simple life and were vocal against the accumulation of wealth and the wealthy.[28] They reached their peak of popularity around the ninth century. Qaraites were in constant

---

[24] Mu`tazilites were the followers of a school of theology based upon reason and logic. They recognized the Qur'an as the main source of access to truth, and they did not believe in the symbolic interpretation of the verses. They also did not consider that the stories in the Qur'an were binding. However, they never replaced faith with reason or religion with science; therefore, they were distinguished from the modern scientific and philosophical approach to access the truth. The Mu`tazilites' doctrine was the official religion of Mammon's caliphate for nineteen years, from 813 to 832 CE.

[25] D. Druck, *Yehuda Halevi* (New York: Bloch, 1941), 66.

[26] K. Armstrong, *Jerusalem: One City, Three Faiths* (New York: Ballantine Books, 1997), 255.

[27] S. D. Goitein, *A Mediterranean Society* (Berkeley: University of California Press, 1999), 76.

[28] Ibid.

conflict with the followers of the Talmud, or in other words the majority of Jews. The clashes between the two on occasion prompted the interference of the government.[29] They not only refused the religious authority of Geonim, but on occasion they denied the administrative role of the exilarch as well. It has been said that many of the Qaraites supporters in the Jewish communities of Iran even refused to pay taxes to the office of the exilarch during this time. Around the twelfth century, however, the number of their supporters gradually declined. The Qaraites were massacred a number of times during their social activities. Finally, in 1149 CE, Jehuda ibn Ezra, who was the steward to the palace of Alfonso VII of Leon and Castile in Spain, turned the power of his government against them. From that point on, no further reference to this sect is noted in the history of Spain.[30]

The Sura academy that was active for more than five centuries was eventually abolished in 1034. The last gaon of the academy, Hai, was arrested in accordance with the caliph's order and executed in 1040. In the meantime, a number of factors increasingly undermined the academies and eventually rendered them obsolete. First, following the fall of the caliphate in Baghdad and the rise of Islamic governments in North Africa and Spain, Jews gradually migrated to these territories, and the population of Jews in and around Baghdad declined. Second, with the outbreak of the Crusades, the Jews were more concerned with the migrations and their survival than seeking advice from the academies over their sectarian differences. Finally, by the twelfth century, other centers of spiritual authority had developed elsewhere in the Diaspora, undermining the role and the importance of the academies in Baghdad. Hence, no academy of this nature was ever established again.

In addition to the office of exilarch and the academies, another institution of authority headed the Eastern Jewish communities between the ninth and sixteenth centuries CE.[31] This territorial authority, *Nagid* in Hebrew and *Ra'is al-Yahud* in Arabic,

---

[29] Ibid., 195.

[30] W. Durant, *The Story of Civilization: The Age of Faith* (New York: Simon & Schuster, 1950), 373.

[31] S. D. Goitein, *A Mediterranean Society* (Berkeley: University of California Press, 1999), 85.

was first established in Egypt and then extended to Morocco and Spain. The appointment of Ra`is al-Yahud was informal; he had to earn the support of the Jewish communities and government to confer on him the title and the honor.[32] The Nagid, in contrast to the exilarch, did not belong to the house of David,[33] but like him was the highest authority of the Jewish community in general, who appointed chief judges and officials, intervened between government officials and the Jewish community, oversaw matters of marriage, divorce, and alimony, and even attended family disputes.[34] Assessment and the collection of poll tax, or *jizya*, the tax that Jews, Christians, and Zoroastrians paid to Islamic institutions of government to protect their lives and properties, was among many functions assigned to the Nagid. Jewish courts usually heard all cases in the Jewish communities. Rarely were judgments of a Jewish court challenged in a Muslim court, an effort that usually justified excommunication of the Jew.[35] Following the abolition of the academies in the eleventh century, the responsibilities of the gaon were also transferred to the Nagid.

Khazar Jewry

The conversion of the king of Khazars to Judaism and the induction of the Jews of non-Semitic origin was a major event of the eighth century. The Khazars were a tribe of Turk origin related to the Caucasian Huns and the Western Turks that migrated west and in the seventh century settled around the eastern shores of the Black Sea. It is said that the Khazars lived around the Caspian Sea and the Caucasus mountains,[36] ruling a territory that at one point extended beyond the Crimea-Caucasus-Volga region. Khazar territories were among the prominent trade centers of the world of the eighth century.[37] The exact date when Khazar leaders converted to Judaism

---

[32] Ibid., 88.
[33] *Encyclopedia Judaica*, "Nagid," CD-ROM, 1997, Judaica Multimedia.
[34] S. D. Goitein, *A Mediterranean Society* (Berkeley: University of California Press, 1999), 91.
[35] Ibid., 192.
[36] *Encyclopedia Americana*, 1979, 16: 391.
[37] W. Durant, *The Story of Civilization: The Age of Faith* (New York: Simon & Schuster, 1950), 447.

is debatable. On the basis of Judah Halevi's famous philosophical dialogue *Kuzari*, the king of the Khazars became a Jew in 740 CE. According to another encounter, the conversion transpired in the aftermath of the conquest of Kharizm in 712 by the Arab commander Muslim ibn Qutayba.[38] However, Al-Masudi believed that the conversion occurred during the reign of Caliphate Harun-al-Rashid between 786 and 809 CE.[39]

The real motivation of Khazar leaders in adopting Judaism is also unclear. A correspondence between Joseph, the king of the Khazars, and Hisdai ibn Shaprut, the known theologian of the tenth century between 954 and 961 CE,[40] two hundred years after the conversion, refers to a religious debate among representatives of Christianity, Judaism, and Islam, after which Khazar leaders had accepted the religion of Israel.[41] This explanation, however, does not seem very plausible, and there are reasons to believe that the conversion was politically inspired. The conversion was preceded by the persecution of Jews in Byzantium who were forced out of the country. Khazaria, the kingdom of the Khazars, embraced the Jews and welcomed the Byzantine arts and crafts as well as a better means of agriculture and trade, which the exile brought with them.[42] It is quite conceivable that the advanced attributes of the Jewish exile that provided opportunities to the Khazar's leadership must have played an important role in the conversion.[43] It seems that rabbinical Judaism did not take the Khazars' conversion seriously and did not show an interest in them on the grounds of an "imperfect Judaism" the Khazars were practicing. Nonetheless, the Khazars, like the Semitic Jews, believed in the Messianic aspiration and the chosenness of their people.[44]

Around the tenth century, the Khazar state came under tremendous pressure by the Russians, who were interested in reaching

---

[38] *Encyclopedia Judaica,* "Khazars," CD-ROM, 1997, Judaica Multimedia.
[39] A. Koestler, *The Thirteenth Tribe: The Khazar Empire and Its Heritage* (New York: Random House, 1976), 66.
[40] Ibid., 65.
[41] *Encyclopedia Judaica,* "Khazars," CD-ROM, 1997, Judaica Multimedia.
[42] A. Koestler, *The Thirteenth Tribe: The Khazar Empire and Its Heritage* (New York: Random House, 1976), 61.
[43] Ibid., 62.
[44] Ibid., 142.

the Caspian Sea. The Russians attacked the Khazars on three occasions in 913, 943, and finally in 965 CE from which the Khazars never did recover. It was in the process of this last attack that the Khazar leaders adopted Islam, conceivably to attract the support of the Arabs. The Khazar state fell sometime around the late tenth century or early eleventh century, but they maintained their independence and their faith up to the thirteenth century before the Mongol invasion.[45] The Khazars traveled west to Constantinople, Poland, Hungary, Lithuania, Ukraine, the Balkans, and eventually into Central Europe, where they established Jewish communities.[46, 47] Furthermore, the rapid growth of the Jewish communities in Germany and France coincided with the fall of the Khazar state and the large-scale migration of Jews westbound, suggesting an Eastern Jewish origin of these communities.[48] There is a body of historical data to support the viewpoint that a substantial portion of modern Jewry has a Caucasian rather than a Semitic origin.[49]

Medieval Jewish Thought and the Influence of Islamic Philosophy

The ongoing war between religion and philosophy reached a new turning point when, under the influence of the Islamic ideology, reason and logic were utilized to defend the faith. While Saadiah ben Joseph and Maimonides were probably the vanguards of this movement, Judah Halevi, on the other hand, opposed using philosophy to prove religion. The two diverse approaches to the religion can be illustrated by understanding the viewpoints of these vanguards.

Saadiah ben Joseph was born in 896 CE in Fayyum, a small town in Egypt. He migrated to Palestine in 915 and again in 928, when he was thirty-six years old. Saadiah became the Gaon of the academy in Sura, translated the Pentateuch into Arabic, and in his

---

[45] Ibid., 141.

[46] Ibid., 151, 180.

[47] *Encyclopedia Judaica*, "Khazars," CD-ROM, 1997, Judaica Multimedia.

[48] A. Koestler, *The Thirteenth Tribe: The Khazar Empire and Its Heritage* (New York: Random House, 1976), 170.

[49] Ibid., chapters. 5, 6, 7.

short lifetime created several masterpieces in Arab literature and logic. Saadiah believed that faith must be based upon reason and historical evidence. According to him, the portions of the Bible that can be explained by reason and logic must be accepted as they are, but one must look for symbolic interpretations for the parts that are not logically explainable. This approach to religion was in part a reflection of the Aristotelian analysis and partly was based upon the method of Islamic Kalam. The latter was an Islamic scholastic theology that had been founded by al-Ashari, a conservative philosopher, who believed in reason and logic to explain the religious codes. Saadiah believed in a conscientious creator possessing eternal life who would not leave righteousness without reward. However, in the opinion of Saadiah, since the reward of righteousness is not always possible in our lifetime, therefore there must be a life after death. Saadiah's writings influenced Maimonides to the point where he wrote, "Were it not for Saadiah, the Torah would almost have disappeared."[50]

Saadiah was a hardheaded man who showed little flexibility over his viewpoints. For instance, when he challenged Exilarch David ben Zakkai, they excommunicated each other for a long while. The struggle between the two lasted for over a decade, up to the death of David. The Muslims assassinated David's successor on the ground that he had defamed Muhammad the Prophet. This time Saadiah selected the victim's son as the exilarch to succeed him, who unfortunately was also a victim of assassination.

Moses Maimonides[51] (1135–1204 CE) was a prominent figure in the cultural life of the Middle Ages. He was born in Cordoba, a city in southern Spain, and achieved such an eminent status among Jews that they said about him, "[F]rom Moses to Moses there arose none like Moses."[52] Although in his childhood he did not show any interest in learning, he later became fascinated by the Torah, medicine, arithmetic, astronomy, and philosophy. At the age of thirteen, when Almohade Muslims took over Cordoba in 1148 CE

---

[50] D. Durant, *The Story of Civilization: The Age of Faith* (New York: Simon & Schuster, 1950), 386.

[51] Maimonides is also known as RaMba`M, an abbreviation of his name and his titles.

[52] W. Durant, *The Story of Civilization: The Age of Faith* (New York: Simon & Schuster, 1963), 408.

and ended the *dhimmi's* life in the western land of Islam,[53] he and his family escaped to Morocco. Under pressure from fanatic Muslims, he lived as a Muslim in Fez, a city in the northern part of Morocco, for nine years. About changing his religion, he wrote: "Muslims themselves know that we utter it insincerely in order to circumvent bigots."[54] In 1165, after a short stay in Palestine, he moved to Alexandria, where he lived the rest of his life. As a special physician to Saladin's eldest son, Nur-ud-Din Ali, and his vizier, al-Qadi al-Fadil al-Baisani, he came very close to central power in Egypt. In 1177 he became the official head of the Jewish community in Cairo. Ten years later, a Muslim jury accused him of deserting Islam and demanded the death penalty for him. To save Maimonides's life, the vizier stated that since Maimonides had converted to Islam by force, he was not a real Muslim; therefore, the death penalty was unjustified.[55]

Maimonides reviewed the work of previous philosophers such as Hippocrates, Galen, al-Razi, and Avicenna in ten manuscripts in Arabic. He also wrote a manuscript about nutrition for Saladin's son, an essay on sexual intercourse for his nephew, al-Mozzafar I, and other works on asthma, hemorrhoids, and drugs.

Maimonides completed his famous work *Guide to the Perplexed*, or *Moreh Nevukhim*, in 1190 CE, which was later translated into Latin and Hebrew. In the introduction to these three volumes, he indeed proposed to reconcile the Mosaic tradition with that of Aristotelian rationality, trying to explain the faith through reason. Maimonides claimed that many of the terms and phrases in the Book of Prophets and the Old Testament should not be accepted literally; rather, their meanings should be sought allegorically. He went on to say that the literal meaning of these statements was contradictory to those who are religious and yet inclined to use reason and logic as the instruments of learning. People should not be forced to choose between reason and faith. Since God created "reason," there should be no conflict between that and God's will. If one saw a

---

[53] J. A. Garraty and P. Gay, *The Columbia History of the World* (New York: Harper and Rowe, 1972), 295.
[54] W. Durant, *The Story of Civilization: The Age of Faith* (New York: Simon & Schuster, 1963), 408.
[55] Ibid.

conflict, it meant that the symbolic meaning of these statements had been ignored. Maimonides, in fact, claimed that Judaism could be properly understood only through Aristotelian thought; otherwise, it was a form of idolatry. He believed that common people were slaves of literal meanings, and he insisted on teaching them the true nature of God.

However, in contrast to Aristotle, who believed in an eternal universe of matter and motion, Maimonides adhered to the concept of creation. He said, "We can neither prove eternity nor the creation of the world; let us therefore hold to our father's faith in its creation."[56] Nonetheless, Maimonides interpreted the story of creation allegorically: Adam was the active form or spirit; Eve was passive matter, which is the root of all evils; and the serpent was imagination. Furthermore, he ridiculed Islam's concept of resurrection and heaven and hell and denied the immortality of the soul.[57] He wrote that "the soul that remains after death is not the soul that lives in a man when he is born";[58] "the latter is a function of the body and dies with it." In fact this was one of the issues for which both Muslims and Jews criticized him. Baruch Spinoza, the seventeenth-century philosopher, while praising Maimonides for his efforts to apply reason to the Bible, criticized him for reading the biblical narratives allegorically. He argued that we must read the Bible for what it exactly says, rather than impose our own perceptions on the text. Maimonides tried to reduce the scriptural miracles to natural events, but he never questioned them the way that Spinoza did. He truly believed that without conviction in the divine origin of moral codes, no social order would be possible. He wrote, "All Israelites are bound to follow everything in the Babylonian Talmud, and we should force the Jews of every land to adhere to the customs established by the Talmudic sages."[59] Nevertheless, he was in some respects more liberal than most Muslims and Christians of his time. He believed monotheistic non-Jews would also go to heaven; however, he was extremely harsh when it came to heretics. He wrote that "any Jew who dismissed the

---

[56] Maimonides, *Guide to the Perplexed*, 2: xvii-f.
[57] S. Zeitlin, *Maimonides* (New York: 1935), p. 103, quoted in W. Durant, *The Story of Civilization: The Age of Faith* (New York: Simon & Schuster, 1950), 413.
[58] Maimonides, *Guide to the Perplexed*, 3: lxx.
[59] S. W. Baron, *Essays on Maimonides* (New York: Columbia University Press, 1941), 117.

Jewish Law should be put to death" or, "according to my opinion, all members of an Israelite community which has arrogantly violated any of the divine precepts must be put to death."[60] Maimonides approved capital punishment for murder, adultery, witchcraft, violent robbery, kidnapping, and the desecration of Sabbath, the way it has been described in the Old Testament.[61] He believed that "[a]ll people will eventually fall except for the Jews who shall remain to eternity."[62] Maimonides believed that the hope for the rise of the Messiah strengthened the spirits of the Jews of Diaspora, and he considered it the thirteenth principle of the religion.

With regard to the relationship between husband and wife, he believed a man must get married when he owns a house.[63] He can have four wives but should not always be with his spouse like a rooster. And finally, he expressed the opinion that a man should fulfill his marital obligation on Friday nights.

Allegorical interpretation of the Holy Scripture, disbelief in immortality of the soul, and the denial of heaven and hell constituted the core of Maimonidean philosophy, which caused a lot of unrest in the Jewish communities. At the time that Christian fanatics were waging a great war against Aristotelian philosophy by burning his books, Rabbi Solomon Ben Abraham of Montpellier also followed the trail of dark-minded Christians and convinced the Church authorities to anathematize the *Guide to the Perplexed* as a heretical work. Rabbi Solomon denounced Maimonides and excommunicated all Jews who were studying philosophy and literature. As a consequence of these events, his followers organized the burning of Maimonides's books in 1234 in Montpellier and eight years later in Paris in public ceremonies. The followers of Maimonides, on the other hand, convicted the other side as informers of the Jews and sought revenge by killing Rabbi Solomon. The atmosphere of social unrest that was created as a result of attacks and counterattacks between both sides attracted many Jews to mysticism and poetry.

---

[60] Maimonides. *Guide to the Perplexed*, 3: xli.
[61] Deuteronomy 23:17; Exodus 31:15.
[62] S. W. Baron, *Essays on Maimonides* (New York: Columbia University Press, 1941), 110.
[63] Mishnah Torah, 54-a.

The influence of Maimonides and Saadiah on Judaism was revolutionary for their times. On the opposite platform was, however, a poet and religious philosopher like Judah Halevi (1075–1141 CE), who opposed the concept of using philosophy in order to prove religion. The serious political developments in Spain in the early twelfth century, where Christians were fighting Muslims and Jews were suffering at the hands of both sides, put him through a religious crisis.[64] As a result, he took a very negative attitude toward philosophy. Like Ghazali,[65] he feared that philosophy was undermining religion, not merely by questioning the dogma, ignoring it, or interpreting it metaphorically, but also by substituting argument for devotion.[66] He advanced the opinion that Judaism was based on revelation and personal experience of God, and therefore he stressed the importance of its fulfillment in a return to Israel.[67] Unlike Saadiah and Maimonides, Judah Halevi did not seek to reconcile Judaism and philosophy, as he maintained the position that Judaism did not need a logical basis.

Jewish Communities of Christendom

The Jewish population of the world was around three million in the early Middle Ages, and only an insignificant number of them were living in Palestine. There was no indication that Jews dispersed in vast areas were about to achieve any form of unity or coalition. Christians were in general under the impression that Judaism would soon come to its closing stage. Moreover, Christian emperors of Rome had abolished many previous Jewish rights throughout the empire. Jews were not allowed to keep Christian slaves, and they could not build new synagogues or repair the old ones, although they

---

[64] K. Armstrong, *Jerusalem: One City, Three Faiths* (New York: Ballantine Books, 1997), 298.

[65] Al-Ghazali, the Muslim theologian of the eleventh century, expressed his opinion on philosophy in his famous work *The Destruction of Philosophy* in the following manner: "Philosophy, logic, science cannot prove the existence of god or the immortality of the soul, only direct intuition can assure us of these beliefs, without which no moral order and therefore no civilization can survive."

[66] W. Durant, *The Story of Civilization: The Age of Faith* (New York: Simon & Schuster, 1963), 406.

[67] *Encyclopedia Americana* (1979), 16: 230.

still had the right of living as Jews and the right of employment in government institutions as teachers or judges. The scope of the Jewish rights in the Christian lands was determined by the officials of the Church and varied under different circumstances. However, it was the official position of the Church, as it had been crystallized in the words of Pope Gregory I, the Great Saint (540–605 CE), that "A Jew has no right to what the law has denied him, but he must not be denied from what the law has conferred upon him."[68] Kings and influential people of Europe more or less abided the guidelines passed by the Church. In essence, the Jews were reluctantly tolerated.

However, none of these restrictions forced the Jews to abandon Judaism or disregard their rituals. If there was no synagogue, there was always a house where they could gather and pray. It is noteworthy that the invasion of the Roman Empire by Vandals, Lombards and Goths, which weakened the empire during this period, had little influence upon Jewish communities.

The fifth, sixth, and seventh centuries witnessed many injustices to the European Jews. A series of forced conversions and massacres, followed by evictions, occurred during this period. In 411 CE, the Jews were evicted from Alexandria, in 592 from Antioch,[69] and in 630 from Jerusalem. In 613 the Jews in Spain were forced to accept Christianity. The forced conversion of Jews spread to Gaul (present-day France) in 633 and to Italy in 661. Some of the Jews accepted Christianity and some pretended that they were Christians while they secretly practiced Judaism. Others migrated to other parts of the world that were more open to the Jews.

By the mid-eighth century, circumstances changed in favor of the Jews. The rise of the second kingdom of Franks in France and the spread of Islam to Spain both inspired the need for the Jewish talents in government and education. As a result of this, most of the Jewish communities were centered in large cities or close to the bishops' headquarters.

During the tenth and eleventh centuries, the great academies were established in large cities in Italy, France, and Germany. Although in these countries, as in Islamic territories, the dominant

---

[68] H. Graetz, *History of the Jews* (Philadelphia: Bella Lowy, 1891), 4: 33.

[69] Antioch was an ancient Syrian city that presently is part of southern Turkey.

culture of the Jewish communities was influenced by the Holy Scriptures and Talmudic interpretations, under the persuasion of these academies the way of life, customs, liturgy, laws, and language in these communities were gradually transformed into a new and different culture of Ashkenazim.[70] The focus of Jewish literature in this era was on religious poetry, interpretation of the Old Testament, mysticism, and the history of religion. This culture gradually reached Spain, where the Jewish community was the most populated and prosperous. In Spain, Jews enjoyed peace and tranquility under the protection of the kings of Aragon and Castile. These Jews contributed to literature and philosophy tremendously. In Western Europe, well-to-do Jews were engaged in commerce while the rest were in agriculture, craft, navigation, trade, and perfumery. Conflict between Jews and Christians was at its lowest level since the seventh century, and if there were small clashes here and there between the two, they usually ended in some form of reconciliation. Certainly no one could predict the pending catastrophe of 1096.

The Crusades and the Jews

Jerusalem as the site of Christ's crucifixion was sacred to Christians. The city had been under the Christian Rome until 614 CE, then under the Persian Sassanid Empire until 629, and had remained in the hands of Muslims since 637 CE. By the eighth century, Islamic forces had conquered North Africa, the eastern shores of the Mediterranean, and most of Spain, greatly reducing the size and the power of the Byzantine Empire. By the eleventh century, the empire had lost most of Asia Minor to the Seljuk Turks, who attacked Syria and Palestine and conquered Jerusalem in 1071.[71] The Crusades[72] were a number of wars initiated by the Christians in Europe to

---

[70] The great-grandson of the biblical figure Noah was named Ashkenaz, and the Bible also refers to Ashkenaz as the people living in the vicinity of Mount Ararat and Armenia. Since the ninth century, however, the Jewish communities that emerged in western Germany and in northern France were called Ashkenazim. The overwhelming majority of Ashkenazi Jews spoke Yiddish. Ashkenazi Jews constituted nine-tenths of the world's Jewish population before 1933.

[71] S. D. Goitein, *A Mediterranean Society* (Berkeley: University of California Press, 1999), 33.

[72] The first Crusades lasted from 1095 to 1099, the second from 1146 to 1148, the third from 1189 to 1192, and the fourth from 1202 to 1204 CE.

recapture Jerusalem and liberate their holy sites from the Muslims. Meanwhile, Europe was growing fast, and there was a tremendous demand for colonial expansion and trade with other countries.[73] In other words, the religious enthusiasm for liberating the Holy Land from the Muslims coincided with the economic interest in trade.

The Church was a centralized power with greater authority, and the appointment of higher echelon clergies such as bishops was no longer in the hands of kings. Therefore, the clergy were able to easily mobilize masses behind themselves, as they did in the first Crusades. It was in this setting that Pope Urban II in a speech in 1095 called upon Christians to free Jerusalem from the Muslims who had recently begun harassing peaceful Christian pilgrims traveling to Jerusalem. The contingents of Robert Flanders took the sea route via Italy and those of Godfrey of Bouillon took the land route around the Adriatic Sea. As Crusaders marched east, masses of men and even women joined them. In 1099, the Crusaders recaptured Jerusalem in a bloody fight in which many inhabitants were massacred.[74] In Jerusalem, Jews stood by the Muslims in defending the city. Once the Muslims were defeated, the Crusaders gathered the remaining Jews in a synagogue and burned them alive.[75] Following the conquest of Jerusalem, the Crusaders came to believe that now they were the real "chosen people," "the elect," and were the heirs to the Jewish holy places.[76]

For many Crusaders, recapturing Jerusalem was the goal, and shortly after this was achieved, the zeal and enthusiasm to continue declined. Soon the realities of maintaining and supplying the soldiers became an important issue. On the other hand, Muslim rulers felt that a concerted military effort was imminent at this time. Thus, in 1187 Yusuf ibn Ayyub,[77] known as Saladin or Salah ad-Din, inflicted a

---

[73] S. D. Goitein, *A Mediterranean Society* (Berkeley: University of California Press, 1999), 35.

[74] K. Armstrong, *Jerusalem: One City, Three Faiths* (New York: Ballantine Books, 1997), 274.

[75] H. Graetz, *History of the Jews* (Philadelphia: Bella Lowy, 1891), 3 308.

[76] K. Armstrong, *Jerusalem: One City, Three Faiths* (New York: Ballantine Books, 1997), 276.

[77] Yusuf ibn Ayyub was the nephew of Nur ad-Din Mahmoud, a devout Sunni Muslim who had every determination to wage a holy war against both Franks and Shiites.

major defeat on the Crusaders and took Jerusalem back. This defeat stunned Europe. In response to the Church's request for another major attack against the Muslims, Richard I of England, Phillip II of France, and Frederick I of the Roman Empire joined in a large-scale attack against the Muslims. Although they succeeded in gaining some territories back, they were unable to free Jerusalem again. In 1199, Pope Innocent III called for another Crusade to recapture Jerusalem, but this effort was again unsuccessful. Indeed, from this point on, Western forces could only gain access to Jerusalem through diplomacy and not through war.

The Crusades were not exclusively anti-Muslim undertakings but were anti-Jewish as well.[78] Early in the Crusades, there were rumors that the Crusaders had every intention to clean up Europe from "Christ killers." In fact, the Crusaders were under the illusion that they must get rid of Jews on their way to Jerusalem. Slogans of this nature revived the deep-seated hatred between the Jews and Christians and encouraged them to attack the Jews. Godfrey, one of the commanders of the Crusades, announced that he would kill the Jews one by one unless they accepted Christianity. In addition to this threat, usury was always used by Christians to justify violence against the Jews. Throughout the Crusades, the sacred unity between Church, state, and the mobs frequently disrupted the social order. The Church usually followed a policy of silence, local governments used the situation to their own advantage, and mobs were always present on the scene to exercise violence against the Jews. In the public opinion, Jews were merely tolerated because of their talent in finances and fund-raising for the kings and nobles. In this environment, kings often wrote off the loans they had obtained from Jews, confiscated the Jewish properties, and later evicted them. Thus, kings and nobles accumulated large sums of wealth. Edward I evicted Jews from England in 1290, and Charles VI expelled them from France in 1394. Landowners often took advantage of the situation, provoking animosity between peasants and Jews, and then people of power intervened seemingly to "protect the Jews" under the condition that Jewish moneylenders wrote off their loans. This was most true with the knights who had participated in the war and consequently felt they had a moral excuse for not paying back the Jewish loans.

---

[78] B. Russell, *A History of Western Philosophy* (New York: Touchstone, 1972), 430.

In summary, the Crusades inflicted many massacres and the destruction of properties of the Jews. On the other hand, the Crusades also promoted a massive cultural exchange between the Christian West and the Muslim East, and brought a handsome economic profit to Western Europe, the wealth that eventually became the economic base for the Italian Renaissance.

The Inquisition and the Jews

Most of the medieval Christians believed that God dictated the Bible, word for word, and it was God's desire that people of the world would eventually convert to Christianity. In other words, faith in other religions was interpreted as disrespect to God. On the other hand, identifying the non-Christians and converting them to Christianity, in the opinion of the Christians, was not only their moral duty but also protected the converters from the torment of hell. The success of the Inquisition was to a great extent due to the wide support of the illiterate masses who had subscribed to this particular viewpoint.

The main objective of the Inquisition was to entice Christians into fundamentalism. Since religious unity was a prerequisite for a powerful central government, this endeavor was also widely supported by the states. In essence, Church and State agreed that heresy was treason and must be punished by death.

The doctrine of the Inquisition was based on a simple code in the Old Testament:

> If there is a prophet among you, or one who claims to foretell the future by dreams, and if his predictions come true but he says, "Come, let us worship the gods of the other nations," do not listen to him. For the Lord is testing you to find out whether or not you really love him with all your heart and soul. You must never worship any god but Yahweh; obey only his commands and cling to him. The prophet who tries to lead you astray must be executed, for he has attempted to foment rebellion against the Lord your god who brought you out of slavery in the land of Egypt. By executing him you will clear out the evil from among you. If your nearest relative or closest friend, even a brother, son, daughter, or beloved wife whispers to you to come and worship these foreign gods, do not consent nor listen, and have no pity. Do not spare that person from

the penalty; do not conceal his horrible suggestion. Execute him! Your own hand shall be the first upon him to put him to death, then the hands of all the people. Stone him to death because he has tried to draw you away from the Lord your god who brought you from the land of Egypt, the place of slavery.[79]

It was on the basis of these verses, the words of God in the eyes of the average Christians, that the Inquisition justified violence against heretics and those people who dared to express a different interpretation of the religion.

In 1227, Pope Gregory IX placed inquisitors under the special jurisdiction of the papacy. The office of inquisitor was entrusted almost exclusively to the Dominicans because of their superior training in theology and their supposed freedom from worldly ambition. The word *Dominicans* originated from the Latin *Domini canes,* meaning the "dogs of the Lord," and was applied to this group because of their strict religious morals and their little or no mercy for nonbelievers.

The usual procedure was for the inquisitor to encourage people in towns and cities to identify their heretic friends and relatives. Before receiving the charges, the accused were given the opportunity to confess. Torture was an effective instrument to obtain confession. After the confession, the accused were encouraged to be an informant. Except for nursing mothers, no one was spared from torture. If the accused, for any reason, were released, they were not allowed to talk to anyone about their experience in prison. Sometimes the inquisitor even prosecuted the dead, confiscated the property of their heirs, and gave one-third of the property to the informants. The accumulation of wealth not only tempted state employees but also informants and church authorities. Therefore, the love of wealth usually replaced the love of God. Burning was the worst form of punishment. This was not only used to frighten people but to remind them of the fire of hell. The burning ceremonies were usually carried out on special days such as the weddings of the kings and victory at wars. The officials used to position the accused people in the center of a large gathering area, burn them, and then throw their ashes into the rivers or farms. Since the inquisitors believed that the Church must

---

[79] Deuteronomy 13:1–10.

not shed blood, if the accused did not confess they would return them to the prison and first suffocate them and then burn them. In this manner, the priests and Church were convinced that they had done their duties before God. The persecution of Christians by Romans in the first three centuries after Christ was very mild and more humane when compared with the persecutions of heresy in Europe from 1227 to 1492. The Inquisition of those years once again reminds us that blind faith is the most horrifying enemy of mankind.

The Marranos, or New Christians, were among those who suffered most as the victims of the Inquisition. *Marranos*, meaning "swine" in Spanish, were hated and rejected by both Jews and Christians. Jews rejected them because, in their opinion, they had abandoned the religion of their fathers. Christians disliked them since, thanks to their new religion, converted Jews were maintaining high-ranking government positions and the opportunities that belonged to Christians. Indeed, the accomplishments of the Inquisition were partly due to the hatred of average Christians for Marranos. The population of Marranos gradually grew as persecution of the Jews increased, and as a result, the anti-Marranos movement achieved new dimensions.

In short, the outbreak of the plague known as the Black Death started in southwestern Europe in 1347, and by 1351 had spread to the most eastern parts of Poland. The disease wiped out almost one-third of the European population and opened a new avenue of accusations against the Jews. Jews were accused of contaminating water wells and therefore causing the spread of the disease. Thousands of Jews were massacred as a result of these accusations in 1391, and many thousands saved their lives by accepting Christianity. However, many of those who were forced to convert, both during this period and thereafter, in fact continued to practice Judaism in private. Christians, however, understood that such baptism was binding, and an open relapse of Marranos to Judaism was indeed considered heresy.

The Spanish Inquisition, distinct from the medieval Inquisition, was established with papal approval in 1478 at the request of King Ferdinand V and Queen Isabella I of Spain. The principal goal of the Spanish Inquisition was to identify and eliminate the Marranos. Use of the Mosaic code in the preparation of food, respect for the Sabbath, celebration of Judaic feasts, circumcision of male newborns, selection of a Hebrew name for children, discussion about the Messiah, ignoring the cross sign as a gesture of blessing, and turning the dead to the wall at the burial service were among the indicators of a return to Judaism. However, after 1502, the Spanish Inquisition turned its attention to new converts from Islam and in the 1520s to persons suspected of Protestantism. Within a few years of the founding of the Inquisition, the papacy relinquished virtually all supervision of this operation to the state, and the Spanish Inquisition became more an instrument of the state than an apparatus of the Church, although Dominicans always functioned as its officers.

In 1483, on Queen Isabella's recommendation, Pope Sixtus IV appointed Tomas Torquemada (1420–1498) as the first inquisitor general of Castile, who in 1487 became the grand inquisitor for all of Spain. Torquemada was a Spanish monk and became known for his ruthless administration of the Inquisition. He was a deeply religious and zealous Catholic who strongly believed that Marranos and non-Catholics could destroy both the church and the country, and therefore he obliged himself by eliminating Marranos, Moors,[80] and others on an unprecedented scale. During his eleven years in the office, more than two thousand people were burned at the stake.

Eviction of Jews from Spain

The Jewish community of Spain, the most populated and prosperous community of Jews in Europe, had enjoyed a prolonged and peaceful life for over three centuries prior to the establishment of the Inquisition. The peaceful and friendly atmosphere made possible the active participation of Jews in almost every aspect of cultural and social life. During this period, known as the golden age of Spanish Jewry, many Jews of culture and wealth soared to positions of influence.

However, by the end of the fourteenth century, due to the Dominican preaching, ritual accusations against Jews and the devastation of the Black Death, for which Jews were blamed, eventually unsettled these communities and interrupted their peace and tranquility.

---

[80]The Moors were the mixed Arab-Berbers of North Africa; however, the Spaniards applied this term to all Muslims and called their culture Moorish.

King Ferdinand of Spain was quite aware of the financial and economic capabilities of Spanish Jewry. Therefore, he resisted eviction of the Jews from Spain, even though it was often recommended by the Church. However, a number of stories eventually changed his mind. Rumors were spread that the special physician to the king, Ribas Altas, who was a Marranos, wore a necklace that was disrespectful to Christ. This accusation was a sufficient excuse for burning the physician.[81] Moreover, Christian fundamentalists forged a letter from the head of the Jewish community in Constantinople to Spanish Jews suggesting that they must poison as many Christians as they could.[82] In another event, a Marrano confessed under torture that he and six others had killed a Christian boy for his heart to prepare poisonous syrup for killing Christians. They burned four of the Marranos, in spite of contradictions in the story and the fact that neither a missing child nor his body was ever reported.[83]

Then in 1487 Tomas Torquemada became the grand inquisitor of all Spain. He believed that the presence of the Jews was the main excuse for the Marranos to regress to Judaism. Therefore, he was determined to separate the Jews from the Marranos. He finally convinced King Ferdinand in 1492 to sign the decree for the eviction of the Jews from Spain. Moreover, in 1491, when the Muslims lost Granada to the Christians, the Jews also lost their economic status. Thus, there was no further reason for Ferdinand to refuse to implement the Torquemada's recommendation.

According to the edict that Ferdinand and Isabella signed on March 31, 1492, all Jews who were not baptized by that time would have to leave Spain by July 31 of the same year. Should they decide to return, they would face the death penalty. During the short period between March and July, Jews were allowed to sell their properties and take their movable items, except for gold, silver, and currency, with them. They were expected to pay all taxes due that year, but the loans to Christians would be collected at their maturity dates.

---

[81] H. C. Lea, *History of the Inquisition in Spain.* (New York: 1906), 1: 133, quoted in W. Durant, *History of Civilization: The Reformation* (New York: Simon & Schuster, 1957), 217.
[82] Ibid.
[83] Ibid.

However, they could sell these loans to Christians at a lower value. According to Will Durant, in this four-month period a home was exchanged for a donkey and a vineyard for a suit. Some of the Jews burned their homes to ashes, and many donated them to the city. Synagogues were converted to churches. In other words, all that the Spanish Jews had accumulated during several centuries of staying in Spain evaporated before their eyes. About 50,000 of them converted to Christianity, and the remaining 150,000 left Spain on horses, donkeys, carts, or bare feet. Many good-hearted Christians encouraged them to convert in order to stay. Rabbis, on the other hand, assured them that the God of Israel would save them and take them across the sea to the Promised Land, as he had done so for their fathers.[84] Some of the Jews waited at the shore hoping for the waters to part so they could walk to Africa. Since the miracle did not occur, they paid dearly to travel by ship. But storms pushed back many of the ships into Spanish shores, and many of the passengers preferred Christianity to storms and seasickness. The only official accusation against Jews was their inclination to entice the Marranos back to Judaism. It is noteworthy that Pope Alexander VI acknowledged King Ferdinand and Queen Isabella for their efforts in evicting the Jews, and conferred the title of The Catholic upon them.[85]

The Jews left Spain, but the religious unity that the Catholic Church and Isabella were dreaming of never crystallized. Eleven years later, the Moors were forced to either convert to Christianity or follow in the footsteps of the Jews out of Spain. The Moors strongly objected to this decree, claiming that when their fathers were governing Spain, they recognized the rights of Christians, and so in exchange, the Christians must respect the rights of Muslims. Nevertheless, the state had no intention or desire to pay attention to this logic. In spite of the fact that Cardinal Richelieu called the decree a savage proclamation, more than three million Muslims left Spain in the early sixteenth century.

About eighty thousand Spanish Jews migrated to Portugal. The migration of this magnitude alarmed King John II, and he set

---

[84] W. H. Prescott, *History of the Reign of Ferdinand and Isabella, the Catholic* (Philadelphia: 1891), 1: 514, quoted in W. Durant, *History of Civilization: The Reformation* (New York: Simon & Schuster, 1957), 218.

[85] *Encyclopedia Americana* (1979), 16: 65.

forth a deadline of eight months for all the Jews to leave Portuguese soil. Moreover, an outbreak of the plague among Jewish immigrants and the concern over the spread of the disease to the Christian population were also good excuses to evict Jews as quickly as possible. John II provided inexpensive ships to transport the Jews to the southern coasts of the Mediterranean Sea. The crews of the ships robbed the Jews, raped their wives and daughters, and sold many of them as slaves to the Moors.[86]

The outcome of those Jews who elected to stay in Portugal after the eight-month deadline was no better. Most of them were sold as slaves, and the younger children were separated from their parents and transported to Saint Thomas Island to be brought up as Christians. Many Jewish mothers drowned themselves with their children in order to avoid the pain and the suffering of separation.[87] In May 1497, Emmanuel, John's successor, abandoned prosecution of the Marranos for a period of twenty years. However, in 1506, Portuguese Christians attacked and slaughtered two thousand Marranos whom they viewed as their economic competitors.

In 1532, Pope Clement VII laid down a more humane recommendation in handling the Marranos. He argued:

> Since they were dragged by force to be baptized, they cannot be considered members of the Church and to punish them for heresy and relapse was to violate the principles of justice and equity. For the sons and daughters of Marranos the case is different. They belong to the Church as voluntary members. But they have been brought up by their relatives in the midst of Judaism, and have had this example continually before their eyes; it would be cruel to punish them according to the canonical law for falling into Jewish ways and beliefs. They must be kept in the bosom of the Church through gentle treatment.[88]

The Portuguese Inquisition was reinstated in 1536 but with the condition that the accused must be confronted by the accuser, a provision that was never practiced during the Spanish Inquisition.

---

[86] H. Graetz, *History of the Jews* (Philadelphia: Bella Lowry, 1891), 4: 369.

[87] Ibid., 371.

[88] Ibid., 531.

The Jews who were evicted from Spain and Portugal in the fifteenth and sixteenth centuries are known as Sephardic[89] Jews. At the time of their eviction from Spain and Portugal, the doors of many countries were closed to Jews. Eviction of Jews was not a phenomenon only of the fifteenth century. Jews had been evicted from England in 1290, from Normandy in 1296, from France in 1306 and again in 1394, and finally in 1492 from Spain and Portugal. In fact, the Ottoman Empire, Italy, and Poland were the only countries that accepted Jews. Holland joined them later after its independence from Spain.

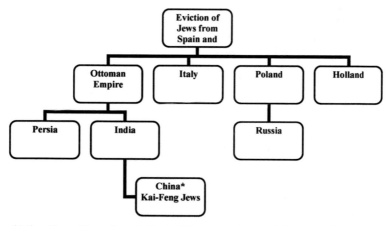

*Migration of Jews from India to China started around the eleventh century

Eviction of Jews from Spain and Migration of the Sephardic Jews to the East

Toward the end of the fifteenth century, the Ottoman Empire not only included Turkey and the Near East but also large parts of Northern Africa and Eastern Europe. The migration of the Sephardic Jews occurred during the reign of Sultan Bajazet II. Those who migrated to the Ottoman Empire scattered throughout the empire, and

---

[89] The word "Sephardic," originating from the term "Sepharad" in the Book of Obedia, has been applied to the region of Lydia in Asia Minor. However, in the Aramaic translation of the Old Testament, it has been applied to Spain. The Spanish Jews called themselves Sephardim and traced their origin to the tribe of Judah.

from there some migrated to Iran. However, most of the Jews settled in Constantinople, and soon it was recognized as the largest Jewish community in all of Europe. It is said that Ferdinand of Spain believed that Sultan Bajazet, by accepting the Jews, might bankrupt the Ottoman Empire and indirectly support the kingdom of Spain. Nevertheless, the Jewish population in the Ottoman Empire grew quickly, and due to relative social tranquility, the Jews built a prosperous community that was only second to the Spanish settlements. Here, Jews had careers in business and medicine and functioned as civil servants in the government and the courts. For a distinct minority of the Jews, the condition was such that they could write and promote their viewpoints or enjoy certain privileges. One of these Jews was Joseph Caro, who wrote the famous manuscript of *Shulhn Arukh*[90] in the sixteenth century in Constantinople. Another example was Solomon Hamitsri, the special physician of Ottoman Sultan, who was the only Jew with the right to ride a horse. Nevertheless, the Jewish masses were living in poverty and were often the subject of the political persecution.

Jews of the Ottoman Empire managed their own communities. The council of rabbis usually selected the managers of these communities. However, Sultan Selim I changed this arrangement and demanded that residents of Jewish communities elect a rabbi or a religious leader locally who was responsible for the management of each community. As in other Islamic countries, Jews used to pay a special tax known as jizya, and in exchange they did not serve in the army.

By 1516, when Ottoman Turks conquered Jerusalem, Palestine had only a modest Jewish population. Ottoman sultans generally allowed the small-scale migration of Jews to Palestine. However, since Muslims and Christians also viewed Jerusalem as a sacred city, the government usually prevented overpopulation of the city by Jews. It was during this period that some Jewish residents of Palestine put forward the ambitious plan of reviving the council of Sanhedrin, but because of the dispersion of Jewish communities and

---

[90] Shulhn Aruch, or "the prepared table," is a collection of Jewish laws and rituals. The manuscript consists of four parts: *Orah Hayyim* on prayers, Sabbath, festivals and fasts; *Yoreh De'ah*, about dietary codes; *Even ha-Ezer*, on women and marriage; and *Hoshen Mishpat*, focusing on civil and criminal codes.

the diversity of their spoken languages, the plan did not receive wide support.

Those Jews who migrated to Italy settled in the northern towns. Their social condition was always dependent on the deeds of the popes and dukes. For instance, in Naples and Milan, two cities that were under the political influence of Spain, Jews experienced tremendous hardship, whereas in Pisa and Livorno, they enjoyed more freedom and tranquility. Indeed, the Inquisition and government servants were prohibited from causing problems for Jewish merchants in Livorno as early as 1593. As a result of this, the city turned into a prosperous Jewish center in Italy. Livorno was also the only major Italian city in which a Jewish ghetto was never established.[91] A number of Italian Jews achieved high positions in trade, finance, and craft. In spite of the efforts to evict them, the government supported them as the benefactors of trade and finance. Jews were engaged in trading silk and wool from Spain and spice and pearls from India. Eventually, as in Constantinople, an elite circle of Jews appeared who, similar to influential people of Italian society, became fascinated with the culture and literature of the Renaissance.

Poland was the third country to accept the Sephardic Jews. The Jewish population of Poland was about fifty thousand by the end of the fifteenth century. These were mostly the Jews who had been evicted from England and France. After the expulsion of Jews from Spain and Portugal, the Jewish population of Poland grew significantly and was over half a million by 1648. In Poland, kings took advantage of Jewish talent for collecting taxes and managing properties. For instance, Stephen Bathory passed a decree in 1576 conferring the right of trade to the Jews in Poland and condemning any prosecutions against them. However, following the economic rivalry between Christians and Jews, the old animosities were revived, and anti-Jewish sentiments reached their peak in 1648. The conflict was initially among Cossacks, peasants, and Polish landowners, but Jews were pulled in as scapegoats. It is said that the massacres of the Jews in Poland turned very ugly. The uprising of peasants under the leadership of Bogdan Chemielnicki between 1648 and 1649 destroyed many Jewish communities in Poland and

---

[91] G. D. Wigoder, *The New Standard Jewish Encyclopedia* (New York: Facts on File, 1992), 585.

Ukraine. According to a Russian historian, the massacre of Jews in Poland was preceded with extreme torture. Jews were skinned alive, burned on the coal rack, or boiled in water. Thousands of Jewish children were buried alive.[92] It is estimated that about thirty-four thousand Jews were massacred in these events in Poland. Eventually, Chemielnicki brought the massacre to an end by receiving a large sum of money. The remaining victims of these outrageous massacres tried very hard to migrate to Russia, but for all practical purposes no Jew reached Russia before the annexation of Poland in 1772. Peter the Great, in response to the many requests of Jews for migration, used to say: "I know Jews and Russians very well. I do not think that the time has yet come that these two people live together. I realize Jews will contribute tremendously to Russia, but I do not recommend Jews and Russians become neighbors at present."[93]

Holland was the fourth country to absorb the evicted Spanish and Portuguese Jews. The relative freedom to practice religion and tolerance of non-Christians in Holland attracted many Jews. The first Jews to enter Holland were the Marranos, who practiced religious rituals in Hebrew but spoke Spanish and Portuguese in their day-to-day activities. They initially settled in Rotterdam, Harlem, and Amsterdam in 1590. Jews in Holland participated mainly in commerce, soon establishing Holland as a center of commerce in Europe. In 1645, Jews were officially allowed to practice Judaism in Holland, but they were still prohibited to marry Christians. Soon a distinct minority of wealthy Jews grew among the Sephardic population of Amsterdam. Due to their wealth, they acquired great social power and monopolized the management of Jewish life. They supervised the synagogues, education, and charity and were instrumental in running Jewish communities.

By the mid-seventeenth century, German Jews migrated to Amsterdam and introduced the Ashkenazi culture to these communities. The Ashkenazi population that had arrived in Holland was culturally less sophisticated than the Sephardic counterpart that had entered previously. The former spoke Yiddish, a blend of medieval German, Hebrew, and Slavic elements, written in Hebrew

---

[92] S. M. Dubnow, *History of the Jews in Russia and Poland* (South Brunswick, NJ: T. Yoseloff, 1967), 1: 145.
[93] Ibid., 246.

lettering.[94] Sephardic Jews, however, because of their cultural superiority, viewed Ashkenazi Jews as secondhand people, and in general did not show any interest in socializing with them. Nonetheless, Amsterdam slowly evolved into a prominent Jewish cultural and commercial center of Europe.

The Ghettos and the Jews

The term *ghetto*, Italian in origin, meaning "segregation" and "divorce," was first applied to the Jewish quarter of Venice in 1517. However, the idea of segregating Jews in Christendom shows up in 1179 and again in 1215, when the Catholic Church officially forbade the Jews and Christians from living together. The establishment of ghettos in Italy and their expansion to other European countries, however, was the result of both intolerance of Jews practiced by the Christians and the desire of the Jews to maintain their unity and exclusiveness.[95] For all practical purposes, the separate living quarters were within the fabric of the Jewish communities of Europe for over seven centuries and were only abolished in 1917.

The legal decree issued by Pope Paul IV in 1555, among other restrictions, forced Jews to live in a separate quarter in Rome. Following the papal order, similar ghettos were established in most of Europe through the next three centuries. These quarters were known as *judengasse* in Germany, *judenstadt* in Prague, *carriere* in France, and *juderias* in Spain. The land of the ghettos was usually assigned to the Jewish community for an annual taxation. In some instances, however, Jews were allowed to purchase the land.[96] Ghettos were surrounded by grim walls and gates where tens of thousands of Jews were forced to live in a square kilometer.[97] The ghettos were barred from spreading out; therefore, houses were built on top of each other so the ghettos could not expand laterally.[98] Gates were closed at

---

[94] A. Koestler, *The Thirteenth Tribe: The Khazar Empire and Its Heritage* (New York: Random House, 1976), 172.

[95] *Encyclopedia Encarta*, "Ghetto," CD-ROM, 2000, Microsoft Corporation.

[96] *Jewishencyclopedia.com* "Ghetto."

[97] W. Durant, *The Story of Civilization: The Reformation* (New York: Simon & Schuster, 1963), 735.

[98] A. Eban, *Heritage: Civilization and the Jews* (New York: Summit Books, 1984), 191.

midnight and opened at dawn, except for Sundays and Christian holy days, during which they were closed all day. Christian gatekeepers guarded the gates, and Jews were compelled to pay their salaries. Inhabitants could only leave the ghettos under special circumstances with permission from the authorities, and they were not allowed to invite guests into the ghettos. Ghettos were generally located in the poor sections of the city. They usually suffered a higher mortality rate than surrounding communities as a result of overpopulation and unhealthy living conditions, increased risk of infectious diseases, and fire. Being deprived of contact with the outside world, these small independent communities stifled many talents and tended to produce individuals who were delusional and living in denial. On the other hand, within the walls of the ghettos the Jewish inhabitants expressed more than usual responsibility toward each other.

In order to be distinguished in public outside the ghettos, Jewish men were forced to wear a yellow hat and Jewish women a yellow veil while traveling. According to Will Durant, the segregation of Jews into ghettos was not the most insulting blow to them. They even could tolerate poverty. But the cruelest insult was to enforce them to wear the yellow hat, veil, or patch. On this subject, Heinrich Graetz (1817–1891), the Jewish historian, wrote, "Wearing the yellow patch was an invitation for the public to insult the Jews. Yellow patch encouraged the mob to insult, to injure and even kill the Jews. Moreover, wearing the yellow patch carried infamy and disgrace for Jews and deprived them of their self-confidence."[99]

Living in the Jewish quarters was not always forced upon Jews. In fact, some Jews voluntarily elected to live separately from others.[100] The right to live in a separate quarter surrounded by a wall was granted to the Jews of Speyer, a town in Germany, in 1084 at the request of the Jews themselves.[101] The voluntary preference of Jews to live in separate quarters to some extent was prompted by the needs of these communities. Fear of being accused, attacked, injured, or even murdered often enticed Jews to live in separate quarters. Living separately was instrumental in providing assistance to each other at the time of attack in a hostile environment, made it more convenient

---

[99] H. Graetz, *History of the Jews* (Philadelphia, Bella Lowy, 1891), 3: 511.
[100] *Encyclopedia Judaica*, "Jewish Quarter," CD-ROM, 1997, Judaica Multimedia.
[101] Ibid.

to maintain a quorum for prayers, and granted an atmosphere where they could observe their religious rituals and laws.[102] The desire of the Jews to maintain their unity and exclusiveness has been cited by Bertrand Russell as yet another incentive for living in separate quarters. He wrote, "After the foundation of Alexandria, great numbers of Jews settled in that city; they had a special quarter assigned to them, not as a ghetto, but to keep them from danger of pollution by contact with gentiles."[103]

Nevertheless, the ghetto was an inherent part of Jewish life until the French Revolution. The revolution drastically changed the social status of Jews, and it was through this process that they were socially emancipated and Christians came to tolerate them as a minority. In the aftermath of the French Revolution, ghettos disappeared in France, and again under the influence of the revolution they vanished in Italy and gradually in other European countries.[104] In Russia, the Pale of Settlement, that was similar to ghettos in Western Europe, continued to exist until the October Revolution of 1917.

In the land of Islam, Jewish living quarters had a different configuration. Initially, Islam did not impose a special restriction upon the *dhimmis*' (non-Muslim people of the Book) areas of residence. Therefore, ghettos, like those in Europe, did not appear in Islamic countries until the early eighteenth century. In the Ottoman Empire, ghettos were always built voluntarily and remained so.[105] In the city of Istanbul, Jewish quarters were in fact scattered all over the city. Muslims had a vague and nonsystematic approach toward this issue. In other words, the initial provision was to distance Jews from the vicinity of mosques. Later, Jews were prohibited from building houses above a certain size or height. With the economic decline, these Jewish quarters with smaller houses gradually became slums.

In Shiite-predominant countries like Iran, the situation was different. From the onset of acquiring power, the Safavid governments established distinct Jewish quarters very similar to the

---

[102] Ibid.

[103] B. Russell, *A History of Western Philosophy* (New York: Touchstone, 1972), 321.

[104] The ghettos that were established by the Nazis from 1939 to 1942 in Europe were in fact living quarters for the Jews before their annihilation. In addition, these camps were designed for weakening the spirits of Jews before their death.

[105] *Encyclopedia Judaica*, "Ghetto," CD-ROM, 1997, Judaica Multimedia.

European ghettos, where their gates were locked at night and on Saturdays. These living quarters, called *mahallas* in Iran, later were extended to Yemen and Morocco, where they were called *qa'at al-Yahud* and *mellah,* respectively. The segregation of Jews in these countries was based upon the religious connotation of ritual uncleanness of Jews.[106] From the beginning of the twentieth century, affluent Jews left the ghettos, and only poor Jews continued to live there.

Characteristics of the Medieval Jews

Jewish communities of the Middle Ages attained certain characteristics that more or less distinguished them from previous periods. These characteristics were not exclusive to the Jewish communities of Europe but were also noted in the rest of the world. These features generally stemmed from (a) the prolonged history of living as a distinct minority in more or less isolation, (b) from being scattered almost all over the world, and (c) the collective distinctiveness of the Jewish communities evolved in the aftermath of the Babylonian Talmud being established as the governing body in these communities. This period lasted for almost ten centuries, from the eighth to the eighteenth century CE, and has been named Classical Judaism by Israel Shahak and Normative Judaism and Rabbinical Judaism by others.[107] The foremost characteristics of Classical Judaism are as follows:

Medieval Jewish communities enjoyed a relative autonomy and were exclusively controlled by the religious institution. The internal affairs of the Jewish communities were administered by their own members. A council of influential figures whose members were often selected among rabbis, managers of synagogues, and the wealthy usually supervised these communities. The council was responsible for collecting taxes, fixing prices on goods, and above all enforcing the law. Religion, and in particular its Talmudic interpretations, was considered the highest authority. One

---

[106] Ibid.
[107] I. Shahak, "The Jewish Religion and Its Attitude to Non-Jews," *Khamsin* 8 (1981): 58.

of the council's functions was to oblige members of the Jewish communities to abide indisputably with the religious laws.

Rabbis used excommunication as an instrument to enforce the law in the Jewish communities. Herem,[108] or complete excommunication, was the cruelest punishment, which usually began with accusations and cursing and ended with complete isolation of the individual from the rest of the community.[109] Members of the community were usually encouraged to avoid the excommunicated person, and many did this as a gesture of good faith. In addition, the excommunicated individual was not allowed to appear in synagogue and was not permitted to bury his dead in the community's cemetery. The ceremony of excommunication was usually held in the synagogue and consisted of turning off candles, one after another, as a symbol of ending the spiritual life of the excommunicated. Then several biblical curses were invoked upon the excommunicated. This form of punishment was often used for the purpose of collecting taxes or discouraging individuals from learning science or philosophy. Women were rarely excommunicated, since their responsibilities were laid upon the male head of household.[110] Religious leaders had their own agents to carry out these ceremonies, although average people also willingly participated, considering it a virtue. In addition to excommunication, expulsion from town was tried as late as the seventeenth and eighteenth centuries in the Jewish communities.[111] This mode of punishment was usually exercised with no regard for the time of year and the financial hardship that might have been inflicted upon the family of the accused. Sometimes violent behavior like flogging and imprisonment followed excommunication. In some countries, like Spain and Poland, where courts were under the jurisdiction of rabbis, even capital punishment in its cruelest form, stoning, was practiced. The government did not usually question these

---

[108] The term *herem* originates from the Aramaic word *haruma* meaning "forbidden." This word was first used in verse 19, chapter 22, of Exodus in reference to the punishment of those who worshipped other gods instead of Yahweh. In the Talmud, however, a milder form of excommunication, or *niddui*, has also been described. In this case, the excommunicated individual wears mourning attire and is prohibited from social activity for seven days to a month.

[109] *Encyclopedia Judaica*, "Herem," CD-ROM, 1997, Judaica Multimedia.

[110] *JewishEncyclopedia.com*, "Excommunication."

[111] I. Shahak and N. Mezvinsky, *Jewish Fundamentalism in Israel* (London: Pluto Press, 1999), 130.

extreme practices. In fact, both Christian and Muslim governments, under the banner of restoring order, supported these kinds of violent acts simply because it was profitable. For example, during the thirteenth and fourteenth centuries, the National Archives of Spain revealed that the Catholic kings of Castile and Aragon always encouraged their agents to collaborate with rabbis in enforcing the rituals of Sabbath. The incentive for this collaboration was essentially profit. For instance, if a Jew was convicted for an offense by a rabbi, nine-tenths of the penalty the Jew paid to the Jewish community was credited to the king's treasury.

Rabbis were exempt from paying taxes. The relationship between the king and the council or the leaders of the Jewish communities was in general friendly. The friendship was sometimes so deep that the king at times sacrificed the local government agent for it. It is said that Emperor Theodosius I, who was a fanatical Christian, executed the Roman commander of Palestine because he had insulted a religious Jewish leader. To illustrate this special relation, around a hundred years before the establishment of the Inquisition, Pedro I, the Christian commander of Castile, gave rabbis the right to establish a countrywide inquisition against the Jews.[112] In the larger Jewish communities such as those in Poland, the special relation between rabbis and the wealthy promoted a form of rabbinical despotism and tyranny over the average Jews. Thus, it was not surprising that Rabbi Moshe Sofer, known as Hatam Sofer (1762–1839) of Bratislava in Austria, once said: "Had I ever learned that a Jew dared to show in his shop on Sabbath, I immediately sent the police to arrest him." The story of a Jew who was flogged to death because of his relation with a gentile woman was only one example of this kind of violence.[113] In another instance, when Maimonides was in charge of the Jewish community in Egypt, he gave an order to flog in public those Jews who had married gentiles until they had divorced their wives.[114] This indisputable subjugation to rabbinical oligarchy was not only widely practiced in European medieval Jewish

---

[112] I. Shahak, "The Jewish Religion and Its Attitude to Non-Jews, *Khamsin* 9 (1981): 12.

[113] Talmud, Baba Pethra 8-a, Nidah 10-b and 20-b.

[114] I. Shahak, "The Jewish Religion and Its Attitude to Non-Jews," *Khamsin* 9 (1981): 11.

communities but also in Islamic and Eastern European countries up to the end of the nineteenth century.

Medieval Jewish communities were characteristically dependent on kings and nobles. Jewish communities dealt directly with the king's representative instead of going through the usual government hierarchy. The king was the only one who could guarantee the relative independence of these communities and confer upon them protection and the privilege of trade. In other words, the relationship between the Jewish communities and the king was based upon a contract according to which these communities paid an annual sum of money to the king in exchange for the privilege of trade and usury.

Manifestly there was no conflict between the Talmudic teachings and this special arrangement. Indeed, the Talmud praises the power of the state and considers exceptions to certain practices for the men of power. On the admiration of the state power, it was stated that "the law of the State is law,"[115] and there was a recommendation to "pray for the welfare of the government, for were it not for the fear thereof, one man would swallow up alive his fellow man."[116] Similarly, praising of Muslim rulers and attributing their acts of cruelty and injustices to the God's will was customary,[117] and they were almost never criticized in the Mediterranean Jewish communities. Communal prayers for the rulers, usually on the Day of Atonement, were held in these communities as early as the eleventh century.[118]

One of the exceptions that are advanced only to the kings and nobles is the subject of the desecration of the Sabbath. Desecrating the Sabbath means doing works that would otherwise not be allowed on Saturday.

For instance, a Jewish midwife or a physician was forbidden from attending a gentile patient on Sabbath. However, the Talmudic law has allowed exceptions in the cases of kings and nobles and, in

---

[115] Talmud, Baba Kaman 113-a.
[116] Mishnah, Mas Avoth, ch. 3: 2.
[117] S. D. Goitein, *A Mediterranean Society* (Berkeley: University of California Press, 1999), 164.
[118] Ibid., 165.

fact, encourages Jewish midwives and physicians to do their best in these cases.[119]

This special arrangement with kings and nobles, on the other hand, put the Jewish communities in a precarious position and made them more vulnerable than ever.[120] Kings and nobles often took advantage of this special relation and exploited these communities to the utmost. In this regard and as an example, the approach of the French kings toward the Jews is noteworthy. In 1306, Jews were evicted from France, and nine years later, on the condition that they pay two-thirds of their profits from loans to the king, they were readmitted into the country. In 1321, after the king had collected a large sum of money, they were evicted again. Later, the Jews were readmitted into France, blamed for the Black Plague, and once again evicted in 1349. In 1360, France invited the Jews back to financially assist in paying the ransom for the release of the king, who was in British detention. Finally, in 1394, Jews were accused of killing a Marrano, who had disappeared mysteriously, and as a result were evicted again by King Charles VI. Moreover, the special arrangement with the kings, in the eyes of the average Christian population, was interpreted as a practice of favoritism of the Jews and often provoked their animosities against Jews.

Medieval Jewish communities were characteristically unfamiliar with land and agriculture. The separation of Jews from land and agriculture, their migration to the cities and towns, and their fascination with trade and finance was a process that took place during the Middle Ages. This transition was not the choice of the Jews and in fact was forced upon them for variety of reasons.

At the onset of the Diaspora, Jews enjoyed the right of land ownership. Most Jews, like other people, were involved in agriculture and livestock. Although in general Jews were not legally prohibited from owning land, a turn of events gradually forced them to relinquish their land and agriculture. These events became more vigorous by the fourth century, when Christianity achieved state power. Indeed, in some respects, Christian Rome imposed more

---

[119] I. Shahak, *Jewish History, Jewish Religion* (London: Pluto Press, 1997), 53.
[120] H. Arendt, *Anti-Semitism: Part One of the Origins of Totalitarianism* (New York: Harvest Books, 1968), 54.

restrictions upon Jews living within the empire than its pagan predecessor.

While living in Christian lands, Jews were not allowed to keep slaves; initially this restriction only applied to Christian slaves and later to slaves in general. Moreover, according to the Old Testament and the Talmud, they were prohibited from having Jewish slaves. On the other hand, it was extremely costly to recruit the labor force in the free market. Furthermore, according to the Mosaic Law, Jews were prohibited from working on Saturday, but Christians considered Sunday as their holiday, thereby eliminating two workdays per week and deteriorating the farming productivity. By depriving them of adequate and inexpensive access to a workforce, large-scale Jewish agriculture was almost impossible.

Soon after Christianity achieved state power, the Church advanced the attitude that positions of authority or honor should be denied to Jews. This provision automatically excluded Jews from the established feudal system. Accordingly, Jews were not allowed to carry arms and fight for the eminent landowners, and indeed the laws of almost all Christian states forbade Jews from carrying arms.[121] Achieving a position in that system required a Christian oath and military service, neither of which was feasible for Jews. To these obstacles, one must add the periodic confiscation of Jewish properties by kings, dukes, and popes. These factors altogether discouraged Jews from the ownership of land and agriculture and gradually forced them to migrate to towns where trade and crafts were the sole source of living. Thus, by the end of the eighth century, agriculture was a marginal Jewish occupation.

However, Jews participated in agriculture and farming whenever the legal and social circumstances allowed them. For instance, after Muslims conquered Spain in 711, many North African Jews migrated to Spain and were attracted to farming. As late as the eleventh century, Jews of the Mediterranean communities were engaged in agriculture.[122] Also, with the development of the leasehold

---

[121] W. Durant, *The Story of Civilization: The Age of Faith* (New York: Simon & Schuster, 1963), 375.
[122] S. D. Goitein, *A Mediterranean Society* (Berkeley: University of California Press, 1999), 220, 234–5.

system in Poland in the fourteenth century, a substantial number of Jews were again absorbed into farming and agriculture.[123]

As Jews achieved prominent positions in trade, the competition with Christians became an issue. As a result of this, the Christian governments, one after another, passed more regulations against Jews and in support of their Christian population.

Later, some of the Jews who were actively involved in trade moved into large-scale commerce, and by the eleventh century Jewish merchants appeared to have commerce in their hands. Indeed, Jews functioned as the middle person between the Islamic world and Christian Europe. Jews demonstrated a great patience and fortitude in learning commerce. They also enjoyed the hospitality and the guidance of local Jews all over the world, a phenomenon that helped them achieve extraordinary success. The financial attractiveness of trade over agriculture was yet another factor that was not overlooked in the Talmudic teachings. Along these lines, Rab, a Babylonian Talmudist, explained, "Trade with a hundred florins, and you will afford meat and wine, put same sum into agriculture, and at most you may have bread and salt."[124]

Due to the confiscations that frequently threatened Jews, they had no choice other than to convert their wealth into a liquid form that could be easily carried from one place to another. Thus, Jews gradually became involved in finance and exchange, a profession with large rewards and great insecurity that could only succeed when conducted by the people with group solidarity.[125] In the beginning, finance was confined to the exchange of money, but soon usury also became prevalent. In spite of the fact that both the Pentateuch[126] and the Talmud[127] had condemned usury, it was generally understood that lending to gentiles was justified. With the development of industry and the expansion of commerce, the demand for capital increased to such an extent that even Jews loaned money to each other through Christian mediators. Since the Qur'an and New Testament had

---

[123] *Encyclopedia Judaica*, "Agriculture," CD-ROM, 1997, Judaica Multimedia.
[124] W. Durant, *The Story of Civilization: The Age of Faith* (New York: Simon & Schuster, New York, 1963), 376.
[125] E. Hobsbaum, *The Age of Extremes* (New York: Pantheon Books, 1994), 338.
[126] Deuteronomy 23:20.
[127] Talmud, Baba Metzia 61-a.

condemned usury, Jews who participated in this kind of activity became more visible.

Moneylenders, regardless of their religious affiliation, were subject to heavy taxes. But in the case of Jews, in addition to heavy taxes, there was always the risk of confiscation. Kings often allowed high interest rates in order to confiscate the usurers for their higher gains. Sometimes, to gain popularity from the public, kings wrote off the interest or even the principal that people owed to usurers. This was most true in the case of British kings, who forced Jewish usurers of the thirteenth century into bankruptcy.[128] Moreover, since collecting loans was extremely difficult, lenders had to bribe government agents to assist them in this endeavor, a practice that often ignited the public opinion against Jews.

In summary, economic and cultural factors forced the Jews to part from land and agriculture and enter into trade, exchange, and finance. This economic character of Jewish communities, along with their dependence upon kings and nobles, was one of the key factors in provoking anti-Semitic sentiments.

Medieval Jewish communities characteristically enjoyed a strong social cohesiveness. As long as Jews lived in the Jewish communities, they would not starve.[129] Each member was obligated to contribute to the community funds to provide for the care of the poor, elderly, patients, and orphans.[130] Therefore, there were homes for the poor and the elderly, hospitals, and orphan houses in every community. Charitable services and dedications to common good were entirely done on a voluntary basis, with the understanding that they were given to God.[131] The historic background of these services dates back to the second century CE.[132]

Medieval Jewish communities, like other societies, consisted of the rich and the poor. Rabbis, however, were emphatic that the rich

---

[128] H. Graetz, *History of the Jews* (Philadelphia: Bella Lowy, 1891), 3: 588

[129] S. W. Baron, *Social and Religious History of the Jews* (New York: Columbia University Press, 1941), 2: 99.

[130] S. D. Goitein, *A Mediterranean Society* (Berkeley: University of California Press, 1999), 121.

[131] Ibid., 126.

[132] G. F. Moore, *Judaism in the First Centuries of the Christian Era* (Cambridge, MA: Harvard University Press, 1932), 2: 174–175.

must assist the poor. In spite of Rabbi Eleazar Ben Azariah's insistence that "all human beings, from women to slaves and poor were equal before god,"[133] rabbis in general believed that the rich were somehow different and were obliged to give more. In many Jewish communities, the weekly distribution of bread among the poor and gifts of clothes to women was an old custom.[134] Loan, gift, partnership, and employment were other forms of charitable services provided to the needy.[135]

Parents usually arranged marriages.[136] Since people married at a younger age, prostitution was infrequent in these communities. Most men married around their twentieth birthday and women around their fifteenth. The father was the head of the household and was instrumental in promoting cohesiveness among the members of the family. He had the right to excommunicate his children and physically punish his wife. The family and the cohesiveness among its members were the basic principles of the social life in the Jewish communities. The more these communities were persecuted, the more cohesiveness there was among Jews.

The morals and ethics of medieval Jews were a reflection of the circumstances in which they were living. Discrimination, insults, persecution, and massacres undoubtedly left a footprint in the hearts and minds of Jews. For this reason, medieval Jewish communities had deep contradictions in their surroundings. These conditions promoted a lack of trust between the Jewish communities and the gentile world around them. Influenced by this contradiction, the Talmud teachings sometimes define two different value systems for Jews and gentiles. For instance, the murder of a Jew was considered a capital offense and, along with adultery and idolatry, the three dreadful sins, was punishable by death. A Jew who indirectly caused the death of another Jew was, however, only guilty of what according to the Talmud was a sin against the "law of Heaven," to be punished by God

---

[133] F. Foakes-Jackson and K. Lake, *Beginnings of Christianity* (London: 1920), 1: 76, quoted in W. Durant, *The Story of Civilization: The Age of Faith* (New York: Simon & Schuster, 1963), 378.

[134] S. D. Goitein, *A Mediterranean Society* (Berkeley: University of California Press, 1999), 139–140.

[135] Ibid., 144.

[136] Ibid., 355.

and not by man.[137] In the case of a gentile murdered by a Jew, this sin was also considered against the law of heaven. Sexual intercourse between a married Jewish woman and any man other than her husband was also one of the three heinous sins punishable by death for both parties. However, the Talmud has a different view of sexual intercourse between a gentile woman and a Jew. The Talmud argued that since there was no matrimony for the gentile woman, therefore this sin was not considered adultery.[138]

The discussion on the topic is not however complete if one does not point out that the Islamic penal code similarly discriminates against Jews by granting them 'blood money' instead of enforcing the 'law of retaliation' or *Ghesas* in the case of a Jew murdered by a Muslim.[139]

Chronology:

613 CE	Forced conversion of Jews in Spain
630 CE	Eviction of Jews from Jerusalem
633 CE	Forced conversion of Jews in France
637 CE	The rise of Islam and declaration of Codes of Omar
661 CE	Forced conversion of Jews in Italy; proclamation of Mu`awiya as the sole caliph of Islamic Empire
750 CE	Abbasid dynasty
756 CE	The establishment of Umayyad dynasty in Spain
762 CE	The beginning of the Qaraites movement
786 CE	Conversion of Khazar leadership to Judaism
896 CE	Saadiah ben Joseph was born
965 CE	The fall of Khazar state
1034 CE	Hai, the last gaon of Sura, was arrested and the academy was abolished
1071 CE	Byzantine Empire loses Asia Minor to the Seljuk Turks

---

[137] Maimonides, "Laws on Murderer," Mishnah Torah, 2:11, quoted in I. Shahak, *Jewish History, Jewish Religion* (London: Pluto Press, 1997), 76.
[138] Talmud, Berachoth 78-a.
[139] M. Adjudani, *Mashroutehe Irani* (Teheran, Akhtaran Books, 2003), 406

1095 CE	The call of Pope Urban II for Christians to free Jerusalem
1099 CE	Crusaders capture Jerusalem
1135 CE	Moses Maimonides was born
1149 CE	The end of the Qaraites movement
1187 CE	Yusuf ibn Ayyub "Saladin" defeats the army of Crusaders and takes Jerusalem back
1199 CE	Pope Innocent III calls for another Crusade
1227 CE	Pope Gregory IV places Inquisition under the jurisdiction of papacy; persecution of heresy in Europe
1258 CE	The fall of Abbasid dynasty to Mongols
1290 CE	Eviction of Jews from England
1347 CE	Outbreak of plague in Europe
1391 CE	Accusation of Jews and their massacre
1394 CE	Eviction of Jews from France
1478 CE	Establishment of Spanish Inquisition
1483 CE	Appointment of Tomas Torquemada as the inquisitor general of Spain
1492 CE	Expulsion of Jews from Spain
1516 CE	The conquest of Jerusalem by Ottoman Turks
1517 CE	The establishment of the Jewish quarter ghetto in Venice, Italy
1536 CE	Reinstating the Portuguese Inquisition
1555 CE	Pope Paul IV decree to force Jews into ghetto in Rome
1590 CE	Settlement of Jews in Amsterdam, Holland
1648 CE	Massacre of Jews in Ukraine and Poland under the leadership of Bogdan Chemielnicki

Chapter Four

THE DAWN OF MODERNITY
Unrest in the Jewish Communities

The seventeenth century is a turning point in the Jewish history. Through antiquity and the Middle Ages, the Jewish history was traditionally viewed as an unfolding divine drama destined to come to its conclusion in the messianic era. Within the context of this viewpoint, the historical events were indeed the reflections of God's will. The exile, or Diaspora, was viewed as the consequence of Jews revoking the divine covenants, and would not end until the coming of the Messiah, when the Jews will be redeemed.

The seventeenth and eighteenth centuries witnessed considerable changes in Judaism and in the Jewish communities. The nature of these changes varied significantly, but they all were challenging the traditional religious establishment and the rabbinical authority of that period. It seemed that strong storms were blowing from all directions at the religion that the rabbis had maintained under their strict control for more than fourteen centuries. The Jewish communities were tired of the status quo and were looking for new vital alternatives.

From one side, the people's desire and hopes for a return to the Promised Land provided a ripe condition for the rise of self-claimed messiahs who were taking advantage of the Jewish masses. Indirectly, by relaying the message that the masses must "follow the messiah and not the rabbis," they were a great challenge to the authority of the religious leaders. This messianic vision later in the nineteenth century, however, evolved into a Jewish nationalism and eventually into Zionism. From the other side, the Hasidic movement, by preaching the "theology without rabbis," attracted the poor Jewish masses and challenged the rabbinical authority by calling for simplicity and straightforwardness in worship. Finally, a wave of heresy questioned the medieval Jewish philosophy, and by waging a struggle between faith and reason, it paved the road toward modernity. Influenced by these three upheavals, the political, economic, and social position of Jews drastically changed and a new horizon in the understanding by Jews of their own identity and tradition opened before them.[1] It was in this manner that modern Jewish thought was molded through the next three centuries. Within the context of modernity, the Jewish history was then assessed as an ever-evolving process influenced by social, political, and economic forces.

The Rise of the Messianic Desire

The term *Messiah*, or its Hebrew equivalent, *Mashiach*, had wide applications for centuries, before the conceptual meaning of *savor* was attached to it. In the Old Testament, this term was first applied to Aaron, the brother of Moses, who was called the Messiah of the god.[2] The word *Messiah*, its Greek translation *Christos* and its English equivalent *Christ*, all carried the meaning of "anointed" or blessed, and were used for the saints and the religious leaders for centuries.[3] Later, after the establishment of kingdoms, the word *Christ* was applied to kings as well. Initially, the meanings of *savor* and *redemption* were not derived from *Christ*. However, centuries later, when human injustices were not compensated by worldly rewards, serving justice was postponed until the coming of the Messiah, and

---

[1] D. B. Ruderman, *Jewish Intellectual History: 16th to 20th Century* (Chantilly, VA: Teaching Company, 2002), Part 1.
[2] Exodus 28:41.
[3] Leviticus 4:3, 5, 16.

then the meaning of *savor* was applied to this term. In this regard, Isaiah the Prophet taught a utopian scenario where, by the coming of a prince from the house of David, there would be no more cruelty and social injustice, and "The Lord will settle disputes among nations; all nations will convert their weapons of war into implements of peace. . . . [I]n that day the wolf and the lamb will lie down together, and the leopard and goats will be at peace. Calves and fat cattle will be safe among lions, and a little child shall lead them all."[4] After the destruction of the Temple and the dispersion of the Jews around the world, the unification and return of Jews to Jerusalem and the construction of the Temple were among the functions that were added to the Messiah's duties.

The followers of Simon bar Kokhba, the leader of the Jewish uprising against Rome in the second century CE, considered him the Messiah. Indeed, throughout the history of the Diaspora, whenever Jews were in a major social crisis, their desire for the arrival of the Messiah as the final solution to the calamity was sensed more than ever. However, following the defeat of this uprising and its devastating outcome, and out of fear for its recurrence, religious leaders took a different position on the subject of the Messiah. That is, they generally ruled out the coming of the Messiah in the near future and excommunicated those who claimed to be *savors*, calling them false messiahs. In spite of this strategy, sometimes the rabbis and the religious leaders themselves were influenced by these false messiahs. Nonetheless, throughout the history of the Diaspora, a number of self-proclaimed figures presented themselves in the guise of messiahs and took advantage of the religious illusions of the Jewish masses.

The hopes and expectations for the coming of the Messiah probably started during the Babylonian exile and reached a peak toward the end of the Second Temple period and the rise of Christ. Since Christ's ancestors belonged to the house of David, it was not surprising for his disciples to call him the Messiah.

In addition to Christ, who in the eyes of the Pharisee Jews claimed himself as the Messiah and for the same reason was crucified, there have been many self-claimed *savors* throughout

---

[4] Isaiah 2:4, 11:6.

history. In 720 CE, a man from Syria named Serene claimed to be the Messiah, and under the banner of regaining Jerusalem from the Muslims, attracted a large number of Jews to himself. It was not long before he was executed by the order of Caliph Yazid II.

Thirty years later, Obadiah Abu Issa Al-Isfahani, from Isfahan in Iran, claimed to be the immediate predecessor of the Messiah and gathered around him more than ten thousand Jews. He prohibited drinking wine, proposed seven daily prayers instead of three, and acknowledged the prophecies of Christ and Muhammad. He led his supporters in a rebellion against the Abbasid caliphs and was killed in battle. After his death, the Jews of Isfahan suffered dearly, and the Qaraites sect absorbed many of his followers.

David Alroy, the leader of another Messianic movement, enticed the Mesopotamian Jews and promised them a return to Jerusalem around 1121 CE. In fact, the movement was started by his father, and David, who was intellectually superior, took over the movement and proclaimed himself the Messiah. Alroy moved his headquarters to the mountains of Kurdistan, a western province in Iran. However, his father-in-law, who was deeply concerned about the outcome of this movement, slaughtered him in 1160 CE.

Due to the rise of Protestantism, vigorous discussions about the imminent end of the world or providence,[5] and the spread of Jewish mysticism among the European Jews, the sixteenth and seventeenth centuries witnessed more *savors* than in other previous periods. Moreover, there was a general belief among the followers of Jewish mysticism that the Hebrew calendar year of 5335 (the year of providence) would be fateful for the people of Israel.[6] Therefore, the desire for the arrival of the Messiah in the decades around 1574 CE, which coincided with the Hebrew date of 5335, reached its peak.

In 1524 CE, the Vatican received a handsome man from Arabia, named David Reubeni, who was riding on a white horse. Reubeni, while calling Pope Clemens VII a brother, introduced himself as the leader of the lost tribe of Reuben. He claimed he was

---

[5] S. D. Goitein, *A Mediterranean Society* (Berkeley: University California Press, 1999), 304.
[6] G. Wigoder, *The New Standard Jewish Encyclopedia* (New York: Facts on File, 1992), 773.

leading an army of over three hundred thousand swordsmen, and with the support of the pope and European kings, he would regain Jerusalem and evict the Muslims from Palestine. The Jews were truly impressed, seeing that a Jew was being received in the Vatican, and many, including the Marranos, believed that Reubeni was the real Messiah. John III, the king of Portugal, welcomed Reubeni's suggestion of reclaiming Jerusalem and invited him to Portugal. It is said that Diego Pires, a baptized Jew and an official of the Portuguese court, was so persuaded by the event that he became circumcised, changed his name to Solomon Molcho, and traveled to Turkey to inform the Jewish masses of the imminent arrival of the Messiah. Reubeni's behavior made John III suspicious. Meanwhile, Reubeni escaped to Spain, where he was arrested and poisoned in prison in 1536. Solomon, who was under the protection of the Vatican for a while, ultimately considered himself the Messiah. He was arrested while interviewing Emperor Charles V and was burned at the stake during the Inquisition.

Among the proclaimed *savors* that appeared during the history of the Diaspora, none enjoyed the vast support of the Jewish masses as much as did Sabbatai Zevi. Sabbatai was born in Izmir, Turkey, in 1626. He was a tall, handsome man who was obsessed with physical cleanness. He washed himself in seawater and wore perfumes. Sabbatai had a pleasant singing voice and often gathered youngsters around him and sang mystical songs to them. He did not have much of an interest in women. Although he married once, the marriage did not last long.[7]

After reading the Zohar[8] and the book of Jewish mysticism, the Cabbala, Sabbatai decided the coming of the Messiah would be in 5408 of the Hebrew calendar, or 1648 CE. He was twenty-two years old on the day that he proclaimed himself the *savor*. In the beginning, a large number of Jews in Izmir supported him, but the religious leaders of the city excommunicated him. Sabbatai left Izmir for Salonica, another city in Turkey, and through a special ceremony,

---

[7] H. Graetz, *History of the Jews* (Philadelphia: Jewish Publication Society of America, 1891), 5: 119–166.

[8] Zohar (brightness) is the principal Cabbalist work whose author is not clearly known. The authorship of this work has been ascribed to Simeon bar Yohai of the second century by some and to Moses de Leon of Spain in 1280 to 1286 by others.

announced his sole devotion to the Torah. He then traveled to Athens, Cairo, and Jerusalem. There he met with Nathan of Gaza, who proclaimed himself Elijah, who had the responsibility of paving the way for Sabbatai's imminent arrival as the Messiah.

Sabbatai returned to Izmir in 1665 and appeared in the main synagogue on Rosh-Ha-Shanah, and reaffirming himself as the Messiah. This time a larger crowd welcomed him. It did not take long before his voice reached the Jewish communities of Western Asia, Eastern Europe, and North Africa. Some of the Jews were skeptical about him, but nonetheless, many of them believed him. Even some Christians believed that Sabbatai was the risen Christ. Soon the great rabbi of Amsterdam was called Sabbatai the Messiah and held an extravagant celebration in his honor. In preparation for his arrival in the Promised Land, pamphlets were distributed to educate the Jewish masses about the ceremonies and rituals. Hearing about these events, many Jews in Poland left their homes, impatiently awaiting the arrival of Sabbatai. Some of his emotionally charged disciples went so far as to suggest the substitution of Yahweh with Sabbatai Zevi and celebrations on the official Jewish mourning days. It is said that in Amsterdam, those under the illusion of the imminent arrival of Sabbatai engraved his initials on the entrance of synagogues, and in the Jewish communities of Hamburg, routine daily life came to standstill.

It did not take long before Sabbatai himself was influenced by the mass hysteria surrounding him. He selected leaders for the ten lost tribes of Israel that were supposed to reappear and march toward the Promised Land. In addition, he announced that he would go to Constantinople and would take off the crown of the Ottoman Empire from the sultan and put it on his head. In this way, Sabbatai planned to commence the divine kingdom on earth. Following this announcement, he, along with a group of his disciples, arrived in Constantinople on January 1, 1666, and was immediately arrested by Ottoman officials.

Officials of the Ottoman Empire were deeply concerned with the mass hysteria surrounding Sabbatai, and they feared that his execution might provoke a more serious reaction from the Jewish masses. After weeks of hesitation, they suggested to Sabbatai that he accept Islam in order to save himself from death. Sabbatai, the self-proclaimed redeemer, converted to Islam on September 14, 1666, and at the recommendation of the Ottoman sultan, he changed his name to Aziz Mohammad Afendi. In the beginning, the Jews of Europe, Asia, and Africa did not take Sabbatai's conversion to Islam seriously, but soon sadness and despair took over these communities. While Muslims and Christians ridiculed the Jews for their naiveté and simple-mindedness, the devoted followers of Sabbatai argued that his action was only a tactical maneuver to attract other Muslims to Judaism.

Following these events, Sabbatai did not sit idle. He convinced the Ottoman officials that by appearing in the main synagogue of the town, he would convert Jews to Islam. At the same time, through his disciples, Sabbatai informed the Jews that he was still committed to lead the people to the Promised Land. Soon the officials of the Ottoman Empire, who had learned about his tricks, sent him into exile to Albany, where he stayed until his death in 1676. Interestingly, for almost half a century after his death, many simple-minded people were still hopeful that one day Sabbatai would come back to life and fulfill his promises.

Marranos who had migrated to Eastern Europe constituted the bulk of the Sabbatean followers. It has been argued that they viewed Sabbatai as a Christ-like figure who would bring their redemption.[9]

Jacob ben Judah Leib, known as Jacob Frank (1726–1791), was another proclaimed *savor* who was born into a religious Jewish family in Podolia. Frank was fascinated by the Zohar in his early youth and joined the Sabbatean circle. Although he studied the Torah as well, he did not show an interest in the Talmud when he was young. Throughout his career, he always took advantage of his ignorance of the Talmud and boasted of being a simple and unsophisticated man. In 1756, a year after the former followers of Sabbatai had predicted the imminent arrival of another messiah, Frank arranged a religious ceremony and was arrested by the Turkish government officials. He was released a few months later and officially converted to Islam.[10] In 1757, while moving to Poland, the

---

[9] D. B. Ruderman, *Jewish Intellectual History: 16th to 20th Century* (Chantilly, VA: Teaching Company, 2002), Part 1.

[10] *Encyclopedia Judaica*, "Frank Jacob and the Frankists," CD-ROM, 1997, Judaica Multimedia.

Sabbatean followers gathered around him, and being an extremely ambitious man, Frank foresaw a bright future for himself. In fact, many Sabbatean followers now believed in Frank as the reincarnation of the divine soul of Sabbatai Zevi. However, the rabbis excommunicated him and his followers, saying that his teachings were against the Torah. Frank, though, was smarter than his predecessors. He approached the Catholic Church, and by introducing his movement as a "contra-Talmudic" that was compatible with the principles of Christianity, he sought protection from his persecutors.[11] Church officials were also hopeful that by supporting this movement, they would succeed in attracting the Jewish masses to Christianity. While the members of the movement, often against their will, were encouraged by the Church officials to engage in anti-Jewish preaching, Frank separated himself from these activities and appeared only as the spiritual leader.[12]

Toward the end of 1756, Frank followers put together an ambiguous statement and requested that the Church oversee a debate between them and the rabbis about the document. This nine-item declaration was as follows:

1. Belief in the Torah of Moses
2. Belief that the Torah and the Prophets were obscure books that had to be interpreted with the aid of God's light from above and not simply by the light of human intelligence
3. Belief that the interpretation of the Torah to be found in the Talmud contained nonsense and falsehood, hostile to the Torah of the Lord
4. Belief that God is one and that all the worlds were created by him
5. Belief in the trinity of the three equal "faces" within the one God
6. Belief that God manifested himself in corporeal form, like other human beings, but without sin
7. Belief that Jerusalem would not be rebuilt until the end of time
8. Belief that Jews waited in vain for the Messiah to come and raise them above the whole world, and

---

[11] Ibid.
[12] Ibid.

9. Belief that, instead, God would himself be clothed in human
    form and atone for all the sins for which the world had been
    cursed, and that at his coming the world would be pardoned
    and cleansed of all iniquity.[13]

In the text of the document, instead of referring to Sabbatai as
the *savor,* they had deceivingly referred to Christ. Initially, the rabbis
refused to attend this ideological debate. Finally, the debate
commenced in June 1757. On October 17, 1758, the Church passed
judgment in favor of the Frank followers with the message that the
Talmud was worthless and corrupt. Following this victory, it is said
that Frank's followers attacked the Jews, looking for copies of the
Talmud in their houses. What they found they burned. Meanwhile, the
rabbis declared a fast in memory of this event in the Jewish
communities.

A year later, in 1759, Frank proclaimed himself the divine
power that was committed to complete the mission of Sabbatai Zevi.[14]
He called himself "the true Jacob," comparing himself with the
patriarch Jacob, and attached titles such as the Great Brother or the
King of Kings to his name. He selected twelve men who were
considered to be his disciples, and twelve women, "the Sisters," who
were in fact his concubines. He proclaimed to his followers, "The
place to which we are going is not subject to any law, because all that
is on the side of death; but we are going to life." In order to achieve
this goal, it was necessary to abolish and destroy the laws, teachings,
and practices that constricted the power of life, but this had to be done
in secret.[15] He insisted that believers had to taste different religions
and change from one to another like changing an old jacket for a new
one, and it was only through this approach that one might achieve
"the secret faith." In this way, Frank prepared his followers to accept
Christianity as the final stage of faith. Nevertheless, his teachings
promoted a form of anarchy and disorder in religion.

One of Frank's disciples advanced yet another allegation
against rabbinical structure in February 1759. This time the subject

---

[13] Ibid.

[14] *JewishEncyclopedia.com,* "Frank, Jacob and Frankists."

[15] *Encyclopedia Judaica,* "Frank Jacob and the Frankists," CD-ROM, 1997, Judaica
Multimedia.

was the blood libel, the old allegation that Jews utilized the Christian children's blood in the Jewish ritual ceremonies. His goal of reviving this issue was nothing but embarrassing to the European Jewish communities before the Church hierarchy, a behavior that under the circumstances could provoke Christians against Jews and produce a devastating outcome for these communities. Following this event, Frank encouraged his followers to accept Christianity, a proposal that was not well received by all.

The priests who were skeptical about the sincerity and reliability of Frank's followers watched them closely. Many of his followers who had been baptized claimed that they viewed Frank as the living incarnation of God. Frank was arrested on February 6, 1760, and the court exiled him to a fortress in the south of Poland, where he stayed for thirteen years. He was released in August of 1772, after the partition of Poland, and again concentrated his efforts in promoting Christianity. Interestingly, Frank and his daughter visited Joseph II, the Austrian king, in March 1775 and discussed with him the necessity of a world revolution.[16] Following this meeting, as a gesture of his preparedness for such an endeavor, Frank asked his followers in Moravia to put on military uniforms. During the last years of his life, Frank spread the word that his daughter Eva was the illegitimate daughter of Queen Catherine of Russia. Indeed, some of Frank's followers believed that Eva was a princess of the Romanoff royal family.

Jacob Frank died in December of 1791. Based upon what has been written about him, one could argue that he was a despotic leader, popular prophet, and a skillful crook. In the opinion of the Jewish masses that did not join his camp, Frank was a demonic power. As it was pointed out previously, a great number of Frank's followers accepted Christianity. Some despaired of his fake promises and returned to the traditional Jewish communities. A number of them were attracted to Jewish mysticism or Kabbalah, focusing on the nature of the universe and the destiny of humanity.[17] A smaller group of his followers, known as the Abrahamites, live in seclusion in Romania to the present day.

---

[16] Ibid.

[17] Z. S. Halevi, *Kabbalah: Tradition of Hidden Knowledge* (New York: Thomas & Hudson, 1979), 4.

The traditional messianic desire of the Jews for a return to their homeland, as had blossomed in the Sabbatean movement, was instrumental in the rise of Zionism in the second half of the nineteenth century.

The Hasidic Movement: Judaism without Rabbis

Hasidism was the last religious movement in Judaism before the Jews entered the modern world.[18] The founding father of the Hasidic movement, Israel ben Elizer Ba`al (1700–1760), known as Shem Tov, was born in a poor Jewish family in the village of Okup in southern Poland. In his youth he engaged in menial jobs such as a doorman in a synagogue and a ditch digger in the Jewish cemetery. In contrast to the rabbis of his time, Shem Tov strongly believed that even a simple human being, through honest worship, might access God. He objected to the conspiracy between the rich and the rabbis and was convinced that one cannot have access to God through mediation of the rabbis or by following the religious rituals in synagogue. His simple and unsophisticated lifestyle attracted many poor Jewish peasants in Poland and later Eastern Europe. He traveled from one place to another, read stories to children, and was quite happy with his simple life.

He preached to his followers to set aside the Talmudic rituals and the synagogue's recommendations and instead pray honestly in their own simple language. He taught his followers to look into nature for the manifestations of God. Instead of mourning for past sins, he told them to enjoy life today. It is said that once a Jewish man complained of the ill behavior of his son to Shem Tov. He advised the man to "show more kindness than ever to your son."[19] In this regard, there was some resemblance between the teachings of Shem Tov and those of Christ, for example, that prayer plays a more important role in the core of Hasidic teachings than studying and learning.[20]

---

[18] A. Hertzberg and A. Hirt-Manheimer, *Jews: The Essence and Character of a People* (New York: HarperSanFrancisco, 1998), 155.

[19] L. Browne, *The Wisdom of Israel* (New York: Random House, 1945), 551.

[20] D. B. Ruderman, *Jewish Intellectual History: 16th to 20th century* (Chantilly, VA: Teaching Company, 2002), Part 1.

Shem Tov did not leave any written material behind. In fact, his disciples put together his teachings after his death. In 1780, Jacob Joseph of Polonnoye, one of these disciples, gathered Shem Tov's teachings and interpretations under the title of *Toledot Ya`akov Yosef.*[21] Opponents, however, argued that Shem Tov's Hasidic ideology was nothing new, and that in fact these same teachings could be found in the Pentateuch where God calls upon Israelites and says, "If you carefully obey all the commandments I give you, loving the Lord your god, walking in all his ways, and clinging to him, then the Lord will drive out all the nations in your land, no matter how much greater and stronger than you they might be."[22]

The Hasidic movement and its popularity among the poor Jewish masses was due to many factors, which included (a) the Chemielnicki massacres[23] and the Haidamacks rebellion[24] that left several thousands of dead Jews behind, (b) the defeat of the false messianic promises of Sabbatai Zevi, Jacob Frank, and others, (c) the simple lifestyle of the Jewish masses in Poland in the eighteenth century, and (d) the brutal power of rabbinical authorities in the Jewish communities of Eastern Europe. To this list one must also add the tenacity and perseverance of Shem Tov's followers in promoting their ideology.

In any event, the spread of the Hasidic movement among the poor Jewish masses of Eastern Europe was a concern of the hierarchy of the Jewish religious establishment, which eventually excommunicated the movement in 1781: "They must leave our communities with their wives and children. . . and they should not be given a night's lodging. . . . It is forbidden to do business with them and to intermarry with them, or to assist at their burial." The anti-

---

[21] *Encyclopedia Judaica*, "Hasidism," CD-ROM, 1997, Judaica Multimedia.

[22] Deuteronomy, 11:22–23.

[23] The uprising of peasants against landowners under the leadership of Bogdan Chemielnicki between 1648 and 1649 destroyed many Jewish communities in the Ukraine and Poland. Eventually, Chemielnicki, after taking a large bribe, brought the massacre to an end.

[24] The Haidamcks rebellion was a series of peasant uprisings against landowners in 1734, 1750, and 1768 that were supported by the Russian Cossacks. These movements, which had carried the banner of "death to the landlords and the Jews," left behind many thousands of dead in Russia and Poland.

Hasidic movement was revived by Elijah ben Solomon Zelman,[25] the gaon of Vilna, who encouraged other Jewish community leaders to impose similar restrictions upon Hasids following the same. He accused the movement of ignoring the study of the Torah as the main path to God, promoting idolatrous worship of human beings, and preaching an overturn of Jewish values. Zelman was also against philosophy and science, and he challenged the Haskalah intellectual movement as well.

Hasidism evolved into a reactionary movement. In the aftermath of the great French Revolution and the rise of Napoleon, Hasidic leaders opposed the emperor's expansive wars. It is said that they encouraged their followers to spy against Napoleon's army in Europe. They argued that the victory of Napoleon would increase the number of well-to-do Jews and consequently take the heart of the Jews far away from God.[26]

Hasidism also took a strong antagonistic position against Haskalah, an intellectual Jewish movement that originated in Western Europe in the mid-eighteenth century. The strongest response of Haskalah to Hasidic opposition appears in the satirical writings of Joseph Perl in 1816, titled *Ueber das wiesen der Sekte Chassidim aus ihren eigenen Schrifteen gezogen in Jahre* or *The Essence of Hasidic Wisdom According to Their Writings*. In Perl's opinion, Hasidism was a reactionary, isolated, and idle movement. In his manuscript, Perl asked the Austrian authorities to impose mandatory education on Hasidic followers in the state-run schools with the hope that they would give up their anti-progressive mentality.[27]

Modern Hasidism neither got along with the political Zionist movement of the early twentieth century nor encouraged their followers to migrate to Israel. Samuel Joseph Ish-Horwitz, an early twentieth-century Zionist, best portrayed the conflict between Zionism and Hasidism in a series of articles. Horwitz wrote that "the Hasidism of the Ba`al Shem Tov is depicted as a wild, undisciplined movement, while Ba`al Shem Tov himself is shown as a charlatan influenced by his rustic surrounding and by the Haidamacks

---

[25] A. Hertzberg and A. Hirt-Manheimer, *Jews: The Essence and Character of a People* (New York: HarperSanFrancisco, 1998), 154.
[26] *Encyclopedia Judaica*, "Hasidism," CD-ROM, 1997, Judaica Multimedia.
[27] Ibid.

rebellion." According to Horwitz, "Hasidism contributed no new truths or ways of looking at the world; it simply appropriated to itself the vocabulary of the Kabbalah without fully understanding its implications, and colored it with quasi-philosophical notions belonging to the household mentality and chronic psychology of the ghetto."[28]

In spite of the Hasidic tenet of promoting simple worship to God and carrying the banner of theology without the mediation of rabbis, their societies were based upon a central figure, the leader or zaddik. Ironically, the zaddik was the mediator between God and the Hasidic followers. He was the one who provided the spiritual illumination for individual members of the society. Since the beginning of the nineteenth century, zaddikim, or the position of leadership, has been hereditary in Hasidic societies. Hasidism strongly believed in miracles, and its followers expected them from some of the zaddikim. Hasidic teachings focused on worship and love for God, the God who was omnipresent. And every Hasid could find it everywhere, even in ugliness. In fact, it was the followers' duty to make beauty from ugliness and create a virtue out of an evil. The Hasidic followers were expected not only to keep God in their thoughts but also to do their deeds in his service. After the fall of the Second Temple of Jerusalem, Hasidism was the first religious thread in Judaism, which had a self-defined way of life and recognizable rite of worship.[29]

Present-day Hasidic followers observe stringent dietary and ceremonial rites of the Sabbath, despite Shem Tov's preaching of a simple worship of God and strong Hasidic objections to traditional Judaism in general and Talmudic rituals in particular. The rites of worship are a mixture of Ashkenazi and Sephardim ceremonies. Optimism, joy, and closeness, along with a simple lifestyle and incessant worship of God, are characteristics of Hasidic societies. In these communities, the rich are obligated to assist the poor, and people are expected to participate in the happiness and sorrow of each other. The zaddiks always accept responsibility for the sins committed by the members. The principal tenets are obedience to God's commands and following the instructions of the Torah. Hasidic

---

[28] Ibid.
[29] Ibid.

men dress in black. They cover their heads at all times and spend a significant part of their time worshipping God. Hasidic women wear a simple dress and always cover their hair. In spite of the fact that women play a secondary role in Hasidic societies, prominent women have often appeared in the history of the movement. They include Adel, Shem Tov's daughter, and Hannah Rochel (1805–1892), known as the Maiden of Ludomir, the only woman in the three-hundred-year history of Hasidism who achieved the status of zaddikim.

The growth of the Hasidic camp and the gradual migration of the leaders to the position of power in the late nineteenth century turned the movement away from its original spiritual character. Moreover, some of the zaddikim, who migrated from Europe to the United States during the great migration of 1880–1925, lost contact with their followers, causing a major setback to the movement. Finally, strong Hasidic opposition to the rising forces such as Zionism and the Jewish worker movements in the first half of the twentieth century further diminished the Hasids' influence on the Jewish masses. By the time of the rise of the Nazis in Germany and during World War II, Hasidism suffered tremendously, and many of their communities in Poland and Russia were completely destroyed. In the aftermath of these events, some of the zaddikim, such as Aaron Rokah, Abraham Mordecai Gur, and Joseph Isaac Liubavich, escaped to Tel Aviv, Jerusalem, and New York: respectively. Among them, only the Hasidic movement of Liubavich, through its expansive propaganda against nonreligious education, antagonism toward the state of Israel, and promotion of fundamentalism among Jews, is more visible. In general, because of the tendencies toward the secularization of Jewish life, during this century Hasidism has turned from its initial offensive position to a more defensive one. At present, the Hasidic population of the world is estimated to be around a quarter of a million followers.

Heresy in Judaism

While Eastern European Jewry was preoccupied with the messianic promises of Sabbatai Zevi, Jacob Frank, and the Hasidic movement of Shem Tov, another major challenge to rabbinical authority was brewing in Western Europe. The Italian Renaissance restored the Greco-Roman culture that had been suppressed by the Catholic Church for centuries. This cultural revolution, which commenced toward the end of the fourteenth century (about the time that the Black Death epidemic was subsiding), spread throughout Europe and reached its peak by the end of the sixteenth century. The Renaissance eventually penetrated the traditional Jewish communities. Influenced by this phenomenon, some members of the communities were attracted to philosophy and nonreligious subjects. Soon a number of Jewish philosophers appeared who tried to apply logic and reason to the rabbinical teachings and the Talmud. These new developments obviously undermined the position of the religious establishment of the time.

The rabbis, on the other hand, argued that the Jewish communities were surrounded by hostile forces and religion was the sole support of these communities. In their opinion, without religion and a strict adherence to it, the very life of these communities was in danger. Therefore, they declared that the study of nonreligious subjects and philosophy was not only a threat to the religious establishment but also to the Jewish communities as a whole. It was within this context that Joel ben Samuel Serkeis (1561–1640), the great rabbi of Krakow in Poland, viewed "philosophy as the mother of atheism," and in the light of this viewpoint, he excommunicated those Jews who dared to study philosophy. Rabbinical authorities always sought support for their position in the Talmud, which insisted that one must study philosophy and nonreligious subjects when it is neither day nor night.[30] In spite of the opposition expressed by the religious authorities, many Jews studied philosophy, courageously challenged the rabbinical teachings, and contributed significantly to our present-day understanding of nature. It is noteworthy to review the lives of some of these Jews.

Leone ben Isaac Modena's (1571–1648) family was among the Jews who had been expelled from France. They eventually settled in Venice, Italy. In spite of being an exceptionally sharp and intelligent man, he changed occupations many times and was always on the verge of poverty. It is ironic that Modena was often surrounded by bad company and was deeply engaged in gambling.

---

[30] Talmud, Menachoth 99-b.

Primarily, Leone was a teacher and writer. He composed many poems in both Italian and Hebrew. His Talmudic knowledge was extensive, and he knew the Old Testament well. Although initially he followed the traditional teachings of the Talmud, later in life he changed his view completely. In one of his manuscripts, he attacked the rabbis for their deviation from the principles of the Old Testament. In another article, in 1637, he claimed that many of the religious ceremonies did not serve their original purpose and therefore were irrelevant. Finally, in a manuscript titled *Kol Sakhal* that was published after his death in 1648, he made the most bitter and overwhelming case against the oral interpretation of the Old Testament and rabbinical Judaism. In this document, he encouraged people to set aside the rabbinical teachings and instead follow the basic principles of the Bible.

Joseph Solomon Delmedigo (1591–1655) was born in Crete, Italy. He studied science along with the Talmud in his youth. In spite of his initial interest in medicine, he attended the University of Padua and studied mathematics under Galileo Galilee. There he set aside some of his religious dogmatism. In 1620, fascinated by the Renaissance, he visited Poland and was surprised to see that, consistent with the rabbis' recommendation, science and nonreligious subjects had been removed from the Jewish schools' curriculum. He disappointingly wrote, "Ignorance and darkness is everywhere."[31] This was probably the first objection expressed about the rabbinical domination in education.

After a while, he traveled to Cairo and Constantinople and was enchanted by the doctrine of the Qaraites. At this point in his life, he essentially separated himself from the Talmud and denied everything outside the Old Testament. However, toward the last years of his life, Delmedigo fluctuated between science and Jewish mysticism. His writings contain numerous contradictions.[32] Eventually, in order to earn a living, he joined the rabbis' circle again, this time defending the Kabbalah. He died an unknown physician in 1655 in Prague.

---

[31] S. M. Dubnow, *History of the Jews in Russia and Poland* (South Brunswick, NJ: T. Yoseloff, 1967), 1: 133–134.

[32] G. Wigoder, *The New Standard Jewish Encyclopedia* (New York: Facts on File, 1992), 264.

Uriel da Costa (1585–1640) was born Gabriel da Costa into a Marrano family in Portugal. The family migrated to Amsterdam in 1617, where Uriel became a minor church official. Later he indicated in his autobiography that by studying the Bible, he was attracted to Judaism. He became fascinated by philosophy and soon found that his version of Judaism was different from that of the Jewish establishment. He was surprised by the fact that the Catholic Church considered the Old Testament as divine scripture and that Christ and his disciples had accepted the Mosaic Law and yet Christians had mistreated Jews throughout history. He was unhappy with Saint Paul, who separated Christianity from Judaism and proposed that one must not be a Jew before becoming a Christian. Soon the same rebellious soul that had caused da Costa to distance himself from the Church and join Judaism now forced him to struggle with the religious establishment of the synagogue. He courageously attacked all the religious rituals and ceremonies that had no basis in the Old Testament, and ridiculed the Talmudic teachings and their values. Da Costa insisted that many of the rabbinical claims were baseless. He criticized the Pharisees of Amsterdam as too rigid and ritualistic, and he denied the value of an institutional religion.[33] As a result of these bold words, the great rabbi of Amsterdam excommunicated him, and consequently his friends also left him, many of whom later took part in his persecution.

Throughout these difficult periods of isolation, da Costa attacked the ideological basis of almost all the people of his time. He questioned the immortality of the soul and wrote that the soul, or the spiritual life that flows in our vessels, dies with our body.[34] He believed that the doctrine of the immortal soul did not derive from the Bible.[35] Samuel da Silva, a Jewish physician, attacked da Costa's position on the immortality of the soul and called him an incapable and ignorant man. The religious leaders complained to Church authority that by attacking Judaism, da Costa had questioned the very foundation of Christianity as well. City officials arrested Uriel, issued a large fine against him, and burned his books. Under social and financial pressures, and because he was responsible for the care of his

---

[33] *Encyclopedia Judaica*, "Costa, Uriel Da," CD-ROM, 1997, Judaica Multimedia.
[34] H. A. Wolfson, *Philosophy of Spinoza* (Cambridge, MA: Harvard University Press, 1948), 2: 323.
[35] *Encyclopedia Judaica*, "Costa, Uriel Da," CD-ROM, 1997, Judaica Multimedia.

younger brothers, da Costa surrendered to the synagogue in 1633, promised to give up his claims, and, according to his own words, he became "an ape among apes."[36] He thereafter questioned the divine nature of the Mosaic Law and insisted that religions were human interventions. In 1639, for the second time, the synagogue and the Jewish community of Amsterdam excommunicated him. This time his brother, Joseph, also joined the camp of opposition.[37]

After seven years, da Costa showed interest again in reconciling with the synagogue. However, because of his insistence upon his viewpoints, the religious leaders proposed the most astringent terms to him. They forced him to confess his sins before the entire congregation, to abide with all Judaic teachings and rituals, and to live like a "real Jew" ever after. Then, according to the Portuguese Inquisition, he received thirty-nine lashes and prostrated himself so that the entire congregation, including his brother Joseph, could walk over him.[38]

Da Costa could not handle the insult of this magnitude. He went into seclusion for three days and wrote the harshest critique of the rabbinical hegemony and the institutional religion in a manuscript known as *Exemplar Humanae Vitae* before he committed suicide. This satirical writing, which in fact is a summary of his viewpoints about religion and nature, was published after his death in 1687. In it he wrote that all human sufferings is due to ignorance and lack of understanding of the natural law.[39] He compared nature with that of religion, writing, "The former teaches us love and kindness and the latter preaches hate and cynicism." Da Costa is considered a hero of religious tolerance, a modern Bible critic, and a major source of inspiration for Spinoza.

Baruch Benedictus Spinoza (1632–1677) was born on November 4, 1632, in Amsterdam. His ancestors were among the Jews who under the pressure of the Spanish Inquisition had adopted

---

[36] Ibid.
[37] H. Graetz, *History of the Jews* (Philadelphia: Jewish Publication Society of America, 1891), 5: 64.
[38] Ibid., 63.
[39] I. Zangwill, *Dreamers of the Ghetto* (New York: 1923), 112, quoted in W. and A. Durant, *The Story of Civilization: The Age of Louis XIV* (New York: Simon & Schuster, 1963), 478.

Christianity. His father and grandfather first traveled to Portugal, then to southern France, and, because of the relative religious freedom in Holland, eventually to Amsterdam. His grandfather was actively involved with the local Jewish affairs and in 1628 became the head of the community of Sephardic Jews of Amsterdam. His father was the school administrator for the Portuguese Jews. Baruch lost his mother at age six and lived thereafter with his stepmother.

Baruch, like other children of his time, learned the Torah and the Talmud in synagogue but, unlike many of them, also acquainted himself with the work of the Jewish philosophers and theologians. Since his father wanted him to enter a trade, he learned nonreligious subjects at home, such as Portuguese, Latin, French, Dutch, and Italian. He excelled in mathematics, particularly in geometry. Baruch lost his father at age twenty-two, and except for a bed, his father gave all of his property to Baruch's stepsister, who claimed the father's entire inheritance. Baruch earned his living through polishing glass, making eyeglasses and lenses for microscopes and telescopes.

Spinoza was an intelligent young man with a curious mind who would focus on controversial issues for days. Among the subjects that attracted his probing mind were (a) the perplexing issues Maimonides had raised on the interpretation of the Old Testament and the immortality of the soul, (b) the comment of Hasdai Crescas (1340–1410), the chief rabbi of Aragon, that one cannot prove the existence of God and the immortality of the soul through reason, (c) the ideas of Levi ben Gershom,[40] the Jewish philosopher and mathematician, that the miracles of the Bible were the product of natural events, and his claim that the Torah cannot prevent us from applying reason and logic, and (d) the story of Uriel da Costa and his heartbreaking destiny.

He later became acquainted with the work of great philosophers such as Descartes, Bacon, Hobbes, and Thomas Aquinas, and gradually lost his interest in traditional Judaism. It is said that his uncertainty about the traditional concepts of the religion had started when he was younger, but out of respect to his father, he

---

[40] Little is known about the life of Levi ben Gershom (1288–1344), a Bible and Talmud critic. However, *Milhamot Adoni*, or *The Wars of the Lord*, is considered his most impressive work.

kept this to himself as long as his father was alive. Eventually, he confessed to his disbelief, and people reported him to the synagogue.

Saul Levi Morteira (1596–1660), the rabbi of Amsterdam, sent him a reconciliatory note, saying that his ex-teachers were disappointed with his comments about God and religion. He invited Spinoza to retract his words and set aside his heretical viewpoints. In this note Morteira also pointed out how much time and effort he had advanced toward Spinoza's education as a teacher.

The anger of the religious leaders toward the viewpoints of Spinoza and other heretics were based on two things. First, these heretics were undermining the foundation of Jewish faith, and by doing so, they created a hurdle in the management of these communities. Second, by raising fundamental questions about God, the origin of humans, creation, and the body and soul, they not only weakened the faith in Judaism but also in Christianity. In this manner, they were also provoking the Christians against the Jewish communities.

It is said that the leaders of the synagogue were prepared to pay Spinoza an annual pension, provided he set aside his criticism of the religion and show up in the synagogue periodically.[41] In any case, on July 24, 1656, the religious leaders of the Jewish community of Amsterdam excommunicated him. In the report to the Spanish Inquisition in 1658–1659, Spinoza was officially charged for "denying the Mosaic Law and immortality of the soul, and holding that god only existed philosophically."[42] He was then cursed:

> *"Cursed shalt thou be in the city, and cursed shalt thou be in the field. . . . Cursed shall be the fruit of thy body, and the fruit of thy land. . . . Cursed shalt thou be when thou comest in, and cursed shalt thou be seen thou goest out. . . . The Lord shall smite thee with consumption, and with a fever, and with an inflammation. . . . The Lord will smite thee with the botch of Egypt, and with the tumors, and with the scab, and with the itch, whereof thou canst not be healed. The Lord shall smite thee with madness, and blindness, and astonishment of heart. . . . Also every*

---

[41] H. Graetz, *History of the Jews* (Philadelphia: Jewish Publication Society of America, 1891), 5: 93.

[42] *Encyclopedia Judaica*, "Spinoza, Baruch de," CD-ROM, 1997, Judaica Multimedia.

sickness and every plague, which is not written in the Book of this Law,
them with the Lord bring upon thee until thou be destroyed."[43]

The text of the excommunication of Spinoza was copied from the curses Yahweh waged against those who did not obey him.[44] After reading the excommunication, Morteira asked the officials to expel Spinoza from the city. Spinoza left the city temporarily and moved in a village close by, but soon he returned to Amsterdam.

Why did the Jewish community of Amsterdam excommunicate Spinoza? Why did he neither enjoy the trust of Jews nor of Christians? Why did many call him an atheist even though his philosophy was focused upon the very idea of God?

One can find the answers to these questions in his famous manuscript *Theological-Political Treatise,* where he expressed his most powerful critique of traditional Judaism and the revealed religions in general. He insisted that religion must be judged on the basis of reason and it is meaningful only when is universally shared by all human beings. He considered the Bible a human document and the miracles as impossible events. In contrast to Maimonides, who tried to reconcile faith and reason by reading and interpreting the Bible allegorically, Spinoza read the Bible "naturally," for what it exactly said.[45]

He argued that nature is governed by the natural laws: "Nothing can be contrary to natural laws." In his opinion, "what is contradicting with being and existence is in contradiction with reason, and what is in contradiction with reason is absurd."[46] This was probably the most courageous statement a philosopher had expressed up to that point in history: the statement that was probably the core of the excommunication of Spinoza and the uneasiness that came afterward. Nonetheless, Spinoza had a clear understanding that he had denied the very foundation of the traditional Jewish faith. Thereby he

---

[43] W. Durant, *The Story of Civilization: Our Oriental Heritage* (New York: Simon & Schuster, 1935), 311.
[44] Deuteronomy 28:16–28.
[45] D. B. Ruderman, *Jewish Intellectual History: 16th to 20th century* (Chantilly, VA: Teaching Company, 2002), Part 1.
[46] Spinoza, *Tractatus Theologico-Politicus* (New York: Dover, 1951), 6: 92.

set the groundwork for secular Judaism and accepted the consequences as a fact of life.[47]

Spinoza believed that God was omnipresent in everything and that everything was omnipresent in God. He held the opinion that one may worship God, but God neither can hear the prayer nor can render a reward for one's prayers. God is not a purposeful being. He lacks nothing and he needs nothing. He just is, and due to his being, everything happens, and happens of necessity.[48] Like Thomas Aquinas, Spinoza believed that the use of the masculine gender for the name of God was meaningless and was only recruited for convenience. Like Maimonides, he assumed that humanity has attributed many of its own characteristics to God. "Describing the God as the authority, legislator, just, forgiver. . . is only originating from incomplete understanding of the average people. . . . God does not show emotion and excitement and is not influenced by happiness and sorrow. . . . Many cannot distinguish between the human and divine characters and readily attribute their own characters to him"[49] God is not an old man with a gray beard leaning upon the clouds and holding the strings of the puppet show called the universe in his hand. There is no creation other than that of the infinite flow of matter and spirit that are ever changing and evolving.

However, in Spinoza's opinion, revealed religions can only serve one useful purpose. Teaching moral values through stories, alleged prophecies, threats, and promises can have an important social impact on the unenlightened and ignorant masses. In the same context, Spinoza, like Thomas Hobbes, believed that the social institutions of religion played an important role as the moral pillars of the society and must therefore be under the state control. However, he believed that the wise person needs the religion of reason. He maintained that philosophers must be free to search for the truth. He advocated, "Man must be free to judge for himself and interpret religion the way he is comfortable."[50] Spinoza was adamant that the

---

[47] A. Hertzberg and A. Hirt-Manheimer, *Jews: The Essence and Character of a People* (New York: HarperSanFrancisco, 1998), 138.

[48] *Encyclopedia Judaica*, "Spinoza, Baruch de," CD-ROM, 1997, Judaica Multimedia.

[49] Spinoza, *Tractatus Theologico-Politicus*, 65, quoted in W. Durant, *The Story of Civilization: The Age of Louis XIVth* (New York: Simon & Schuster, 1963), 639.

[50] Spinoza, *Tractatus Theologico-Politicus* (New York: Dover, 1951), 7: 118.

state must not take advantage of religion for political purposes. Nevertheless, not having a clear understanding of state power, he did not further the concept of the separation of religion and state in his time.

As a biblical scholar, Spinoza believed that the interpretation of the Bible is everyone's right and does not require supernatural illumination or special authority.[51] Contrary to the understanding of Maimonides, Spinoza believed that we are not allowed to impose our interpretations on biblical text. In his opinion, the Bible must be interpreted in the same way we interpret nature. By citing numerous verses that were repetitive and contradicting, he concluded that scripture was not the work of a single author, and even though some portion of the Pentateuch was originated by Moses, the book as a whole appeared many centuries later. Referring to the tenth verse in chapter 34 of Deuteronomy—"There has never been another prophet like Moses, for the Lord talked to him face to face"—he wrote, "It is . . . clearer than the sun at noon that the Pentateuch was not written by Moses, but by someone who lived long after Moses."[52] He believed that the Mosaic Law had been legislated for the Hebrew society of Moses's time and could not be applied to other people, or even to the Jews who were living outside that society. In his opinion, only the moral issues embedded in the Ten Commandments enjoyed general acceptance.[53]

On the subject of Jews as the chosen people,[54] he took the position that God's election of the Jews depended upon their behavior in revealing the "true virtue." Since the only standard of judgment for Spinoza was reason, he proclaimed, "Therefore there is absolutely nothing that Jews can arrogate to themselves beyond other people."[55] In his opinion, all humanity is one, and people are chosen on the basis of their behavior rather than their ethnic origin.[56]

---

[51] Ibid.

[52] R. E. Friedman, *Who Wrote the Bible?* (New York: HarperSanFrancisco, 1987), 21.

[53] Spinoza, *Tractatus Theologico-Politicus* (New York: Dover, 1951), 5.

[54] Jeremiah, 31:36.

[55] A. Hertzberg and A. Hirt-Manheimer, *Jews: The Essence and Character of a People* (New York: HarperSanFrancisco, 1998), 138.

[56] Spinoza, *Tractatus Theologico-Politicus* (New York: Dover, 1951), 54–56.

Spinoza categorically rejected the knowledge gained by authority, sense information, or hearsay as incomplete or inadequate. He thought that we perceive things through their essences or contiguous causes. In this way, one may learn why something is what it is, why it has the nature it has, or what made it what it is.[57] Skepticism occurs only because of poor understanding. He insisted that "there couldn't be a common ground between philosophy and religion, since the former is searching the truth and the latter demands an indisputable obedience."[58]

On Judaism, Spinoza has used the most radical and revolutionary vision to replace the traditional religious thinking with the determinism of the Age of Enlightenment.[59] His ideas have remained the basis of naturalistic thinking and scientific reasoning, and he is thought of as a great hero of modern and free-thinking people. He was instrumental in providing the fundamental ideologies for the modern secular world. According to Wolfson, Spinoza's uniqueness lay in his being the first individual in the Judeo-Christian world to construct a universal view that was not based on revelation. In other words, he offered the basis for a thoroughly secular understanding of the universe.[60] It was not until almost a century after his death that his ideas were recognized as the most persistent influence on all modern philosophers. Indeed, his philosophical heritage was the core of the modern Jewish experience that evolved through the next three centuries.

The sacred coalition between the Jewish and Christian establishment in the persecution of Spinoza was not an unexpected event. Some of his persecutors even sought out the state authorities to burn his books, which in their opinion were destroying human minds. Some called him a "devil in the outfit of man" who was determined to

---

[57] *Encyclopedia Judaica*, "Spinoza Baruch de," CD-ROM, 1997, Judaica Multimedia.

[58] Spinoza, *Tractatus Theologico-Politicus* (New York: Dover, 1951), 14: 189.

[59] The Age of Enlightenment was an intellectual movement of the eighteenth and nineteenth centuries that characteristically stood for the power of human reason. Philosophical rationalists such as Baruch Spinoza and Rene Descartes, political philosophers such as Thomas Hobbes and John Locke, and skeptical thinkers such as Pierre Bayle, Jean Jacques Rousseau, Voltaire, Immanuel Kant, and David Hume contributed to the movement.

[60] *Encyclopedia Judaica*, "Spinoza Baruch de," CD-ROM, 1997, Judaica Multimedia.

"ruin the religion."[61] And finally, some believed Spinoza was the "most famous atheist" of their time.[62] Baruch Spinoza died of tuberculosis at age forty-four on February 20, 1677, and was buried without any religious ceremonies.

In summary, the seventeenth century was a turning point in Jewish history. Prior to this date, Jewish communities were homogenous, the Jewish identity was well defined, and in the eyes of Jews, Jewish history was predetermined. After this date, influenced by the three intellectual movements reviewed in this chapter, the Jewish communities lost their homogeneity, Jewish identity was a subject of interpretation, and Jewish history was viewed as a dynamic process that was deeply influenced by social, political, and economic forces.

Chronology:

720 CE	Serene of Syria claims himself the Messiah
750 CE	Obadiah Abu Isaac Al-Isfahani claims himself the immediate predecessor of the Messiah
1121 CE	David Alroy promises the return of Jews to Jerusalem
1524 CE	Vatican receives David Reubeni; Marranos trust him as the real Messiah
1585 CE	Uriel De Costa is born into a Marrano family in Portugal
1620 CE	Joseph Delmedigo criticizes the curriculum of the Jewish schools in Poland
1632 CE	Baruch Spinoza is born
1633 CE	Uriel de Costa surrenders to the synagogue's demand
1637 CE	Leone ben Isaac Modena attacks rabbis for deviation from the principles of the Old Testament
1639 CE	Jewish community of Amsterdam excommunicates

---

[61] R. Kayser, *Spinoza: Portrait of a Spiritual Hero* (New York: 1946), 249, quoted in W. and A. Durant, *The Story of Civilization: The Age of Louis XIV* (New York: Simon & Schuster, 1963), 630.

[62] R. W. Meyer, *Leibniz and the 17th Century Revolution* (London: Cambridge University Press, 1952), 46–47.

Uriel De Costa for the second time

1656 CE	Jewish community of Amsterdam excommunicates Baruch Spinoza
1658 CE	Charges against Spinoza are proclaimed: denying Mosaic Law and immortality of the soul, and holding that God only existed philosophically
1665 CE	Sabbatai Zevi proclaims himself as the Messiah in Izmir
1665 CE	Sabbatai Zevi converts to Islam
1676 CE	Sabbatai Zevi dies
1677 CE	Baruch Spinoza dies
1700 CE	The birth year of Israel ben Elizer Ba`al, known as Shem Tov, founding father of the Hasidic movement
1756 CE	Jacob Frank is arrested by the Turkish government
1757 CE	Frank proclaims himself as the Messiah and challenges rabbis for a debate
1758 CE	Church passes judgment in favor of Frank over the debate
1759 CE	Frank proclaims himself as the divine power committed to complete the mission of Sabbatai Zevi
1775 CE	Frank visits Joseph II, the Austrian king, and raises the necessity of a world revolution
1780 CE	Jacob Joseph of Polonnoye, a follower of Shem Tov, gathers his teachings and interpretations
1781 CE	Rabbinical authority excommunicates the Hasidic groups
1791 CE	Jacob Frank dies
1816 CE	Joseph Perl writes a satire in opposition to the Hasidic viewpoints

Chapter Five

EMANCIPATION OF THE JEWS

The Jewish communities of the Diaspora were in general self-contained societies more or less separate from the larger communities of the non-Jews. As previously mentioned, the rabbis enjoyed a great deal of authority in these communities and maintained the Jewish population well under control. In these communities the synagogue was not only a center of worship but also an institution of government.

The Five Books of Moses fulfilled the role of the Constitution, and the Talmud served as the Supreme Court for these communities. The larger society of the non-Jews surrounding these communities was in constant conflict with the Jews. In addition to the forceful segregation of the Jews, mandatory conversion to Christianity, interference with their religious practices, and physical assault on their homes and businesses during the periods when the non-Jews had strong religious fervor was common practice.

Emancipation was the abolition of these restrictions and disabilities, and the recognition of Jews as equal to all other citizens. This effort was indeed a reflection of the social, political, and economic changes that occurred in the aftermath of Renaissance in Europe and evolved through three periods in the history of the Jewish Emancipation.

Tolerance of Jews before the French Revolution

A number of developments were instrumental in easing the atmosphere of hate and dislike for the Jews and in promoting tolerance in the period preceding the French Revolution.

Toward the end of the Black Death (or the plague) that wiped out almost one-third of the European population by the fourteenth century, the intellectual movement of the Renaissance intervened. The Greco-Roman culture that had been suffocated for centuries under the influence of the Catholic Church gradually became rejuvenated. This Cultural Revolution that originated in Italy and reached its zenith toward the end of the sixteenth century was not confined to Italy. Moreover, Italy was not the sole contributor to this cultural process. The Renaissance, in essence, revived the concepts of curiosity, objectivism, and individualism.

At the outset of the sixteenth century, the Catholic Church was the strongest social institution in Europe. Through a multitude of priests across Europe and in colonies, the Church baptized the Christian children, taught them the meaning of the "faith," and solidified their systems of belief and thought through their lifetime. In this regard, rich and poor, nobles and serfs, kings and ordinary people were equally influenced by the rules of the Church.

In October 1517, Martin Luther questioned the indulgences of the Catholic Church, and in a period of less than fifty years, from 1517 to 1564, when John Calvin died, Catholicism went through many changes. The rights of priests, as the exclusive group who could understand and interpret the religion and who could ask for redemption, were curtailed; the mass religious ceremonies were considered unnecessary; and many new sects with their own congregations appeared in Christianity. Thus, the unity of the Catholic Church that had been maintained for over a millennium was shattered, and Protestantism was founded.

Later in the seventeenth and eighteenth centuries, as an extension of the ideals of the Renaissance and due to the efforts of philosophers and original thinkers like Baruch Spinoza, Rene Descartes, Thomas Hobbes, Voltaire, John Locke, Emmanuel Kant, and Pierre Bayle, mankind emerged out of centuries of darkness and ignorance into a new Age of Enlightenment.[1] For the first time, humanity came to realize that through reason, endless progress could be achieved in knowledge, technical advancements, moral values, and an understanding of the laws of nature and society. This new way of thinking was based upon three core principles. First, humans have to have faith in reason, and what cannot pass the test of reason is absurd; second, humans may access the truth only through the observation of nature rather than through reading authoritative sources like the Bible and Aristotle; and finally, human aspirations must focus upon improving the life in this world rather than on redemption in the next life.

Soon experimental science and scientific methods of analyzing nature, first in astrology, then in physics, and later in biology, appeared. This giant step forward was, on one hand, due to the application of ancient Greco-Roman and Islamic philosophical resources and, on the other hand, due to the Renaissance, which freed science from the yoke of religion.

The century that separated Baruch Spinoza from Moses Mendelssohn witnessed many changes in Western Europe. As a result of these developments, a group of Christians, though in the minority, gradually emerged who questioned the wisdom of punishing a people for generations because their ancestors had allegedly mistreated Christ centuries ago. Again, in light of the Renaissance and the Age of Enlightenment, many Christians viewed the New Testament from a different perspective and understood things differently. They learned that although it was true that Jesus was in conflict with the Pharisees and the leaders of the Temple of Jerusalem, he never retracted his affiliation to Judaism and he remained a Jew. In addition, those Christians who were familiar with history came to realize that Christianity had systematically persecuted the Jews through the Middle Ages and beyond, a behavior that did not look pleasant in the Age of Enlightenment. Therefore, many thinkers of this period, Jews and non-Jews, tried hard to put the hatred between the Jews and the Christians aside and look for new avenues of understanding between them. The industrious efforts of Manasseh ben Israel (1604–1657) in

---

[1] The French Revolution, Industrial Revolution, Declaration of Human Rights, modern discoveries, and inventions are all considered the lasting heritage of the Age of Enlightenment.

reconciling Jews and Christians were among the first endeavors of this kind.

Ben Israel tried hard to prove that the Christian allegation of "blood libel,"[2] where Jews allegedly used the blood of Christian children in the preparation of Passover unleavened bread, was absurd. In his manuscript he reasoned that the Jews who were convicted in the past had confessed under torture, and therefore their confessions were not valid. Moreover, most Jews who were executed because of this accusation were exonerated later. In the meetings that he held with the leaders of the Church, he vigorously attempted to convince them that Jews were neither interfering in Church affairs nor were interested in converting Christians to Judaism. In this manner, he tried to repair the wide gap between the two peoples. His efforts as a representative of European Jewry in opening the British Empire to the Jews, which because of the anti-Jewish sentiments of the English had been closed for over four centuries, were rather unsuccessful. As a matter of fact, between their eviction in 1290 until 1649, when Oliver Cromwell achieved power in England, no Jew ever reached the British Isles. Eighty-five years later, in 1734, the number of Jews living in that country was six thousand and increased to twenty-six thousand by 1800.

It is noteworthy that the efforts of non-Jewish intellectuals like John Toland (1670–1722) were also instrumental in preparing the spirit of tolerance in England and Ireland. Toland was an Irish-born deist who was actively involved in the theological and political controversies in England at the beginning of the eighteenth century. *Reasons for Naturalizing the Jews in Great Britain and Ireland on the Same Footing with all Other Nations* was among his many manuscripts that were published anonymously in London in 1714. The focus of his paper was a plea for facilitating the naturalization of foreign-born Jews and thereby attracting them to England. The

---

[2] Throughout history, this argument has led to scores of trials and massacres of Jews. The origin of blood libel probably dates back to the Hellenic period between the fourth and second centuries BCE. Apion, an Alexandrian writer and orator, reported the incident involving a Greek victim in the Jewish temple who was fattened for sacrifice. Many, however, believe that the story was initially fabricated and spread by King Antiochus in order to prepare the public before replacing the altar of Yahweh with that of Zeus in 168 BCE. A similar accusation was used by pagan Rome against Christians, and later, when Christianity penetrated the popular consciousness, Christians used it against Jews.

economic and philosophic arguments Toland used to demonstrate the utility of the Jews to the country represented genuine tolerance well in advance of his day. Most of the Jews who moved to England were among the poorest migrants from Poland. In May 1753, the British Parliament passed the "Jew bill" conferring the right of citizenship to Jews of England. In the aftermath of this legislation, widespread anti-Jewish sentiments resurfaced, and because of this public outcry, the bill was revoked in December of the same year. Instead, the right of citizenship was conferred upon a minority group of wealthy Jews only.

In France the situation was somehow different. Here the social and political atmosphere for emancipation of the Jews was primed, and the voice of the intellectuals of the Enlightenment made the emancipation a reality. Voltaire (1694–1778), the French philosopher, probably contributed more than any other to the destruction of the traditional system of beliefs and gave the French Revolution its final momentum. Voltaire and his followers were the most radical anti-Christians of their time, and they did not hesitate to pour scorn on Christianity by criticizing its Jewish origins. It was from this angle that Voltaire categorically questioned the Old Testament.[3] Nonetheless, he was quite aware of the difficulties the Jews had experienced through their history in exile, and he vigorously condemned any persecution of the Jews. He admired the disciplined living style of the Jews and was quite comfortable with the notion that their interest in usury was only a reflection of their circumstances. He praised the Jews for their ancient disbelief in immortality and for their tolerance.[4] Historically, Voltaire's philosophical convictions were instrumental in creating the environment that made emancipation of the Jews possible, in spite of the fact that his *Dictionnaire Philosophique* contained numerous offensive statements against Jews.[5] Isaac de Pinto, the Portuguese philosopher, wrote and criticized Voltaire in his book titled *Apologie pour la Nation Juive* and suggested that Voltaire owed an apology to the Jews.

Jean Jacques Rousseau (1712–1778), the French writer, praised the eminence of the Mosaic Law on the basis of its

---

[3] *Encyclopedia Judaica*, "Voltaire," CD-ROM, 1997, Judaica Multimedia.
[4] W. and A. Durant, *The Story of Civilization: Rousseau and Revolution* (New York: Simon & Schuster, 1967), 150.
[5] Ibid., 630.

preservation when he wrote in support of the Jews: "The laws of Solon,[6] Numa[7] and Lycurgus[8] are dead; those of Moses, much more ancient, continue to live. Athens, Sparta and Rome have perished and left no offspring on the earth. But Zion, destroyed, has not lost her children; they are preserved, they multiply, they spread throughout the world. . . . [T]hey mingle with all peoples, yet are not confused with them; they have no rulers, yet they are always a people. . . . [W]hat must have been the force of a legislator capable of effecting such marvels! Of all the systems of legislation now known to us, only this one has undergone all tests, has always been steadfast."[9]

In Austria, Queen Maria Theresa was religiously committed to inflict more hardship on the Jews, but her son, Emperor Joseph II, had a remarkably more open-minded view of the Jewish question. Joseph, who was influenced by the social developments in France in 1781, praised the Jews of Austria, Hungary, and Bohemia as useful people. He encouraged Christians to look upon Jews as Austrian citizens and discontinue troubling them. Following this announcement, Jews were allowed to freely practice their religion, and their children were admitted to the public schools. They were also encouraged to learn the country's official language and use it in administrative and legal affairs. However, they still did not have the right of land ownership and were prohibited from launching their independent social institutions. By the time of Joseph's death in 1790, the new order to a great extent had been established, and Vienna was among the few communities where cooperation between Christians and Jews was possible. The improved relations between these two groups in Austria were achieved in spite of strong objections from the extremes. Christian merchants saw the emancipation of Jews as economic competition for themselves and considered it a premature

---

[6] Solon (628–539 BCE) was an Athenian legislator and statesman who has been considered the founder of the Athenian democracy. He believed each social class must enjoy privileges according to the social responsibilities they carry.
[7] Numa Pompilius (715–673 BCE) was considered the wisest and most religious Roman emperor. The revised version of the Roman calendar is one of his contributions.
[8] Lycurgus (396–325 BCE) was Plato's pupil and an Athenian statesman who oversaw the construction of famous buildings such as the Dionysus Theatre.
[9] W. and A. Durant, *The Story of Civilization, Rousseau and Revolution* (New York: Simon & Schuster, 1967), 629.

endeavor.[10] On the other hand, rabbis opposed the attendance of Jewish children in public schools, seeing it as a threat to their religion.

In Germany, Christian Wilhelm von Dohm (1751–1820), a historian and diplomat, proposed the right of worship and access to the system of education for the Jews. In his famous work *On the Improvement of the Jews as Citizens*, he reviewed the history of the Jewish people and pointed out that the continuing deterioration of their situation was a consequence of the oppression they were subjected to through their lives in exile. Dohm wrote, "The Jews have wisdom, a sharp intellect, they are assiduous, persevering, and are able to find their way in every situation. . . . On the other hand this nation has an exaggerated tendency to look for gain in every way, a love for usury, defects which are further aggravated in many of them by their self-imposed segregation owing to their religious precepts as well as rabbinical sophistry. . . . [I]f our reasoning is correct, we shall find the oppression from which they still suffer. . . are the true reasons for their shortcomings."[11] Dohm advanced the proposal that Jews must enjoy equal civic rights as Christians. He wrote, "Deprivation of civic rights from Jews is a sign of barbarism, and contradicts the spirit of the age of enlightenment."[12] This latter issue provoked many Christians, who accused him of using his pen at the service of Jews.

Moses[13] Mendelssohn (1729–1786) was probably the first Jewish voice from the heart of the ghetto demanding modernity. His doctrine was a response to Spinoza's philosophical argument and in fact was an effort to bring Judaism in line with the Age of Enlightenment. Therefore, he is recognized as the founding father of Haskalah, the enlightenment movement of European Jewish society.

Mendelssohn began the usual Talmudic education at age fourteen. Later, however, he abandoned the old tradition and pursued the secular education. During this period, he met Lessing, the German Christian writer and dramatist, and developed a strong friendship with him. In 1754, Lessing published a play, *Die Juden,* or *The Jew,* with

[10] Ibid., 631.

[11] *Encyclopedia Judaica*, "Dohm, Christian Wilhelm Von," CD-ROM, 1997, Judaica Multimedia.

[12] H. Graetz, *History of the Jews* (Philadelphia: Bella Lowy, 1891), 5: 355.

[13] Because of his vast contributions in improving the civic status of Jews, Moses Mendelssohn has been named Moses the III, after Moses the prophet and Moses Maimonides.

the sole purpose of showing that a Jew could be wise, sophisticated, and enlightened.[14] About Mendelssohn, Lessing wrote the following: "In spite of the fact that he does not have higher education, he has access to philosophy, mathematics, language and poetry at age twenty-five. His philosophical talent along with his courage reminds me of Spinoza. I think if his coreligionists allow him to grow further and show his talent, he will be of our national pride."[15]

Mendelssohn, like Spinoza, believed that eternal truth is based on reason and not on revelation. However, in contrast to Spinoza, he viewed the Bible as historical truth, and he further reasoned that religious ritual and ceremonial practice made Jews morally and ethically more sensitive.[16] In other words, he reconciled individual freedom, which is an attribute of the Age of Enlightenment, with the freedom of practicing Jewish ritual ceremonies. On this subject, he wrote, "Let every man who does not disturb the public welfare, who obeys the law, acts righteously toward you and his fellow men be allowed to speak as he thinks, to pray to God after his own fashion or after that of his fathers, and to seek eternal salvation where he thinks he may find it."[17]

Mendelssohn defended the existence of God and the immortality of the soul in *Phaedon,* his philosophical work. He wrote that if we believe in God, then we must accept that He neither conceives us nor gives us false hope. The human soul is constantly improving. Since the evolution of the soul is not possible during our lifetime, then the soul must be immortal. Mendelssohn believed that without God and the immortality of the soul, "man is like a lost person in a stormy night, hopeless of finding a shelter."[18] His argument in favor of the religious laws and ceremonies and his conviction that these practices made one a better Jew was unpersuasive, and he failed to convince others to accept his version of

---

[14] A. Eban, *Heritage: Civilization and the Jews* (New York: Summit Books, 1984), 224.
[15] *Encyclopedia Judaica,* "Mendelssohn, Moses," CD-ROM, 1997, Judaica Multimedia.
[16] D. B. Ruderman, *Jewish Intellectual History: 16th to 20th Century* (Chantilly, VA: Teaching Company, 2002), Part 1.
[17] *Encyclopedia Judaica,* "Mendelssohn, Moses," CD-ROM, 1997, Judaica Multimedia.
[18] W. and A. Durant, *The Story of Civilization, Rousseau and Revolution* (New York: Simon & Schuster, 1967), 639.

Judaism. Nonetheless, he was recognized as the model of a Jew who can completely exercise his faith in the gentile world.

In 1782, at the peak of his fame, Mendelssohn appealed to the rabbis not to excommunicate those who pursued a secular education and who might think differently. A year later, in a manuscript titled *Judaism and the Authority of Religion*, he encouraged young Jews to leave ghettoes and join the ranks of Western civilization. Although both Jewish and Christian fundamentalists of his time rejected this paper, it served to emancipate the Jewish masses. Mendelssohn's teachings persuaded many Jews, who courageously left the traditional Jewish communities, obtained a secular education, and contributed vastly to science, philosophy, and literature.

Rabbi Moshe Sofer, who believed "anything new is forbidden by Torah,"[19] proclaimed Mendelssohn as the ultimate heretic who had come to ruin Judaism. As the gaon of Vilna, he forbade Jews from adopting Western dress or manners or using a language other than Yiddish. The rabbi's followers distributed flyers blaming Mendelssohn for bringing Jews in contact with gentiles and their culture, which consequently would ruin the Jews. As a final point, Mendelssohn's argument that ceremonial practice somehow made Jews more moral was unconvincing to many, including most of his children, who converted to Christianity and gave the rabbis a good excuse to condemn their father's viewpoints publicly.

It has been widely assumed that Mendelssohn was the founding father of the Haskalah. This cultural movement was founded in Germany in the mid-eighteenth century and spread to the whole of Europe in spite of fierce opposition from the rabbis. Haskalah was, in essence, a rationalistic cultural trend like Enlightenment and followed the principle that *reason is the measure of all things*. And in order to conciliate between Judaism and the Enlightenment, Mendelssohn stressed that there was nothing in the Jewish faith that opposed reason.

The followers of the movement, who were called "maskilim," or intellectuals, contributed significantly to the emancipation of Jews through different approaches. One can summarize their aspirations and objectives in five categories as follows:

---

[19] A. Hertzberg and A. Hirt-Manheimer, *Jews: The Essence and Character of a People* (New York: HarperSanFrancisco, 1998), 186.

1. Promoting secular education. The classical Jewish communities in Europe and elsewhere were strictly under the control of rabbinical authorities up to the sixteenth century. As mentioned previously, education was exclusively confined to the study of the Torah and the Talmud. In general, rabbis fiercely opposed teaching philosophy and secular subjects. They viewed philosophy as an effort to undermine the pillars of these communities, and they did not hesitate to show their objections by excommunicating the secular students or teachers. In general, the rabbis' opinion on the subject was in full compliance with the Talmudic teaching that suggested, "Go then and find a time that is neither day nor night and learn then Greek wisdom."[20] In fact, the traditional Jewish communities viewed secular studies as a tendency toward distancing from Judaism.[21] The Haskalah followers, on the other hand, believed that secular education was the road to a complete and equal partnership with Christian Europe. They regarded secular culture as the prerequisite for Jewish emancipation. Therefore, it was not surprising that maskilim characteristically entertained a strong anti-Talmudic position on this subject. Both Mendelssohn and Naphtali Herz Wessely, one of the prominent maskilim, tried to demote the Talmud in their writings. In fact, Wessely wrote a two-volume book in 1848 titled *The Talmud in Its Emptiness* and argued that though the Talmud was historically important, its legal decisions were socially and spiritually outdated, and therefore they were no longer binding.

The followers of Haskalah promoted a rational education, so they focused on changing the curriculum and the methods of teaching. The first school of this kind, the Freischule, or "free school," was established in 1778 in Berlin. The new curriculum consisted of German and French, arithmetic, geography, history, natural sciences, and art. A few hours were set aside for Bible study, but study of the Talmud was entirely discarded. Although this curriculum aroused the rabbinical opposition, it was in general well received by the Jews, particularly those of the upper social strata.

Later, these free schools were established in other parts of Germany, then France and other Western European countries. Soon governments intervened in Jewish education. The most prominent

---

[20] Talmud, Menachoth 99-b.
[21] *Encyclopedia Judaica*, "Haskalah," CD-ROM, 1997, Judaica Multimedia.

ruling of this kind was the edict of Emperor Joseph II of Austria issued in 1781 that ordered Jews either to establish modern schools or to send their children to the state schools. Jews were also allowed to enter high schools and universities, and those who studied the Talmud before they completed their school curriculum were punished by imprisonment.[22] As a result of this edict, many schools with modern curriculum were established in Bohemia, Moravia, Hungary, and Austria at the turn of the century. Maskilim were also concerned about the education of girls. While wealthy girls received private education at home, poor girls were deprived of education. From 1790 on, Haskalah opened schools with similar curriculum for all girls.

2. The impact of Haskalah on the traditional Judaic ideology. By considering reason as the measure of all things and by promoting the path of logic as the means to reach the truth, Haskalah indeed influenced the Judaic ideology. Some of these approaches radically changed previous thinking. One of the most prominent ideologies in classical Judaism was the idea of the Messiah, or the expectation of a savior that would free Jews of the Diaspora and restore their ancient glory. Maskilim, with their rationalistic approach, in fact eroded this hope, and in time they weakened old concepts such as divine intervention in favor of Israel, the myth of the chosen people, and the future mission of Israel. It was in response to this shakeup in ideology that some searched for a symbolic definition of the messianic hope, equating it with the reign of universal peace. After the messianic hope declined, as we shall see in chapter 7, maskilim in fact paved the road for the rise of political Zionism. Haskalah also made efforts to convince Jews to consider their birthplace their home, a sensitive issue that in the past was a source of conflict between Jews and gentiles. Finally, the Haskalah cultural movement must be viewed as the very foundation of the Jewish Reform movement of the nineteenth century.

3. Linguistic reform. In Western Europe, particularly in Germany and France, well-to-do Jews had started teaching their children German and French as early as the seventeenth century. This effort was aimed at easing communication with non-Jews in both business and social affairs. But the proclamation of the maskilim to

---

[22] Ibid.

use Yiddish in day-to-day conversations introduced an element of distrust between Jews and gentiles. In fact, German writers had previously claimed that Jews, by employing Yiddish or Hebrew, were able to deceive non-Jews. Haskalah, therefore, maintained a position against using Yiddish in public, proposed Hebrew as the language of worship, and encouraged Jews to communicate in their native language. They discouraged using Yiddish or Hebrew in bookkeeping and business transactions. The Jewish communities of Western European countries received these recommendations with more enthusiasm than those in Eastern Europe.

4. Productivization of Jewish occupation. Circumstances forced Jews away from farming and agriculture and gradually moved them toward trade and money lending during the Middle Ages. A poor participation of Jews in labor in general and in agriculture in particular served as a scapegoat in the hands of gentiles against Jews throughout the history of the Diaspora. Haskalah made some effort in different areas to attract more Jews to labor and agriculture in order to change the Jewish occupation mix. However, these efforts were met with resistance on the part of the Jewish masses.

5. Assimilation in dress and manner. In many European countries, language reform was accompanied with improvements in dress and in public manners. Through its numerous publications, clubs, and societies, Haskalah played a prominent role in changing the public manners and dress code of European Jewry, characteristics that were most typical of life in ghettoes and had been carried from generation to generation. For instance, Haskalah took a strong position against wearing head covers, prayer shawls, and long coats in public.

In 1783, the followers of Haskalah started the publication of *Ha-Me`assef,* which continued until 1811. They published *Bikkure Ha-Ittem* from 1820 to 1831, *Ha-Halutz* from 1859 to 1889, and *Kerem-Hermed* from 1853 to 1857. The ultimate goal of these periodicals was to advance secular education among Jews.[23]

In spite of the assiduous efforts of the followers of Haskalah, this cultural movement remained exclusive only to the higher strata of

---

[23] *Encyclopedia Americana* (1979), 16: 92.

the Jewish intellectuals and never included the masses. Haskalah was finally blamed as a culture of assimilation and was denounced as a betrayal of Jewish identity.[24] As we shall see in chapter 6, lack of wide support for Haskalah among Jewish masses was a prominent factor in the spread of modern anti-Semitism, on one hand, and the enticement of Jews around the issue of Jewish national identity and Zionism, on the other hand. Nonetheless, a more realistic assessment of the Haskalah movement and its overall positive impact on the Jewish emancipation has only been addressed in recent decades.

The French Revolution and Emancipation of the Jews

Whereas the intellectual interactions of the seventeenth and eighteenth centuries paved the road for the emancipation of European Jews, it was the great French Revolution that in fact advanced social freedom to Jews and granted them the right of citizenship. Jews were not actively involved in the French Revolution, but they willingly supported the principles of this social uprising.

The ideals of the Enlightenment became evident in numerous lengthy debates and political deliberations on Jewish emancipation, which occurred during the Revolution. It was then legislated that "it shall be the objective of every political organization to protect the natural rights of man"; therefore, "all citizens have the right to all the liberties and advantages of citizens, without exception." Furthermore, it was stressed that deprivation of Jews from these rights and keeping them in a politically and socially inferior status would be contradictory to the principle of the "natural rights" of humans, and hence would undermine the civic equality that constituted the core of the Revolution.[25] On December 23, 1789, during the debate in the National Assembly, Comte de Clermont-Tonnerre, a nobleman from Paris and an advocate of Jewish emancipation, declared, "The Jews should be denied everything as a nation, but be granted everything as individuals. ... [T]here cannot be a nation within a nation." He proposed that the Tenth Article of the Declaration of the Rights of Man and of the Citizen, which states that "no man should be persecuted for his religion," should include all Jews in France.

---

[24] G. Wigoder, *The New Standard Jewish Encyclopedia* (New York: Facts on File, 1992), 418.
[25] *Encyclopedia Judaica*, "Emancipation," CD-ROM, 1997, Judaica Multimedia.

Abbe Henri Gregoire (1750–1831), a Catholic clergy and an activist of the French Revolution, asked, "Are there any ways of making the Jews of France happier and more useful?" As the remedy, he then suggested the full integration of Jews in French society. He went far enough to advocate the abolition of the fundamental factors that had separated Jews from Christians. He proposed closing down all Jewish quarters, providing communal autonomy for Jews, and making the effort to eliminate the "superstitious beliefs" to which the Jews adhered because they were misled by their rabbis.[26] He also discarded the traditional Christian claim that Jews must suffer because of their sins. Gregoire played an active and vigorous role in bringing the Jewish question to the French National Assembly until emancipation was granted to them on September 27, 1791.

Comte de Mirabeau (1749–1791), the French statesman, strongly argued that Jews were reacting to the circumstances they were living in and they must not be blamed. He stressed, "The Jew is more of a man than he is a Jew." In the debate of December 24, 1791, Mirabeau rejected the assertion that Jews did not regard themselves as citizens of France.

Influenced by the supreme aspirations of the Revolution, many Jews now looked upon France as the Promised Land: "France, our Jerusalem, your hills our Zion mount and your waterways our Jordan River, let us drink from your sanction the blessing of freedom."[27] And on this same subject, in 1791, Berr Isaac Berr, a member of the Assembly of Jewish Notables, proclaimed, "By Divine mercy and the government of the people, we have become not only men, not only citizens, but also Frenchmen."[28]

Accordingly, on that date, the French Constitutional Assembly conferred equal rights of citizenship on all Jews. These rights were first enforced by the army of the French Revolution and later by the military machine of Napoleon Bonaparte in 1796 in the Netherlands, in 1797 in Venice, in 1798 in Mainz, in 1801 in Rome, and in 1811 in Frankfurt. It was in this manner that European Jewry left the dark days of the Middle Ages behind.

---

[26] *Encyclopedia Judaica*, "Gregoire, Henri Baptiste," CD-ROM, 1997, Judaica Multimedia.

[27] Letter to the editor of *La Chronique de Paris* in 1791.

[28] *Encyclopedia Judaica*, "Haskalah," CD-ROM, 1997, Judaica Multimedia.

In 1806, in an effort to create an atmosphere of better understanding between Jews and Christians, Napoleon advanced a number of questions to a council of 111 rabbis and Jewish leaders. In essence, he was interested in knowing the response of the Jewish community to the following questions: Do Jews practice polygamy? Were they allowed to marry Christians? Do rabbis willingly abide with the rulings of the court in cases of marriage and divorce? Do Jews participate in usury? The council of rabbis responded that polygamy and usury were against Mosaic Law;[29] they did not have a problem with the marriage between Jews and Christians; and they accepted the court rulings on the matter of marriage and divorce. These were exactly the responses Napoleon expected. Following this intercourse, Comte Louis-Mathieu Mole, the representative of Napoleon, suggested that the rabbis revive the Grand Sanhedrin, the assembly of religious leaders, which had not met since 66 CE. Jews announced this event with a proud and happy proclamation: "A great event is about to take place, one which, through a long series of centuries, our fathers, and even we in our own times, did not expect to see. The 20th of October has been fixed as the date for the opening of a Great Sanhedrin in the capital of one of the most powerful Christian nations, and under the protection of the immortal prince who rules over it. Paris will show the world a remarkable scene, and this ever memorable event will open to the dispersed remnants of the descendants of Abraham a period of deliverance and prosperity."[30] The Great Sanhedrin did not achieve anything significant. The council of seventy-one rabbis and religious leaders convened on an irregular basis from July 26, 1806, through April 6, 1807, and issued a nine-item declaration to the Jewish communities throughout Europe on February 9, 1807. "It is a religious obligation for every Israelite in France . . . to regard from now on civil marriage as a civil obligation, and therefore forbids every rabbi or any other person in the two lands to assist in a religious marriage without it having been established beforehand that marriage has been concluded according to the law before a civil officer. The Grand Sanhedrin declared further that marriages between Jews and Christians which have been contracted in accordance with the laws of the civil code are civilly legal, and that,

---

[29] H. Graetz, *History of the Jews* (Philadelphia: Bella Lowy, 1891), 5: 491.
[30] W. Durant, *The Story of Civilization: The Age of Napoleon* (New York: Simon & Schuster, 1975), 276.

although they may not be capable of receiving religious sanction, they should not be subject to religious prosecution."[31] Since then, the rulings over marriage and divorce in the Jewish communities of the Western world have remained the same. The civil law of the state regulates marriage and divorce, while the religious authorities are free to impose their own rules only upon those Jews who accept their authority.

The Grand Sanhedrin also recommended that Jews engage in farming, love their birthplace as their home, and defend it against foreign enemies. Napoleon also suggested that Jews select family names for themselves. Following this prelude, starting in 1808, synagogues across France actively participated in the recruitment of Jews into Napoleon's army.[32] Through these encounters, Napoleon tried to ease the tension between Jews and Christians, on the one hand, and took advantage of the Jewish soldiers in his army, on the other hand. However, it is said that in the latter part of his reign, Napoleon imposed restrictions against full emancipation of the Jews.[33]

The Impact of Emancipation on the Jewish Communities

The emancipation of Jews and the advancement of civic rights to them had an extraordinary impact on their social and cultural lives. By leaving ghettoes and joining modern European life, Jews gradually tore down the walls that rabbis and Jewish fundamentalism had built around them for over eighteen centuries. While many Jews freed themselves from the Talmudic educational system and made important contributions to Western culture and civilization, some did not see this as sufficient, and converted to Christianity in order to nurture their talents in the Christian world. Many of the latter group viewed their conversion to Christianity only as "the entrance ticket to European society"[34] and the sole prerequisite for full acceptance in Christian Europe. Among those we can name a few.

---

[31] A. Hertzberg and A. Hirt-Manheimer, *Jews: The Essence and Character of a People* (New York: HarperSanFranciso, 1998), 195.
[32] *Encyclopedia Americana* (1979), 16: 84.
[33] *Encyclopedia Judaica*, "Emancipation," CD-ROM, 1997, Judaica Multimedia.
[34] P. Johnson, *A History of the Jews* (New York: HarperPerennial, 1987), 312.

Benjamin Disraeli was born in 1804 and was baptized when he was thirteen years old. His father, Isaac Disraeli, the historian, had profound disagreements with the traditional Jewish system of education. He described the Talmud as a "complete system of barbarous learning of the Jews" in his book *Curiosities of Literature*.[35] He wrote that ten centuries had not produced ten great men. He broke with Judaism and baptized all of his children, without which his son could not have gotten into the British Parliament. Benjamin, having a great social and political ambition, entered the House of Commons at age twenty-three and became the prime minister in 1873. He served in this capacity until 1880. Through his political career, Disraeli vigorously supported British conservatism. He believed that only a coalition between Church, aristocracy, and kingdom could guarantee the prosperity for England. Hence, in 1831 he founded the movement of "Young England" and tried to organize the British workers in support of the Church and kingdom, an effort that was later defeated. Historians have expressed opposing views about Disraeli's political career. Some thought of him as a capable politician, while others called him a political adventurer. Nonetheless, his efforts to heal the conflict between Jews and Christians were to a great extent fruitful. His theories on the supremacy of the Semitic race never received the support of the scientific circles.[36] He blamed Christians for not recognizing the virtues of Judaism and blaming the Jews for not grasping the Christianity that he called "complete Judaism." In order to justify his conversion to Christianity, he loved to remark, "I am the missing page between the Old Testament and New."[37] In 1863, he wrote, "I look upon the Church as the only Jewish institution remaining, I know no other. . . . If it were not for the Church, I do not see why the Jews should be known. The Church was founded by Jews, and has been faithful to its origin. It secures their history and their literature being known to all. . . . The Jews owe everything to the Church."[38]

Seven years after the baptism of Benjamin Disraeli, Karl Marx was baptized in 1824 at age six. His grandfather and uncle were both in the circle of rabbis, but his father was a student of the

---

[35] Ibid., 311.
[36] *Encyclopedia Judaica*, "Disraeli, Benjamin," CD-ROM, 1997, Judaica Multimedia.
[37] P. Johnson, *A History of the Jews* (New York: HarperPerennial, 1987), 324.
[38] Ibid.

Enlightenment and a devoted follower of the Haskalah movement.
Moses Hess (1812–1875), the German social philosopher and a
prominent activist of political Zionism, in a letter to Berthold
Auerbach, the German writer, introduced Karl Marx with these
words: "He is a phenomenon that has made an enormous impression
on me; even though I am active in the same field. . . . [H]e is still a
young man (about 24 years old at most), who will give medieval
religion and politics their deathblow. He combines with the deepest
philosophical earnestness the most biting wit. Imagine Rousseau,
Voltaire, Holbach, Lessing, Heine and Hegel united in one person."[39]

At a young age Marx was dedicated to Hegel's philosophy. In
fact, he joined a radical group known as the Young Hegelians. Later,
however, he further advanced the Hegelian philosophy and arrived at
the concept of "man, the product of labor." In his works, he
envisioned the emancipation of humans in a free society where they
are not controlled by state and is not alienated by labor. From 1852 to
1861, Marx served as the London correspondent of the *New York
Tribune*. There are numerous contradictions in his writings about
Jews. On one hand, in his manuscript titled *On the Jewish Question,*
he strongly supported the emancipation of the Jews and rejected the
viewpoint of Bruno Bauer, the Hegelian philosopher, who believed
Jews ought to give up Judaism in order to achieve emancipation.[40] On
the other hand, he made numerous remarks with anti-Semitic
connotations in his private letters. For instance, in *Thesis on
Feuerbach*[41] and in his debate with Ferdinand Lassalle,[42] he used
insulting language. On July 30, 1862, in a letter to his friend Friedrich
Engels, he wrote about Lassalle, "It is now perfectly clear to me that,
as the shape of his head and the growth of his hair indicates, he is

---

[39] E. Kamenka, *The Portable Karl Marx* (New York: Penguin Books, 1983), 22.
[40] Ibid., 96–114.
[41] Ludwig Feuerbach (1804–1872), German philosopher and Hegel's disciple,
believed in human need as the sociopolitical foundation of society.
[42] Ferdinand Lassalle (1825–1864), one of the leaders of socialism in Germany, son
of a Jewish merchant, was first interested in literature but later was fascinated by
history and philosophy. He actively participated in the German revolution of 1848.
He then engaged in a series of correspondence with Marx after the defeat of the
revolution. At a young age, he was a devoted Jew, but later he departed from Judaism
and denied it as a "living reality." Influenced by the Hegelian philosophy, Lassalle
believed in the historic mission of Judaism but did not judge it as an effective
element in modern history.

descended from the Negroes who joined in Moses' flight from Egypt. This union of Jew and German on a Negro base was bound to produce an extraordinary hybrid."[43] And in his *early writings,* he derogatorily wrote, "Money is the jealous God of Israel, besides which no other god may exist. Money abases all the gods of mankind and changes them into commodities. Money is the self sufficient value of all things. ... Money is the alienated essence of man's work and existence: this essence dominates him and he worships it. The god of the Jews has been secularized and has become the god of the world."[44] Based on this and his other early writings, it seems that Marx viewed Judaism as equivalent to that of capitalism, and attributed his hatred for the latter to the former.[45] Interestingly, some of his ideological adversaries in the First International, like Bakunin,[46] took advantage of Marx's Jewish background to undermine him.

Heinrich Heine (1797–1856), the famous German writer and the greatest poet after Goethe,[47] converted to Christianity in 1825. He openly justified his religious conversion as "an entrance ticket to European society."[48] He declared, "I make no secret of my Judaism, to which I have not returned, because I never left it."[49] In spite of the fact that he supported Jews and their cause in different ways in his writings, the traditional Jewish society never accepted him. Heine created a vast collection of poems, essays, and lyrics. By 1912 alone, there were over four thousand musical settings of his poems by great German and Austrian composers such as Wagner, Schumann, Schubert, and Rubinstein.[50] Heine was another disciple of Hegel who

---

[43] *Marx-Engels Werke*, 3: 259, quoted in P. Johnson, *A History of the Jews* (New York: HarperPerennial, 1987), 350.

[44] P. Johnson, *A History of the Jews* (New York: HarperPerennial, 1987), 351.

[45] *Encyclopedia Judaica*, "Marx, Karl Heinrich," CD-ROM, 1997, Judaica Multimedia.

[46] Mikhail Alexander Bakunin (1814–1876) was the principal theoretician and founder of anarchism. He was one of the ideological adversaries of Karl Marx who had an anti-Semitic viewpoint. By introducing Marx as the "modern Moses," he tried to present the movement of social democracy as a Jewish plot.

[47] A. Hertzberg and A. Hirt-Manheimer, *Jews: The Essence and Character of a People* (New York: HarperSanFrancisco, 1999), 225.

[48] P. Johnson, *A History of the Jews* (New York, HarperPerennial, 1987), 312.

[49] *Encyclopedia Judaica*, "Heine, Heinrich," CD-ROM, 1997, Judaica Multimedia.

[50] Ibid.

was in contact with many European philosophers and politicians of the nineteenth century like Nietzsche, Metternich, and Bismarck.

Henri Bergson (1859–1941), the French philosopher, was the Nobel laureate of 1927 in literature who was later attracted to philosophy and politics. He served as the head of the French delegate to the United States. Bergson's views appear in his theories on the functions of instinct, intellect, and intuition.[51] Though he converted to Catholicism later in his life, he protested vigorously against the anti-Jewish legislation of the Vichy government after the fall of France in 1940.

Finally, we can name Felix Mendelssohn, the pianist and composer and grandson of Moses Mendelssohn, who converted to Protestantism, along with other members of his family, in his early childhood.

In contrast to those who converted to Christianity, a larger segment of Jews welcomed Western civilization without leaving Judaism. They viewed religion as a private and personal matter that, in their opinion, was not in conflict with them associating with gentiles. Many of them set Talmudic education aside, learned nonreligious subjects, and contributed significantly to European science and to the fine arts.

Among this latter group, we might begin with Hermann Cohen, the German philosopher who introduced a new interpretation of Kant's philosophy and founded the school of neo-Kantianism. Hermann was born in an orthodox Jewish family in 1842 and initially became fascinated by theology and with the goal of becoming a rabbi. Later he became interested in philosophy, particularly that of Plato and Kant. Cohen believed that in order to arrive at reality, our thought processes have to follow certain principles; and since these principles are ever changing, we therefore can never have a final knowledge of reality. In his opinion, the concept of God played a central role in ethics. Hence, for him, God was an idea or concept, rather than an existent being.[52] Later, however, he changed his position on this subject and proposed that reality is rooted in God and man's reason

---

[51] G. Wigoder, *The New Standard Jewish Encyclopedia* (New York: Facts on File, 1992), 137.

[52] *Encyclopedia Judaica*, "Cohen, Hermann," CD-ROM, 1997, Judaica Multimedia.

also originated in God. In 1879, when Heinrich von Treitschke, the historian, attacked the German Jews by defining their religion as the "national religion of an alien race" and demanding rapid assimilation of Jews into German society, Cohen in his rebuttal manuscript titled *Ein Bekenntnis zur Judenfrage* proposed the complete integration of German Jewry into German society *without any double loyalty*, yet demanded that Jews take their religion seriously. Interestingly, Cohen rejected Zionism as a betrayal of the ideal.

Sigmund Freud, the founder of psychoanalysis, was born in 1856 in Moravia. He completed his training at the University of Vienna, and in 1882, because of financial difficulties, he left the academic environment for the practice of medicine. He started his scientific career as a neurologist and founded the method of psychoanalysis that revolutionized the understanding and treatment of psychiatric illnesses. Later, he applied his method of psychoanalysis to primitive cultures, mythology, and religion. About the latter subject, he wrote that his parents were Jews and he remained a Jew himself.[53] Freud denied the material truth of religion but accepted its historical impact. He wrote, "Nothing can withstand reason and experience, and the contradiction which religion offers to both is only too palpable."[54] He considered religion as an irrational manifestation of the human mind that could be traced by psychoanalysis to early personal conflicts.[55] In his last year of life, he ventured outside the field of psychoanalysis into Egyptology and explored the possible link between Moses and Egyptian monotheism. In his controversial book titled *Moses and Monotheism,* he pointed out the similarities between Aten, the universal god of Akhenaten, and the God of Israel. He suggested that Moses might have been a noble in Akhenaten's court who taught monotheism to the Israelites. In his book, Freud claimed that the Israelites rebelled against Moses. In his view, some of the Jewish character was derived from Jews' guilt feelings about Moses, their symbolic father. Nonetheless, the book produced a strong reaction from many Jews and non-Jews. Following the Nazi occupation of Austria in 1938, Freud and his daughter Anna left

---

[53] *Selbstdarstellung: An Autobiographical Study*, 1925, quoted in *Encyclopedia Judaica*, "Freud, Sigmund," CD-ROM, 1997, Judaica Multimedia.

[54] *Encyclopedia Judaica*, "Freud, Sigmund," CD-ROM, 1997, Judaica Multimedia.

[55] G. Wigoder, *The New Standard Jewish Encyclopedia* (New York: Facts on File, 1992), 345.

Vienna. Freud was a critic of Zionism and was skeptical about Palestine ever becoming a Jewish state.[56] He died in London after a long battle with cancer in 1939.

Albert Einstein was born in Ulm, Germany, in 1879 and completed his education in Switzerland. In 1914, he became professor of physics at Berlin University. During the rise of National Socialism in 1933, he came to the United States and was appointed professor of theoretical physics at the Princeton Institute of Advanced Study. Einstein published his theory of relativity in 1913 and won the Noble Prize in 1921 for his contribution to the quantum theory. Einstein's theory of relativity revolutionized the concepts of space and time and their application to both physics and philosophy.

Einstein was an attentive Jew and a supporter of the scientific institutions of Israel. However, like Moses Maimonides and Spinoza, he rejected the notion of anthropomorphism, or the idea of a personal god, refusing to attribute human physical traits and feelings to God. Although he was deeply influenced in his thinking by Spinoza,[57] unlike Spinoza, who identified God with nature, Einstein believed that God manifested himself "in the laws of the universe as a spirit vastly superior to that of man."[58]

On the basis of his lectures and writings, it seems Einstein believed in a "cosmic religion" that was incompatible with the doctrines of the "revealed religions" such as Judaism.[59] He rejected the concept of a personal god, but he believed in the metaphysical needs of humans. On the relation between theology and science he wrote, "Science without religion is lame, religion without science is blind."[60] On ethics he wrote that "the ethical conduct of man should

---

[56] S. Freud, "Letter to the Keren Hajessod of the Palestine Foundation Fund," in A. Shatz, *Prophets Outcast* (New York: Nation Books, 2004), 54.

[57] M. Jammer, *Einstein and Religion* (Princeton, NJ: Princeton University Press, 1999), 247.

[58] On the same subject, Steven Hawking went one step further and concluded, "The boundary condition of the universe is that it has no boundary. The universe would be completely self-contained and not affected by anything outside itself. It would neither be created nor destroyed. It would just BE." See S. W. Hawking, *A Brief History of Time*. (New York: Bantam Books, 1988), 136.

[59] M. Jammer, *Einstein and Religion* (New York: Princeton University Press, 1999), 149.

[60] Ibid., 51.

be based effectually on sympathy, education and social ties and needs; no religious basis is necessary."[61] Meanwhile, he praised the founders of the great religions at the National Conference of Christians and Jews in 1947: "If the believers of the present day religions would earnestly try to think and act in the spirit of the founders of these religions, then no hostility on the basis of religion would exist among the followers of the different faiths."[62] By denying a personal god, Einstein provoked the religious fundamentalism more or less in the same manner as Maimonides and Spinoza.[63]

To the group of conscious Jews who contributed to Western culture and science we can name several Nobel Prize laureates: Adolf Von Baeyer (1835–1917), chemistry in 1905; Henry Moissan (1852–1907), chemistry in 1906; Albert Abraham Michelson (1852–1931), physics in 1907; Elie Metchnikoff (1845–1916), medicine in 1908; and Enrico Fermi (1901–1954), physics in 1938. In arts, we have Amedeo Modigliani (1884–1920); Camille Pissarro (1830–1903), the founder of Impressionism in painting; Marc Chagall (1887–1985); and Jacob Epstein (1880–1959). In literature we have Solomon Rabinovich (1859–1916), who wrote under the pen name of Shalom Aleichem.

It was in this manner that within a period of less than a century, the bulk of European Jews left their ghettoes, set aside the Talmudic traditions in education, and joined the arena of Western civilization and "as individuals" notably contributed to mankind's

---

[61] Ibid., 87.

[62] Ibid., 150.

[63] Einstein received numerous hostile letters in his lifetime. The most strongly worded one was from the founder of the Calvary Tabernacle Association in Oklahoma City, who wrote: "Professor Einstein, I believe that every Christian in America will answer you, 'We will not give up our belief in our God and His Son Jesus Christ, but we invite you, if you do not believe in the God of the people of this Nation, to go back where you came from.' I have done everything in my power to be a blessing to Israel, and then you came along and with one statement from your blasphemous tongue do more to hurt the cause of your people than all of the efforts of the Christians who love Israel can do to stamp out anti-Semitism in our Land. Professor Einstein, every Christian in America will immediately reply to you, 'Take your crazy, fallacious theory of evolution and go back to Germany where you came from, or stop trying to break down the faith of a people who gave you a welcome when you were forced to flee your native land.'"

humanities and science.[64] In a period of eighty-five years, from 1905 to 1990, 109 Jews or half-Jews were elected as Nobel Prize laureates.

Reform in Judaism

Political emancipation of the Jews prompted a new interpretation of Judaism in order to meet the spiritual needs of contemporary Jews. Reform Judaism is the heritage of the German Ashkenazi Jews.

Israel Jacobson (1768–1828), a German Jew, was the first to propose modifications in the religious education and praying rituals in the synagogue. Influenced by the values and viewpoints of the Enlightenment, he believed that the elimination of the cumbersome details of the Judaic rituals was a big step in giving up Jewish otherness and therefore in promoting a better understanding between Jews and Christians. He insisted that Jews should abandon the praying style of the ghetto and behave in a way similar to the Protestants. In 1801, he established a school in Brunswick, Germany,[65] where Jews and Christians could jointly attend, and nine years later he launched the first Reform synagogue, where sermons were delivered in German instead of Yiddish.[66] Soon a group of Jews in Hamburg, Germany, proposed to abandon everything in the Jewish tradition that might compromise their claim for being good German Jews; the most important of all was the concept of Jews as a distinct people waiting for a return to the Promised Land. Neither Jacobson nor the Hamburg group was promoting assimilation. On the contrary, their emphasis was on the manner of worship, and indeed they were trying to preserve Judaism by wrapping it in a universally acceptable dressing.[67]

Among orthodox Jews, some insisted that Jews must enter the modern world without giving away even the slightest bit of the

---

[64] B. Russell, *The History of Western Philosophy* (New York: Touchstone, 1972), 323.
[65] G. Wigoder, *The New Standard Jewish Encyclopedia* (New York: Facts on File, 1992), 498.
[66] *Encyclopedia Judaica*, "Jacobson, Israel," CD-ROM, 1997, Judaica Multimedia.
[67] A. Hertzberg and A. Hirt-Manheimer, *Jews: The Essence and Character of a People* (New York: HarperSanFrancisco, 1998), 195.

traditional religion. However, they believed that modern Jews need to gain secular knowledge and participate in the social world.[68] This school of thought was founded by Rabbi Samson Raphael Hirsch (1808–1888). He, like other orthodox rabbis, believed that religious laws, written and oral, were divinely revealed and therefore were not changeable. Hirsch insisted that Judaism was not in need of reform— the Jews were. He adamantly argued that Christians had always dreamed of the Second Coming, and that did not make them less of a German or Hungarian. Why, then, should the dream of Jews for the Messiah make them less patriotic citizens? Nonetheless, his followers were modern in appearance and manner, yet they observed the rituals of the Bible and the Talmud and viewed Halakhah as the unchangeable divine laws. Hirsch himself elected to conduct services wearing a robe in the style of Protestant ministers while a choir sang in his synagogue. In other words, Hirsch succeeded in advancing his Protestant style of service and his flexible attitude toward secular education for Jews, called the Neo-Orthodoxy, to many countries in the world.

The formula that Hirsch used, however, did not satisfy those Jews who were after real change. Orthodoxy in any form or shape was no longer acceptable by the group of Jews who did not consider the Torah as the literal word of God and viewed the Bible as a human document, though divinely inspired. Therefore, they believed that a human document could be changed. Abraham Geiger (1810–1874), a brilliant rabbi, courageously argued that the orthodox ritual laws were great for the Middle Ages when Jews were living defensively in seclusion. Now Jews have entered into an era of modern pluralism. In this setting, the observance of ritual laws would further separate them from the rest of mankind. Therefore, it was time to free them from these restrictions.[69] He further argued that if the Pharisees introduced the Oral Laws by interpreting the Mosaic Codes, Jews could also reinterpret them to meet their post-emancipation needs. In other words, Reform Jews are the equivalent of the modern-day Pharisees.[70]

---

[68] D. B. Ruderman, *Jewish Intellectual History: 16th to 20th Century* (Chantilly, VA: Teaching Company, 2002), Part 1.
[69] A. Hertzberg and A. Hirt-Manheimer, *Jews: The Essence and Character of a People* (New York: HarperSanFrancisco, 1998), 190.
[70] D. B. Ruderman, *Jewish Intellectual History: 16th to 20th Century* (Chantilly, VA: Teaching Company, 2002), Part 1.

Again, the radical reform of Abraham Geiger was distinct from that of assimilation. He believed that Jews must identify themselves as Jews, maintain their historic connection, abandon the cumbersome religious rituals, and focus on the moral values of Judaism. In his opinion, the ceremonial laws were created by human beings, and therefore individual Jewish consciences would decide to what extent they would be followed. However, Geiger, near the end of his life, softened his position and included some Hebrew in his sermons and kept the Sabbath worship on Saturday instead of Sunday. In essence, the cardinal difference between the Neo-Orthodoxy of Hirsch and the Reform movement of Geiger is the fact that the former only tolerates, while the latter identifies with, Western culture.[71]

Rabbi Zacharias Frankel (1801–1875), the pioneer of *conservative Judaism* and a prominent Jewish scholar, took a position somewhere between that of Geiger and Rabbi Hirsch on the subject of reform.[72] He argued that Jews are a unique people and they must not be considered just one people among many. The collective historic experience of the Jews defines their character as Jews and separates them from the rest. He believed that the essence of Judaism had evolved in the course of their long history and must remain untouched, and at any given time, the community of Jews, rather than individual Jews, is the ultimate authority on the extent of what ceremonial laws are practiced. Geiger, however, criticized Frankel as being old fashioned and someone who was so deeply entangled in the Talmud that he failed to see the necessities of the modern age.

Reform Judaism, through its journey to the United States, went through another twist. The mastermind of this transformation was a man named Isaac Meyer Wise (1819–1900). Wise was born in Bohemia and joined the circle of rabbis in 1843. He migrated to the United States in 1846. Although Beth Elohim in Charleston, South Carolina, was the first Reform congregation in America since 1825, indeed the industrious efforts of Isaac Wise were instrumental in the promotion of the Reform movement in this country. Wise strongly believed that Judaism was going through an ongoing transformation in order to adapt to the new environment. He argued that traditional

---

[71] Ibid.
[72] G. Wigoder, *The New Standard Jewish Encyclopedia* (New York: Facts on File, 1992), 341.

Judaism was not flexible enough to meet the challenges of the time, and if Judaism is expected to have a positive impact on modern society, then it must change.[73] In order to give an impetus to the Reform movement, he founded the Union of American Hebrew Congregations in 1873, the Hebrew Union College in 1875, and the Central Conference of American Rabbis in 1889. These organizations were the first of their kind in the United States. Wise, as a measure to advance the concept of Reform Judaism, published two weekly periodicals, *The Israelite*" in English and *Die Deborah* in German. He also established the first training institution for Reform rabbis in 1889.

In 1885, Wise chaired a conference in Pittsburgh, Pennsylvania, to formulate the vision and viewpoint of Reform Judaism. The platform in essence represented reconciliation between the American and German viewpoints of the Reform movement. Following is the declaration of the conference, known as the Pittsburgh Platform:

> First, we recognize in every religion an attempt to grasp the infinite, and in every mode, source, or book or revelation held sacred in any religious system, the consciousness of the indwelling of God in man. We hold that Judaism presents the highest conception of the God idea as taught in our Holy Scriptures and developed and spiritualized by the Jewish teachers, in accordance with the moral and philosophical progress of their respective ages. We maintain that Judaism preserved and defended, midst continual struggles and trials and under enforced isolation, this God idea as the central religious truth of the human race.

> Second, we recognize in the Bible the record of the consecration of the Jewish people to its mission as priest of the one God, and value it as the most potent instrument of religious and moral instruction. We hold that the modern discoveries of scientific researches in the domains of nature and history are not antagonistic to the doctrines of Judaism, the Bible reflecting the primitive ideas of its own age, and at times clothing its conception of Divine Providence and justice, dealing with man in miraculous narratives.

> Third, we recognize in the Mosaic legislation a system of training the Jewish people for its mission during its national life in

---

[73] Ibid., 791.

Palestine, and today we accept as binding only the moral laws, and maintain only such ceremonies as elevate and sanctify our lives, but reject all such as are not adapted to view and habits of modern civilization.

Fourth, we hold that all such Mosaic and rabbinical laws as regulate diet, priestly purity, and dress originated in ages and under the influence of ideas altogether foreign to our present mental and spiritual state. They fail to impress the modern Jew with a spirit of priestly holiness; their observance in our days is apt rather to obstruct than to further modern spiritual elevation.

Fifth, we recognize, in the modern era of universal culture of heart and intellect, the approaching of the realization of Israel's great messianic hope for the establishment of the kingdom of truth, justice and peace among all men. We consider ourselves no longer a nation, but a religious community, and therefore expect neither a return to Palestine, nor a sacrificial worship under the sons of Aaron, nor the restoration of any of the laws concerning the Jewish state.

Sixth, we recognize in Judaism a progressive religion, ever striving to be in accord with the postulates of reason. We are convinced of the utmost necessity of preserving the historical identity with our great past. Christianity and Islam being daughter religions of Judaism, we appreciate their providential mission to aid in the spreading of monotheistic and moral truth. We acknowledge that the spirit of broad humanity of our age is our ally in the fulfillment of our mission, and therefore, we extend the hand of fellowship to all who operate with us in the establishment of the reign of truth and righteousness among men.

Seventh, we reassert the doctrine of Judaism, that the soul of man is immortal; grounding this belief on the divine nature of the human spirit, which forever finds bliss in righteousness and misery in wickedness. We reject as ideas not rooted in Judaism the beliefs both in bodily resurrection and in *Gehenna* and *Eden* (Hell and Paradise) as abodes for everlasting punishment or reward.

Eighth, in full accordance with the spirit of Mosaic legislation, which strives to regulate the relation between rich and poor, we deem it our duty to participate in the great task of modern times, to solve on the basis of justice and righteousness, the problems by the contrasts and evils of the present organization of society.

The Central Conference of American Rabbis adopted the Pittsburgh Platform as the principal doctrine of Reform Judaism in 1889. Following are the principal philosophical tenets of Reform Judaism.

First, Reform Judaism rejected the traditional concept of "messiah." According to Judaic teachings, Jews are awaiting the coming of the Messiah, who miraculously gathers Jews from all over the world and leads them to the Promised Land and restores their past glory. The founders of the Reform movement who were deeply influenced by the thoughts and visions of the Enlightenment replaced the restoration of social justice and peace in human community with that of the Messiah. Hence, in their opinion, it was up to the Jews to decide for their own future rather than awaiting the Messiah to do it for them.

Second, Reform Judaism disallowed all ritual elements that might further separate Jews from gentiles. It is due to this tenet that they proposed a number of improvements in the area of worship and public manner. In essence, the Reform movement strongly believed that religious rituals not only must serve a purpose but must also meet the general public acceptance; otherwise, they are cumbersome and must be abandoned. Therefore, Reform Judaism confined prayer to the Sabbath and the first day of Jewish festivals, promoted English as the language of worship, and discouraged men from wearing head covers in public. While Reform Judaism believed in theological differences between Jews and Christians, adherence to the dietary laws was viewed as an old-fashioned and out-of-date practice.[74] Lastly, influenced by the precept of compatibility between Jews and gentiles, the Reform movement initially opposed the Zionist movement, viewing the latter as a dividing force.

Third, Reform Judaism rejected "Halakhah" or Judaic legal codes as an outdated legal system that had outlived its purpose.[75] Instead, Reform Judaism supported a system of secular law, arguing

---

[74] G. Wigoder, *The New Standard Jewish Encyclopedia* (New York: Facts on File, 1992), 792.
[75] K. Crim, *The Perennial Dictionary of World Religions* (New York: HarperSanFrancisco, 1981), 602.

against every justification to wrap social relations in an aura of holiness. In essence, Reform Judaism did not view human mistakes and errors equal to those of sins, a principle upon which Halakhah was structured. They only considered the Jewish moral laws as binding.[76]

Following the massive migration of Eastern European Jews, who were considerably more religious than German Ashkenazim, to America at the turn of the century, Reform Judaism gradually reversed its position on a number of issues, and the Pittsburgh Platform was extensively revised in 1937. Furthermore, the Central Conference of American Rabbis that in 1897 had unanimously disapproved any attempt to establish a Jewish state adopted a position of neutrality toward Zionism in 1935.[77] Later, in the aftermath of the Holocaust and after the establishment of the State of Israel, and also the decline of anti-Semitism, Reform Judaism also entered into a compromised understanding with Zionism. At present, many Reform Jews are strong supporters of the Zionist movement in spite of the fact that Reform Judaism as an institution has not expressed an official opinion on this subject.

Reconstructionist Judaism was pioneered by Mordecai Menahem Kaplan (1881–1983) in 1934.[78] Kaplan argued that Jews adhered to the traditional Judaism and expected salvation after life. Since, in his opinion, this is not a credible conviction, therefore, Judaism must be transformed in order to accomplish salvation in this world. He proposed that humans have much unexploited capacities and there are sufficient world resources to achieve worldly happiness. He viewed Judaism not merely as a religion but as a civilization, which, like any other civilization, has a history, a language, a literature, an art, music, and standards of conduct, moral values, and a religion.[79] Reconstructionists do not view ritual ceremonies as religious laws, but as a way to maintain group identity and survival. Their *Guide to Jewish Rituals,* published in 1941, has been put

---

[76] Ibid., 292.
[77] D. Friedman, "The Transformation of Reform Judaism," *Humanistic Judaism* 28:1–2 (2000): 18.
[78] K. Crim, *The Perennial Dictionary of World Religions* (New York: HarperSanFrancisco, 1989), 601.
[79] *Encyclopedia Judaica*, "Reconstructionism," CD-ROM, 1997, Judaica Multimedia.

together with this principle in mind. For instance, any references to the Jews as a chosen people and a personal messiah have been removed from this guide. Moreover, they leave it to individual Jews to decide what part of the rituals they must practice to suit their spiritual needs. Their understanding of the Israel mission is summarized in the Jewish commitment to liberal social issues and the separation of church and state. Although the Reconstructionist movement had a significant impact on the educated strata of the Jewish communities, it did not succeed in attracting the Jewish masses. Presently, the followers of Reconstructionist Judaism are estimated to be about five thousand families in North America.

The Evolution of Modern Jewish Thought

Inspired by	Position Statements
Moshe Sofer (1762–1839) *Orthodoxy*	Anything new is forbidden in Torah. Torah is a supernatural law conferred upon a "chosen people."
Samson Raphael Hirsch (1808–1888) *Neo-Orthodoxy*	Jews must enter the modern world without giving away even the slightest bit of traditional religion; modern-day Jews may gain secular knowledge.
Zacharias Frankel (1801–1875) *Conservative Judaism*	The essence of Judaism must remain untouched, and the community of Jews at any given time has the authority to judge what portion of ceremonial laws should be practiced.
Abraham Geiger (1810–1875) *German Reform Judaism*	Orthodox ritual laws were great for the period when Jews were living defensively in seclusion. Now Jews have entered into an era of modern pluralism; it is the time to free them from these restrictions.
Isaac Meyer Wise (1819–1900) *American Reform Judaism*	Traditional Judaism is not flexible enough to meet the challenges of modern time and must change. Maintain only such ceremonies as elevate and sanctify our lives, but reject all such as

are not adapted to the views and habits of modern civilization. Judaism is a progressive religion, ever striving to be in accord with the postulate of reason.

We are convinced of the utmost necessity of preserving the historical identity with our great past. We extend the hand of fellowship to all who operate with us in the establishment of the reign of truth and righteousness among men.

Mordecai Menahem Kaplan (1881–1983)

Reconstructionist Judaism

Salvation after life is not a credible conviction; therefore, Judaism must transform in order to accomplish worldly salvation. Judaism is not a mere religion, but a civilization.

Baruch Spinoza (1632–1677)

Secular Judaism

One can be moral without religiosity.

And what is in contradiction with reason is absurd.

Religion is meaningful when shared by all human beings.

In this way, Jews who were marginalized throughout the Middle Ages were emancipated and gradually entered into the mainstream of gentile society.

Chronology:

1517 CE   Martin Luther protested the indulgence of the Catholic Church.

Manasseh ben Israel (1604–1657)   He tried industriously to reconcile Jews and Christians.

1714   Publication of John Toland's manuscript, *Reasons for Naturalizing the Jews in Great Britain and Ireland on the Same Footing with All Other Christians*.

1753	British Parliament passed the "Jew Bill" conferring the right of citizenship to Jews in England.
Voltaire (1694–1778)	The French philosopher praised the Jews for their ancient disbelief in immortality and for their tolerance.
Jean Jacque Rousseau (1712–1778)	Jean Jacques Rousseau praised the Mosaic Codes.
1781	Emperor Joseph II of Austria acknowledged Jews as useful people.
Christian Wilhelm von Dohm (1751–1820)	In his famous work *On the Improvement of the Jews as Citizens,* he proposed the right of worship and access to public education for Jews.
Moses Mendelssohn (1729–1786)	He appealed to rabbis not to excommunicate those Jews who pursue secular education and may think differently.
1778	Haskalah establishes the first "free school" with a secular curriculum in Berlin.
1789	Comte de Clermont-Tonnerre, an assemblyman and advocate of Jewish emancipation, declared, *"The Jews should be denied every right as a nation, but must be granted everything as individuals. . . . [T]here cannot be a nation within a nation."*
Abbe Henri Gregoire (1750–1831)	French assemblyman who advocated the abolition of the fundamental factors that had separated Jews from Christians.
Comte de Mirabeau (1749–1791)	The French statesman stressed, "The Jew is more of a man than he is a Jew."
September 27, 1791	The French National Assembly grants the article of emancipation to Jews.
1796	Napoleon enforces the article of emancipation in the Netherlands.
1797	The article of emancipation is adopted in Venice.
1801	Rome adopts the article of emancipation.
1801	Israel Jacobson establishes the first school in

	Brunswick where Jews and Christians jointly attend.
1804	Benjamin Disraeli is baptized.
1806	The opening of the Great Sanhedrin in Paris.
1808	Samson Raphael Hirsch, the founder of Neo-Orthodoxy in Judaism, is born.
1808	Synagogues recruited Jewish soldiers for Napoleon's army.
1810	Abraham Geiger, the founder of German Reform Judaism, is born.
1811	The article of emancipation is adopted in Frankfurt.
1819	Isaac Meyer Wise, the founder of American Reform Judaism, is born in Bohemia.
1824	Karl Marx is baptized.
1825	Heinrich Heine converts to Christianity.
1856	Sigmund Freud is born in Moravia.
1873	Benjamin Disraeli becomes the prime minister of England.
1873	Isaac Meyer Wise founds the Union of American Hebrew Congregations.
1879	Albert Einstein is born in Ulm, Germany.
1885	Declaration of the Pittsburgh Platform.
1934	Mordecai Menahem Kaplan argues in favor of Judaism as a civilization: the birth of the Reconstructionist Movement.

Chapter Six

ANTI-SEMITISM

Wilhelm Marr, a German journalist, was the first to introduce the term "anti-Semitism" in 1879.[1] The term "Semite" is applied to the descendants of Shem, the elder son of Noah, the biblical figure.[2] Historically, however, Semites are the ethnic groups of different ancestry[3] who were residing in Assyria, Araem, Babylon, Canaan, and Phoenicia, and spoke Semitic languages.[4] The origin of the Semites is not well understood, but most historians believe that prior to city dwelling, these ethnic groups were the habitants of southwestern territories of Asia, the Arabian Peninsula, and Mesopotamia. Genetic and archaeological data suggests that the Semites, like the rest of modern humans, originated in eastern Africa and gradually left the uncultivated deserts and eventually settled

---

[1] H. Fast, *The Jews: Story of a People* (New York: Dell, 1968), 281.

[2] Genesis 10:21–22.

[3] D. K. Shipler, *Arab and Jew: Wounded Spirits in a Promised Land* (New York: Times Books, 1986), 314.

[4] The Semitic group, part of Afro-Asiatic family of languages, have been classified into four groups: (1) the Acadian or Assyria-Babylonian language, which was the speaking language of the people of Mesopotamia from the third millennia to the fourth century BCE; (2) the ancient and modern Hebrew language group, which included the Aramaic and Phoenician languages; (3) the ancient and modern Arabic; and (4) the Ethiopian group of languages.

around the eastern coast of the Mediterranean Sea and Northern Africa.[5] The three prominent Semitic religions, Judaism, Christianity and Islam, and the use of the alphabet in writing are among the achievements of the ancient Semitic people.

Although the term "anti-Semitism" denotes hostility toward the Semites in general, it in fact stands for enmity exclusively against the Jews. Glock and Stark, who have offered the most comprehensive definition of the term, have described anti-Semitism as "the hatred and persecution of Jews as a group; not the hatred of persons for other reasons who happen to be Jews, but rather the hatred of persons because they are Jews."[6]

The theoretical foundation of anti-Semitism is based upon the erroneous assumptions of Europeans of the colonial era. By discovery and incursion, Europeans of that period not only had access to the vast natural resources in the colonies but also got the opportunity to utilize an abundance of cheap slave labor. Moreover, by their arrival in the colonies, Europeans spread their cultural values and civilization among native inhabitants. Prosperous people usually attribute their success to their intrinsic qualities that have made them superior and in this regard Europeans were not an exception.[7] The sharp contrast between the European civilization and the colonies was simply explained on the basis of the intelligence and astuteness of the former. Joseph-Arthur Comte De Gobineau (1816–1882), the French statesman, and Ernest Renan (1823-1882), the philosopher, both proclaimed they could divide mankind into distinct racial groups. They asserted that intelligence and moral and social behaviors were among predetermined biological characters separating Caucasians from black Africans.[8] They further subdivided the Caucasians into those with light skin or *Aryan stock* and dark skin or *Semitic stock*. This classification was based upon the physical characteristics of each group and their spoken language.[9] Accordingly, the whites that spoke

[5] L. L. Cavalli-Sforza, *Genes, Peoples and Languages* (New York, North Point Press, 2000), 61

[6] G. I. Langmuir, *Toward a Definition of Anti-Semitism* (Berkeley: University California Press, 1990), 317.

[7] L. L. Cavalli-Sforza, *Genes, Peoples and Languages* (New York, North Point Press, 2000), 6

[8] Ibid., 76

[9] E. W. Said, *Orientalism* (New York: Vintage Books, 1994), 99.

the Aryan group of languages[10] were considered of superior stock, while those who spoke Semitic languages were assessed as inferior stock. To express it in different words, those who spoke the Aryan group of languages were considered the Aryan race and those who used Semitic languages as the instrument of communication were viewed as the Semitic race. However, in this artificial classification, they ignored the fact that millions of dark-skinned people in India were speaking Sanskrit, a prominent language of the Aryan group. Others further expanded on the controversy about language and race and, in spite of numerous inconsistencies, invented the Aryan and Semitic races.[11]

The "Aryan myth" is based upon two erroneous conclusions. The first is that Jews represented a distinct race. It is impossible to separate humans into distinct races.[12] Therefore, modern social scientists prefer to use the term "ethnic or sociogeographic groups" over that of "human races." In other words, race refers not to a process of nature but to an artifact of human consciousness, an artifact that does not exist outside the mind of those people who invented it.[13] The idea that biological traits in a group of people have been carried contingently throughout history and have not been influenced by geographic and environmental factors is only a fallacy.[14] Racial boundaries are not more distinct than geographic or cultural precincts; as the latter is constantly changing, so does the former. Indeed, marriage and the pattern of intercourse between men

---

[10] The Aryans were the peoples who spoke and spread Indo-European family of languages to many territories including Europe. Germans by no means were Aryans and calling them 'Aryans' was only a fantasy on the part of Germans. The modern classification of Indo-European group of languages consists of Albanian, Armenian, Germanic, Celtic, Italian, Greek, Slavic, and Indo-Iranian. The English language is a subgroup of Germanic. The Indo-European languages probably originated in north of Black and Caspian Seas in Caucasus around 5000 years ago. The spread of Indo-European languages coincides with the spread of agriculture economy from Middle East toward Europe in northwest direction and eastbound toward Iran, Pakistan and India.

[11] S. D. Goitein, *A Mediterranean Society* (Berkeley: University of California Press, 1999), 292.

[12] L. L. Cavalli-Sforza, *Genes, Peoples and Languages* (New York, North Point Press, 2000), 13

[13] G. I. Langmuir, *Toward a Definition of Anti-Semitism* (Berkeley: University of California Press, 1996), 313.

[14] L. L. Cavalli-Sforza, *Genes, Peoples and Languages* (New York, North Point Press, 2000), 29

and women are determined not only by a biological process but also by geographic and cultural contacts with other peoples. Human population has significant physical, biological and genetic variability often greater than differences noted among the "racial groups."

Jews, therefore, represent an ethnic community that has maintained certain cultural identity for over nineteen centuries. However, in light of numerous migrations to different geographic areas,[15] incessant persecutions exercised against them by other peoples, and imposition of various cultural values upon them, Jews in spite of their higher rate of inbreeding, could not have remained uninfluenced by environmental factors.[16] Indeed, anthropological measurements of Jews from different parts of the world clearly indicate that they differ immensely from one another in terms of important physical and biological characteristics such as stature, skin color, head measurements, facial features, and blood groups. In fact, the similarity between Jews and their surrounding gentiles is more pronounced than between Jews living in different geographic locations,[17] a process that has been attributed by modern science to the genetic exchange between Jews and the neighboring population.[18] Jews who have lived in so many regions and walked through scores of cultures, and in the course of history have been repeatedly invaded, could not have maintained a distinct race, even though some of them show certain physical characteristics.[19]

Indeed, we can recognize many typical physical features of all ethnic groups among Jews.[20] According to Leibowitz, the sons of Abraham, Isaac, and Jacob had no racial peculiarities that distinguished them from the Ishmaelites, Edomites, Arameans, and Moabites.[21] In essence, in contrast to the popular view, most historians and anthropologists have questioned the very concept of a

---

[15] Ibid., 49

[16] G. I. Langmuir, *Toward a Definition of Anti-Semitism* (Berkeley: University of California Press, 1996), 312.

[17] A. Koestler, *The Thirteenth Tribe* (New York: Random House, 1976), 182.

[18] L. L. Carvalli-Sforza, *Genes, Peoples, and Languages* (New York: North Point Press, 2000), 12

[19] A. Koestler, *The Thirteenth Tribe* (New York: Random House, 1976), 186.

[20] Y. Leibowitz, *Judaism, Human Values and the Jewish State* (Cambridge, MA: Harvard University Press, 1997), 82.

[21] Ibid.

distinct Jewish race in spite of a relatively higher rate of inbreeding among them.[22, 23, 24, 25]

The second fallacy in the Aryan myth is that Jews were inferior to the Aryans. Advances in genetics and behavioral biology have questioned the relation between the physical or physiological characteristics and brain function or behavior in mankind. It is impossible to attribute the cultural or mental capacity of certain human groups exclusively to their physical characteristics such as stature, skin pigmentation, or the shape of their noses. Moreover, by eliminating the social and geographic factors that have been instrumental in the historic decline and economic backwardness of certain human groups, the cultural differences among them would have been trivial. Therefore, certain stereotypical characteristics of the Jews as an ethnic group are probably due to numerous devastating social and geographic factors they have been subjected to through their rough historic pathway rather than a predetermined biological inferiority.

Finally, in the background of this philosophical exchange, Carl Duhring (1833–1921), the German philosopher and economist[26] who had subscribed to the Aryan myth, expanded upon it by adding the notion that Jews were behind a world plot to ruin the "supreme Aryan race." It was in this manner that the Aryan group of languages was interpreted as the Aryan race, biological features like the color of skin were linked to cultural and intellectual values, and the social and geographical factors responsible for the backwardness of certain ethnic groups were completely ignored.

---

[22] *JewishEncyclopedia.com*, "Anthropology/Purity of Race."

[23] *Encyclopedia Britannica*, 12: 1054, 1973.

[24] In spite of this consensus, two groups insist upon a racial distinction of Jews. First, white supremacists consider Jews as a distinct race in order to justify the persecutions that have been exercised upon them throughout history. Second, Jewish fundamentalists, on the basis of their interpretation of the Bible, also consider Jews as a distinct race to substantiate their sanctity.

[25] L. L. Cavalli-Sforza, *Genes, Peoples and Languages* (New York, North Point Press, 2000), 74

[26] Eugene Karl Duhring believed in a form of socialism where, in contrast to Marxism, there was a compatibility and harmony between labor and capital. Friedrich Engels, in his work *Anti-Duhring*, criticized his viewpoints in 1878. Most of Duhring's writings enjoy a deep nationalist fervor and intense anti-Semitic sentiments.

Historic Roots of Hatred and Persecution of Jews

Although the term "anti-Semitism" is fairly new, the hatred and persecution of Jews dates back many centuries. The very nature and character of anti-Semitism has varied considerably from time to time throughout history. The character of the pagan anti-Semitism is very different from the anti-Semitism of early Christianity, from that of Martin Luther and from the anti-Judaic understanding of National Socialism. However, in most circumstances, the driving force behind anti-Semitism has been economic factors, which often have been wrapped in a cultural coating.[27]

Before the rise of Christianity, anti-Semitism was presented in an erratic, heterogeneous, and unstructured format. The anti-Judaism of the pagan period usually focused on the peculiar Jewish rituals and customs.[28] In this phase of history, Persians, Greeks, and Romans, who essentially represented the power of the world, had their own social and cultural values. Moreover, their independent identity had no Judaic cultural influence. They could ridicule or insult Jews without belittling their own culture. They hated Jews merely because they maintained a separate identity of their own.[29] This point has been vividly demonstrated in the writings of Tacitus, the Roman historian of the first century BCE:

> New religious customs were introduced by Moses, which are opposed to those of other mortals. Among them everything is profane that to us is holy; and everything is permitted among them that is abhorrent to us. . . . They defend these religious customs, whatever may have been their origin, on the ground of their great antiquity. Other repulsive and abhorrent customs came into force by reason of their wickedness; for thus they brought it about that the worst persons became faithless to the religion of their fathers and brought them contributions and gifts; thus the wealth of the Jews increased. Which is also due to the fact that among themselves the most stringent honesty and a most solicitous charity prevail, combined with a hateful hostility to all others.

---

[27] W. Durant, *Story of Civilization: The Age of Faith* (New York: Simon & Schuster, 1950), 385.

[28] G. I. Langmuir, *Toward a Definition of Anti-Semitism* (Berkeley: University of California Press, 1996), 57.

[29] Ibid., 6.

They segregate themselves from the latter in their meals, they refrain from cohabiting with women of other faiths, but among themselves there is nothing that is not permitted. They introduced circumcision as a means of distinguishing themselves from others. Those joining their ranks also accept circumcision, and are filled with nothing but contempt for the gods, renunciation of their fatherland, disrespect for parents, children and brothers, and they are constantly attempting to increase their numbers, and to kill one's posterity appears to them as a crime. The souls of those killed in battle, or executed because of their religion, are considered immortal; thence their tendency to beget children and their contempt for death. . . . Such people pray only to the clouds and to a god in Heaven. They believe that the flesh of pigs is not different from human flesh, because their father did not eat pig's flesh. Soon they part with their foreskins and despise the laws of the Romans. But they learn, and obey, and honor the Jewish laws, everything, in short, that Moses handed down in his secret scrolls. They will not show the way to one who has lost it except to worshipers of the same faith, they will lead only the circumcised to the spring for which the thirsty languish. Such is the influence of a father for whom every seventh day was a day of rest, on which he refrained from any expression of life.[30]

Ancient Rome, leaning on a strong military apparatus, did not tolerate any popular movement, even the most benevolent one. In this setting, Roman emperors were just looking for an excuse to punish the entire group. Because of the Jews' separate identity and distinction, Rome viewed them as a movement of common people, handled them with distrust, and generally had misgivings about them. Josephus Flavius depicted the persecution of Jews under the Emperor Tiberius in this manner:

In Rome there was a Jew, an exceedingly godless man, who had been accused of many offenses in his native country, and had become a fugitive to escape the penalty. This man set himself up to be a teacher of the Mosaic Law, and together with three confederates persuaded Fulvia, an aristocratic lady who had accepted the Jewish faith, and had put herself under his instruction, to forward a present consisting of gold and purple to the Temple in Jerusalem. Having received this present from the lady they used it for themselves, for no other had been their purpose. Saturninus, Fulvia's husband, complained of this to his

---

[30] K. Kautsky, *Foundations of Christianity* (New York: Monthly Review Press, 1972), 265–266.

friend, the Emperor Tiberius, at her request, and Tiberius immediately ordered all Jews to be banished from Rome. Consequently, four thousand Jews were made soldiers and sent to Sardinia.[31]

The disparities between the Jews and the gentiles of the pagan period, in terms of their practice of rituals and customs, did extend into the Christian era. Since the Romans had their own independent culture, which contained little or none of the Judaic tone, the difference between them and the Jews seemed more visible. In this setting, the Jewish customs appeared at odds with the rest of the community. For instance, when the Christians were fasting, the Jews were eating, and when the Christians were eating, the Jews were fasting. Jews did not work on Saturdays, whereas Christians were working. On the contrary, Christians were resting on Sundays, when Jews were working. Jews celebrated Passover about the same time that Christians were mourning for Christ's crucifixion. Finally, Christians viewed the Mosaic dietary codes, which had been legislated centuries before the rise of Christianity and obliged Jews not to eat or drink the food and wine prepared by gentiles,[32] as an insult on the part of the Jews.

For the common people, particularly at times of social and economic difficulties, attacking and insulting Jews was a way of expressing their social dissatisfaction. If the masses did not have access or could not attack the aristocrats, the usurers, the generals, and the despots on the throne, instead they could attack the defenseless Jews who were present almost everywhere.

The rise of Christianity introduced a new perspective to anti-Judaic activities. The anti-Judaism of Christianity, because of the close dependence of the two religions, has been the most extreme of all kinds.[33] The anti-Judaic sentiments of Christianity can be addressed in three separate and distinct contexts: doctrinal, legal, and popular.

---

[31] *Antiquities, xviii, 3, 8* quoted in K. Kautsky, *Foundations of Christianity* (New York: Monthly Review Press, 1972), 269–270.

[32] I. Abraham, *Jewish Life in the Middle Ages* (Philadelphia: 1896), 411, quoted in W. Durant, *The Story of Civilization: The Age of Faith* (New York: Simon & Schuster, 1950), 386.

[33] G. I. Langmuir, *Toward a Definition of Anti-Semitism* (Berkeley: University of California Press, 1996), 57.

First, doctrinal anti-Judaism of Christianity is based upon the assumption that most Jews before and all Jews after the rise of Christ were inferior to Christians, and in the opinion of more radical elements, they were the enemy of Christianity.[34] In other words, Christians are the real Israel, and the rise of Christianity is in complete contradiction with the existence of Judaism.[35] The root cause of the Christian hatred for Judaism is not the myth of Christ's life or his alleged crucifixion by the Jews.[36] This myth originated in the Christian understanding that Christ was a Jew by birth, remained a Jew to the last minute of his life, and in his teachings repeatedly insisted he had no intention of introducing a new religion but instead wanted to "advance" Judaism.[37] In the opinion of Christian fundamentalism,[38] "advanced Judaism" is nothing but Christianity, and hence these two may not coexist. Leibowitz believes this perspective has spilled into the collective conscience of many Christians, even those liberal intellectuals of the Age of Enlightenment like Voltaire, Kant, and Hegel. He also believes that there cannot be an honest dialogue between Judaism and Christianity.[39] He admits that liberal elements of Judaism and Christianity may enter into common understandings, but there can be no reconciliation between the theological principles and the fundamental elements of the two religions. This peculiar relation between Judaism and Christianity, however, does not apply to Islam.

Legally, the anti-Judaic sentiments of Christianity can be summarized (1) in measures that separated Jews from Christians and curtailed contact between them, (2) in procedures that diminished the social status of the Jews, and (3) in efforts that prevented Jews from exercising control over Christians. Forcing Jews into separate living quarters, excluding Jews from the feudal system of production, and

---

[34] Ibid., 58.

[35] E. Abrams, *Faith or Fear* (New York: Free Press, 1997), 86.

[36] Y. Leibowitz, *Judaism, Human Values, and the Jewish State* (Cambridge, MA: Harvard University Press, 1992), 254.

[37] Matthew, 5:17–19.

[38] The infallibility of the Bible, the virgin birth and the divinity of Christ, the sacrifice of Christ as the atonement for the sins of all people, the physical resurrection and the second coming of the Christ, and finally, the bodily resurrection of believers constitute the principles in the belief system of Christian fundamentalism.

[39] Y. Leibowitz, *Judaism, Human Values, and the Jewish State* (Cambridge, MA: Harvard University Press, 1992), 255.

preventing them from carrying arms are among the legal manifestations of anti-Judaism.

However, the popular aspect of the anti-Judaic movement, as I reviewed in more detail in chapter 3, became fashionable only in the eleventh century, coinciding with the beginning of the first Crusade. It was not until then that an intense and popular anti-Judaism emerged in the Christian world. In other words, prior to this date, the anti-Judaic activities were confined to higher social circles, and it was more or less after this date that a vast Christian audience was interested in listening to accusations against Jews.[40]

Early accusations usually focused on stereotypical ideas such as *Christ killers, rejection of Christianity,* and *usury.* In each, some element of the truth could be found. However, by the eleventh century, new accusations were added that had no basis in truth. These included *ritual murder, host desecration,* and *well poisoning.*[41] The latter series of accusations were not true representations of an anti-Judaic ideology of Christians. Rather, they usually erupted as a result of a social and psychological reaction of the majority toward an "inferior minority" in a rapidly developing society.[42]

The accusation of Jews as Christ killers dates back to the early Christian era. To understand the public Christian support for this accusation, we must realize that average Christians were quite comfortable in blaming an entire people for the alleged wrong behaviors of some Jews centuries earlier in Jerusalem. This was in spite of the fact that the New Testament repeatedly recounts the idea that a large crowd of Jews grieved upon Jesus's crucifixion and expressed their sorrow thus: "Then the crowds spread out their robes along the road ahead of him, and as they reached the place where the road started down from the Mount of Olives, the whole procession began to shout and sing as they walked along, praising God for all the wonderful miracles Jesus had done."[43] And "Great crowds trailed along behind, and many grief-stricken women."[44] Also, "And when the crowd that came to see the crucifixion saw that Jesus was dead

---

[40] Ibid., 61.
[41] Ibid.
[42] Ibid., 62.
[43] Luke 19:36–37.
[44] Luke 23:27.

they went home in deep sorrow."[45] However, these encounters, which represented the sympathy of the crowd for Christ, were usually dismissed, and because of the Roman influence the role of the Roman commander in this process was always minimized.[46] Nonetheless, Christian priests often cited the verses of the New Testament where Jews had proclaimed, "His blood be on us and on our children!",[47] as a justification for the harsh treatment of Jews.

Obviously, on the sacred days, priests, with passionate fervor, preached the story of the crucifixion of Christ, and Jews, concerned that their presence in public on these days might provoke the Christians, used to hide in their homes.

The early Christians, who viewed Jesus as the manifestation of God in human form, wondered why his own people rejected him. According to the Church, the Jews must have believed in Jesus as the Messiah more than other people because he was one of their own, but nonetheless they rejected him. The great Jewish sin, however, was not Christ killing, it was rejection of Christ.[48]

It was on this ground that the Church denounced the Jewish religion as the "Synagogue of Satan," a characterization that first appeared in Revelation of the New Testament: "I know how much you suffer for the Lord, and I know all about your poverty. . . . I know the slander of those opposing you, who say that they are Jews, the children of God, but they aren't, for they support the cause of Satan."[49] Indeed, traditional Jews had only a few verses in the Old Testament they could offer up in their defense against Christianity: "The prophet who tries to lead you astray must be executed, for he has tempted to foment rebellion against the Lord your God who brought you out of slavery in the land of Egypt."[50] In response to this, the Church always maintained the position that Christ was only teaching the "true Judaism." In fact, Christian fundamentalists still uphold the position that the Jews will be saved only by asserting their

---

[45] Luke 23:48.

[46] *Encyclopedia Judaica*, "Anti-Semitism," CD-ROM, 1997, Judaica Multimedia.

[47] Matthew 27:25.

[48] A. Hirt-Manheimer and A. Hertzberg, *Jews: The Essence and Character of a People* (New York: HarperSanFrancisco, 1998), 81.

[49] Revelation 2:9.

[50] Deuteronomy 13:5.

faith in Christ.[51] This theological argument has been the cornerstone of hatred for the Jews in the long course of history.

Usury is the third sore and stinging account in the history of anti-Judaism. As I previously reviewed in chapter 3, the departure of Jews from agriculture and their fascination with finance were not their choice and were indeed forced upon them in the Middle Ages. At the beginning, finance was limited to the exchange of money, but soon lending and collecting interest became prevalent. Even though both the Pentateuch[52] and the Talmud[53] had condemned usury, the public perception justified lending to gentiles. However, it was not until late in the eleventh century, at the outset of the Crusades, that Jews were stereotyped as "usurers" in addition to "Christ killers."[54]

The opposing forces in the first and second Crusades, Christians and Muslims, both enjoyed the banking assistance and services of Jewish court bankers and moneylenders.[55] By devising the *suftaja*, bill of exchange, the court bankers could have access to the savings and economic activities of the entire Jewish merchant class rather than depending solely on the fortunes of the rich.[56] Around the eleventh century, when borrowing from Jewish moneylenders reached its peak, so did the hatred for Jews. Steven Runciman elucidated the anti-Semitism of the Crusaders in this manner: "Their [Jews] unpopularity grew throughout the eleventh century, as more classes of the community began to borrow money from them; and the beginnings of the crusading movement added to it. It was expensive for a knight to equip himself for Crusade; if he had no land and no possessions to pledge, he must borrow from the Jews. But was it right that in order to go and fight for Christendom he must fall into the clutches of members of the race that crucified Christ?"[57] Or, for that

---

[51] A. Hertzberg and A. Hirt-Manheimer, *Jews: The Essence and Character of a People* (New York: HarperSanFrancisco, 1998), 83.

[52] Deuteronomy 23:20.

[53] Talmud, Baba Metzia 61-a.

[54] G. I. Langmuir, *Toward a Definition of Anti-Semitism* (Berkeley: University of California Press, 1996), 60.

[55] S. Runciman, *A History of Crusades* (Cambridge, UK: Cambridge University Press, 51), 1: 135.

[56] *Encyclopedia Judaica*, "Banking and Bankers," CD-ROM, 1997, Judaica Multimedia.

[57] G. I. Langmuir, *Toward a Definition of Anti-Semitism* (Berkeley: University of California Press, 1996), 63.

matter, even return the money he had borrowed from the Jews? In fact, popular Crusaders were motivated not only by their Christianity but also by their greed. It has been concluded that "[a]s in the persecutions of the later Middle Ages, the argument that the Jews, as enemies of Christ, deserved to be punished was merely a feeble attempt to conceal the real motive: greed."[58]

In addition, knights, dukes, and great landowners used their property as collateral toward loans they had transacted with Jews. Average Christian peasants viewed this arrangement with a great deal of displeasure. In their minds, they were working hard on the land, yet part of their effort was dispatched to Jewish pockets. Their dissatisfaction with their work conditions was easily transformed into a hatred for Jews. In circumstances such as these, every minor conflict was a sufficient excuse for them to act against the local Jewish population. Furthermore, landowners and those in positions of power often took advantage of the situation, provoked the animosity between peasants and Jews, and then intervened to protect the Jews on the condition that Jewish moneylenders write off their loans. In England, Henry III, who had borrowed 422,000 pounds from Jews, forced them to disregard the loan as a gesture of support for the government and its coronation of Richard I in 1190. In the same year, Richard de Malabestia, who owed a large sum of money to Jews, arranged for the destruction of the Jewish quarter in Burk, where over three hundred and fifty Jews were killed, thereby managing to not pay his due. In another instance, Phillip Augustus arrested a number of Jews in 1180, accusing them of well poisoning. The Jews were released only after they agreed to pay a large sum of money to him.

Even a theologian and philosopher like Thomas Aquinas justified this kind of conduct against Jews on religious grounds. He proclaimed: "It is true, as the Law declares, that Jews in consequence of their sin, are or were destined to perpetual slavery: so that sovereigns of states may treat their goods as their own property, with the sole proviso that they do not deprive them of all that is necessary to sustain life."[59]

The Christian masses were neither sophisticated enough to understand these philosophical viewpoints nor were eager to get involved with issues that concerned the people in power. They merely

---

[58] Ibid., 64.

[59] *Encyclopedia Judaica*, "Aquinas, Thomas," CD-ROM, 1997, Judaica Multimedia.

tolerated the Jews lending money and conceptualized that by doing that, they saved Christians from usury, which they viewed as "moral corruption." They tolerated Jews in more or less the same way that they had put up with prostitution, a measure that in their opinion was necessary to protect marriage and avert homosexuality. In the final analysis, the economic necessities that forced Jews into usury were always ignored, while Christians often used usury to prove that the Jews were an inferior minority.[60]

Ritual murder, host desecration, and *well poisoning* were false accusations with no basis of truth that were later added to the original accusations against Jews.

Ritual murder has been defined as the killing of a human not merely out of hatred but for religious purposes.[61] The allegation that Jews murdered non-Jews in order to obtain blood for Passover and other rituals, known as blood libel, was an effort to incriminate Jews as nonhuman and different.[62] Throughout history, this issue has led to scores of trials and many massacres of Jews. The origin of blood libel probably dates back to the time of conflict between the Jews and Greeks, from the fourth to the second centuries BCE. According to Apion, an Alexandrian writer and orator, a Greek victim was found in the Jewish temple who had been fattened by the Jews for sacrifice. Many, however, believe that the story was spread by King Antiochus to prepare the public for replacing the altar of Yahweh with that of Zeus, the act that led to the Maccabees' uprising in 168 BCE. As Christianity penetrated the popular consciousness, Christians used the blood libel accusation against the Jews in the same manner that pagan Rome had previously used against the Christians. The initial accusation that Jews killed a young boy every year in order to insult Christ surfaced around the mid-twelfth century. Later the accusation changed, proclaiming that Jews killed a Christian child, usually around Easter or Passover of each year, to obtain the blood they needed in their rituals. Fabrications of this kind were usually constructed when Christian children were missing or children's bodies were found. Then the gentile believers elaborated on the story, a Jewish massacre usually followed the incident, and often shrines

---

[60] G. I. Langmuir, *Toward a Definition of Anti-Semitism* (Berkeley: University of California Press, 1996), 60.

[61] Ibid., 240.

[62] *Encyclopedia Judaica*, "Blood libel," CD-ROM, 1997, Judaica Multimedia.

were constructed at the site of the alleged murder or disappearance. The first distinct case of blood libel is that of William of Norwich in 1144 CE. This is the first recorded medieval accusation against the Jews, an accusation that spread widely and caused many massacres of Jews and influenced Martin Luther and Adolph Hitler, among many others.[63] The cases of young Harold of Gloucester in 1168, Richard Pontoise of Paris in 1179, Domingo of Val in the state of Aragon of Spain in 1250, Little Saint Hugh of Lincoln[64] in 1255, Simon of Trent in 1475, and "the Holy child of La Gaurdia" in 1491 are a few additional examples.[65] Most of these tales originated in England. In fact, by the mid-thirteenth century, there were five shrines of this kind, four of them in England. These cases merely represented irrational beliefs of gentiles about Jews, and in most cases, particularly in the case of Hugh of Lincoln, investigations clearly demonstrated how these rumors originated, who the figures were behind the rumors, and how they took advantage of circumstances.[66]

In spite of the fact that many scholars[67] wrote against it, blood libel persisted in Eastern Europe well into the nineteenth century, and

---

[63] G. I. Langmuir, *Toward a Definition of Anti-Semitism* (Berkeley: University of California Press, 1996), 210.

[64] The story of the ritual murder of Hugh of Lincoln is probably the most popular story of this kind. According to the tale, Hugh, the singing boy, was taken to the Jewish quarter and crucified in preparation for the Passover feast in the midst of an excited crowd of Jews. Soon after this rumor spread, armed groups of Christians entered the Jewish quarter. They dragged the Jewish rabbi behind a horse and then executed him, along with eighteen other Jews. Simple-minded average Christians converted the Church of Lincoln into a shrine in memory of little Hugh. Today, however the following statement is visible at the entrance to the Church of Lincoln: "Different versions of this tale have been expressed both in England and elsewhere. They all are reflections of superstition, dogmatism and hatred against Medieval Jews. There is no base to the story of ritual killing of Christians and use of their blood for Passover. . . . Since the 13th century, the Church has always supported Jews against these kinds of accusations."

[65] G. Wigoder, *The New Standard Jewish Encyclopedia* (New York: Facts on File, 1972), 160.

[66] G. I. Langmuir, *Toward a Definition of Anti-Semitism* (Berkeley: University of California Press, 1996), 240–242.

[67] Ahad-Ha'am, the cofounder of political Zionism, expressed the opinion that "every Jew who has been brought up among Jews knows as an indisputable fact that throughout the length and breadth of Jewry, there is not a single individual who drinks human blood for religious purpose. . . . [L]et the world say what it will about our moral inferiority, we know that its ideas rest on popular logic, and have no real scientific basis."

the Church maintained a vacillating position on the subject. For instance, when Jacob Frank proclaimed his messianic mission in 1759, the Church, in exchange for supporting his followers, encouraged him to officially announce the validity of blood libel. Time to time, there were also vicious people who used to take advantage of the irrational beliefs of the public on this matter. In 1716, a converted Jew named Serafinovich, in his book titled *Exposure of Jewish Ceremonies,* accused the Jews of using Christian blood in their rituals. He proclaimed that Jews smeared Christian blood at their entrances to protect their homes or bring business success. He also claimed that Jews used blood in the preparation of unleavened bread for Passover. The Jewish community requested the Church to arrange a meeting before rabbis and priests where Serafinovich could defend his allegations, but he did not show up.[68] Polish Jews appealed to Pope Benedict XIV, who announced that the allegations were unfounded. The blood libel, however, persisted, and announcements of this kind had little impact on the public's irrational beliefs.

The charge of *desecration of the host,* the sacred wafer, was an allegation against Jews as serious as desecration of the image of Christ[69] in the Roman Catholic world. An explanation of the accusation was that Jews, like Christians, identified the host with the body of Christ, and by breaking or piercing the host, they imagined they were crucifying him one more time.[70] In essence, some circle of Christianity believed that Jews, by the desecration of the host, had replaced the holy by the profane and therefore their deeds were blasphemous, justifying their persecution and massacre. The first record of this allegation was at Belitz near Berlin in 1243, where a group of Jews, men and women, were burned at the stake.[71] The charge of desecration of the host was the prelude to a number of expulsions and massacres of Jews in Europe.

Finally, the *well poisoning libel* in the fourteenth century during the plague triggered a new wave of persecutions and

---

[68] W. and A. Durant, *The Story of Civilization: Rousseau and Revolution* (New York: Simon & Schuster, 1967), 633.
[69] *Jewishencyclopedia.com,* "Host, Desecration of."
[70] Ibid.
[71] *Encyclopedia Judaica,* "Host, Desecration of," CD-ROM, 1997, Judaica Multimedia.

massacres of European Jews. The plague epidemic reached Europe in 1346 and, from ports on the Black Sea, rapidly spread to Constantinople and Venice, and from there to Northern and Eastern Europe. The twelve-year epidemic killed from one-quarter to one-third of the European population. It is noteworthy that well poisoning was neither the sole explanation for the epidemic nor were Jews the first ethnic group to be accused. In fact, Pope Clement VI advanced the notion that the Black Death was God's affliction upon Christian people.[72] Not having a clear understanding about the infectious origin of the epidemic, people viewed it as an artificially induced malady. Although monks and nobles were also blamed for well poisoning, and they were also mistreated in some countries, the Jews in particular were charged. The first allegation of this kind against Jews surfaced in 1348 with a Jew who, according to the story, was instructed by a rabbi to poison wells: "See, I give you a little package, half a span in size, which contains a preparation of poison and venom in a narrow, stitched leathern bag. This you are to distribute among the wells, the cisterns, and the springs about Venice and the other places where you go, in order to poison the people who use the water."[73] The accusation of well poisoning spread all over Europe like wildfire and created an atmosphere of terror. Accordingly, Jews were tortured to confess their participation in the poisoning. Nobles and upper-class Christians intervened unsuccessfully in support of the Jews. They had a difficult time convincing the public that their assumption that well poisoning, as the cause of the plague, was baseless, since many Jews themselves had died during the plague. Meanwhile, the massacre of Jews and the destruction of their properties continued throughout the epidemic. In several locations, after Jews had exercised every possible avenue to come to terms with Christians but did not succeed, in an act of frustration the Jews set fire to their homes. In one account in Mainz, over six thousand Jews perished in fire.

Well poisoning libel not only resulted in the annihilation of thousands of Jews and destruction of their properties, but it also lowered the status of Jews in Europe. It is true that many of those Jews who had been expelled from their homeland as the result of well poisoning slanders were resettled, but they ended up in shoddier conditions and certainly were more isolated.

---

[72] *Encyclopedia Judaica*, "Black Death," CD-ROM, 1997, Judaica Multimedia.
[73] Ibid.

The Protestant Reformation and Anti-Semitism

At the commencement of the sixteenth century, the Catholic Church was the most prominent landowner in Europe. It owned about one-fifth of the European fertile land and enjoyed an unchallengeable political power. Across Europe and in the colonies, the priests of this grand religious institution baptized children upon their birth, preached to them a system of beliefs, molded their way of thinking throughout their lives, and finally escorted them ceremonially to their graves. Rich and poor, noble and serf, king and common were all under the influence of the Church. It was under these circumstances that Martin Luther, who started initially as a monk, challenged the validity of indulgences of the Catholic Church. Indulgences were official letters from the pope that promised the remission of sins and guaranteed arrival in heaven in exchange for a sum of money. [74] In fact, Luther challenged the pope to a debate on the subject when he posted his famous ninety-five theses on the entrance of the university church in October 1517.

With the invention of the printing machine and the distribution of the Bible in large numbers among Christians in Europe, the Church gradually lost its monopoly of dictating religious issues. Moreover, the unethical and often self-serving behavior of priests had eroded the solidarity of the Church as a unified institution. Within half a century, from 1517, when Luther proclaimed his opposition to the Church, until 1564, when John Calvin died, the very foundation of the Catholic Church was shattered. The Church hegemony was questioned, the right of priests as the only people who could understand and interpret the Bible was discarded, ceremonial mass prayer was proclaimed unnecessary, and many new religious sects and denominations surfaced in Christianity. Therefore, the solidarity and cohesiveness of Christianity that had been maintained for over fifteen centuries collapsed.

Luther, because of his opposition to the Catholic Church, was counting on Jewish support. In 1523 he wrote, "If I had been a Jew and had seen such idiots and blockheads ruling and teaching the Christian religion, I would rather have been a sow than a Christian.

---

[74] P. Carey, *Great Minds of the Western Intellectual Tradition* (Chantilly, VA: Teaching Company, 2000).

For they have dealt with the Jews as if they were dogs and not human beings. They have done nothing for them but curse them and seize their wealth. . . . I would advise and beg everybody to deal with the Jews and to instruct them in the Scriptures; in such a case we could expect them to come over to us."[75] However, when the Jews declined his doctrine of Protestantism, he furiously condemned them. In 1543 he wrote, "What then shall we Christians do with this damned, rejected race of Jews? . . . Since they live among us and we know about their lying and blasphemy and cursing, we cannot tolerate them if we do not wish to share in their lies, curses, and blasphemy. . . . First, their synagogues or churches should be set on fire, and whatever does not burn up should be covered or spread over with dirt so that no one may ever be able to see a cinder of stone of it. . . . Secondly, their homes should likewise be broken down and destroyed. . . . Thirdly, they should be deprived of their prayer books and Talmud in which such idolatry, lies, cursing and blasphemy are taught. Fourthly, their rabbis must be forbidden under threat of death to teach anymore."[76]

    In order to understand the depth of Luther's hatred for Jews, we ought to review this disturbing passage from his famous pamphlet titled *The Jews and Their Lies*:

"We do not curse them but wish them well, physically and spiritually. We lodge them, we let them eat and drink with us. We do not kidnap their children and pierce them through; we do not poison their wells; we do not thirst for their blood. How, then, do we incur such terrible anger on the part of such great and holy children of God? There is no other explanation for this than . . . that God has struck them with 'madness and blindness and confusion of mind.' So we are at fault in not avenging all this innocent blood of our Lord and of the Christians which they shed for three hundred years after the destruction of Jerusalem, and the blood of the children they have shed since then (which still shines forth from their eyes and their skin). We are at fault in not slaying them."[77]

---

[75] J. R. Marcus, *The Jew in the Medieval World* (Cincinnati, OH: Sinai Press, 1938), 166, quoted in A. Hertzberg and A. Hirt-Manheimer, *Jews: The Essence and Character of a People* (New York: HarperSanFrancisco, 1999), 128.
[76] Ibid., 167.
[77] G. I. Langmuir, *Toward a Definition of Anti-Semitism* (Berkeley: University of California Press, 1996), 309.

Teachings of this kind clearly demonstrated that the anti-Judaism of Protestantism did not differ significantly from that of Catholicism.[78]

In spite of sharp differences between Catholicism and Protestantism, both sects subscribed to the common doctrine that the conversion of Jews to Christianity must be pursued.[79] However, the two branches of Protestantism, Calvinism and Lutheranism, were somehow different in implementing this common doctrine. Calvinism, according to Max Weber, was "the spirit of capitalism," and from the beginning emphasized individual responsibility and respect for social values, while Lutheranism, on the other hand, believed in justification through faith. Therefore, since Lutherans had a more antagonistic attitude toward the Jewish faith,[80] the anti-Semitism of Lutheranism was more vicious and fierce. Lutheranism was a prominent factor to persuade public German opinion to accept the Holocaust a few centuries later.[81]

On the other hand, the Catholic Church suspected that Jews were behind the reformation movement, and in fact the segregation of Jews in the ghettoes in the mid-sixteenth century was the reaction of the papacy to this erroneous notion.[82]

Islam and Anti-Judaism

The rejection of the prophet Muhammad and his teachings by the Jewish tribes of Medina was the core of the conflict between Muslims and Jews.[83] Historically, the ideological differences between the two religions had remarkably less impact. In the beginning, the prophet advanced the principle of "*la ekrahe fe l dinne*" ("faith which has been adopted unwillingly is not a faith"),[84] according to which the

---

[78] W. Durant, *The Story of Civilization: The Reformation* (New York: Simon & Schuster, 1957), 727.
[79] A. Hertzberg and A. Hirt-Manheimer, *Jews: The Essence and Character of a People* (New York: HarperSanFrancisco, 1999), 129.
[80] *Encyclopedia Judaica*, "Anti-Semitism," CD-ROM, 1997, Judaica Multimedia.
[81] W. Durant, *The Story of Civilization: The Reformation* (New York: Simon & Schuster, 1957), 727.
[82] G. Wigoder, *The New Standard Jewish Encyclopedia* (New York: Facts on File, 1992), 792.
[83] D. K. Shipler, *Arab and Jew: Wounded Spirits in a Promised Land* (New York: Times Books, 1986), 163.
[84] Qur'an, 2:255.

rights of the Jews, Christians, and Pagans were respected. Muhammad, like Christ, initially claimed that his intention was not to abolish Judaism but to adjust the Judaic teachings according to new divine commandments revealed to him. However, since the Jews did not see a substantial difference between his teachings and their own,[85] they objected to his prophecy[86] and ridiculed his messianic claim. In exchange, verses revealed to the prophet of Islam indicated that the Jews had distorted the Bible,[87] had murdered their prophets,[88] and had mocked the coming of the Messiah.[89]

The Jewish tribes of Medina were the descendants of those Jews who, after the destruction of the Second Temple of Jerusalem and in the aftermath of Simon Bar Kokhba's uprising, had migrated to the Arabian Peninsula. As a gesture of dissatisfaction toward Jews, the prophet changed the Kiblah from Jerusalem to Mecca in 624 CE. Following the verbal arguments, military conflicts arose. When the Jewish tribes of Medina, Banu-Qaynuqa, Banu-Nadir, and Banu-Qurayza, unanimously rejected Muhammad, he was bitterly disappointed and decided to break up the coalition between the Jews and Arabs and expel them from the Arabian Peninsula. The tribe of Banu-Qaynuqa was the first to suffer. After their surrender, they were forced to leave Medina, and shortly afterward they migrated to Syria. The Banu-Nadir submitted to Muhammad's forces and proceeded into the sanctuary in Khyber, north of Medina. The Banu-Qurayza suffered the worst fate. All their men were put to death, and the women and children sold into slavery. The last Jewish opposition to Muhammad was in Khyber, where Jews formed a coalition with local Arabs. However, Muhammad conquered the sanctuary in 628, and Jews were allowed to remain there but were forced to pay heavy taxes.[90]

The relations of the prophet of Islam with the Jewish tribes had been clearly reflected in verses revealed to him before and after his departure from Mecca to Medina. Prior to his departure, the verses

---

[85] S. D. Goitein, *A Mediterranean Society* (Berkeley: University of California Press, 1999), 303.

[86] Qur'an, 2:118–119.

[87] Qur'an, 2:73.

[88] Qur'an, 2:91.

[89] Qur'an, 2:101.

[90] E. Barnavi, *A Historical Atlas of the Jewish People* (New York: Schocken Books, 1992), 75.

had a modest and a friendly attitude toward non-Muslims, whereas after his departure, they were generally more hostile, with tougher wording such as "The worst enemies of Muslims are Jews and pagans."[91] "Fight against those who have been given the Scripture as believe not in Allah nor the Last Day, and forbid not which Allah has forbidden by His messenger, follow not the religion of truth, until they pay the tribute and being brought low."[92] In accordance with this, the prophet Muhammad raised the issue of the poll tax, or jizya, in 632 CE.

Since then, the Islamic institution of government obliged itself to protect the life and property of Jews, Christians, and Zoroastrians and guaranteed them the freedom of religious practice in exchange for paying the poll tax. The people of the book, or *dhimmis*, acknowledged the political supremacy of Muslims on terms and conditions not dissimilar to those imposed by conquerors onto their subjects.[93] Since the poll tax was a substantial source of income, Islamic governments generally preferred that Jews not convert to Islam and maintain their status as a protected minority.[94, 95]

Dhimmis usually were expected to pay jizya with humiliation and degradation. The agent who collected jizya usually asked dhimmis to stand before him, hit him on his back, and shout at him, "Oh non-Muslim, pay your toll tax." The payer then brought his tax out of his pocket and offered it to the agent. When handing over the money, his hand must never be raised above the agent's hand. After receiving the tax, the agent would then grant to him a lead seal that dhimmis carried around their necks, indicating that they had paid the toll tax. Muslims were allowed to watch these ceremonies in order to acknowledge the glory of Islam.[96]

The contract between the dhimmis and the Islamic state could be revoked under the following three conditions: if a dhimmi insulted

---

[91] Qur'an, 5:82.

[92] Qur'an, 9:29.

[93] A. Eban, *Heritage: Civilization and the Jews* (New York: Summit Books, 1984), 131.

[94] J. L. Esposito, *The Oxford History of Islam* (New York: Oxford University Press, 1999), 307.

[95] J. A. Garraty and P. Gay, *The Columbia History of the World* (New York: Harper & Row, 1972), 264.

[96] A. Zarin-Koob, *Du Gharn Sokoot* [Two Centuries of Silence] (Teheran: Javidan, 1951), 283–284.

Islam or the prophet Muhammad in public; if a dhimmi refused to pay jizya; or if a dhimmi had married or had a relation with a Muslim woman. Under these circumstances, the dhimmi was either executed or was sold as a slave.[97] Sometimes such events were interpreted as a cancellation of the contract between the Islamic state and the entire Jewish community.[98] In that case, the community was in danger of persecution and more suffering.

The restrictions that collectively applied to Jews and Christians are known as the Covenant of Omar. The commitments that dhimmis reluctantly gave to the second Caliph consisted of the following:

> We shall not build synagogues and... in towns and their surroundings and we shall not repair the old ones, and . . . we promise to serve generously any Muslim who may enter in our house for three nights. . . . [W]e do not reveal our religion to him and we shall never try to convert him to our religion and . . . if any of our relatives accepted Islam, we shall not discourage him and we promise to respect Muslims and we rise as a gesture of respect before them and . . . do not speak about them and . . . do not imitate their names and . . . we promise not to ride on a horse, do not carry sword or other arms and . . . not to sell wine or encourage Muslims to drink and we shall shave the hair of forehead and do not carry cross around the neck and . . . not to sound loud in our churches and not to sing in front of Muslims and not to mourning loud for our dead and . . . we shall not bury our dead near to those of Muslims and we shall not accept the ownership of the slaves owned by Muslims and we shall not look at the Muslim homes.[99]

In addition to the poll tax and double rate of custom duties,[100] there were a number of allegations that further tainted the attitude of Muslims toward Jews. Among them was the perception of uncleanness of the Jews.

Islam from the very beginning considered idolatresses unclean or *najis*.[101] Islamic theologians of the Umayyad period,

---

[97] I. Petrochevsky, *Eslam dar Iran* (Teheran: Payam, 1972), 195.

[98] Ibid.

[99] R. Reis-Nia, *Az Mazdak ta baad* (Teheran: Payam, 1979), 58.

[100] S. D. Goitein, *A Mediterranean Society* (Berkeley: University of California Press, 1999), 296.

[101] Qur'an, 9:28.

however, distinguished between idolatresses and dhimmis, and viewed the Jewish prophets as comparable to that of Mohammad ibn Abdollah. Later, however, they considered Judaism and Christianity forms of paganism that were practicing a kind of idolatry[102] and consequently were considered unclean. Likewise, Shiites assessed non-Muslims as unclean.[103] The concept of uncleanness that initially meant "spiritual uncleanness" later was literally interpreted to suggest "physical uncleanness" as well.[104] Jews were labeled physically unclean in spite of the fact that the Jewish religious codes of hygiene were more stringent when compared with those of Islam.[105] It is said that Yemeni Shiites, who are relatively moderate, also considered Jews unclean, and used to speak with Jews through a funnel in order to protect themselves from their saliva.[106] On the other hand, some Islamic theologians have only considered those people of the book who hesitated to accept the prophecy of Muhammad as unclean, referring to the Jewish tribes of Medina.[107]

The allegation that Jews were unclean had many historic ramifications. For instance, enforcing Jews to wear the colored patch, belt, or headgear[108] for identification purposes was merely designed to protect Muslims against the "uncleanness of Jews." Women were often forced to wear one red and one black shoe and carry a bell to be distinguished from Muslims.[109] In many communities, again as a consequence of this allegation, Jews were forced not to leave home in rainy days lest they may "unclean" their fellow Muslims.[110] As early as the eighth century, Jews were required to identify themselves by

---

[102] I. Petrochevsky, *Eslam dar Iran* (Teheran: Payam, 1972), 107.

[103] A. Netzer, ed., *Padyavand* (Costa Mesa, CA: Mazda, 1996), 1: 236.

[104] Ibid.

[105] Ibid., 233.

[106] Ibid., 236–237.

[107] The three Jewish tribes of Medina—Banu-Nadhir, Banu-Qurayza, and Banu-Qaynuqa—found a lot of resemblances in Prophet Muhammad's teachings and their own, and therefore they did not accept his prophecy. Following verbal arguments, several military interchanges occurred among them. In the final attack, the tribe of Banu-Qurayza, as mentioned earlier, was defeated in Khyber; the men were killed and the women and children enslaved.

[108] S. D. Goitein, *A Mediterranean Society* (Berkeley: University of California Press, 1999), 295.

[109] Ibid., 296.

[110] H. Nategh, *Karnamehe farhangui e farangui dar Iran* (Paris: Khavaran, 1996), 127.

wearing the yellow patch on their sleeves.[111] These kinds of restrictions, which were not enforced during the Fatimid and early Ayyubid dynasties,[112] were widely implemented during the reign of Harun-al-Rashid and Caliph al-Motavakel of Abbasids Caliphate. It was during this period that in addition to a yellow patch, Jews were forced to identify their homes by fixing a caricature of a devil's face on their entrances.[113] In Iran, as late as 1897, Jews were attacked for not wearing a red patch for the purpose of identification.[114]

As previously mentioned, singling out the Jews in this manner in fact was an invitation to others to further insult them. The issue of uncleanness was often a strong excuse to exercise violence against Jews and their communities. For example, sometimes the clergy took advantage of this allegation to provoke Muslims against Jews in order to gain status for themselves. At other times, the allegation was used to settle the financial conflicts between a fellow Muslim and a Jewish counterpart. In addition, the allegation of uncleanness was instrumental in forcing Jews away from mosques and other religious facilities into less desirable quarters that eventually were converted to Jewish ghettoes.

The blood libel, yet another allegation that Jews used a Muslim's blood in their rituals, periodically surfaced through Middle Eastern countries.[115] The Islamic version of this accusation that was adapted from Christendom was similar to the European original, with minor differences.[116] Sadly, this kind of allegation slipped into the school curriculum in a number of Islamic countries and achieved nothing more than to glorify hatred.[117]

In spite of this, the Arabs were in general more tolerant of Jews in the Islamic territories than Christians in Spain and Portugal.[118]

---

[111] A. Eban, *Heritage: Civilization and the Jews* (New York: Summit Books, 1984), 132.

[112] S. D. Goitein, *A Mediterranean Society* (Berkeley: University of California Press, 1999), 295

[113] I. Petrochevsky, *Eslam dar Iran* (Teheran: Payam, 1972), 105.

[114] M. Adjudani, *Mashroutehe Irani* (Teheran, Akhtaran Books, 2003), 274

[115] D. K. Shipler, *Arab and Jew* (New York: Times Books, 1986), 317.

[116] Ibid., 318.

[117] Ibid., 323.

[118] H. Nategh, *Karnamehe farhangui e farangui dar Iran* (Paris: Khavaran Publishers, 1996), 127.

Hence, Islam treated Jews more humanely,[119] and the persecution of Jews by Muslims on religious grounds has been infrequent.[120] Overall, Jews did not suffer more than Christians because of prejudice imposed upon them under Islam.[121] Although Jews were encouraged to convert to Islam, forced conversion of Jews was not common.[122] Certainly, ugly organized activities like the Inquisition never surfaced in the Islamic countries.[123] Even in the modern time, the fundamentalist Islamic movements and their sponsoring states that often use the language of genocide against Jews have often a tendency to depict the Arab-Israeli conflict as a root for the clashes between Muslims and Jews.[124]

Ethnic Characteristics of the Jews and Anti-Semitism

Not ignoring the economic and cultural factors that were instrumental in promoting anti-Jewish behavior and activities, we must not also overlook certain ethnic characteristics of Jews that made them an attractive prey to anti-Semitism throughout history. Nonetheless, the world powers often took advantage of these ethnic characters as the scapegoats, particularly during social and economic upheavals.

The sine qua non of this ethnic character is a prominent contradiction where the destiny of the Jews is somehow linked to that of mankind and Jews have set a high goal not only for themselves but for all human beings on earth, and yet they have avoided almost all political actions of the past twenty centuries. To understand this contradiction, we must go back to the Hebrew Bible and reexamine the story of the relationship between the two main characters, the Lord and the people of Israel. This special relationship has been defined through "covenants," or agreements that bind these two

---

[119] B. Russell, *A History of Western Philosophy* (New York: Touchstone, 1972), 323.
[120] G. Wigoder, *The New Standard Jewish Encyclopedia* (New York: Facts on File, 1992), 477.
[121] S. D. Goitein, *A Mediterranean Society* (Berkeley: University of California Press, 1999), 293.
[122] Ibid., 301
[123] B. Russell, *A History of Western Philosophy* (New York: Touchstone, 1972), 323.
[124] A. M. Dershowitz, *The Vanishing American Jew* (New York: Simon & Schuster, 1997), 136.

elements together.[125] In the biblical sense, the covenants stood for the special relationship between God and Israel. Each covenant was usually accompanied by one or more external symbols.[126] The most important of these covenants is that of Sinai, between God and the children of Israel.[127] According to this covenant, God called upon Israel, saying, "Now therefore, if ye will obey my voice indeed, and keep my covenant, then you shall be a peculiar treasure unto me above all people; for all the earth is mine."[128] The Sinai covenant is symbolized by the Sabbath,[129] the Ten Commandments,[130] and "the tables of the Covenant."[131]

On the basis of this covenant, the people of Israel stand in a special and unique relationship to the universal deity.[132] In other words, in the heart of the myth of the "chosen people" is a well-defined concept of history, where the Jews have been considered an intermediary between God and the rest of humanity and have a conscious resolution for achieving a high goal for mankind on

---

[125] P. Cary, *Great Minds of the Western Intellectual Tradition* (Chantilly, VA: Teaching Company, 2000), Part 2.

[126] G. Wigoder, *The New Standard Jewish Encyclopedia* (New York: Facts on File, 1992), 245.

[127] Four other important covenants have been described in the Old Testament of the Bible. First, the covenant between God and Noah: "I have placed my rainbow in the clouds as a sign of my promise until the end of time . . . and I will remember my promise to you and to every being that never again will the floods come and destroy all life" (Genesis 9:13–17). Second, the covenant between God and Abraham: "And I will give all this land of Canaan to you and them, forever . . . that every male among you shall be circumcised. . . . This will be the proof that you and they accept this covenant" (Genesis 17:8–12). Third, the covenant through which God promised the monarchy to remain exclusively in the house of David: "Your family shall rule my kingdom forever" (Samuel II 7:16), and "And it is my family he has chosen. Yes, God has made an everlasting covenant with me; his agreement is eternal, final, sealed" (Samuel II 23:5). Finally, the covenant between God and Aaron, Moses's older brother, by which priesthood was conferred on him and his family: "Now because of what he has done—because of his zeal for his God, and because he has made atonement for the people of Israel by what he did—I promise that he and his descendants shall be priests forever" (Numbers 25:12–13).

[128] Exodus 19:5.

[129] Exodus 31:13.

[130] Exodus 24:7.

[131] Deuteronomy 9:9.

[132] *Encyclopedia Judaica*, "Chosen People," CD-ROM edition, 1997, Judaica Multimedia.

earth.[133] This concept has been central to the history of Jewish thought that has been further elaborated in the Talmudic era, and indeed has many philosophical and mystical ramifications. On the basis of this covenant and other verses,[134] some medieval theologians have elaborated on the distinction of Jews from others. For instance, Judah Halevi, the eleventh-century theologian and poet, passed judgment that the children of Israel depended on a divine providence, while the rest of humanity was subject to the laws of nature.[135] Likewise, Moses Maimonides, the prominent theologian of the twelfth century, believed that "all people will eventually fall except for the Jews who shall remain to eternity."[136] It is noteworthy that as late as the mid-eighteenth century, even enlightened people like Moses Mendelssohn stressed that Jews were recipients of the special message of God, which they would in turn pass on to the nations of the world.[137] By the same token, present-day Jewish fundamentalists view the people of Israel as an intermediary between God and the rest of humanity, and have tried to segregate Jews from gentiles.[138]

On the other hand, some theologians, by referring to the latter part of the following verse—"Of all the people of the earth, I have chosen you alone. That is why I must punish you the more for all your sins"[139]—have argued that the covenant did not imply that God shall confer special privileges to the children of Israel, but instead demanded more responsibilities and obligations from them. Similarly, the Talmud has taken the position that the term "chosen people" did not refer to a special group of people but to certain characteristics or behaviors such as humility, loyalty, and obedience that signified the true Jew.[140]

---

[133] H. Arendt, *Anti-Semitism: Part One of the Origins of Totalitarianism* (New York: Harvest Books, 1968), 8.

[134] Exodus 19:6, Genesis 32:28, Jeremiah 31:36, Leviticus 19:2 and 20:24.

[135] *Encyclopedia Judaica*, "Chosen People," CD-ROM edition, 1997, Judaica Multimedia.

[136] S. W. Baron, *Essays on Maimonides* (New York: Columbia University Press, 1941), 110.

[137] *Encyclopedia Judaica*, "Chosen People," CD-ROM edition, 1997, Judaica Multimedia.

[138] H. Arendt, *Anti-Semitism: Part One of the Origin of Totalitarianism* (New York: Harvest Books, 1968), viii.

[139] Amos 3:2.

[140] Talmud, Yevamoth 79-a, Beitzah 32-b.

Throughout the Middle Ages, the interpretation of the doctrine of the chosen people has been a reflection of how Jews have been treated in the gentile world. The more the Jews were oppressed and persecuted, the more exclusive interpretation of this doctrine was suggested by Jewish thinkers. This kind of interpretation was indeed a psychological defense mechanism through which Jews could make their sufferings bearable and intelligible. The myth of the chosen people was most visible during the fifteenth and sixteenth centuries, when the relations between Jews and gentiles were at their lowest point.[141]

Influenced by an exclusive interpretation of this doctrine, Jews maintained a stronger position against mixed marriages than gentiles. Similarly, by obeying the Mosaic dietary laws, Jews were uncomfortable eating at the same table with gentiles.[142] Again influenced by the same doctrine, Jews, in contrast to Christians and Muslims, did not promote the conversion of non-Jews.[143] Indeed, during the three millennia of Jewish history, the conversion of gentiles to Judaism was only promoted during the reign of David and for a short period in the Maccabees' era. It was abandoned because of the strong opposition of the priests and was probably the clue to the disproportionate poor growth of world Jewry. Along the same lines, in a recent opinion survey, only one-quarter of American Jews had any interest in the conversion of non-Jews through intermarriage.[144] Finally, persuaded by this covenant, traditional Jews have distinguished between those who were born of a Jewish mother from those who converted to Judaism. These and other stringent implementations of the covenant have often been an instrument in the hand of anti-Semitism. Needless to say, even gentiles came to believe that the difference between them and Jews was not merely a matter of different faith but was instead a racial distinction.[145] Nevertheless, in essence this very exclusive interpretation, or misinterpretation, of the

---

[141] H. Arendt, *Anti-Semitism: Part One of the Origin of Totalitarianism* (New York: Harvest Books, 1968), vii.

[142] S. D. Goitein, *A Mediterranean Society* (Berkeley: University of California Press, 1999), 291.

[143] P. Johnson, *A History of the Jews* (New York: HarperPerennial, 1987), 168.

[144] R. M. Geffen, "Intermarriage and the Premise of American Jewish Life" *American Jewish Congress Monthly,* March/April 2001: 8.

[145] H. Arendt, *Anti-Semitism: Part One of the Origins of Totalitarianism* (New York: Harvest Books, 1968), viii.

covenant has nurtured one of the deadliest forms of anti-Judaism, known as "modern anti-Semitism." Indeed, anti-Semitic movements have found this kind of analysis an attractive instrument to unveil and legitimize their claim to *Jewish superiority* and present it to the public as a basis upon which an alleged *Jewish conspiracy for world domination* was in process.

The grouping of the two elements, the conscious resolution for achieving a high goal for the mankind and lack of participation in almost all political actions of the past twenty centuries, has served as the foundation for Jewish vulnerability throughout history, what Hannah Arendt has referred to as "aloofness without a policy."[146] Indeed, when these two factors come together, it often disrupts the fabric that ties humans together in every society.[147]

In fact, Jews behaved as a "separate body" from the rest of the people not only because of the aforementioned theological considerations but also due to the lack of political ability[148] that probably had stemmed from their demographic dispersion and harsh persecutions through the Middle Ages.[149]

Jews were landless minorities who were denied the right to carry arms.[150] Therefore, under these circumstances, they depended solely upon the gentile establishment for their physical protection. In the events that led to violence, no matter for what reason, Jews were defenseless, and it was only natural that they were beaten repeatedly.[151] This was particularly true for the centuries prior to the Enlightenment when Jewish communities were isolated and had the least contact with the gentile world.[152] Being a distinct and visible minority[153] in a setting of helplessness created the worst scenario for the Jews of the pre-emancipation era.

---

[146] Ibid., 5.

[147] Ibid., 4–5.

[148] H. Arendt, *Anti-Semitism: Part One of the Origins of Totalitarianism* (New York: Harvest Books, 1968), 8.

[149] B. Russell, *A History of Western Philosophy* (New York: Touchstone, 1972), 323.

[150] Y. Leibowitz, *Judaism, Human Values, and the Jewish State* (Cambridge, MA: Harvard University Press, 1992), 82.

[151] H. Arendt, *Anti-Semitism: Part One of the Origins of Totalitarianism* (New York: Harvest Books, 1968), ix.

[152] Ibid.

[153] G. I. Langmuir, *Toward a Definition of Anti-Semitism* (Berkeley: University of California Press, 1996), 315.

Trusting in a well-defined and predetermined concept of history, what may have been yet another ramification of the myth of the chosen people has enforced a tradition of optimism in history among Jews. This optimism, while it has provided moral support, on occasion has turned out to be detrimental.[154] The optimist vision of history has been inductive to error in judgment and has left Jews often unprepared for unforeseen events.[155] The misunderstanding of the past has been partially responsible for the underestimation of the unparalleled forthcoming danger.

Finally, the historic dependence of the Jews upon the special arrangements with people of power like kings and nobles and their prejudices in favor of authority has only added fuel to the fire of political anti-Semitism.[156]

This combination of factors has led Jews to a precarious condition of being at the mercy of unpredicted forces through centuries. This background has in fact preceded many major anti-Semitic activities of modern time.[157] Indeed, it was in the same setting that Jews were simply presented to the masses as "social parasites" and could be blamed for all social evils in the period preceding the Holocaust.

The *eternal anti-Semitism*, or the notion that as long as there are Jews there shall be anti-Semitism, is yet another facet of the Jewish ethnic characteristic. After all, the concept that anti-Semitism glues the Jews together and protects them in the world of the gentiles has prompted many to subscribe to the notion of an eternal guarantee of Jewish survival.[158] The theory of eternal anti-Semitism that Hannah Arendt calls a "superstition" might have served to bring Jews together, but at the same time it exonerates the Jew-haters as innocent people who are merely behaving as the pawns of an eternal order. At the heart of the theory again resides the conviction of Jewish chosenness and the messianic vision. Furthermore, the theory leaves

---

[154] R. Hilberg, *The Politics of Memory: The Journey of a Holocaust Historian* (Chicago: Ivan R. Dee, 1996), 137.

[155] H. Arendt, *Anti-Semitism: Part One of the Origins of Totalitarianism* (New York: Harvest Books, 1968), 8.

[156] Ibid., 54.

[157] Ibid., 4.

[158] H. Arendt, *Anti-Semitism: Part One of the Origins of Totalitarianism* (New York: Harvest Books, 1968), 7.

the Jews in a state of helplessness: within the framework of the theory, the victims of anti-Semitism cannot do anything that might change their fate.

Modern secular Jews, however, do not believe that Jews constitute a divinely chosen people, and generally subscribe to the notion that Jews are people among people. They strongly believe that the interpretation of the myth of the chosen people ought to remain in the realm of theologians.[159]

Anti-Semitism as a Political Instrument

The first political parties that incorporated anti-Semitism in their platforms surfaced in the mid-nineteenth century. This phenomenon was most visible in Germany, France, and Austria, and characteristically coincided with the growth of capitalism in Western Europe. The utilization of anti-Semitism as a political instrument resulted from a number of factors that had come together at a historic juncture.

The old feudal mode of production evolved into capitalism from the sixteenth to the eighteenth century.[160] By the early nineteenth century, following three revolutions, the American Revolution, the French Revolution, and the Industrial Revolution in England, the capitalist mode of industrial development was eventually established.[161] In the process of capitalist growth, the lower strata of the middle class, or small property owners, suffered most and were threatened to lose their very existence. The middle lower class was in fact descendants of craftsmen, artisans, and tradesmen who in the old feudal system of production were protected against market competitions. The expansion of capitalism opted more and more to liquidate small property owners or the petite bourgeoisie, who learned quickly that if they did not pull up to the upper class, they would be forced into the ranks of the lower class, or the proletariat. Therefore, the market competition was a matter of life and death to them.[162]

---

[159] *Encyclopedia Judaica*, "Chosen People," CD-ROM edition, 1997, Judaica Multimedia.

[160] M. Beaud, *A History of Capitalism* (New York: Monthly Review Press, 1983), 17.

[161] Ibid., 74.

[162] H. Arendt, *Anti-Semitism: Part One of the Origin of Totalitarianism* (New York: Harvest Books, 1968), 36.

About the same period, particularly following the French Revolution, this was instrumental in Jewish emancipation. Many Jews left ghettoes, appeared in the social arena, and indeed participated in a fierce competition in the market that was most unkind to the lower middle class than ever. Therefore, it seemed only natural for the lower middle class to identify their economic and social hardships with the presence of the Jews in the social arena and name them as the source of their pain.

Moreover, the aristocracy and nobility, the central players of the old feudal system of production, were quite unhappy about the rise of capitalism, since they had lost their privileges and were not shy about taking advantage of every opportunity in their favor against the bourgeoisie.[163] Consequently, they eagerly supported the unhappy lower middle class in their opposition to the Jews. On the basis of this scenario, Friedrich Engels once said that the anti-Semitic movements of this time were conducted by noblemen and were supported by a chorus of a howling mob of petite bourgeoisie.[164] It is noteworthy that the Catholic Church in France and Austria and the Protestant establishment in Germany were backing the nobility in this sacred war. The central leaders of these movements soon learned that their anti-Semitic slogans were quite attractive to the masses, through which they could easily mobilize them, and therefore they simply took advantage of the circumstances.

Finally, in the process of its expansion, industrial capitalism was acutely in need of capital. The providers of capital and credit were bankers; sadly, many were Jews because of their age-old experience in finance and money lending. According to Hannah Arendt, the nation-states that emerged in the aftermath of the French Revolution did not allow Jews to merge into the social class system. Instead, by granting certain privileges to a minority of Jews, which often must have been enforced against the will of society, they preserved them as a separate group.[165] In other words, Jews neither formed a class of their own, nor did they melt into the class system in their countries of birth. They were usually defined as being Jews, separate from other social classes. Nonetheless, the interest of the

---

[163] M. Beaud, *A History of Capitalism* (New York: Monthly Review Press, 1983), 48.
[164] H. Arendt, *Anti-Semitism: Part One of the Origins of Totalitarianism* (New York: Harvest Books, 1968), 37.
[165] Ibid., 13.

nation-states in preserving Jews as a separate group and preventing their assimilation into class society was combined with the Jewish interest in self-preservation and group survival.[166] In the final analysis, the emancipation of the Jews did not eliminate all the restrictions and privileges for all Jews; instead it eradicated some restrictions for all Jews while granting certain privileges to a small group of Jews. It was not surprising that Christian Wilhelm Dohm, the prominent advocate of Jewish emancipation of the eighteenth century, strongly opposed such contradictory practices of the nation-states.[167] Hence, the masses simply viewed the exclusive group of Jews in charge of finance and banking as yet another justification for their dismal economic condition, and the hatred for bankers and financial capitalism soon converted to resentment against Jews. The rise of the house of Rothschild to a prominent European financial position certainly nourished the anti-Semitic mentality of this period. The founder of the house, Meyer Amschel Rothschild, a court Jew, started his career under the authority of the Austrian emperor. He established his five sons in the five financial capitals of Europe: Frankfurt, Paris, London, Naples, and Vienna. They entered into enormous business activities during the last years of the Napoleonic wars. After the defeat of Napoleon, when European nation-states were in need of credit for reorganization, the house of Rothschild enjoyed the monopoly of handling state loans. Between 1815 and 1828, the total capital of the house jumped from 3.3 million to 118.4 million francs.[168] Their financial activities lasted for three generations, and they succeeded in beating all Jewish and non-Jewish competitors in the entire financial market during that period. To the gentile world, Arendt believed, the life story of the house of Rothschild became a symbol of the working reality of Jewish internationalism. The popular notion that the Jews, and not other peoples, were tied together by supposedly closer bonds of blood and family connections was to a great extent stimulated by the reality of this one family.[169]

---

[166] Ibid.

[167] Ibid., 12.

[168] *Encyclopedia Judaica*, "Banking and Bankers," CD-ROM edition, 1997, Judaica Multimedia.

[169] H. Arendt, *Anti-Semitism: Part One of the Origins of Totalitarianism* (New York: Harvest Books, 1968), 27.

Later, imperialism or capitalism on a world scale[170] challenged the institution of nation-states. In this stage of economic development, during the fall of nation-states, the Jews also lost their exclusive position in finance, and their importance as a group declined accordingly.[171] In spite of the fact that individual Jews in high financial positions represented Jewry as a whole in the eyes of the gentile world, the Jewish community disintegrated and was no longer financially organized. The individual Jews in top financial positions, however, were sufficient to shape public opinion around the notion that Jews were controlling the economy, a perception that can be substantiated with little if any substance.[172] In conclusion, because of their close relationship to the state source of power in the past, the Jews were invariably identified with power, and because of their detachment from society and their attentiveness upon the closed family sphere, they were invariably suspected of working for the destruction of all social structures.[173]

The blending of these factors, at the historic juncture of the last decades of the nineteenth century in Europe, generated "modern anti-Semitism," one of the ominous forms of anti-Judaism. The foundation of modern anti-Semitism is set upon the scapegoat theory, according to which, Jews were to be blamed for all economic difficulties and social despair. Consequently, Jews were viewed as secret forces behind states and were introduced as the true leaders of the world economy.

In order to legitimize the scapegoat theory, history has been forged time after time. The most widely cited forged document of historical importance is the *Protocols of the Learned Elders of Zion*. This manuscript was first published by Sergei Nilus in Russian in 1905, and it has been translated into most languages since then.[174] The main theme of the document is the Jews, liberals, and Freemasons[175]

---

[170] M. Beaud, *A History of Capitalism* (New York: Monthly Review Press, 1983), 143.
[171] H. Arendt, *Anti-Semitism: Part One of the Origins of Totalitarianism* (New York: Harvest Books, 1968), 15.
[172] Ibid.
[173] Ibid., 28.
[174] B. W. Segel, *A Lie and a Libel: The History of the Protocols of the Elders of Zion* (Lincoln: University of Nebraska Press, 1995), 60.
[175] Freemasonry was a fraternal secret society that revealed itself in 1717. Original Freemasons firmly believed in a Supreme Being, accepted men of all religions into

are behind a conspiracy to overthrow the Christian world. The manuscript, aimed at an audience alien to a thoughtful approach to history, is the work of many hands in the conservative Christian camp. In essence, the text is sympathetic to the nobility who lost their privileges in the aftermath of the French Revolution, who were frightened by the dismantling of traditional values and hierarchies, and who confused the Jews with the rising bourgeoisie class in Europe. The book charges that *Liberty, Fraternity, and Equality*, the famous slogan of the French Revolution, was a Jewish invention;[176] that the elders of Zion, by raising the land tax, paved the way for the fall of nobility;[177] that the Jews were inherently the destructive agents of social decomposition;[178] and more. The success of the *Protocols of the Learned Elders of Zion* in attracting a broad audience was based on its ability to offer a simple answer to the perplexing mysteries of modern world affairs.[179]

The major source document of the book was found to be a satire of Napoleon III by Maurice Joly, the French writer, who published it under the title of *Dialogue between Machiavelli and Montesquieu in Hell* around 1864.[180] In this satirical article, Joly tried to depict the ambitious agendas of Napoleon III for the conquest of the world.[181] According to Philip Graves, a reporter for the *Times of London* who researched the subject in 1921, the source document was forged in 1897 by the Tsarist Russian secret police, substituting Napoleon III with that of the Elders of Zion in Joly's satire. The

---

their membership, had high moral values, were dedicated to charity, and were committed to constant self-improvement. They played a prominent role in the Great French Revolution. Like Jews, they have been accused of being behind subversive plots to overthrow governments, and at times they were labeled as anti-Christ. Indeed, their policy of admitting men of different faiths, particularly non-Christians, as brothers into their membership has been the focus of much criticism, predominantly by the Roman Catholic Church. In 1933, Hitler denounced Freemasonry and blamed them for subversive activities that led to World War I and ordered the dissolution of the Masonic organizations in Germany. Today, Freemasonry membership exceeds six million worldwide.

[176] B. W. Segel, *A Lie and a Libel: The History of the Protocols of the Elders of Zion* (Lincoln: University of Nebraska Press, 1995), 81.
[177] Ibid., 83.
[178] Ibid., 9.
[179] Ibid., 7.
[180] Ibid., 67.
[181] Ibid., 84.

Protocols was first published in 1905 as an effort to defeat the social uprising in Russia. Indeed, Benjamin Segel proclaimed that without the Russian Revolution at the turn of century, the *Protocols* would have remained unknown to the world.[182] According to Segel, the most conservative elements of the Christian world, concerned over the international communist movement, fabricated Joly's satire to create the saga of "Judeo-Bolshevism." The Russian autocracy and their supporters, who fled with the *Protocols* to Europe in the aftermath of the October Revolution, truly believed that the Revolution was the work of a Jewish conspiracy. Nonetheless, the *Protocols* grasped the imagination of millions all over the world.

The simple and incredible hypothesis of Louis Ferdinand Celine (1894–1961), the French novelist and physician, is yet another example of forging history. Celine, in his book *Ecole des Cadavres*, alleged that Jews were behind all European wars since 843 CE, they promoted the hostility between France and Germany, and they were instrumental in preventing European unity.[183] He went so far as to blatantly recommend the massacre of all Jews as the final solution. For the most part, French politicians viewed him as a charlatan and did not take his opinions seriously, but Celine's book was published in the first months of World War II and was widely used by the Nazi propaganda machine.

It was within the context of modern anti-Semitism and the scapegoat theory that political institutions and parties included anti-Semitism in their platforms and justified their anti-Judaic sentiments.

Adolf Stoecker was the first political leader to exploit anti-Semitism as a political instrument to mobilize the masses in Germany.[184] He initially tried to attract workers around his Christian Socialist Workers' Party by raising the issues of Christian moral values and reconciliation between state and workers in 1878. However, when he failed in this endeavor, in order to attract the lower middle class, he founded the "anti-Semitic students' movement" in 1881. Stoecker was eventually elected to the German Reichstag, and his victory corresponded with the First International Anti-Jewish

---

[182] Ibid., 17.

[183] H. Arendt, *Anti-Semitism: Part One of the Origins of Totalitarianism* (New York: Harvest Books, 1968), 49.

[184] *Encyclopedia Judaica*, "Anti-Semitic Political Parties and Organizations," CD-ROM, 1997, Judaica Multimedia.

Congress that convened in Dresden in 1882. More than three thousand delegates from Germany, Austria, Hungary, and Russia participated in this convention.

In 1883, Otto Boeckel, known as the "Hessian King of Peasants," founded his Anti-Semitic People's Party and, along with three of his followers, was elected to the Reichstag in 1890. Boeckel owed his victory to the peasants in Hessian province who invariably hated the nobility and Jews: they hated the nobility that owned too much land and they disliked Jews upon whose credit the peasants depended.[185]

Adopting anti-Semitism as a political instrument was not confined to the conservative parties. Indeed, liberal and sometimes even left-wing parties of this period found anti-Semitism quite effective in mobilizing the masses. For instance, the German Liberal Party that represented the lower middle classes and was headed by Georg Ritter Von Schoenerer, by attacking the Rothschild's financial conglomerate, achieved a tremendous popularity and succeeded in mustering large student movements. In fact, he, more than others, influenced young Adolf Hitler in his future endeavors.[186] According to Arendt, the political activities of the anti-Semitic parties characteristically were not limited to one country. In other words, in spite of their nationalist slogans, they extended their activities all over Europe; that is, from the very beginning, they aimed at an ambitious goal of an inter-European upheaval.[187]

In France, Catholicism was widely supported by the lower and lower middle classes, and Freemasonry was initially used as a scapegoat. However, the political parties soon learned that anti-Semitic slogans were remarkably more powerful in mobilizing the masses. Even the socialists who were influenced by the teachings of Fourier (1772–1837) and Proudhon (1809–1865), the French philosopher and the socialist, adopted the image of the Rothschilds as the icon of financial capitalism, and they simply confused anti-Semitism with the struggle against capitalism. This confusion has

---

[185] H. Arendt, *Anti-Semitism: Part One of the Origins of Totalitarianism* (New York: Harvest Books, 1968), 38.
[186] *Encyclopedia Judaica*, "Anti-Semitic Political Parties and Organizations," CD-ROM, 1997, Judaica Multimedia.
[187] H. Arendt, *Anti-Semitism: Part One of the Origins of Totalitarianism* (New York: Harvest Books, 1968), 39.

been vividly presented in the work of Cesare Lombroso on anti-Semitism: "The small shopkeeper needs credit, and we know how badly organized and how expensive credit is these days. Here too the small merchant places the responsibility on the Jewish banker. All the way down to the worker—*i.e.* only those workers who have no clear notion of scientific socialism—everybody thinks the revolution is being advanced if the general expropriation of capitalists is preceded by the expropriation of Jewish capitalists, who are the most typical and whose names are most familiar to masses."[188]

Subsequent to the introduction of modern anti-Semitism, Jews were no longer blamed merely as the Christ killers or the people who had distinguished themselves by a different belief system and religious rituals; rather, they were viewed as the impetus behind the world's economy and were therefore responsible for all social and political troubles.

State Anti-Semitism and the Persecution of Eastern European Jews

In the mid-nineteenth century, the world Jewish population was about 4.5 million, 72 per cent of them living in Eastern Europe. In contrast to Germany, where the Jews worked exclusively in usury and finance, in Eastern Europe they were involved in a variety of occupations. These opportunities to a great extent were possible through a special arrangement between the Jewish communities and kings, dukes, and nobilities.[189] These Jewish communities, called kehillas, were typically managed by several wealthy and influential members of the community known as kahals. Kehillas usually entered into a contract directly with the king or nobility, according to which they were allowed to participate in certain occupations and enjoy security in exchange for an annual sum of money. The governing body of the community directly dealt with the king or had close legal relations with his agent, and usually bypassed the usual administrative hierarchy. Outside this special arrangement, these communities were

---

[188] C. Lombroso, *Anti-Semitism in Light of the Modern Science* (1894), quoted in H. Arendt, *Anti-Semitism: Part One of the Origins of Totalitarianism* (New York: Harvest Books, 1968), 48.

[189] E. Barnavi, *A Historical Atlas of the Jewish People* (New York: Schocken Books, 1992), 134.

self-sufficient units that were totally alien to the surrounding gentile world.

The managerial council of the Jewish communities by and large supervised the slaughterhouse, oversaw the operation of the synagogue and school, and collected taxes from the members of the community. The council also functioned as a judicial system enforcing the laws and articles of the Talmud as a supreme legislation.

In addition, because of their extensive experience in finance and tax collection, the king and nobilities often called upon the Jews to manage their properties and collect revenues and taxes. This provoked the antagonistic attitude of Christian peasants against the Jews.[190] The peasants, being unhappy about their working conditions, could not articulate their anger against the king and nobility, but they could easily express it against the Jews. In essence, the peasants perceived the Jews as the agents of the king and nobility who imposed the hard working conditions upon them. They also perceived the Jews as those who were taking away what the peasants had produced through their hard work. For this reason, most peasant uprisings in Eastern Europe often had anti-Jewish elements, sometimes ending with the massacre of Jews.[191] The massacre of Jews as part of the peasantry movement under the leadership of Chemielnicki between 1648 and 1649 in the Ukraine and Poland is only one example of the atrocities perpetuated upon the Jews. The massacres came to an end after Chemielnicki was paid a large sum of money. Another atrocity was the peasant uprisings in 1734, 1750, and again in 1768 known as the Haidamacks Rebellion. These movements, which were supported by the Russian Cossacks, commenced under the banner of "death to the landowners and Jews" and left many thousands of Jews dead in Russia and Poland.[192]

The special charter between kings, nobilities, and Jews were often influenced by social and political circumstances. Sometimes

---

[190] B. Avishai, *The Tragedy of Zionism: How its Revolutionary Past Haunts Israel Democracy* (New York, Helios Press, 2002), 16.
[191] E. Barnavi, *A Historical Atlas of the Jewish People* (New York: Schocken Books, 1992), 154.
[192] S. M. Dubnow, *History of the Jews in Russia and Poland* (South Brunswick, NJ: T. Yoseloff, 1967), 1: 182–186.

kings declined to enter into contracts with Jewish communities or cancelled their agreements and denied the protection of Jews in order to restore the public trust in the government. For instance, in 1698, Peter the Great, in response to Jews' request for migration to Russia, said, "I know Russians and Jews well. In my opinion, it is not the time for the two peoples to conjoin. I am certain that Jews shall serve Russia vastly, but I do not think it would be appropriate for them to become neighbors."[193] In the aftermath of the French Revolution and the rise of nation-states in Europe, efforts to turn Jews into ordinary citizens and abolish the special arrangement between the nobilities and Jews did not succeed, and the untenable social position of Eastern European Jewry extended well into the early twentieth century.

It was not only the Christian lower middle class that often expressed their social and economical dissatisfaction by attacking Jews, but it was also the states that often took advantage of the weak and indefensible status of the Jews as well. By promoting anti-Semitism, states either cashed in on Jews or tried to divert the attention of the Christian lower middle class away from the social and economic problems of the country. Over twelve hundred new legislations were passed against Russian Jews between 1649 and 1881, almost half of them during the reign of Tsar Nicolas I (1825–1855),[194] when the country was on a most dire economic and social course. Based upon these legislations, the Jews were deprived of land ownership and liquor sales, and their sales taxes were twice as much as Christians'. During this same period, conscription of twelve-year-old boys was enforced, and these young Jews were sent to distant locations to keep them away from the Jewish culture. According to the conscription law of 1827, ten out of one thousand of the Jewish population had to serve in the military for thirty-two years, whereas the figures for non-Jews were seven out of one thousand for twenty-five years.[195]

In order to divert the people's attention away from social and economic difficulties, Eastern European states often allowed, and at times supported, the periodic assault and destruction of the Jewish quarters. The Russian term "pogrom," meaning storm, was first

---

[193] Ibid., 246.
[194] *Encyclopedia Americana*, 16: 81, 1979.
[195] Ibid.

applied to the destruction of the Jewish quarters and the massacre of Jews in Odessa in 1871. The following two stories illustrate the role of state anti-Semitism in these events.

In the process of these pogroms, the state was not only the provocateur but also behaved as a silent bystander while looting, destruction, and killings were going on. Moreover, the state, by issuing edicts known as "May Laws," frequently urged Jews in the thousands to be expelled from large cities to small towns. [196]

State anti-Semitism outraged many responsible individuals of that period, among them Leo Tolstoy, the famous Russian writer. He blatantly condemned the Russian government because of its role and lack of accountability in one of the massacres that occurred in Kishinev in 1903. He wrote of the "burning feeling of pity for the innocent victims of the cruelty of the populace, amazement of the bestiality of all these so-called Christians, revulsion at all these so-called cultured people who instigated the mob and sympathized with its actions. But I felt a particular horror for the principal culprit, our Government with its clergy, which fosters in the people bestial sentiments and fanaticism, with its horde of murderous officials. The crime committed at Kishinev is nothing but a direct consequence of that propaganda of falsehood and violence which is conducted by the Russian government with such energy. ... Like the Turkish Government at the time of the Armenian massacres, it remains entirely indifferent to the most horrible acts of cruelty, as long as these acts do not affect its interests." [197]

State anti-Semitism was the most important factor in the migration of Eastern European Jewry to the United States. In a period of less than forty years, between 1890 and World War I, more than two million Russian and Polish Jews migrated to America.

Anti-Semitism and American White Supremacy

A belief in the superiority of the white race over other ethnic groups is the essence of the concept known as white supremacy. Joseph-Arthur Comte de Gobineau (1816–1882), French diplomat

---

[196] H. Fast, *The Jews: Story of a People* (New York: Dell, 1968), 284.
[197] Ibid., 331.

and social philosopher, was probably one of the pioneers of the theory of white supremacy. In his famous work titled *Essay on the Inequality of Human Races,* he strongly argued that the Aryan or white race was superior to all other races. Later, Houston Stewart Chamberlain (1855–1927), an Anglo-German writer, advanced the concept of "racial purity" and proclaimed superiority of the German people as the descendants of the superior Aryan stock.

The concept of white supremacy, which had a longer history in Europe,[198] for all practical purposes surfaced in the latter part of the nineteenth century in the United States, concurrent with the great migration of Eastern European Jews. In addition to the scattered small migrations of Sephardic Jews through the second half of the seventeenth century, mainly from Central and South America, there was a large-scale migration of German Ashkenazi Jews to America around 1840. Nonetheless, for a number of reasons, neither the early small migrations nor this large wave of migration of Jews to the United States triggered significant anti-Semitic sentiments. Religious heterogeneity, diversity of the ethnic strains in the colonies, and the principle of separation of state and religion, as was reflected in the First Amendment of the U.S. Constitution, were among the important factors.[199] However, following the persecutions and massacres of Eastern European Jews in 1880, another large wave of migration to the United States took place. Consequently, the Jewish population of the United States, which was about a quarter million in 1880, increased to three million within forty years. The fast growth of the Jewish population was exclusively due to the migration of Jews of Eastern European origin. Eastern European Jews, in contrast to German Ashkenazi Jews, were less sophisticated in their lifestyle and social behavior, their culture and religion had remained unchanged from the medieval period, and the Enlightenment had barely influenced them. Nevertheless, the large-scale resettlement of Eastern European Jews in the United States within a short period was instrumental in reviving anti-Semitism in the country. While one of every six Jews in America had an Eastern European background in 1880, the ratio changed dramatically to five out of six in 1920.

---

[198] G. M. Fredrickson, *White Supremacy: A Comparative Study in American and South African History* (New York: Oxford University Press, 1981), 100.
[199] J. A. Garraty and P. Gay, *The Columbia History of the World* (New York: Harper & Row, 1972), 673.

Therefore, it was not surprising that the Ku Klux Klan,[200] as the most visible white supremacy organization in America, reentered the political arena and demanded restrictions on immigration in 1915.

The Ku Klux Klan and other white supremacy organizations generally pursued the doctrine of the British Israelites known as the *racist theology of identity,* which in essence restored the scapegoat theory. British Israelites believed that Anglo-Saxons and their ethnic folks throughout the world were the true descendants of the lost ten tribes of Israel.[201] This proclamation, which surfaced in the mid-Victorian era in seventeenth-century England, was the foundation upon which the white supremacy movements advanced a biblical justification for their anti-Semitic activities. They believed in the biblical account of the messianic mission of Israel and in the political-spiritual task of the "chosen people." But they viewed white Anglo-Saxon Protestants as the "true Israelites,"[202] whereas colored people and Jews were satanic forces. According to the racist theology of identity, God's first creation produced Jews and colored people, the descendants of a union between Eve and the serpent. In their opinion, Adam, a white man, was the product of a second creation.[203] They also envisioned that God's law must be established on earth through an inevitable apocalyptical great war, Armageddon, between the white "true Israelites" and all the satanic forces. The racist theology of identity also maintains that America was the "new Jerusalem," after its architect, Richard Brothers (1757–1824).[204]

Influenced by the racial theology of identity, the Klan and other white supremacy movements only acknowledge the first ten

---

[200]The Ku Klux Klan was founded by six former Confederate Army officers in 1865, following the American Civil War in the South. The membership of the organization was open to native-born, white, Protestant males, sixteen years or older. Roman Catholics, blacks, and Jews were excluded from membership and were often the targets of persecution by the Klan. The Klan generally viewed all non-Protestants and liberals as aliens and the trade unionists as subversives. The Ku Klux Klan reached its peak of popularity in the 1920s with a membership of over three million.

[201] *Jewishencyclopedia.com,* "Anglo-Israelism."

[202] Christian identity churches, by carrying names like Church of Christ in Israel, Church of Israel, Church of True Israel, Israel Bible Society, Mission to Israel, Old Order Israelites, Virginia Christian Israelites, Christian Israel Church, and Wisconsin Church of Israel, usually identify their members as true Israelites.

[203] *Klanwatch Intelligence Report* (Southern Poverty Law Center, 1995), 79: 3.

[204] *Encyclopedia Judaica,* "Brothers, Richard," CD-ROM edition, 1997, Judaica Multimedia.

amendments of the U.S. Constitution and the Articles of Confederation. In their opinion, the Fourteenth Amendment, according to which the right of citizenship is extended to all people born or naturalized in the United States, is illegal, and the government is illegitimate and de facto since 1868, when it ratified this amendment.[205]

Moreover, within the context of their theology, identity followers viewed Jews as satanic forces who were the source of the entire world's evil, quite similar to the scapegoat concept, previously discussed in more detail under Anti-Semitism as a Political Instrument, above.

Therefore, it was not unexpected that in the aftermath of the Communist revolution, the Klan accused the Jews of being the agents of international Bolshevism.[206] Along the same lines, fearful of the extension of revolution to the West, Mitchell Palmer, the attorney general of the United States in 1919 and 1920, warned against the "Red scare," declaring that over sixty thousand Trotskyites had infiltrated the political parties in America. In one publication, his supporters alleged that (1) the leadership of the Bolshevik Party, except Lenin, were all Jews, (2) out of 388 members of the Petrograd Council, only 16 were non-Jews, and (3) the tsar's government was in fact overthrown by a group of New York Jews,[207] among them the millionaire Jacob Henry Schiff.[208] As a result of this anti-Semitic propaganda, the Congress of the United States passed three legislations within a period of four years, all aimed at imposing restrictions on minorities entering the United States: in 1917 the

---

[205] *Klanwatch Intelligence Report* (Southern Poverty Law Center, 1995), 79: 4.

[206] E. Barnavi, *A Historical Atlas of the Jewish People* (New York: Schocken Books, 1992), 218.

[207] P. Johnson, *A History of the Jews* (New York: HarperPerennial, 1987), 459.

[208] Jacob Henry Schiff (1847–1920) migrated to America at age eighteen and eventually was named the head of the Kuhn and Loeb financial institution in 1885. He was essentially involved in advancing floating loans to the government at home and to foreign nations. His most spectacular and controversial endeavor was a bond issue of $200,000,000 for Japan at the time of the Russo-Japanese War in 1904–1905. Schiff was deeply angered by the anti-Semitic policies of the czarist regime in Russia; hence, he was delighted to support the Japanese war effort against Russia. He consistently refused to participate in loans on behalf of Russia, and used his influence to prevent other firms from underwriting Russian loans. Schiff strongly opposed Zionism and rejected the movement as a secular, nationalistic perversion of the Jewish faith that, in his opinion, was incompatible with American citizenship.

Espionage Act, in 1918 the Sedition Act (both associated aliens with treason), and in 1921 the Quota Act, restricting the number of immigrants to the United States.[209] By 1924, after fifteen years of debate, Congress came to the conclusion that Jews, Slavs, Italians, Greeks, and other non-Aryans were corrupting American racial stock,[210] and for all practical purposes the Jewish migration to America virtually ended.[211] It was within this political atmosphere that prominent universities like Harvard and Columbia adopted quota policies to restrict the admission of Jewish students to their medical schools.[212] There was a widespread banning of Jewish employment in industry as well, and job announcements often included the statement "Gentiles Only."[213]

Anti-Jewish sentiments continued to grow through World War II. A *Fortune* magazine poll in April 1939, at the onset of war, found that 94 percent of Americans disapproved of the Nazis' treatment of Jews, yet 83 percent opposed lowering immigration quotas.[214] And President Franklin Roosevelt, influenced by public opinion, postponed any action against Nazi atrocities until January 1944.

By the beginning of 1945, the attitude toward the Jews drastically changed. In 1950, only 5 percent of Americans viewed Jews as a threat compared to 24 percent in 1944, and the percentage of Americans who believed Jews had too much power dropped from 67 percent in 1944 to 17 percent in 1962.[215] This radical change of attitude toward Jews was due to a number of factors. First, by the end of the war and in the aftermath of the allied triumph, there was general sympathy for Jewish suffering. Second, the booming economy that transpired in the decade after the war curtailed anti-Semitic activities to a great extent. Third, the birth of the state of Israel was instrumental in wiping out the old stereotypical image of

---

[209] P. Johnson, *A History of the Jews* (New York: HarperPerennial, 1987), 460.
[210] J. J. Goldberg, *Jewish Power: Inside the American Jewish Establishment* (Reading, MA: Addison-Wesley, 1996), 110–111.
[211] Ibid., 104.
[212] Ibid., 112.
[213] Ibid.
[214] Ibid.
[215] Ibid., 117.

Jews[216] and helped their acceptance in the gentile world. Last, but probably the most significant factor, was the concerted efforts of organized American Jewry in eliminating discrimination immediately after the end of World War II. In a crusade to fight discrimination over a broad range of issues, Jewish organizations mobilized media and academia to discredit prejudice in any form or shape. They entered into civil rights movements, antiwar groups, and feminist societies. Postwar Jewish organizations enjoyed a high degree of open-mindedness, and obliged themselves to fight discrimination wherever it occurred and help whoever was the victim. Organized American Jewry, in a coalition with other liberal social institutions such as the National Association for the Advancement of Colored People (NAACP) and the American Civil Liberties Union (ACLU), through many legal struggles, achieved great results.[217] Equal housing opportunities, legislation against job discrimination, and the abolition of school prayer were among their prime achievements. The prominent Jewish organizations of this period, like other liberal social institutions, viewed school prayer as an "establishment of religion," which in their opinion violated the First Amendment of the U.S. Constitution. Therefore, they made an unyielding effort to convince the U.S. Supreme Court to rule that the "union of government and religion tends to destroy government and to degrade religion," as transpired in June of 1962.[218] In this manner, the active role of postwar American Jewry, in collaboration with other democratic institutions, brought the social revolution for religious equality to a final triumph.

During the past two decades, white supremacy, in both the United States and Europe, has revamped its ideological composition to attract the young, particularly those of the lower middle class. These organizations often communicate with youth through rock music and the Internet.[219] A number of economic and social factors have been instrumental in these organizations becoming popular with the young lower middle class in recent years in the United States: (1)

---

[216] P. Rosenwasser, "Historical U.S. Anti-Semitism," in Reframing Anti-Semitism: Alternative Jewish Perspective (Oakland, CA: Jewish Voice for Peace, 2004), 59.
[217] J. J. Goldberg, Jewish Power: Inside the American Jewish Establishment (Reading, MA: Addison-Wesley, 1996), 122–123.
[218] Ibid., 124.
[219] Reconstructing Nazis (Southern Poverty Law Center Intelligence Report, 1999), 96: 21.

income inequality is at its historic peak,[220] (2) there is rising child poverty in young families,[221] (3) there is growing unemployment among the uneducated,[222] and (4) America's white majority is dissipating.[223]

Subtle Forms of Anti-Semitism

Hatred and enmity against Jews is often subtle. Restrained anti-Semitic activities are generally allegations focused upon two principal themes: (1) overstating Jewish wealth and introducing Jews as the sole representatives of financial capitalism who control the world economy and (2) exaggeration of the role of Jews in the state apparatus.

Overstating Jewish Wealth and Introducing Jews as the Sole Representatives of Financial Capitalism Who Control the World Economy: As was discussed in more detail in this chapter, in a period from the early seventeenth century to the latter part of the nineteenth century, coinciding with the development of capitalism in the nation-states, the call for capital invited the services of Jewish court bankers. European monarchies preferred to confer certain privileges on small groups of well-to-do Jews in order to take advantage of their expertise in finance and banking. The exclusive position of the house of Rothschild, a family of bankers, with close ties to the French, the Austrian, and the British governments, was sufficient to further reinforce the fanatic concept that the Jews controlled world finance. According to Hannah Arendt, "The popular notion that the Jews, in contrast to other people, were fastened

---

[220] Congressional Budget Office data indicate that within twenty-two years, from 1977 to 1999, the average income of the lowest 20 percent of the population has declined, while the average income of the upper 20 percent has increased by 50 percent in the same period.

[221] Data from the Center for Labor Market show that the percentage of minor children in poverty has doubled in twenty-one years, from 1973 to 1994.

[222] Data from the U.S. Bureau of Labor Statistics reveal that in an interval of twenty-six years, from 1970 to 1996, the youth jobless rate has increased by almost 50 percent among high school dropouts, and the real wages of young workers have declined 21.7 percent in the same period.

[223] Whites constituted 72.1 percent of the population in 1999. The U.S. Census Bureau projects that whites will make up only 52.8 percent of the population by the year 2050.

together by the supposedly closer bonds of blood and family ties was to a large extent stimulated by the reality of this one family, which virtually represented the whole economic and political significance of the Jewish people."[224] However, toward the end of the nineteenth century, along with the rise of imperialism in Europe, the nation-states gradually fell, and countries were now able to run their finance and business without the Jewish backing. Indeed, the Jews were neither the major buyers nor sellers of the workforce in capitalist production,[225] and the Jewish wealth played an insignificant role in this period.[226] A study in 1939 in fact revealed that only 0.6 percent of ninety-three thousand bankers in the United States were Jews.[227] Another survey in 1970 found 1 Jew among 377 high banking executives.[228] It is noteworthy to mention that the Jewish finance and banking influence has further declined at an accelerating rate since World War II.[229] Moreover, wealthy Jews have always formed a small group when compared to those of Christian nobles and merchants. For instance, in the United States, Catholics own about 50 percent, Protestants 43 percent, and Jews less than 7 percent of the total assessed value of possessions.[230] A more recent survey found that the top 20 percent of the U.S. population, which includes the ruling class, are primarily white and Christian.[231] Finally, one must remember that capital, by its nature and regardless of the capitalist's religious affiliation, is always after profit. A Jew, like a Christian or a Muslim, invests in order to make a profit; they will not and cannot invest merely to satisfy their or their coreligionist's belief system. Therefore, an overstatement of Jewish wealth or exaggeration of their role in the world economy only confuses an issue that is not based on strong data but is a subtle reference to the scapegoat theory. In general, Jews, like

---

[224] H. Arendt, *Anti-Semitism: Part One of the Origins of Totalitarianism* (New York: Harvest Books, 1968), 27–28.

[225] Ibid., 34.

[226] Ibid., 15.

[227] *Encyclopedia Judaica*, "Banking and Bankers," CD-ROM edition, 1997, Judaica Multimedia.

[228] P. Rosenwasser, *"Historical U.S. Anti-Semitism" in Reframing Anti-Semitism: Alternative Jewish Perspectives* (Oakland, CA.: Jewish Voice for Peace, 2004), 62.

[229] *Jewishencyclopedia.com*, "Banking."

[230] J. K. Conrad, *The Pillars of Religion* (Brighton, CO: Adams Press, 1978), 143.

[231] P. Rosenwasser, *"Historical U.S. Anti-Semitism" in Reframing Anti-Semitism: Alternative Jewish Perspectives* (Oakland, CA: Jewish Voice for Peace, 2004), 64.

Episcopalians and Presbyterians, belong to the upper income brackets in the United States.[232] Urban living traditions, their attraction to certain lines of occupation, their intellectual achievements, and their social success as a minority have played a role in the creation of an illusion that Jews have monopolized the economy and politics.

Exaggeration of the Role of Jews in the State Apparatus: Through the Middle Ages, aside from the court Jews who served periodically both in Islamic and Christian states, the role of Jews as legislators and men of power has generally been scanty. The allegation that Jews are the real forces behind state power in essence seems to be a white supremacy invention.[233] Many white supremacy groups believe that Jews are secretly running the U.S. government, hence labeling it a "Zionist-occupied government." In fact, the hate groups in America and Europe, instead of blaming the multinational corporations for their excesses, intentionally condemn Jews for an unproven conspiracy, simply because it is easier to pick on a historical scapegoat.[234]

In general, the voting power of the Jews, as a mechanism to influence a state, is negligible.[235] Except for the state of Israel, the Jews constitute distinct minorities elsewhere. Besides, in many parts of the world, a parliamentary mode of government is only a façade, and even the voting power of the majority is blatantly ignored. In Western countries and the United States, where people's votes are acknowledged, Jews usually have some impact in local elections. In the United States, there are only a few congressional districts that have a constituency of over 1 percent Jewish population, and in only twelve states Jews make up more than 3 percent of the population.[236] Therefore, the Jewish vote has a modest impact on the U.S. presidential election only when the race is extremely close.[237] The voting power of Jews in parliamentary elections in Europe is no more

---

[232] D. J. Bogue, *The Population of the United States: Historical Trends and Future Projections* (New York: Free Press, 1985), 659.

[233] R. Blazak, *Youth and Hate* (Southern Poverty Law Center Intelligence Report, 1999), 96: 24.

[234] Ibid., 25.

[235] J. J. Goldberg, *Jewish Power: Inside the American Jewish Establishment* (Reading, MA: Addison-Wesley, 1996), 32.

[236] P. Findley, *They Dare to Speak Out* (Chicago: Lawrence Hill Books, 1985), 323.

[237] Ibid.

impressive. Nonetheless, Jews have often used their wealth and influence in past decades to gain parliamentary support on the issues of their concern as an ethnic group.[238] This is not only to support the campaign fund for those who are pro-Israel, but also to defeat the lawmakers who might have crossed a certain line regarding Israel.[239] Professor Organski, a political scientist, has argued that the support of the U.S. Congress for Israel is more ideological than economic.[240] In his opinion, this special relation is not merely because of Jewish money but more because of Israel's democratic image, Arab unpopularity, and Christian sympathy for the Holy Land. He further argues that American Jewish leaders, the state of Israel, U.S. policymakers, and opponents of Israel, each for different reasons, like to exaggerate the impact of the pro-Israel lobby.[241] In fact, the Jewish component of pro-Israeli lobby, when compared with those of Christian Zionists and large corporations, is negligible.[242]

However, the supporters of these two viewpoints often allude to their own anecdotal experience or unsubstantiated stories, rather than scientific data, to justify their positions on Jewish wealth and power. Nonetheless, Jews are overrepresented among writers, producers, publishers, and editors. In fact, over one-quarter of this "elite media" in United States are Jews, making the public media, television and newspapers, the stronghold of Jewish power.[243] Jews conceivably exercise their influence in the society through this avenue. This assumption is probably credible in spite of the claims that most Jews in entertainment and the news media are "apostate Jews,"[244] meaning they are more businesspeople than they are Jews. In other words, they are more interested in their professional success than they care for their faith. Conversely, we must not overlook the impact of those Jews in the media who have courageously presented

---

[238] J. J. Goldberg, *Jewish Power: Inside the American Jewish Establishment* (Reading, MA: Addison-Wesley, 1996), 266.

[239] Ibid., 269.

[240] Ibid., 267.

[241] A.F.K. Organski, *$36 Billion Bargain*, reviewed by D. Pipes at danielpipes.org/article/604.

[242] M. Plitnick, *Myth and Reality: Jewish Influence on US Middle East*, Jewish Voice for Peace June Newsletter, 2005

[243] J. J. Goldberg, *Jewish Power: Inside the American Jewish Establishment* (Reading, MA: Addison-Wesley, 1996), 280.

[244] Ibid., 281.

the stories of social wrongdoing, injustice, and discrimination in our system of government.[245]

Finally, one must keep in mind that in every community, both the achievements and shortcomings of the minorities are more likely to come into the spotlight than those of the majority and Jews are no exception to this general rule.

Chronology:

624 CE	The prophet Muhammad changed Kiblah from Jerusalem to Mecca
628	The last Jewish opposition to Muhammad in Khyber was defeated.
632	Prophet Muhammad raised the issue of poll tax or jizya
1346	Black plague in Europe
1348	The first allegation of "well poisoning"
1517	Martin Luther posted his famous ninety-five theses at the entrance to the university church
1564	John Calvin died
1648	Peasantry movement of Chemielnicki in Ukraine and Poland
1864	Maurice Joly published the satire of Napoleon III under the title of *Dialogue between Machiavelli and Montesquieu in Hell*
1871	Massacre of Jews in Odessa
1879	Wilhelm Marr introduced the term "anti-Semitism"
1881	Adolf Stoecker established the anti-Semitic students' movement
1882	The First International Anti-Jewish Congress convened in Dresden, Germany
1883	Otto Boeckel founded his anti-Semitic People's Party
1897	The source document of the *Protocols of the Learned Elders of Zion* was forged by Tsarist Russian police
1903	Massacre of Jews in Kishinev
1905	Sergei Nilus published the *Protocols of the*

---

[245] Ibid., 282.

	Learned Elders of Zion.
1915	Ku Klux Klan demanded restriction on immigration
1917	U.S. Congress passed the Espionage Act
1918	Congress passed the Sedition Act
1919	Mitchell Palmer, attorney general of the United States, warned against "Red scare"
1921	Philip Graves searched the source of the *Protocols*
1921	Congress passed the Quota Act
1924	Jewish immigration to the United States ended

Chapter Seven

JEWS IN MODERN TIME

J ews entered the twentieth century with aspirations and fear. They had every reason to be hopeful that the world of the gentiles, having gone through the Protestant Reformation, having experienced the Age of Enlightenment, having struggled through the French Revolution, and having achieved the Declaration of the Rights of Man, would treat Jews like all other citizens. On the other hand, having gone through a turbulent history, Jews also feared that the values of Western civilization might fail to protect them. Nevertheless, Jews embraced the twentieth century to meet a number of grave challenges.

Zionism

Through the centuries of the Diaspora, the desire and aspiration for returning to the original homeland was embedded not only in the fabric of Judaism but also in the collective conscience of the Jewish communities. Indeed, the concept of redemption in Judaism was bundled together with the messianic vision and the return to Zion.[1] The Jews, as late as the eighteenth century, believed

---

[1] Zion is the name of a stronghold in Jerusalem that was captured by King David. In the Maccabean period, Mount Zion was identified by the Temple of Jerusalem.

that the coming of the Messiah and the return to Jerusalem were essential prerequisites for the Jewish redemption.[2] And the desire for a return to Zion or the homeland was usually enhanced when the intensity of the Jewish persecutions were increased. The cultural or religious Zionism that probably dates back to the Babylonian captivity in the sixth century BCE once again was defeated in the failed uprising of Simon Bar Kokhba in 135 CE and resurfaced in the messianic movement of Sabbatai Zevi in 1626.

In contrast to cultural Zionism, political Zionism is a modern development of the late nineteenth century. Nathan Birnbaum, the Austrian philosopher, first used the term "Zionism" in 1893 for a movement to establish a national homeland for Jews. The political Zionist movement was similar to other national movements of nineteenth-century Europe, but it lacked the two preconditions of national identity, namely a unified language and sovereign borders.[3] In contrast, European nation-states of that period had both their national territory and unified language while they were striving for political independence.

The development and growth of political Zionism were due to two prominent social forces of emancipation and modern anti-Semitism that interacted in the historic juncture of the late nineteenth century.

The first force was the emancipation of Jews and the Enlightenment movement of Haskalah, which produced an intellectual stratum of Jews who came to realize that Jews must take their fate into their own hands. This was a concept in sharp contrast with the traditional Talmudic teachings of the messianic vision. As a result of this new vision and understanding, the many-centuries-old messianic dictum that invited Jews to show patience for the arrival of the Messiah was either set aside or was reinterpreted to invite the masses of Jews to participate in a struggle for the establishment of a homeland.

In this manner, the issue of a national identity as a solution to the Jewish question came into the spotlight. Therefore, without Jewish emancipation and the growth of the intellectual Jewish

---

[2] Y. Leibowitz, *Judaism, Human Values, and the Jewish State* (Cambridge, MA: Harvard University Press, 1992), 125.
[3] A. Hertzberg, *The Zionist Idea* (Philadelphia: Jewish Publication Society, 1997), 15.

movements, the rise of political Zionism was inconceivable.[4] In other words, the traditional medieval Talmudic teachings could not envision the concept of self-emancipation, which was the cornerstone of political Zionism.

The doctrine of self-emancipation in the form of a movement to establish a Jewish homeland was due to the efforts and contributions of many intellectuals.

Moses Hess pictured Jews as a distinct race in his 1862 book titled *Rome and Jerusalem.* He wrote, "Reform, conversion, education, and emancipation—none of these open the gates of society to the German Jew; hence his desire to deny his racial origin. . . . [A]nd the tendency of some Jews to deny their racial descent is equally foredoomed to failure. Jewish noses cannot be reformed, and the black, wavy hair of the Jews will not be changed into blond by conversion or straightened out by constant combing. The Jewish race is one of the primary races of mankind, and it has retained its integrity despite the influence of changing climatic environments."[5] In another passage he proposed, "[B]ut despite enlightenment and emancipation, the Jew in exile who denies his nationality will never earn the respect of the nations among whom he dwells. He may become a naturalized citizen, but he will never be able to convince the gentiles of his total separation from his own nationality."[6]

In his opinion, the Jewish question cannot be addressed in the absence of a sovereign border or a Jewish state. His viewpoint was distinctly different from those of the disciples of the Jewish assimilation who were suggesting a conscious surrender of Jews to the values of the majority in exchange for civil rights in the modern world. As Arthur Hertzberg puts it, the doctrine of assimilation in essence recommended, "Let the Jew become like everybody else, yielding up his claim to chosenness and being relieved of his role as scapegoat. Let society run on its universal and immutable principles, rooted in reason and natural law, which know neither positive nor negative exceptions for the Jew."[7] The doctrine of assimilation also

---

[4] H. Arendt, *Anti-Semitism: Part One of the Origins of Totalitarianism* (New York: Harvest Books, 1968), 56.
[5] A. Hertzberg, *The Zionist Idea* (Philadelphia: Jewish Publication Society, 1997), 121.
[6] Ibid.
[7] Ibid., 27.

sharply contrasted the viewpoints expressed by Karl Marx and the Haskalah on the Jewish question.

Along the same lines, Leo Pinsker, who was probably the first Zionist theoretician, in an 1881 pamphlet titled *Auto-Emancipation,* wrote, "[T]hey [Jews] are everywhere foreigners and nowhere hosts in their own national rights; they are in economic competition with every majority within which they live. To hope for better days in Russia or wherever else the Jews were under serious attack, was, therefore, a delusion, and piecemeal emigration to a variety of underdeveloped lands which might be hospitable for a moment meant merely to export and exacerbate the problem. There was only one workable solution: the Jews must organize all their strength and, with whatever help they could muster from the world as a whole, they must find a country of their own where the bulk of Jewry would at last come to rest."[8] In his opinion, Jews cannot trust the cultural achievements of mankind to safeguard their rights as citizens.

Theodore Herzl (1860–1904), the decisive and central figure in the history of Zionism, was an Austrian journalist. Like most Jewish intellectuals of his time, he was most impressed by the cultural triumph of Europe and viewed the Jewish assimilation in these achievements inevitable. In a critique to the work of Edouard Drumont (1844–1917), the French author whose writings had violent anti-Semitic sentiments, he viewed the anti-Semitism merely as an instrument in the hands of the state to divert the revolutionary rage of the masses. However, it was after the Dreyfus affair that he changed his position and viewed the Jewish question as a national issue. Herzl, after the intellectuals of his generation, deployed a dialectical approach in analyzing anti-Semitism. In his opinion, the *thesis* was anti-Semitism, omnipresent and disturbing to public order; the *antithesis* was the world of liberal nationalism that could not ignore the disruptive role of anti-Semitism forever and could not force Jews back into the ghettoes again. Therefore, the inevitable *synthesis* of the two, in his opinion, must lead to Zionism.[9] On the basis of his analysis, he proposed, in his 1896 book *Jewish State*, that European governments should be appealed to for support. However, Herzl's Jewish state was not welcomed by the Ottoman Empire. British

---

[8] Ibid., 43.
[9] A. Hertzberg, *The Zionist Idea* (Philadelphia: Jewish Publication Society, 1997), 50.

government, on the other hand, suggested part of Uganda as a new homeland for the Jews in 1903, a proposal that was presented to the first World Zionist Congress and was defeated by the Russian members under the leadership of Chaim Weizmann.

Herzl was distinguished on two principles from the other Zionist theoreticians of his time and most of those who appeared later on. First, he initially opposed and never gave more than a reluctant consent to the efforts of his East European followers to develop Zionist colonization in Palestine.[10] Second, Herzl never envisioned modern Hebrew as the official language of the future state, and regarded that as a semiprivate affair, which certain circles could be permitted to promote with the broad framework of his political nationalism.[11] In essence, through the Zionist movement, he merely envisaged a homeland "for the Jews," solely as a response to the anti-Semitism of the nineteenth century.

The next prominent figure in the Zionist movement was Asher Ginsberg, also known as Ahad Ha'am (1856–1927), who was indeed the most vocal critic of Theodore Herzl. Ha'am, a writer and philosopher, was born in the Ukraine and was the editor of *Ha-Shiloah* between 1896 and 1903, through which he attacked philosophical positions of Herzl on Zionism. In 1917 he participated in the negotiations that eventually resulted in Balfour's declaration. On the rights of Jews in Palestine, Ha'am was a true hardliner. He strongly believed in the revival of Judaism as the prerequisite for the Jewish emancipation, a traditional Judaism that promoted an absolute obedience of the revealed Law, and a patient waiting for the Messiah.[12] In contrast to Herzl, who viewed Zionism as a national movement toward the establishment of a state for the Jews, Ha'am believed in a Jewish state that first met "the need of Judaism."[13] He trusted that the Jewish state would be established only after the past glory of Judaism had been restored and Jews had settled in Palestine. Hence, Ha'am did not refer to Zionism as a response to anti-Semitism in the same way that Theodore Herzl did. In essence, the ideological difference between the two was that Ha'am did not trust the gentile world while Herzl did.

---

[10] Ibid., 74.
[11] Ibid., 49.
[12] Ibid., 64.
[13] Ibid., 51.

Ha'am not only distrusted the gentile world, but he was also suspicious of the Jewish masses. Indeed, he envisioned a utopian Jewish society where "the men of the spirit" were to be admired.[14] Like Plato, he knew he could not trust the masses to elect the philosopher-kings, or in his case, "the men of the spirit." However, he failed to realize that revolutions of the nineteenth century had ended the supremacy of the nobility and the clergy in the European societies, and in turn the traditional Jewish societies had revolted against the old hierarchy of the synagogue. He was also unable to recognize that for the first time in the history of European Jewish societies, an intellectual class was on the rise whose concerns were the Jewish masses, democracy, and nationalism, all of which were in conflict with his vision of the eminent men of spirit.[15] The doctrine of Ha'am, understandably, has been also referred to as "spiritual Zionism."

Some disciples of political Zionism, influenced by the classic Marxism of the early twentieth century, proposed "Labor or Socialist Zionism." Among them was Ber Borochov (1881–1917), who sought the answer to anti-Semitism and the Jewish question in the victory of the proletariat and the institution of a classless society. Borochov illustrated the need for a Jewish state within the popular framework of nineteenth-century dialectical materialism. He wrote that the Jewish upper bourgeoisie, as a part of world capitalism, is not content with the local market and is always after expansion. This class is not concerned with the Jewish question and indeed prefers the assimilation of Jews into the gentile world. In contrast, the Jewish petite bourgeoisie and proletariat, who pursue a more or less common interest, are after a national market with less competition. They have no interest in the world market and are against the assimilation of Jews. Anti-Semitism, according to Borochov, has a class origin resulting from the struggle between the Jewish and non-Jewish petite bourgeoisie and the proletariat. Then he argues that the Jewish masses are in need of their own territory, where they can promote the class struggle. Palestine, because of its limited resources, does not attract the upper segment of the bourgeoisie, but is quite attractive to the Jewish agricultural proletariat. Hence, Jews, by migrating to Palestine, can promote the proletarian class struggle and take a step

---

[14] Ibid., 59.
[15] Ibid., 61.

forward toward socialism.[16] Labor Zionists, in addition to a Jewish state, were concerned over the class structure of the Jews.[17] Aside from the weaknesses of this theory, in this manner, socialist Zionism justified the Jewish nationalism of the early twentieth century. Indeed, it was on the basis of this kind of analysis that agricultural cooperatives or kibbutzim were established in Palestine that served as the cultural, political, and military backbone of the Jewish communities prior to the establishment of the state of Israel.

Another prominent figure is Martin Buber, the Austrian philosopher and theologian, who was born in 1878 in Vienna. He attended universities in Vienna, Zurich, and Berlin and joined the Zionist movement in 1898. In 1901 he became the editor of *Die Welt*, a weekly periodical through which he stressed the need for Jewish cultural creativity. At age twenty-six, Buber became interested in Hasidic philosophy, and in 1909 he actively participated in public affairs. He established a democratic faction within the Zionist movement opposing Theodore Herzl's position on a number of issues. He focused on two fundamental subjects, the *bi-national state* and Hebrew *humanism*, and actively advocated them through his public career. In the Zionist Congress of 1921, he stressed that the movement must also be sensitive to the needs of the Arabs: "[T]he Jewish people proclaims its desire to live in peace and brotherhood with the Arab People and to develop the common homeland into a republic in which both peoples will have the possibility of free development. . . . [I]t is up to us how to impress Arabs, either as a good neighbor or as an invader."[18] As an upshot of his notion, he indeed advocated the establishment of a bi-national Arab-Israel state.[19] After the outbreak of the Arab-Israel war and following World War II, Buber strongly supported the policy of compromise and understanding between the two peoples, and lectured extensively on this subject outside Israel. Moreover, in response to Mahatma Gandhi's proclamation in 1939 that Palestine belongs to the Arabs and that it is therefore wrong and inhuman to impose the Jews on the

---

[16] Ibid., 355–366.

[17] N. G. Finkelstein, *Image and Reality of the Israel-Palestine Conflict* (London: Verso, 2003), 9.

[18] *Encyclopedia Judaica*, "Buber, Martin," CD-ROM edition, 1997, Judaica Multimedia.

[19] M. Buber, "Zionism and 'Zionism,'" in A. Shatz, *Prophets Outcast* (New York: Nation Books, 2004), 58.

Arabs, Buber wrote, "Here I must add. . . [b]y a genuine peace we inferred and still infer that both people together should develop the land without the one imposing its will on the other."[20] Buber also believed in the idea of "Hebrew Humanism" in place of Jewish nationalism.[21] In this regard he wrote, "By opposing Hebrew humanism to a nationalism which is nothing but empty self-assertion, I wish to indicate that, at this juncture, the Zionist movement must decide either for national egoism or national humanism. If it decides in favor of national egoism, it too will suffer the fate, which will soon befall all shallow nationalism. . . . Israel is not a nation like other nations, no matter how much its representatives have wished it during certain eras."[22] Nonetheless, the concept of Hebrew humanism is the theological interpretation of Buber from the "Jewish chosenness," suggesting that Jews, beyond forming a national unity among them, have responsibilities toward humanity.

The second factor that transformed political Zionism from the realm of a philosophical discussion to a history-making movement was modern anti-Semitism, which reached its climax through the Dreyfus affair in 1895.[23]

Alfred Dreyfus, the sole Jewish officer in the French Army, was accused and convicted of espionage for Germany in 1894. Three years later, evidence was submitted in favor of Dreyfus's innocence and the introduction of Major Walsin-Esterhazy as the guilty party. In 1899, the Court of Appeal reduced the sentence to ten years, and a week later the French president pardoned him. In 1903, Dreyfus requested a new revision trial that was refused until 1906, when Georges-Benjamin Clemaenceau (1841–1929) became prime minister. The Court of Appeal annulled all the charges and acquitted Dreyfus. In 1908, nine years after the presidential pardon and two years after the clearance of Dreyfus by the Court of Appeal, he was attacked at the burial ceremony of the French writer, Émile Zola. The Court acquitted the attacker and released him. In the aftermath of this event, anti-Jewish groups under the leadership of Jules Guerin, the

---

[20] A. Hertzberg, *The Zionist Idea* (Philadelphia: Jewish Publication Society, 1997), 463.

[21] Ibid., 457.

[22] Ibid, 459.

[23] A. Hertzberg, *The Zionist Idea* (Philadelphia: Jewish Publication Society, 1997), 40.

founder of Ligue Antisemite, an anti-Semitic organization, poured into the streets in most of the large French cities, shouting "Death to the Jews." Guerin was the strongest figure in the upheaval against Dreyfus and was supported by two members of the aristocracy: the Duke of Orleans and the Marquis de Mores were supporting him. Every public gathering of Dreyfus's supporters, shored up by liberals and intellectuals, was violently disrupted by Guerin's followers. In these events, the army and church were on the side of the anti-Dreyfus camp. Among Guerin's supporters was a man named Max Regis, who suggested to a cheering crowd in Paris that they "water the tree of freedom with the blood of the Jews."[24] The magnitude of the mob activity was not new, but according to Arendt, exercising these activities under the banner of freedom, France, and patriotism seemed quite unprecedented.[25]

The Dreyfus affair had a prominent impact on the political and social atmosphere in France. These events boosted the popularity of the Third French Republic that came to power in 1889. On the other hand, as a result of the Dreyfus affair, the influence of the army and Church was curtailed. And eventually in 1905, the principle of separation of Church and state for the first time was established in France.[26]

However, consequent to the Dreyfus affair, many Jews arrived at two painful conclusions. First, Jews, even those in prominent social positions like Alfred Dreyfus, lacked civil rights.[27] Second, the social and cultural values of the West, even in a progressive country such as France, are not trustworthy and could not maintain the rights of Jewish citizens. These conclusions were exactly what the Zionist supporters were anxious to hear, and indeed played a key role in the triumph of political Zionism. About the time of the close of the Dreyfus case, Hannah Arendt wrote, "The only visible result was that it gave birth to the Zionist movement—the only political answer Jews have ever found to anti-Semitism and the only

---

[24] H. Arendt, *Anti-Semitism: Part One of the Origins of Totalitarianism* (New York: Harvest Books, 1968), 111.
[25] Ibid., 112.
[26] *Encyclopedia Encarta*, "Dreyfus Affair," CD-ROM edition, 2000, Microsoft Corporation.
[27] H. Arendt, *Anti-Semitism: Part One of the Origins of Totalitarianism* (New York: Harvest Books, 1968), 117.

ideology in which they have ever taken seriously a hostility that would place them in the center of world events."[28]

In essence, the rise of political Zionism was the product of an exchange between two different visions for achieving a single solution toward modern anti-Semitism. The first vision, influenced by the economic, social, and cultural achievements of the West, insisted upon the toleration of Jews more than ever. Therefore, to defeat modern anti-Semitism, social, cultural, and economical exchange between Jews and non-Jews must be promoted and expanded. This viewpoint, which was mainly expressed by Western European Jews, particularly their intellectual strata, also submitted to a symbolic reinterpretation of the messianic promise. The coming of the Messiah was then signified by an age of individual freedom, national liberty, and social and economic justice.[29]

The second perspective subscribed to national identity as the sole remedy to modern anti-Semitism, a viewpoint that was widely supported by the Eastern European Jews. Indeed, two factions could be encountered in this second camp. One faction was relatively more secular and progressive, essentially the followers of Theodore Herzl, and believed in the establishment of "a state for Jews," or for those Jews who were in need of it. This group, historically, maintained a more liberal attitude toward the geographic boundary of the state and did not even stress an official state language.[30] The other group, influenced by the doctrine of Ahad Ha'am, believed in "a state for Judaism" but not merely for the Jews. They strongly believed that Judaism, more than Jews, was in need of being saved.[31] In their viewpoint, the establishment of a Jewish state, revival of the traditional culture, and recapturing of the land of Israel, with the boundaries spelled out in the covenant between God and Abraham,[32] were the prerequisites and only the first step for the coming of the Messiah. It was in this sequence, in their opinion, that anti-Semitism could be eradicated. Nevertheless, the struggle between these two opposing schools of thought is a characteristic of the Zionist

---

[28] Ibid., 120.

[29] A. Hertzberg, *The Zionist Idea* (Philadelphia: Jewish Publication Society, 1997), 18.

[30] Ibid., 49.

[31] N. G. Finkelstein, *Image and Reality of the Israel-Palestine Conflict* (London: Verso, 2003), 9.

[32] Ezekiel 33:24; Genesis 17:8.

movement of the past century, before and after the establishment of the modern state of Israel.

Zionism, in essence, commenced as a revolutionary movement against anti-Semitism, traditional rabbinical authority, and against Medieval Jewish yielding characters.[33] Opponents, however, have criticized Zionism as a tribal doctrine that viewed Jews as a single nation regardless of the circumstances under which they lived and erroneously they assumed Jews always remained alien where they lived.[34] Zionists exaggerated on a 'uniform bond' among Jewish people and ignored the rivalries among Orthodox, Reform, Conservative and Secular Jews,[35] and above all dismissed the class struggle in the Jewish communities.[36]   Others have pointed to a contradiction within the Zionist ideology wherein it tries hard to bring Jews to the level of other nations and yet it separates them from other nations,[37] hence arming the anti-Semites with the theoretical weapons they dream of.[38]

The Communist Movement and the Jewish Question

Before the French Revolution, the Jews undoubtedly enjoyed very little in terms of civil rights. Here and there, usually after victory in wars, governments expressed their appreciation to Jewish bankers and usurers for their support, but for all practical purposes, civil rights did not apply to Jewish communities. Many theoreticians of the social democracy movement of the nineteenth and twentieth centuries viewed the denial of civil rights and seasonal persecutions of Jews from different angles and advanced various remedies to what has been collectively known as the "Jewish question."

In order to understand the subject clearly, one must review not only the viewpoints of Karl Marx and other pioneers of the social

---

[33] B. Avishai, *The Tragedy of Zionism: How its Revolutionary Past Haunts Israel Democracy* (New York, Helios Press, 2002), xvi

[34] H. Draper, *Zionism, Israel and the Arabs* (Berkeley, CA: Center for Socialist History, 1997), 106.

[35] B. Avishai, *The Tragedy of Zionism: How its Revolutionary Past Haunts Israel Democracy* (New York, Helios Press, 2002), 25.

[36] Ibid., 231.

[37] D. B. Ruderman, *Jewish Intellectual History: 16th to 20th Century* (Chantilly, VA: Teaching Company, 2002), Part 2.

[38] A. Leon, "Zionism," in A. Shatz, *Prophets Outcast* (New York: Nation Books, 2004), 116.

democracy movement but also the reaction of Jews toward the left movement, and the attitude and performance of the communist movement toward Jews in general.

The position of Karl Marx on the Jewish question can be found in a critique he wrote of an article by Bruno Bauer, German Hegelian philosopher of the nineteenth century, on the subject in February 1844.

Bauer took the position that

[t]he Jews of Germany want emancipation. What sort of emancipation do they want? . . . No one in Germany is politically emancipated. We ourselves are not free. How shall we emancipate you? You Jews are *egoists* if you demand a special emancipation for yourselves as Jews. You should work as Germans for the political emancipation of Germany and as men for the emancipation of mankind. . . . The *Christian* state knows only *privileges*. In it the Jew has the privilege of being Jew. As a Jew he has rights that Christians do not have. Why does he want rights which he does not have and which Christians enjoy? If the Jew wants to be emancipated from the Christian state, then he is demanding that the Christian state abandon its religious prejudice. But does the Jew abandon his religious prejudice? Has he then the right to demand this rejection of religion from another?[39]

Bauer continues:

The Christian state by its very nature cannot emancipate the Jew. . . . Jew by his nature cannot be emancipated. So long as the state remains Christian and the Jew Jewish, both remain equally incapable of either giving or receiving emancipation.[40]

Marx argues,

On the one hand, Bauer demands that the Jew give up Judaism and that man generally give up religion so that he might be emancipated *as a citizen*. On the other hand, Bauer regards the political abolition of religion as logically implying the abolition of religion altogether. The state that presupposes religion is not yet a true, a real state. 'To be sure religious conceptions reinforce the state. But which state? What kind of state?' At this point the one-sidedness of Bauer's formulation of the

---

[39] F. Kamenka, *The Portable Karl Marx* (New York: Penguin Books, 1983), 96.
[40] Ibid., 97.

Jewish question becomes apparent. It is by no means sufficient to ask: Who is to emancipate? Who is to be emancipated? Criticism has yet a third task. It must ask: *What kind of emancipation* is involved? ... Because Bauer does not raise the question to this level he falls into contradictions.[41]

Marx proceeds:

The Jewish question presents itself in different ways according to the state in which the Jew finds himself. In Germany, where there is no political state, no state as state, the Jewish question is a purely *theological* question. The Jew finds himself in *religious* opposition to a state that acknowledges Christianity as its foundation. The state is theologian by profession. Here, critique is critique of theology, a double-edged critique, critique of Christian theology and of Jewish theology. ... In France, in a *constitutional* state, the Jewish question is the question of constitutionalism, the question of the *incompleteness of political emancipation.* Here the *semblance* of a state religion is preserved, even if only in an empty and self-contradictory formula, in the formula of *the religion of the majority* and the relation of the Jew to the state therefore also retains the *semblance* of a religious or theological contradiction. ... Only in the free states of North America— or at least in some of them—does the Jewish question lose its *theological* significance and become a truly *secular* question. The critique of this relationship ceases to be theological as soon as the state abandons a *theological* posture toward religion. ... [T]hen critique becomes the *critique of the political state.* In the United States there is neither a state religion, nor a religion officially declared to be that of the majority nor a pre-eminence of one form of worship over another. The state is stranger to all forms of worship. ... [T]here are even some North American states where the constitution imposes no form of religious faith and no specific religious practice as a precondition for political rights. Yet people in the United States do not believe that a man professing no religion can be an honest man."[42]

In another passage, Marx continues:

We do not convert secular questions into theological ones. We convert theological questions into secular ones. History has been resolved into superstitions long enough; we can now resolve superstition

---

[41] Ibid., 97–98.
[42] Ibid., 99.

into history. For us the question of the *relation between political emancipation and religion* becomes the question of the *relation between political emancipation and human emancipation.* ... Political emancipation of the Jew, of the Christian, of the religious man generally is the emancipation of the state from Judaism, from Christianity, from religion in general. ... The Jewish question then, is finally reducible to a secular conflict, to the relationship between the political state and its presuppositions, whether these presuppositions be material elements such as private property, or spiritual elements such as education and religion. ... Man emancipates himself from religion politically by banishing it from the sphere of public law into that of private right.[43]

Marx, therefore, does not join Bauer in saying to the Jews that they cannot politically emancipate until they emancipate themselves from Judaism. He rather writes that they can be emancipated politically without renouncing Judaism. Jews can be politically emancipated, earn their civil rights, and remain Jews. This is exactly what Bruno Bauer, by focusing his discussion on the religious state of Germany, denies. In his opinion, emancipation from religion is not a prerequisite of achieving political emancipation. Moreover, in contrast to most theoreticians of the Second and Third International communist movements, Marx does not postpone the political emancipation of the Jews to a successful class struggle and realization of the "classless society" of the future.

Rosa Luxemburg, in contrast to Marx, believed the political emancipation of Jews inevitably had to be postponed until the victory of the proletariat in the class struggle. She was born into a Jewish family in Poland in 1871 and raised at the time of a historic juncture when the "Jew was the slave of the lowest of the low"[44] and Jewish masses were caged in ghettoes and restricted by special laws. She eventually achieved an eminent position in the leadership of the Spartacus League, or the German Socialist party. Luxemburg viewed anti-Semitism as an attribute of the capitalist mode of production that Yonkers in Germany and the tsars in Russia were the real benefactors of.[45] This viewpoint gives the impression that anti-Semitism is an

---

[43] Ibid., 100–104.

[44] P. Frolich, *Rosa Luxemburg: Her Life and Work* (New York: Monthly Review Press, 1972), 1.

[45] H. Arendt, *Anti-Semitism: Part One of the Origins of Totalitarianism* (New York: Harvest Books, 1968), 48.

exclusive feature of capitalism and did not exist in the earlier periods, which was not the case. Moreover, by undervaluing the role of the cultural and political factors on the Jewish question, and focusing exclusively on the class struggle and the capitalist mode of production, where Jews were neither the major providers nor buyers of the workforce,[46] she did not take anti-Semitism seriously. Along these lines she wrote, "Why do you come with your special Jewish sorrows? I feel just as sorry for the wretched Indian victims in Putumayo, the Negroes in Africa. . . . I cannot find a special corner in my heart for the ghetto."[47] Alternatively, her intense focus on human needs enticed her to see anti-Semitism only as a part of humanity's suffering.

On the Jewish question, Lenin in 1903 wrote, "National Jewish identity is a reactionary effort that is promoted not only by the Zionists but also some of social democrats. Jewish nationalism is in conflict with the interest of the Jewish proletariat and directly as well as indirectly hampers the assimilation of the Jews into the community of the non-Jews. This movement solely promotes the spirit of ghetto among the Jews. The slogan of the Jewish national culture in fact is supported by the Jewish capitalists and clergy and is in contrast with the proletarian concern."[48] In his opinion, those who are against the assimilation of the Jews in the community of non-Jews are uncultured nationalists.[49] Aside from his stand against Jewish national identity, Lenin also analyzed the Jewish question in the context of the class struggle and the proletarian interest. Yet in practice, he took a solid position against anti-Semitism, and on July 27, 1918, ordered the Workers, Peasants and Soldiers Commissariat to kill anti-Semitism in any form or shape on the spot.[50]

Nahman Syrkin (1867–1924), the Russian writer and thinker, tried very hard for some form of reconciliation between Jewish political emancipation, class struggle, and Zionism. Like Rosa Luxemburg and Lenin, he assessed the Jewish emancipation within

---

[46] Ibid., 34.

[47] Letter to Mathilde Wurm, 16 February 1917, quoted in P. Johnson, *A History of the Jews* (New York: HarperPerennial, 1987), 449.

[48] V. I. Lenin, *Critical Remarks on the National Question* (*Collected Works*, 1913), 7: 100 ff.

[49] V. I. Lenin, "The Position of the Bund in the Party," *Iskara*, October 22 (1903).

[50] P. Johnson, *A History of the Jews* (New York: HarperPerennial, 1987), 452.

the context of class struggle, but in contrast to Lenin, he viewed Zionism as a solution to the Jewish question. In this regard, he wrote,

> A classless society and national sovereignty are the only means of solving the Jewish problem completely. The social revolution and cessation of the class struggle will also normalize the relationship of the Jew and his environment. The Jew must, therefore, join the ranks of the proletariat, the only element which is striving to make an end of the class struggle and to redistribute power on the basis of justice. The Jew has been the torchbearer of liberalism which emancipated him as part of its war against the old society; today, after the liberal bourgeoisie has betrayed its principles and has compromised with those classes whose power rests on force, the Jew must become the vanguard of socialism.[51] . . . The assimilated bourgeoisie turned away from Judaism because the Jewish people was weak and there was no economic advantage in being a Jew.[52] . . . Socialism will do away with wars, tariffs, and the conflict of economic interests among civilized peoples; it will eliminate the possibility of the oppression of one nation by another, and it will increase commercial and cultural intercourse, this creating a common base of interests and purposes among the civilized nations. This will pave the way for the uniting of their separate histories, which will weld them into one humanity.[53] . . . Nonetheless, the enemy has always considered the Jews a nation, and they have always known themselves as such. Though they were robbed of all external national characteristics—being dispersed, speaking all languages and jargons, possessing no national property or creative national forces—they were a distinct nation whose very existence was sufficient reason for its being.[54] . . . Zionism is a real phenomenon of Jewish life. It has its roots in the economic and social positions of the Jews, in their moral protest, in the idealistic striving to give a better content to their miserable life. It is borne by the active, creative forces of Jewish life. Only cowards and spiritual degenerates will term Zionism a utopian movement.[55]

A number of contradictions are striking in Syrkin's analysis. While he subscribed to socialism as an international movement, in contrast to Lenin's viewpoint, he endorsed a national movement such

---

[51] A. Hertzberg, *The Zionist Idea* (Philadelphia: Jewish Publication Society, 1997), 340.
[52] Ibid., 341.
[53] Ibid., 342.
[54] Ibid., 343.
[55] Ibid., 347.

as Zionism as the solution to the Jewish question. However, he did not foresee the Palestinian Nationalism as a future obstacle to the Zionist movement.[56] He also, for reasons not clear, attributed the assimilation of Jews into the community of non-Jews to the bourgeoisie, and, naturally, fighting against assimilation for him became a class struggle against the liberal bourgeoisie. Finally, like others, his prescription for the political emancipation of the Jews was postponed to the time of the proletarian victory and the establishment of a classless society.

Leon Trotsky, like Lenin and Luxemburg, believed the Jews had a negligible impact on the class struggle and the Jewish question could have only been resolved in the aftermath of a proletarian victory.[57] He once said that neither Judaism nor anti-Semitism had any influence in his conviction to activism. He did not view Zionism as the remedy to the Jewish question when in 1937 he said, "[T]he conflict between the Jews and Arabs in Palestine acquires a more and more tragic and more and more menacing character."[58] Many, however, have blamed Trotsky for his indifference toward Judaism, and some have identified him with the violence and evil behavior of Bolshevism. Finally, some have grumbled that Trotsky, being born in a Jewish family and attaining a prominent position in the Bolshevik party, gave an excuse to the adversaries to hold Jews responsible for the October Revolution.[59]

Nevertheless, Jews proportionately more than other peoples became attracted to Marxism. It has been said that the biblical and Talmudic traditions of social criticism, and the viable Jewish sense of injustice, were instrumental in drawing Jews to the left of the political spectrum and to the Marxism of the nineteenth century.[60] Undoubtedly, the pledge of social justice and provisions to support the rights of the ethnic and religious minorities in the Marxian doctrine must have played important roles. It was in this regard that in 1901, Leon Blum (1872–1950), the French statesman, wrote, "The collective impulse of the Jews leads them toward revolution; their

---

[56] B. Avishai, *The Tragedy of Zionism: How its Revolutionary Past Haunts Israel Democracy* (New York, Helios Press, 2002),74.
[57] L. Trotsky, "On the Jewish Problem," in A. Shatz, *Prophets Outcast* (New York: Nation Books, 2004), 106.
[58] Ibid., 101.
[59] P. Johnson, *A History of the Jews* (New York: HarperPerennial, 1987), 451.
[60] Ibid., 354–355.

critical powers drive them to destroy every idea, every traditional form which does not agree with the facts or can not be justified by reason. . . . In the long, sorrowful history of the Jews, the idea of inevitable justice, the belief that the world would be one day ordered according to reason, one rule prevail over all men, so that everyone gets their due. Is that not the spirit of socialism?"[61] In addition to the keen interest of the Jews to participate in varieties of left organizations on an individual basis, the establishment of the Bund, a political and social organization of Jews, was yet another indication of their enthusiasm for achieving social justice. The Federation of the Jewish workers of Lithuania, Poland, and Russia, or the Bund, was a socialist party that was established in 1897. This organization was in fact a continuation of the clandestine activities of the Russian Jewish workers in the 1880s. The Bund was not only a political party, but also a labor union that was actively engaged in improving the working conditions and expanding the social and political knowledge of the Jewish masses. In the 1890s, Tsarist police banned the Bund organization, and many of its leaders were severely punished. However, the political and social influence of the Bund significantly increased after the defeat of the Russian Revolution in 1905 and when similar parties were established in Rumania, England, and the United States. In the aftermath of the October Revolution in 1917, the Bund was melted into the Soviet Communist party, but the Polish establishments of the organization continued its independent activities until 1947.

As a political party, the Bund more or less followed the generic doctrine of the Communist parties of the late nineteenth and early twentieth centuries of Europe. However, as a Jewish organization, the Bund was adamantly against the concept of Jewish national identity, and discouraged activities around that subject. It was then considered a natural enemy of Zionism. Nonetheless, the Bund actively promoted the German-Jewish Yiddish culture.

Based upon what has been said so far, it was not surprising that a quarter of the leadership of the Bolshevik party was Jews. This was an issue that the media affiliated with the political parties of the right did not shy away from to use against the Jews in the first half of the twentieth century.

---

[61] Ibid., 458.

The social and political institutions of the left movement had quite complicated attitudes and reactions toward Jews. The principal goal of these organizations, as we have encountered in the past, were to advance the production forces in order to achieve socialism. The petite bourgeoisie, within this ideological framework, were considered an impediment, and therefore must have been eliminated. Although anti-Semitism was not in the platform of any of these political organizations, political parties and the so-called socialist states that came to power in the first half of the twentieth century justified discrimination against Jews and persecuted them under the banner that they represented strata of the petite bourgeoisie. It is, however, noteworthy that the bitterness of the left movement toward the petite bourgeoisie was not confined to Jews and, during the reign of Stalin, included millions of non-Jews as well.

During the Soviet civil war that lasted from 1918 to 1921, the Bolsheviks' adversaries utilized the forged document of the *Protocols of the Elders of Zion* and massacred many Russian Jews. The White Army under the leadership of Anton Denikin organized numerous pogroms in more than 160 Jewish communities in the Ukraine alone, resulting in the mass annihilation of over a hundred thousand Jews. It is said that the communists did not counteract these atrocities in the manner that they were expected to.[62]

In contrast to the Marxian analysis of the Jewish question, the Soviet Communist party viewed the Jewish communities as the stronghold of the petite bourgeoisie and therefore stereotyped them as being "nonproductive." Subsequently, separate agricultural collectives were established for the Jews, and they were transferred from the western parts of the country to the central regions. Concurrently, a Jewish section, the Yevsektsiya, was founded within the Communist party that supposedly must have been unaffiliated to religion. The Jewish section of the Communist party, in spite of its very Jewish image, was only an instrument to enforce the dictatorship of the proletariat among the Jewish masses. Furthermore, contrary to the Marxian position on the Jewish question that explicitly proposed banishing religion from the sphere of public law into that of private right, all Jewish religious institutions were closed and Hebrew publications banned in August 1919. Finally, toward the end of 1920,

---

[62] E. Barnavi, *A Historical Atlas of the Jewish People* (New York: Schocken Books, 1992), 214.

the administrations of the Jewish communities were transferred to the Soviet secret police. These oppressive policies were not only aimed at Jewish religious institutions or communities, but they also extended to any social activity that had a Jewish flavor, including the Bund organization. At the time of dissolution of the Socialist Bund party in 1919, in spite of its past social and political achievements, Plekhanov sarcastically commented that they were "Zionists who suffered from seasickness," referring to the exodus of Israel from Egypt and crossing the Red Sea.[63] Finally, in order to make the Jews "productive," a Jewish Autonomous Region was established in Birobidzhan near the Chinese border in 1927, and until 1949 more than four hundred thousand Jews were moved into these working camps.

The irrefutable power of Stalin after April 1922 only added to these atrocities. The discrimination and intimidation of Jews even extended into the Communist party committees and gatherings. These behaviors were so widespread that on March 4, 1926, Trotsky furiously questioned Bukharin about why he should have tolerated the anti-Semitic activities within the party in Moscow.[64] These activities not only were ignored in the Communist party, but also Jews proportionally paid a bigger share of loss. In 1937 and 1938, thousands of Jews were labeled as the agents of "imperialism and reaction" and purged from the Communist party.

In the meantime, once again the *Protocols of the Elders of Zion* came into the spotlight in the aftermath of the October Revolution in the West. This time, the Jewish Bolsheviks were feared as the new rulers of the world and were introduced as *the causes of world unrest.*[65] In essence, many anti-Bolshevik elements in the Western media swiftly subscribed to the content of the Protocols and became anti-Semites overnight. As an example, the *London Times,* in an article titled "Jews and Bolshevism" on November 27, 1919, said, "The essence of Judaism. . . is above all a racial pride, a belief in their superiority, faith in their final victory, the conviction that the Jewish brain is superior to the Christian brain, in short, an attitude corresponding to the innate conviction that the Jews are the chosen

---

[63] Ibid.
[64] I. Deutscher, *The Prophet Unarmed: Trotsky 1921–1929* (Oxford: 1965), 258, quoted in P. Johnson, *A History of the Jews* (New York: HarperPerennial, 1987), 454.
[65] P. Johnson, *A History of the Jews* (New York: HarperPerennial, 1987), 456.

people, fated to become one day the rulers and legislators of mankind."[66] It was ironic that two years later, in August of 1921, it was *The Times* that revealed that the *Protocols* was a forgery.

Therefore, at the outset of World War II, Jews were in an extremely awkward position. Outside the Soviet sphere of influence, they were accused of being "Bolshevik elements," and inside the Socialist camp, they were blamed as "the agents of Imperialism and reaction."

National Socialism, the Holocaust, and the Jews

The economic prosperity of Europe came to an end with a major crisis in 1929. Influenced by this crisis, not only the world economy fell, but also Western civilization and its values were questioned. Young and fragile democracies collapsed and military dictatorships came to power. It was in this social and political milieu that the National Socialist party, on January 31, 1933, slipped into power in Germany.

The annihilation of the Jews was the agenda of the government of the Third Reich from very beginning and was not an accidental event at this historic juncture.[67] When Hitler came to power, the German banks were exclusively in the hands of Jews, and German Jewry was declining rapidly in the eye of the public. In other words, Jews had wealth without having public function. It was in this social environment that the Nazis could introduce Jews simply as "social parasites" and blame them for all social evils.

This vision of history is obviously contradicting the viewpoint of those who believe that the extermination of Jews was organized and carried out by professionals of the Third Reich who did not represent a typical cross section of German society. The fact that Nazis, and on top of it Adolph Hitler, found the idea of Jewish annihilation an attractive one was only one side of the coin. The other and probably more important side was the milieu under which masses found the theory dazzling and could be mobilized around it.

The intellectual roots of the Third Reich can be explored in the scholarly works of philosophers like Johann Gottlieb Fichte,

---

[66] Ibid., 457.
[67] H. Arendt, *Anti-Semitism: Part One of the Origins of Totalitarianism* (New York: Harvest Books, 1968), 3.

Frederick Hegel, Frederick Nietzsche, and statesmen such as Joseph-Arthur Gobineau and Houston Stewart Chamberlain. Though the Nazis embraced these philosophical viewpoints on issues such as power, government, and morality, by no means must it be thought that these intellectuals all had anti-Semitic sentiments. In order to envision the cultural and political institutions of the Nazis, one must put these viewpoints together.

Hegel glorifies the state as supreme in human life. In his opinion, the state is all that matters and world history is no empire of happiness, and in fact, "[t]he periods of happiness are empty pages of history because they are the periods of agreement without conflict." Or, war is the greatest purifier, "the ethical health of peoples corrupted by a long peace, as the blowing of the winds preserves the sea from the foulness which would be the result of a prolonged calm."[68]

Nietzsche wrote, "Society has never regarded virtue as anything else than as a means to strength, power and order. . . . Society is not entitled to exist for its own sake but only as a substructure and scaffolding, by means of which a select race of beings may elevate themselves to their higher duties. . . . There is no such thing as the right to live, the right to work, or the right to be happy: in this respect man is no different from the meanest worm."[69] Nietzsche's viewpoint on war appeared in his famous work *Thus Spake Zarathustra*, in an Old Testament language style: "Ye shall love peace as a means to new war, and the short peace more than the long. You I advise not to work, but to fight. You, I advise not to peace but to victory. . . . Ye say it is the good cause which halloweth even war? I say unto you: it is the good war which halloweth every cause. War and courage have done more great things than charity."[70]

In his famous work *Essai sur l'Inegalite des Races Humaines*, Joseph-Arthur Gobineau expressed his viewpoint on the human races. He wrote, "The racial question suffices to explain the whole unfolding of the destiny of peoples. . . . History shows that all civilization flows from the white race that no civilization can exist without the cooperation of this race. . . . The Aryan German is a

---

[68] W. L. Shirer, *The Rise and Fall of the Third Reich* (New York: Simon & Schuster, 1959), 98.
[69] Ibid., 100.
[70] Ibid.

powerful creature. Everything he thinks, says and does is thus of major importance."[71]

Houston Stewart Chamberlain, the author of *Foundations of the Nineteenth Century*, the work that fascinated many Nazis thinkers, believed Greek philosophy and art, Roman law, and the personality of Christ were the three items that shaped the nineteenth century. In the framework of his thinking, there were also three successors to this foundation, Teutons or ancient Germanic tribes and Jews, as two pure races, and half-breed Latins of the Mediterranean. He wrote, "True history begins at the moment when the Teuton, with his masterful hand, lays his grip upon the legacy of antiquity."[72] Nonetheless, his ideas of "racial purity" significantly influenced the racist theory of Hitler.

On the subject of hatred for Jews, the founder of Protestantism, Martin Luther, contributed greatly in the sixteenth century. He was a prominent anti-Semite and believed in the absolute obedience of political authorities, a blend that was quite palatable to the Nazi taste. It was his desire that Germany get rid of Jews. He recommended that Jews should be deprived from "all their cash and jewels and silver and gold . . . and their synagogues or schools be set on fire, that their houses be broken up and destroyed . . . and they be put under a roof or stable, like gypsies, . . . in misery and captivity as they incessantly lament and complain to God about us."[73] In addition to Luther, many German writers wrote on this subject. Nietzsche, certainly not an anti-Semite,[74] believed that Christians, as much as Jews, were responsible for the slave morality prevalent in the world.[75] Fichte, the chair of philosophy at Berlin University, believed that the Latins, especially the French and the Jews, were the decadent races. Houston Chamberlain wrote, "Whoever claimed that Jesus was a Jew is either being stupid or telling a lie. . . . Jesus was not a Jew."[76] He believed Christ was an Aryan, and he wished he was a member of the Teutons. At one point in his career, Chamberlain contradicted himself, forgot about his previous claim on the racial purity of the

---

[71] Ibid., 104.

[72] Ibid., 106.

[73] Ibid., 236.

[74] B. Russell, *A History of Western Philosophy* (New York: Touchstone, 1972), 764.

[75] W. L. Shirer, *The Rise and Fall of the Third Reich* (New York: Simon & Schuster, 1959), 99.

[76] Ibid., 107.

Jews, and condemned the Aryans for giving the Jews "a halo of false glory." To Hitler, the Jews were not German.

The very first effort of the Third Reich was to arrive at a definition of "Jew". In Nazi doctrine those who had three Jewish grandparents were considered full-Jew, regardless of whether or not they practiced Judaism or were a member of a synagogue congregation. In this framework, those who had married a Jew or were related to the Jewish community were considered half-Jew or *Mischlinge*.[77] According to these definitions, "Jewishness" was not viewed as a belief system or a religion but as a race, biologically predetermined. Jews, in the doctrine of the Nazis, did not belong to the Aryan stock, and therefore they were inferior. Nonetheless, behind these definitions a horrifying plan for Jews was in progress.

By the time of the rise of the Third Reich, Jews gradually lost their social and civil rights as German citizens. Nazis issued laws excluding Jews from public service, the universities, the professions, and on April 1, 1933, they proclaimed a national boycott of Jewish shops.[78] As a protest to this proclamation, the German Jewish newspaper *Judische Rundschau* invited Jews to wear the yellow patch with pride. On September 15, 1935, the Nazis passed what is known as the Nuremberg Race Laws,[79] according to which Jews were completely deprived of their rights as German citizens. It was after this date that the German government officially relinquished its responsibility to protect Jews within German territory.

On November 7, 1938, a seventeen-year-old Jew assassinated the third secretary of the German embassy in Paris. In the aftermath of this event, and as revenge, the German government organized and carried out a huge pogrom on the nights of November 9 and 10, known as Kristallnacht or the Night of Broken Glass. In preparation for the pogrom, Reinhard Heydrich, the man in charge of the Secret

---

[77] B. Engelmann, *Germany without Jews* (New York: Bantam Books, 1984), 291.

[78] W. L. Shirer, *The Rise and Fall of the Third Reich* (New York: Simon & Schuster, 1959), 203.

[79] The Nuremberg laws "for the protection of German blood and German honor" and "for the protection of the genetic health of German people" prohibited marriage and sexual relations between Jews and German citizens. Jews were also barred from employing Aryan women, forty-five years or younger, as household help. According to the Nuremberg laws, German Jews lost their basic civil rights and their status was reduced to that of "subjects."

Service and the Gestapo, instructed the heads of police departments in the following manner:

   a. Only such measures should be taken which do not involve danger to German life or property. (For instance synagogues are to be burned down only when there is no danger of fire to the surroundings.)

   b. Business and private apartments of Jews may be destroyed but not looted.

   c. The demonstrations which are going to take place should not be hindered by the police.

   d. As many Jews, especially rich ones, are to be arrested as can be accommodated in the existing prisons. ... Upon their arrest, the appropriate concentration camps should be contacted immediately, in order to confine them in these camps as soon as possible.[80]

The pogrom that was organized and carried out by the Third Reich resulted in more than twenty-five million marks worth of damage.[81] Following this event, the properties of the German Jews were confiscated and offered to the "Aryan citizens."

The public reaction to the atrocities against Jews inside Germany has been best presented in the notes of William Shirer. He wrote, "Hitler's sickness was contagious; the nation was catching it, as if it were a virus. Individually, as this writer can testify from personal experience, many Germans were as horrified by the November 9 inferno as were Americans and Englishmen and other foreigners. But neither the leaders of the Christian churches nor the generals nor any other representatives of the 'good' Germany spoke out at once in open protest. They bowed to what General von Fritsch called "the inevitable," or "Germany's destiny."[82] Likewise, an appreciable public protest was not noted; indeed, the Germans acted

---

[80] W. L. Shirer, *The Rise and Fall of the Third Reich* (New York: Simon & Schuster, 1959), 430–431.

[81] Contrary to the position of the German government, insurance companies felt obligated to pay for the losses to Jews; otherwise, they were concerned about losing their clients in Germany and abroad. On the other hand, payments of that magnitude would have brought the insurance industry to the verge of bankruptcy. Goering solved the problem by suggesting that insurance companies pay the Jews for the damage, following which the state would confiscate the sums the Jews had collected, and reimburse the insurance companies.

[82] W. L. Shirer, *The Rise and Fall of the Third Reich* (New York: Simon & Schuster, 1959), 435.

as a nation in the destruction of Jews.[83] The outside world, however, was outraged by the barbarism exercised by a nation that had bragged about its records of respect for humanity and Western cultural values for centuries. Nonetheless, Hitler considered it as an exclusively German affair and wrote off the outside reaction as the "Jewish world conspiracy."

Once Jews were expelled from the German economy, the state must have come up with a plan for the people who had lost their jobs and properties. Therefore, the expulsions of Jews to other countries or what Nazis called "forced emigration," living in ghettoes or forced labor in the concentration camps, were options under consideration.

A plan to ship over four million German Jews to Madagascar, the small island off the southeast coast of Africa, was among the first "solutions" the Nazis were entertaining before 1939.[84] During this early phase, merely as a measure to rid Europe of Jews, the Nazis were pursuing a pro-Zionist policy, calling Zionists the "decent" Jews who were thinking in "national" terms, even showing a willingness to provide them with training camps for the future immigrants.[85] On the other hand, a number of Zionist leaders saw the rise of Hitler to power as a decisive defeat of assimilationism; hence it has been argued that they tried to take advantage of the circumstances to promote the migration of European Jews to Palestine.[86] The lack of time, however, forced the Nazis to drop the Madagascar plan from their agenda.[87]

In 1939, at the beginning of World War II, the German army invaded the western part of Poland and thus gained power over more than two million Jewish inhabitants of these areas. A year later, German S.S. police had managed the forced living of over four hundred thousand Polish Jews in the Warsaw ghetto, in two and one-half miles by one-mile area, surrounded by high walls. The administration of the ghettoes was in general under a council of Jews called the Judenrat, who were appointed by German authorities. The

---

[83] R. Hilberg, *The Politics of Memory: The Journey of a Holocaust Historian* (Chicago: Ivan R. Dee, 1996), 126.
[84] H. Arendt, *Eichmann in Jerusalem: A Report on the Banality of Evil* (New York: Penguin, 1994), 76.
[85] Ibid., 60
[86] Ibid., 59–60
[87] Ibid., 77

general directive for the ghettoes was to exploit the residents to the highest extent with the lowest level of expenditure. Hunger,[88] hard work, dense population, and infectious diseases such as typhus and tuberculosis, on average, eliminated 1 percent of the population each month. In general, the Nazis treated the Polish Jews far worse than the German Jews.

Among the Judenrat, as some historians have argued, were those who consciously cooperated with Nazi authorities and provided them indispensable assistance, usually for personal gain. For instance, it has been contended that some members of the Judenrat had prior knowledge about the destination of the trains to death camps, while masses of Jews were under the impression they were only being resettled in eastern provinces.[89] Hence, they obediently embarked on the trains,[90] particularly when they noticed the encouragement of their coreligionists at the Judenrat's capacity. It has been further argued that the Nazis trusted some Jewish Councils officials to provide them with the lists of Jews, their whereabouts, their properties, and how to secure their funds to defray the expenses of deportation and extermination.[91] The case of Rudolph Kastner, a prominent Zionist leader in Hungary, and his peculiar relations with the high-ranking Nazis is probably the most controversial and tumultuous, among others.[92] On the basis of the fragmentary correspondence collected on

---

[88] Comparison of average weekly food allowance (ounces) during World War II:

	Bread	Meat	Sugar	Fat
Germany	80	17.5	8	9.5
Poland	62	9	5.5	2.25
Jews	14	2.5	1.75	0.9

[89] Ibid., 196.

[90] Ibid., 11.

[91] Ibid., 118.

[92] It has been argued that Dr. Rudolph Kastner, who at one point was the vice president of the Zionist Organization in Budapest, negotiated with German authorities for the immigration of a few thousand Jews, mostly prominent members of the Zionist youth organizations, to Palestine in exchange for ensuring a quiet and orderly transfer of several hundred thousand Hungarian Jews to Auschwitz. It has been claimed that his closeness to the Nazis was so genuine that he could travel freely in Nazi Germany without showing any identification papers. Once the state of Israel was established in 1948, Dr. Kastner participated in the new government as an active member of the Labor Party. In 1953, Malkiel Gruenwald, an Israeli citizen from Jerusalem, accused him of collaboration with the Nazis, which hastened the

the Jewish Councils, it has also been argued that Jewish communities desperately pursued a policy of adjustment toward German brutality.[93] The Jewish tradition of respect for laws and contracts and the trust of authority prompted the Jewish institutions and leadership to follow a policy of accommodation and to refrain from resistance.[94] However, the notion that wherever Jews lacked leadership there were fewer deaths, as expressed by Hannah Arendt,[95] has not been shared by other historians.[96]

In June 1941, when the Nazis attacked the Soviet Union, the German police launched a special force, the Einsatzgruppen, or the German mobile killing units or death squads, to identify and kill Jews and Soviet political activists on the spot in the occupied territories.[97] The Einsatzgruppen usually asked the Jewish leaders to call the Jews together and take their valuables, and then the Einsatzgruppen killed them before the eyes of German soldiers and local residents.[98] These operations continued for months before Western countries acknowledged these atrocities.

In October 1941, Field Marshal von Reichenau proclaimed, "The German soldier is not only versed in the art of war, but is a bearer of a ruthless national ideology, and thus must understand the necessity of a cruel but just revenge against sub-human Jewry."[99] The extermination of Jews, even children, was justified as an act of

---

destruction of the Hungarian Jews. Kastner was tried in 1955 and the court accepted most of Gruenwald's allegations. Benjamin Halevi, a district court judge on the case, expressed the opinion that Rudolph Kastner had "sold his soul to the devil." Kastner was assassinated by a young Israeli man in March 1957. (See H. Arendt, *Eichmann in Jerusalem: A Report on the Banality of Evil*, pages 42 and 199, and *Encyclopedia Judaica*, "Kasztner, Rezso Rudolf," CD-ROM edition.)

[93] R. Hilberg, *The Politics of Memory: The Journey of a Holocaust Historian* (Chicago: Ivan R. Dee, 1996), 132.

[94] Ibid., 126.

[95] H. Arendt, *Eichmann in Jerusalem: A Report on the Banality of Evil* (New York: Penguin, 1994), 125, 166.

[96] R. Hilberg, *The Politics of Memory: The Journey of a Holocaust Historian* (Chicago: Ivan R. Dee, 1996), 150.

[97] H. Arendt, *Eichmann in Jerusalem: A Report on the Banality of Evil* (New York: Penguin, 1994), 95.

[98] Ibid., 91.

[99] E. Barnavi, *A Historical Atlas of the Jewish People* (New York: Schocken Books, 1992), 228.

defense to protect the future generations of Germans.[100] By this time, more than a million European Jews in the areas under German influence had lost their lives. The official policies of the Third Reich was to push European Jews eastbound into Poland and the occupied Soviet territories, work them to death, and kill those who survived these harsh conditions.[101] Men were usually separated from their families and were forced to work in road construction and in heavy industry as slave laborers.[102,103] Those with professional expertise or art talent were treated somehow better. From the Warsaw ghetto alone, over three hundred thousand, or three-quarters of the population, were transferred to the concentration camps. The deportation of Jews to these camps, in spite of their numerous administrative and political difficulties, reached its peak in the summer and autumn of 1942. For instance, many controversial opinions were expressed over the handling of half-Jews, and eventually the state decided against their deportation.[104]

Victims were usually transferred by rail to concentration camps. Initially, German police used to pay the price of third-class one-way tickets to the railroad authorities. Later, however, a charter rate was arranged, and thousands of Jews were forced into each railway wagon. The travel conditions were so harsh that the elderly and sick did not generally reach the destination that was usually unknown to them.

The scheme of the complete extermination of European Jewry, the "final solution," was first raised by Hermann Goering, the number two Nazi, in a letter to Heydrich on July 31, 1941, where he charged Heydrich to make preparations.[105] But the idea was originally Hitler's, who had instructed Himmler verbally[106] and had included it

---

[100] N. G. Finkelstein, *Image and Reality of the Israel-Palestine Conflict* (London: Verso, 2003), 107.

[101] W. L. Shirer, *The Rise and Fall of the Third Reich* (New York: Simon & Schuster, 1959), 966.

[102] G. Palast, *The Best Democracy Money Can Buy* (London: Pluto Press, 2002), 129.

[103] T. Bower, *Nazi Gold: The Full Story of Fifty-year Swiss-Nazi Conspiracy to Steal Billions from Europe's Jews and Holocaust Survivors* (New York: HarperCollins, 1997), 335.

[104] H. Arendt, *Eichmann in Jerusalem: A Report on the Banality of Evil* (New York: Penguin, 1994), 113, 159.

[105] R. Hilberg, *The Politics of Memory: The Journey of a Holocaust Historian* (Chicago: Ivan R. Dee, 1996), 78.

[106] Ibid., 80.

in his speech to the Reichstag on January 30, 1939. On January 20, 1942, when the Nazis had almost every indication that they were the victors in the war, Heydrich reported to an assembly of Nazi officials in Wannsee, a suburb of Berlin, that about eleven million Jews would be absorbed into the final solution.

The Nazis did not have a historic model to follow for the mass killing of this magnitude.[107] Millions of tortured, starved, and enslaved people died in the concentration camps across the territories under German influence, but the extermination camps, the Vernichtungslager, were more efficient mass killing machines of the Third Reich. The first of these was built in 1939 for the purpose of mercy killing of incurably sick people. In fact, in a period between 1939 and 1941, about fifty thousand Germans were killed as a part of the "euthanasia program."[108] This program was abandoned in response to public outcry. However, when the same killing machine was used against the Jews, no public protest was expressed anywhere in Europe.[109] The largest of these extermination camps was Auschwitz, with four huge gas chambers and crematoria. It was here that victims were gassed first and then were cremated in mass scale. It has been estimated that over one and one-half million Jews were exterminated in Auschwitz alone.[110] The Jew-killing industry of the Nazis also included the extermination camps with smaller capacities. In Treblinka, 800,000 were massacred, in Belsec over 600,000, in Sobibor 250,000, and in Chelmno 150,000. The number shot to death was 1,400,000, and over 600,000 died of starvation and disease in camps. In this manner, by the end of World War II, around six million Jews had lost their lives. Different methods have been used to arrive at this figure. Dr. Richard Korherr, the chief statistician to Himmler, who maintained the statistics, reported that 633,300 Jews had been exterminated by March 23, 1943, in Russia alone.[111] The total figure comes from comparing the Jewish population, country by country,

---

[107] Ibid., 84.

[108] H. Arendt, *Eichmann in Jerusalem: A Report on the Banality of Evil* (New York: Penguin, 1994), 108.

[109] Ibid., 109.

[110] E. Barnavi, *A Historical Atlas of the Jewish People* (New York: Schocken Books, 1992), 232.

[111] W. L. Shirer, *The Rise and Fall of the Third Reich* (New York: Simon & Schuster, 1959), 963.

before the war with the population after the war.[112] The figure
presented to the Nuremberg tribunal court, 5,700,000, had been
prepared by the World Jewish Organization. Gerald Reitlinger, who
searched this subject extensively, proposed that the true figure was
between 4,194,000 to 4,581,000.[113] Regardless of which estimate is
closer, the figure is substantial.

European countries did not respond to the final solution
similarly. German allies like Slovakia, Croatia, and the government of
Vichy in France fully complied with the German order for deportation
of the Jews. Indeed, the Vichy government showed a great deal of
enthusiasm on the subject by passing a number of anti-Jewish
legislations earlier.[114] Italy postponed a decision on this matter until

---

[112] Statistics on European Jewry exterminated during World War II: Adapted from E.
Barnavi, *A Historical Atlas of the Jewish People* (New York: Schocken Books,
1992), 233:

Country	Jewish population in 1939	Jewish population after War	Exterminated Jews
Poland	3,250,000	400,000	2,850,000
Soviet Union	3,050,000	1,700,000	1,350,000
Rumania	850,000	425,000	425,000
Germany	504,000	254,000	250,000
Hungary	403,000	203,000	200,000
Czech	380,000	100,000	280,000
France	240,000	120,000	120,000
Austria	175,000	55,000	120,000
Lithuania	155,000	20,000	135,000
Holland	120,000	40,000	80,000
Latvia	95,000	9,000	86,000
Yugoslavia	75,000	15,000	60,000
Greece	75,000	13,000	62,000
Belgium	55,000	25,000	30,000
Italy	57,000	45,000	12,000
Bulgaria	50,000	43,000	7,000
Denmark	6,000	4,000	2,000
Estonia	5,000	1,000	4,000
Luxemburg	3,000	1,000	2,000
Norway	2,000	1,000	1,000
Total	9,550,000	3,474,000	6,076,000

[113] W. L. Shirer, *The Rise and Fall of the Third Reich* (New York: Simon & Schuster,
1959), 978.
[114] H. Arendt, *Eichmann in Jerusalem: A Report on the Banality of Evil* (New York:
Penguin, 1994), 162.

September 1943, at the time of the German invasion. Even then, a large majority of Jews, those who had served as war veterans and those who were members of the Italian Fascist Party, along with their children, grandchildren, siblings, parents, and grandparents, were exempted from deportation.[115] In Bulgaria, the parliament and people both stood by the side of the Jews; hence, no Bulgarian Jew was ever deported.[116] In contrast, Rumania pursued a deeply anti-Semitic policy, and their approach toward Jews was one of the ugliest ever reported in Europe. The Rumanians started their Jew-killing machine before the Germans by suffocating them in freight trains that were traveling aimlessly for days.[117] The government of Rumania managed to get rid of close to three hundred thousand of the Jewish population in this manner without any German assistance. The magnitude of mass killings diminished only toward the end of the war, once Rumanians learned that they could sell Jews for a hefty price.[118] Hungary refused to deport Jews until German forces invaded the country in March 1944. However, the deportation of Jews to death camps was nowhere as efficient as in Hungary, where within a period of less than two months, 147 trains carried 434,351 Jews to the gas chambers of Auschwitz.[119] While in Germany and France no public protest to deportations were seen, in Holland a number of strikes against the first deportation were arranged.[120] In Belgium, police refused to cooperate with the Nazis, and railway men arranged ambushes against the Germans. Finally, in Denmark, officials cautioned the Nazis against any anti-Jewish measures that might force the immediate resignation of the entire government. In essence, because of the public support that Jews received, the Jewish loss in Holland, Belgium, and Denmark was remarkably less intense.[121]

Living in dispersion for centuries had erased the idea of an active resistance against Nazis crimes from the social conscience of the Jews. It has been argued that the tradition of Jewish trust and

---

[115] Ibid., 178.

[116] Ibid., 187–188.

[117] Ibid., 191.

[118] Ibid., 193.

[119] W. L. Shirer, *The Rise and Fall of the Third Reich* (New York: Simon & Schuster, 1959), 140.

[120] H. Arendt, *Eichmann in Jerusalem: A Report on the Banality of Evil* (New York: Penguin, 1994), 169.

[121] Ibid., 171.

optimism in history,[122] and the strategy of adjustments and adaptations that Jews had practiced for centuries,[123] made the final solution to be carried out easier, reducing the burden on the German government apparatus.[124,125] But other forms of resistance, such as insisting upon Jewish cultural and religious values, participation in the resistant groups, collaboration with Allied forces, and dying in dignity by committing suicide instead of surrendering to the Nazis, were often encountered through the war years.[126] It is noteworthy that in the death camps, since people were living for only a short period of time, they had no chance of organizing, and an uprising was almost impossible. But in the ghettoes, inmates were living together for a longer period and had a better chance to know each other; therefore, organized resistance against the Germans was more likely to happen. By January 1943, when Himmler visited the Warsaw ghetto, over three hundred thousand of its inhabitants had already perished in gas chambers across Eastern Europe. By this time, for "security reasons," he was determined to liquidate the remaining sixty thousand Jews living in the ghetto. However, he soon found out that the Jews were determined not to passively walk like herds into the gas chambers. On April 19, 1943, they engaged in an uprising against the Nazi police that lasted for four weeks before it was crushed. The Warsaw uprising was an expression of astonishing human courage and sacrifice. Juergen Stroop, the German commander of the ghetto, wrote on this subject, "Within a few days it became apparent that the Jews no longer had intention to resettle voluntarily, but were determined to resist evacuation. ... Over and over again new battle groups consisting of 20 to 30 Jewish men, accompanied by a corresponding number of women, kindled new resistance. . . . I therefore decided to destroy the entire Jewish area by setting every block on fire."[127] May

---

[122] R. Hilberg, *The Politics of Memory: The Journey of a Holocaust Historian* (Chicago: Ivan R. Dee, 1996), 137.

[123] Ibid., 151.

[124] H. Arendt, *Eichmann in Jerusalem: A Report on the Banality of Evil* (New York: Penguin, 1994), 117.

[125] R. Hilberg, *The Politics of Memory: The Journey of a Holocaust Historian* (Chicago: Ivan R. Dee, 1996), 127.

[126] U.S. Holocaust Memorial Museum, *Resistance in Nazi Camps, Resistance during the Holocaust* (Washington, DC: Author, n.d.), 24–25.

[127] W. L. Shirer, *The Rise and Fall of the Third Reich* (New York: Simon & Schuster, 1959), 976–977.

16, 1943, was the last day of the uprising. The number of Jews who had perished in the Warsaw ghetto was 56,065, as was presented to the Nuremberg tribunal. William Shirer speaks of the Warsaw ghetto uprising as the first and only Jewish armed resistance against Nazi crimes and atrocities.[128] In contrast, others believe that in the aftermath of the uprising in Warsaw, Jews revolted against Nazis in the ghettoes of Krakow and Vilna and later in the concentration camps of Sobibor, Trabnik, and Treblinka.[129]

Historians have expressed two viewpoints about the Holocaust. One group believed chaos within the Nazi system of government was the source of atrocities. This group of historians thought that the annihilation of European Jewry was not a thought-out agenda reflected in the Nazi ideology. Nazis, in their opinion, hated Jews, but hatred alone could not have been the root of the process.[130] The Holocaust, the way it happened, occurred because the entire system of the government bureaucracy was in chaos, where bureaucrats in actuality became perpetrators.[131] Under this chaotic condition, laws were gradually interpreted as decrees, then as announcements, then referred to as written orders, oral orders, and finally to no orders.[132] On the contrary, a second group of historians accepted the notion that the Nazis, long before they slipped into power, had a plan for the extermination of European Jewry. In fact, Hitler in his speech to the German Reichstag on January 30, 1939, spoke of the annihilation of the Jewish race throughout Europe. However, except for the agreement between Himmler and Thierack, the minister of justice, dated September 18, 1942, in which men and women were to be "worked to death," there is no official Nazi document on the mass extermination of European Jewry. Even in the original German correspondence between Goering and Heydrich on July 31, 1941, the "final solution" has been expressed as a "desirable solution."[133] On January 20, 1942, when Heydrich reported to a conference of top Nazi officials in Wannsee, he described the final

---

[128] Ibid.

[129] H. Fast, *The Jews: Story of a People* (New York: Dell, 1992), 336.

[130] R. Hilberg, *The Politics of Memory: The Journey of a Holocaust Historian* (Chicago: Ivan R. Dee, 1996), 70.

[131] Ibid., 124.

[132] Ibid., 80.

[133] W. L. Shirer, *The Rise and Fall of the Third Reich* (New York: Simon & Schuster, 1959), 964, 1175.

solution as forcing Jews to the east, separating men and women into labor gangs for hard work under conditions that might naturally shrink their numbers, and those who might survive these conditions must be treated accordingly.[134] Nonetheless, the lack of direct language in the Nazi documents about the final solution has always been a tool in the hands of Holocaust deniers.

It is noteworthy that the Nazis did not overlook the financial gains that were inherent in their Jew-killing industry. The very first legal procedure exercised in many German-occupied territories was to make Jews "stateless"; in that way the state could freely confiscate Jewish properties and other countries could not question their fate.[135] The top-level exchange of big Jewish businesses for the rescue of the owners[136] and the trade of Jews for large sums of money or valuable commodities were frequently encountered during the war.[137,138] However, the more lucrative source of revenue for the Nazis was elsewhere. Upon arrival in the camp, valuables were taken away for "safekeeping," and the first endeavor after opening the heavy metal doors of the gas chambers, and before dragging the bodies to crematories, was a search for gold teeth and jewelry.[139,140] These items were then transferred to the Reich bank and from there to accounts in Swiss banks.[141] Indeed, in the period from 1939 to 1945, the Swiss banking system received 279 tons of German gold.[142] It has been argued that Switzerland, despite its self-claimed neutrality in the war, safeguarded the Nazis' assets by transferring truckloads of German gold to Portugal[143] and Argentina[144] during the same period.

---

[134] Ibid., 966.

[135] H. Arendt, *Eichmann in Jerusalem: A Report on the Banality of Evil* (New York: Penguin, 1994), 115.

[136] Ibid., 142.

[137] Ibid., 144.

[138] T. Bower, *Nazi Gold: The Full Story of Fifty-year Swiss-Nazi Conspiracy to Steal Billions from Europe's Jews and Holocaust Survivors* (New York: HarperCollins, 1997), 62.

[139] W. L. Shirer, *The Rise and Fall of the Third Reich* (New York: Simon & Schuster, 1959), 971.

[140] T. Bower, *Nazi Gold: The Full Story of Fifty-year Swiss-Nazi Conspiracy to Steal Billions from Europe's Jews and Holocaust Survivors* (New York: HarperCollins, 1997), 54.

[141] Ibid., 337.

[142] Ibid., 347.

[143] Ibid., 55.

Another sizable source of revenue was life insurance policies and assets of the heirless Jews. Many insurance companies refused to pay these claims on the ground that death certificates were not submitted.[145] Finally, there are reports to suggest that certain objects of art that belonged to Jews were twice stolen: once during the war by Nazis and again by the Russians in 1945.[146]

The Holocaust, nonetheless, jolted many Jewish theocratic circles. It raised radical questions like God's lack of response, the existence of God, and whether humanity could be trusted. Some theologians, like Richard Rubenstein, went far enough to suggest that Jews can no longer insist upon the myth of the omnipotent God and its corollary or on the particularity of the Jews after the Holocaust.[147] On the other hand, Emil Fackenheim offered a sense of hope and argued that God was not responsible for the evil of the Holocaust; humanity was. Therefore, the Jews must face up and endure the contradiction of Jewish particularity and suffering and move forward.[148] More than half a century later, the controversy between these two opposing schools of thought has not yet been resolved.

The State of Israel

The first Zionist World Congress convened in 1897 in Switzerland and defined its goal as the creation "for the Jewish people of a home in Palestine secured by public law."[149] The delegates in the first Congress proposed to achieve the Zionist goal via (1) encouraging agricultural and industrial Jewish workers to migrate to Palestine, (2) ingathering of world Jewry through local and international organizations, (3) arousing the Jewish conscience around the world, and (4) persuading the support of influential governments toward the Zionist goal. When Soltan Abdul Hamid II of the Ottoman Empire did not welcome the Zionist idea, the followers focused their activities on the British government. Uganda, one of the

---

[144] Ibid., 67.
[145] Ibid., 6
[146] Ibid., 335
[147] D. B. Ruderman, *Jewish Intellectual History: 16th to 20th Century* (Chantilly, VA: Teaching Company, 2002), Part 2.
[148] Ibid.
[149] *Encyclopedia Encarta*, "Zionism," CD-ROM edition, 2000, Microsoft Corporation.

British African colonies, was suggested as the proper site for a Jewish state, but the Uganda scheme was rejected in the seventh Zionist World Congress in 1905. Following the defeat of the Ottoman Empire in World War I, Palestine came under the control of the British and French governments. In 1917, Arthur J. Balfour, then the British foreign minister, assured the Zionist leaders of his government's intention to support the establishment of a homeland for Jews in Palestine. In the context of the Balfour Declaration, the British government accepted this responsibility with the proviso that the civil and religious rights of the non-Jew inhabitants of Palestine would be protected.[150] Through the next two decades, the Zionist leaders, particularly the socialist elements among them, underestimated Arab nationalism and viewed the conflict merely as a class struggle between the peasants and Arab landowners, and hoped for resolution once the peasants realized that the Jewish working class was struggling on their side.[151]

In May 1939, in an effort to calm the Arab communities, the British government assured the Arab majority of Palestine that the migration of Jews into the area would be limited to seventy-five thousand over the next five years, and the approval of the Arab authorities for migration above that number would be required. In addition, the British government committed itself to the establishment of a Palestinian state within the next decade in which the essential

---

[150] Following is the text of the Balfour Declaration (Arthur Balfour and A. Eban, *Heritage: Civilization and the Jews* [New York: Summit Books, 1984], 257:

Foreign Office, November 2, 1917
Dear Lord Rothschild,
    I have much pleasure in conveying to you, on behalf of His Majesty's Government, the following declaration of sympathy with Jewish Zionist aspirations, which has been submitted to and approved by the Cabinet.
    His Majesty's Government view with favour the establishment in Palestine of a national home for the Jewish people and will use their best endeavors to facilitate the achievement of this object. It being clearly understood that nothing shall be done which may prejudice the civil and religious rights of existing non-Jewish communities in Palestine or the rights and political status enjoyed by Jews in other country.
    I should be grateful if you would bring this declaration to the knowledge of the Zionist federation.
[151] A. Shlaim, *The Iron Wall: Israel and the Arab World* (New York: W. W. Norton, 2001), 17.

interests of both Arabs and Jews were to be safeguarded.[152] The content of the correspondence between the British government and the Palestinian authorities, which is known as the "white paper," did not please the Zionist leaders and in fact was interpreted as an indication of British betrayal of their commitment toward the Jewish people. Therefore, in May 1942, a meeting of the Zionist leaders in New York proposed the establishment of a Jewish state on the western rim of Palestine. During World War II, merely because of Nazi atrocities, Jewish-British resentments declined significantly, and except for a few small groups, the majority of Jews in Palestine suspended their hostile activities against the British authorities and actively supported the war.

The harsh experience of the Jews in World War II left them with a sense of despair and distrust of the cultural values of the West. They could neither disregard the crimes and atrocities of the Nazis nor the apathy of large segments of the civilized world that included not only states but also the Vatican and church institutions.[153] In 1942, once the horrible atrocities of the Nazis against the Jews were first confirmed,[154] a number of Jewish guerilla warfare groups that were established in the heart of the Jewish settlements in Palestine attacked the British interests in the region.[155] While one group under the

---

[152] *Encyclopedia Judaica*, "The White Papers," CD-ROM edition, 1997, Judaica Multimedia.

[153] Many believe that Pope Pius XII was a Third Reich puppet, and under his leadership the Vatican did not make the necessary efforts to save the Jews. His prolonged silence against the Nazi atrocities is an issue that many of his critics will not forget. However, he publicly acknowledged the Holocaust on June 25, 1943, and appealed for support of the Jews. It is ironic that fifty-five years later, on March 16, 1998, Pope John Paul II offered an apology to world Jewry for the Vatican's long overdue silence on the Nazi crimes.

[154] B. Avishai, *The Tragedy of Zionism: How its Revolutionary Past Haunts Israel Democracy* (New York, Helios Press, 2002), 159.

[155] Menachem Begin was born in Brest-Litovsk in 1913. It is said that the thirty thousand population of the town in 1939 had been reduced to about ten thousand in 1944, and Jews were not even allowed to bury their dead in public. In fact, a German soldier shot Menachem's father to death at the burial ceremony of his friend. He lost his parents and brother in the Holocaust, which left a profound footprint on his personality. He always viewed Arab hostility as an extension of European anti-Semitism. Young Begin, who had an unforgiving personality, became the leader of the Irgun Zeva'l le'ummi in 1943. The World Zionist Organization fiercely criticized the violent agenda of this paramilitary organization, since it was disruptive of the

leadership of Avraham Stern had focused on the assassination of British authorities in Palestine, another clandestine guerilla group, the Irgun Zeva`I le`ummi, under Menachem Begin, was engaged in the destruction of British administrative facilities as a way of struggle. It is noteworthy that these forms of violent tactics, including blowing up the King David Hotel in Jerusalem, with the loss of many civilian Arabs, Jews, and British lives,[156] as a mode of political struggle, were quite new in the 1940s.[157] The Irgun practice of targeting civilians was later adopted by the Arabs as a means of struggle.[158] It was under these circumstances that the tenacity of the Zionist movement and the persuasion of Western Jews eventually convinced the Allies to consider a homeland for the survivors of Nazi crimes.

Finally, by the establishment of the state of Israel on May 14, 1948, the British-Palestine mandate[159] officially ended. The birth of the state of Israel was due to a number of exceptional factors at this historic juncture. Among them were the world's sympathy for the pains and sufferings of Jews during World War II, the political influence of American Jews to acquire the support of President Truman, the British lack of interest to govern in Palestine, and the relentless efforts of the Zionist movement.

The state of Israel was founded upon the pattern of nation-states formed after the French Revolution, adopting a Western type of parliamentary system of government. The Declaration of Independence signed on May 14, 1948, pledged that

> The state of Israel will be open for Jewish immigration and for the ingathering of the Exiles; it will foster the development of the

---

political solutions to the Jewish issue. Menachem Begin eventually served as the prime minister of Israel from 1977 to 1983.

[156] A. Eban, *Heritage: Civilization and the Jews* (New York: Summit Books, 1984), 324.

[157] P. Johnson, *A History of the Jews* (New York: HarperPerennial, 1987), 521.

[158] D. Schafer, "The Seeds of Enmity," *The Humanist*, September/October (2002): 12.

[159] Within the context of the Versailles Treaty at the end of World War I, through a mandate system, the League of Nations recognized that certain former communities within the Ottoman Empire had reached a stage of development where they could achieve independence. In Class A of the mandates were former Ottoman provinces of Palestine, Iraq, and Syria. Accordingly, the administration of Palestine and Iraq were assigned to Great Britain and Syria to France. The mandates for Iraq ended in 1932 and for Syria in 1936 when both achieved their independence.

country for the benefit of all inhabitants; it will be based on freedom, justice, and peace as envisaged by the prophets of Israel, it will ensure complete equality of social and political rights to all its inhabitants irrespective of religion, race and sex; it will guarantee freedom of religion, conscience, language, education and culture; it will safeguard the Holy Places of all religions; and it will be faithful to the principles of the Charter of the United Nations.[160]

Israel was originally meant to become a secular state. However, because of the influence of religious parties and the historic identification of Judaism with that of Jewish nationality, the state of Israel evolved into a government with a strong religious façade. Nonetheless, some of the Zionist leaders, even in their early stage of struggle, were uneasy about this particular subject.[161] For instance, Lord Rothschild in a private letter expressed his concern over this issue to Theodore Herzl on August 18, 1902.[162] While the separation of church and state, as in the Constitution of the United States, does not apply to the state of Israel, the state is not exclusively governed by the Judaic Halakhah and therefore is not exactly a religious state. The modern state of Israel in general is ruled by civic laws,[163] while the religious courts handle matters of "personal status" such as marriage, divorce, and death.[164] Moreover, the Army institutions observe Sabbath and dietary laws,[165] and religious education is administered by the ministry of religions with the financial support of the state.[166]

From its commencement, the state of Israel had to face numerous issues of social importance, among them the immigration or Aliyah of the Jews of Diaspora to the new homeland. The leaders

---

[160] E. Barnavi, *A Historical Atlas of the Jewish People* (New York: Schocken Books, 1992), 275.
[161] N. Chomsky, "Israel and the Palestinians," in A. Shatz, *Prophets Outcast* (New York,: Nation Books, 2004), 256.
[162] S. Aloni, "One Hundred Years of Zionism, Fifty Years of Statehood," *Humanistic Judaism* 28:1–2 (2000): 37.
[163] Y. Leibowitz, *Judaism, Human Values, and the Jewish State* (Cambridge, MA: Harvard University Press, 1992), 175.
[164] *Encyclopedia Judaica*, "Legal and Judicial System of State of Israel," CD-ROM edition, 1997, Judaica Multimedia.
[165] Y. Leibowitz, *Judaism, Human Values, and the Jewish State* (Cambridge, MA: Harvard University Press, 1992), 180.
[166] Ibid., 182.

of the Zionist movement, who had a common vision of the establishment of the state of Israel and had struggled together to achieve the goal, expressed opposing viewpoints on the necessity of migration of the entire world Jewry to Israel. David Ben-Gurion, the first prime minister, insisted that those who did not resettle in Israel would have no say in the future of the state, in spite of the fact that the state of Israel owes its very existence to their efforts.

On the contrary, Nahum Goldmann, who served as the leader of the World Zionist Organization from 1951 to 1968, believed the resettlement of world Jewry in Israel was an unrealistic expectation. He insisted that the Zionist Organization had obligations toward world Jewry regardless of where they elected to live. Nonetheless, the state of Israel views world Jewry as Israeli citizens in exile,[167] a position that has often been cited against Jews to indicate that they do not consider their birthplace as their homeland.

The migration of Jews of the Diaspora to Israel has been mainly influenced by the political, economic, and social circumstances under which Jews were living. The following table reveals the total Jewish population that migrated to Israel from 1881 to 1994:

Periods	Immigration of Jews to Israel
1881–1914	50,000
1919–1948	412,124
1948–1951	658,654
1952–1960	294,486
1961–1964	224,825
1965–1971	191,402
1972–1979	262,297
1980–1989	149,280
1990–1993	522,276
1994	76,416
Total	2,841,760

Adapted from *Statistical Abstract of Israel 1995*, Jerusalem, cited in *Encyclopedia Judaica*, CD-ROM edition, 1997, Judaica Multimedia.

---

[167] H. Draper, *Zionism, Israel and the Arabs* (Berkeley, CA: Center for Socialist History, 1997), 106.

The data clearly show that the Jewish migration to Israel varied considerably over time and peaked in three relatively distinct periods of 1919–1948, 1948–1951, and 1990–1993, following World War I, the establishment of the state of Israel, and the fall of the Soviet Union, respectively,

A look at the countries of origin and the timing of immigrations, as it is shown in the following table, reveals that the migration of Jews to Israel not only was due to the relatively higher standard of living in Israel but also peaked in the aftermath of social upheavals and unrest in these countries:

Country	Total Jewish Emigrants to Israel	Peak period of Immigration	Number of Jews Emigrated in the Peak Period
Algeria	25,431	1961–1964	9,680
Argentina	43,319	1972–1979	13,158
Canada	7,915	1972–1979	2,178
Cezc/slav	39,751	1919–1948	16,794
Egypt	37,470	1952–1960	17,521
France	31,634	1980–1989	7,538
Germany	70,628	1919–1948	52,951
Hungry	40,371	1919–1948	10,342
India	26,536	1965–1971	10,170
Iraq	129,539	1948–1951	123,371
Iran	78,985	1948–1951	21,910
Libya	36,675	1948–1951	30,972
Morocco	267,159	1961–1964	100,354
Poland	341,598	1919–1948	170,127
Rumania	314,630	1948–1951	117,950
Tunisia	52,944	1952–1960	23,569
Turkey	69,488	1948–1951	34,547
USSR	801,287	1990–1993	462,811
United States	76,192	1972–1979	20,963

Adapted from *Statistical Abstract of Israel, 1995*, Jerusalem, quoted in *Encyclopedia Judaica*, CD-ROM edition, 1997, Judaica Multimedia.

Two general conclusions may be derived from these demographic data. First, like other ethnic minorities, Jews generally migrate only when they are under intense social, political, or economic hardship. Second, even under these circumstances, Jews, like other peoples, approach the issue more rationally and usually migrate to those regions of the world that provide them with more favorable social and economic opportunities. This is true in spite of the fact that in the cultural fabric of Jews, the statement "Leshonoh haba ah birusholayim," meaning "next year in Jerusalem," reflects their twenty-five-centuries-old desire to return to the Holy Land.[168] In other words, strong social, political, and economic factors, rather than faith alone, determine the migration of people from one place to another.

Today Israel is the second largest Jewish community of the world. The world Jewish population has been estimated around thirteen million in 1989; out of this number, 45.5 percent were living in North America and 29 percent in Israel.[169] While the non-Ashkenazi population of the state in 1948 was relatively small, in light of the migration of Oriental Jews from the Middle East and North Africa, the Ashkenazi population declined and stabilized around 40 percent by 1965.[170] The mass migration of Russian Jews to Israel between 1989 and 1993 increased the Ashkenazi proportion to 55 percent and the population of the country to 34 percent of the world Jewry population. Following is Israel's demography based upon the 1996 census:

Population	5,938,000
Jewish	80.1%
Europe/American born	32.1%
Israel born	20.8%
Africa born	14.6%
Asia born	12.6%
Muslim	14.6%
Christian	2.1%
Others	3.2%

Adapted from *The World Factbook 2001*. Retrieved from
http://www.cia.gov/cia/publications/factbook.

Israeli society is not a homogeneous community of Jews. Ashkenazi Jews are mostly white-collar workers of the old European

---

[168] H. Fast, *The Jews: Story of a People* (New York: Dell, 1968), 319.

[169] E. Barnavi, *A Historical Atlas of the Jewish People* (New York: Schocken Books, 1992), 278.

[170] I. Shahak and N. Mezvinsky, *Jewish Fundamentalism in Israel* (London: Pluto Press, 1999), 48.

Zionist establishment; they mainly constitute the industrial and managerial segments.[171] Oriental Jews, the Middle Eastern and North African immigrants, are more represented in agriculture and the blue-collar skilled and unskilled workers. It has been argued the Oriental Jews constitute an underprivileged stratum between Ashkenazi Jews and Israeli Arabs.[172] Russian Jews, on the other hand, are highly visible in high tech industry and contribute significantly to the Israeli science, music and art. Orthodox Jews and Israeli Arabs make the two other segments of the Israeli society. Since 1985 these five demographic factions have behaved variably in time when it comes to major social issues. Under stable economic conditions, the old European Zionist establishment leads the Israeli Arabs, Russian and Oriental Jews and marginalizes the institutional Jewish orthodoxy. However, in the periods of severe social tension, Jewish orthodoxy and Oriental Jews lead the Russian Jews, alienate the Israeli Arabs and force the European Labor Zionists into a form of internal seclusion.[173]

Fifty-some years after the passage of a piece of legislation known as the Law of Return on July 5, 1950, which granted Jews the right of settlement in Israel, almost two-thirds of world Jewry is still living outside the country. Nonetheless, the achievements of Jews in the area of civic rights along with an overall improvement in their economic status are among the most prominent grounds for a decline in immigration to Israel. Therefore, the century-old Zionist expectation for the migration of the entire Diaspora to Israel merely remains as an unachieved ideal.[174] Hence, along these lines, Professor Yeshayahu Leibowitz wrote, "The early Zionists believed that Jews in exile were eternally doomed to be aliens, either as tolerated foreigners or as outcast and oppressed strangers. They could be delivered from this tragic situation by setting up a national home in their own land. This conception does not fit the contemporary scene. We are witnessing the accelerated assimilation of Jews and their complete integration in their host societies. The only ones resisting this process

---

[171] E. Shohat, "Sephardim in Israel," in A. Shatz, *Prophets Outcast* (New York: Nation Books, 2004), 302.

[172] Ibid., 307.

[173] B. Avishai, *The Tragedy of Zionism: How its Revolutionary Past Haunts Israel Democracy* (New York, Helios Press, 2002), 364

[174] Y. Leibowitz, *Judaism, Human Values, and the Jewish State* (Cambridge, MA: Harvard University Press, 1992), 193.

are Jews who do not want it. Zionism today is therefore a matter of a voluntary, deliberate decision by Jews—a minority of them. It has also become evident that Jewish independence affords no guarantee to the well-being and security of the Jewish people, who are threatened in their land more than anywhere else."[175]

Today, while the state of Israel has turned into a gigantic military power, it is confused about its values and structure[176] and has failed to establish a stable and meaningful relation on the basis of coexistence with her neighbors.[177,178] Despite the fact that Israel is not considered the ultimate solution to the world Jewish question and is not the only place where Jews have the right or the capacity to defend themselves,[179] Israel's achievements as a highly developed, multiparty system of government with advanced health and educational services, and a standard of living unmatched by its neighboring countries,[180] conveys high aspirations for world Jewry in many respects. First, cultural and social achievements of Israel in the past fifty years have been instrumental in changing the stereotypical image of Jews in the

---

[175] Ibid., 117.

[176] A. Eban, *Personal Witness: Israel through My Eyes* (New York: G. P. Putnam's, 1992), 604.

[177] E. Hobsbawm, *The Age of Extremes* (New York: Pantheon Books, 1994), 359.

[178] E. W. Said, *Orientalism* (New York: Vintage Books, 1994), xxiv.

[179] B. Klug, "A Time to Speak Out," in A. Shatz *Prophets Outcast* (New York: Nation Books, 2004), 389.

[180] Israel and neighboring countries in statistics:

	Israel	Egypt	Jordan	Lebanon	Syria
Population (million)	5.9	69.5	5.1	3.6	16.7
Gross Domestic Product	$18,900	$4,200	$3,500	$5,000	$3,100
Literacy Rate	95%	51.4	86.6%	86.4	86.4
Unemployment	9%	11.5%	30%	18%	20%
Debt (billion)	$38 b	$31 b	$8 b	$9.6 b	$22 b
Industrial Production Growth Rate	7%	2.1%	3.8%	4.8%	N/A
Percentage below Poverty	N/A	22.9%	30%	28%	25%
Defense: Percentage of GDP	9.6	5.7	7.7	–	7.2
Fertility Rate	2.68	3.07	3.29	2.05	3.95
Life Expectancy	78.6	63.6	77.5	71.5	71.52
Infant Mortality Rate	7.72	60.46	20.36	28.35	33.8

world's public opinion. Considering the circumstances under which Jews lived for over nineteen centuries, they were viewed as cowardly, conservative, and incapable people.[181] It was in the aftermath of the establishment of the state of Israel that this stereotype gradually changed, and once again it became clear that under proper conditions, Jews, like other people, would demonstrate their cultural and social capabilities. Second, the very existence of the state of Israel in the international arena is crucial to point out the needs of Jewish communities scattered around the world. Third, the modern state of Israel offers new Jewish cultural values for those Jews who are not comfortable living with the old traditional values.[182] Finally, the state of Israel was originally founded as a solution to anti-Semitism. Therefore, in times of social crisis in other parts of the world, when anti-Semitic activities are on the rise and not many other countries are receptive to Jews, Israel would be accessible as a homeland to those Jews who need one, as it wasa sanctuary to several hundred thousand victims of Holocaust.[183, 184]

Chronology:

1844	Karl Marx wrote a response to Bruno Bauer on the "Jewish question"
1866	Moses Hess attacked Jewish assimilation in his book *Rome and Jerusalem*
1871	Rosa Luxemburg was born to a Polish Jewish family
1878	Martin Buber was born in Vienna
1881	Leo Pinsker, the first Zionist theoretician, published his manuscript on *Auto-emancipation*
1893	Nathan Birnbaum, Austrian philosopher, cast the term "Zionism"
1895	The Dreyfus affair
1896	Theodore Herzl published *Jewish State*
1897	First Zionist World Congress in Switzerland

---

[181] N. G. Finkelstein, *Image and Reality of the Israel-Palestine Conflict* (London: Verso, 2003), 110.

[182] A. Hertzberg, *The Zionist Idea* (Philadelphia: Jewish Publication Society, 1997), 626.

[183] P. Findley, *They Dare to Speak Out* (Chicago: Lawrence Hill Books, 1985), 317.

[184] E. Abrams, *Faith or Fear* (New York: Free Press, 1997), 141.

1897	Bund, Federation of the Jewish workers of Lithuania, Poland, and Russia, was established
1901	Leon Blum, the French statesman, wrote on Jews and social justice
1903	British government suggested Uganda as the future homeland for Jews
1903	Lenin wrote on "National Jewish identity"
1905	In the aftermath of the Dreyfus affair, the principle of separation of church and state was established in France
1905	Fifth Zionist World Congress rejected "Uganda scheme"
1917	Balfour Declaration
1918	Lenin attacked the Workers, Peasants and Soldiers Commissariat for anti-Semitic activities
1919	Hebrew publications were banned and the Bund party was dissolved in the Soviet Union
1926	Trotsky furiously questioned Bukharin for anti-Semitic activities within the Soviet Communist party
1927	Jewish Autonomous Region of Birobidzhan was established in USSR near Chinese border
1933	Nazis came to power in Germany
1935	Nazis passed the Nuremberg Race Laws
1937	Thousands of Jews labeled as the "agents of Imperialism and Reaction" and were purged from Communist party
1938	Kristalnacht pogrom in Germany
1939	German army invaded the western part of Poland
1939	White Paper restricted the migration of Jews to Palestine
1941	Germany attacked Soviet Union
1942	Deportation of Jews to concentration camps reached its peak
1942	The establishment of a Jewish state on the western rim of Palestine was proposed by the Zionist leaders
1943	The uprising of Warsaw ghetto
1948	British-Palestine mandate officially ended and the state of Israel was established

Chapter Eight

JEWS OF THE POSTMODERN ERA
AND
THE CRISIS OF THE JEWISH IDENTITY

Once the ashes of World War II settled, humanity had to face a new reality. The science that blossomed in the Age of Enlightenment in the seventeenth century and shifted our God-centered thinking to human-centered philosophy could no longer claim that it had the key to the truth and was the answer to every unknown. The *absolute universe,* which had been configured on the Newtonian paradigm, was replaced with the *relativism* of Einstein. Humanity came to understand that within the postmodern vision, nothing is absolute, truth is relative, neither reason nor faith alone can discover the truth, everything is possible and nothing is for certain, one ideology is as good as another, and ideologies ought not to be necessarily rational and could rather be intuitive.[1] In the realm of history, the postmodern era is distinguished by pluralism, by the blending of cultures and a fast expansion of global economy, and by the erosion of the concept of the nation-state.[2] The digital information revolution has torn up the conventional boundaries and has brought

---

[1] W. G. Dever, *What Did the Biblical Writers Know and When Did They Know It?* (Grand Rapids, MI: Eerdmans, 2001), 24–25.
[2] E. W. Said, *Orientalism* (New York: Vintage Books, 1994), 349.

people closer to one another. Concurrently, the shattered concept of the absolute universe and the shortcoming of science to explain everything have created a crisis of meaning and identity.

The postmodern era finds Jews in an open environment of opportunity and acceptance. They are generally free to live and work wherever they like, to communicate with other peoples freely and enjoy the freedom of expression, having the same civil rights as other citizens. Institutional anti-Semitism, for all practical purposes, is on the defensive. Although white supremacy militia groups, primal Eastern European anti-Semitism, and Islamic fundamentalism with its share of anti-Semitism are still around, the anti-Semitism sponsored by government or church institutions is sharply declining. The public opinion in general does not approve of anti-Semitic sentiments, and above all, the conversion of Jews to the religion of the majority is no longer the prerequisite to social acceptance and success in this era.[3] The historic external enemies have been either eliminated or their anti-Jewish outlooks have lost their clout in the eyes of public opinion. In essence, American Jewry in this historical intercept is no longer facing any institutional enemy.[4, 5, 6]

Nonetheless, the crisis of meaning and identity of the postmodern era is haunting Jewish life. The conflict between Israel and its neighbors, the clash between fundamentalist and secular Jews, the mounting trend in intermarriage, secularization, and assimilation, the divergence between Israel and the Diaspora, the changing pattern of Jewish demography in America and elsewhere, the inconsistency in the traditional Jewish agenda and liberalism, and the way Jews are going to reconcile the crisis of Jewish identity are among the viable issues facing world Jewry at a time when the external threat is ever vanishing. If the Jewish problem of the last century was the very survival of Jews against a rabid anti-Semitism, the Jewish problem of the postmodern era seems to be our continued existence in the face of our internal challenges.

---

[3] S. G. Freedman, *Jews vs. Jews: The Struggle for the Soul of American Jewry* (New York: Touchstone, 2000), 28.

[4] A. M. Dershowitz, *The Vanishing American Jew* (New York: Touchstone, 1997), 1.

[5] J. J. Goldberg, *Jewish Power: Inside the American Jewish Establishment* (Reading, MA: Addison-Wesley, 1996), 3.

[6] A. Hertzberg and A. Hirt-Manheimer, *Jews: The Essence and Character of a People* (New York: HarperSanFrancisco, 1998), 274.

Israel and the Arabs

In 1880, the population of Palestine was about 450,000, and over 95 percent of its inhabitants were Arabs.[7] The rise of nationalism in Europe in the nineteenth century and the climax of anti-Semitism in the 1880s intensified the migration of Jews to Palestine. Jews managed to purchase land from the Arab landowners and established agricultural cooperatives. It has been argued that major Arab landowners sold to Jews too willingly, and often the available lands for sale to Jews were more than what Jews could afford.[8] In the meantime, since 1915, the British government had promised Arabs their independence once the Ottoman Empire was defeated, and as of 1917 had pledged support toward a national homeland for the Jews. From 1922 to 1948, the period that Palestine was under British mandate, it became quite clear that the British commitments to both sides were increasingly irreconcilable.[9]

The rise of Jewish immigration to the area and the discussion in some Zionist circles over a Jewish state constituting all of Palestine seemed quite disturbing to the Arabs[10,11,12] They justified their dislike for Zionism principally on two grounds. First, Arabs were extremely unhappy over the promises British authorities were making to Zionist leaders by pledging part of their homeland to a third party without prior consultation with them. This was in spite of a provision Britain had included in the Balfour Declaration of 1917 protecting the civil and religious rights of the non-Jewish inhabitants of Palestine.[13] Second, Arabs were fearful of losing all of Palestine to the Jews.[14] Indeed, the King-Crane Commission, which was charged by U.S. President Woodrow Wilson to study the Palestine issue in 1919, in its

---

[7] *Encyclopedia Encarta*, "Palestine," CD-ROM edition, 1999, Microsoft Corporation.

[8] A. Dershowitz, *The Case for Israel* (Hoboken, NJ: John Wiley, 2003), 25.

[9] F. Hobsbawm, *The Age of Extremes* (New York: Pantheon Books, 1994), 210.

[10] N. Chomsky, *The Fateful Triangle: The United States, Israel and the Palestinians* (Boston: South End Press, 1983), 91.

[11] A. Shlaim, *The Iron Wall: Israel and the Arab World* (New York: W. W. Norton, 2001), 55.

[12] B. Avishai, *The Tragedy of Zionism: How its Revolutionary Past Haunts Israel Democracy* (New York, Helios Press, 2002), 156.

[13] A. Hourani, *A History of the Arab People* (Cambridge, MA: Harvard University Press, 1991), 318.

[14] N. G. Finkelstein, *Image and Reality of the Israel-Palestine Conflict* (London: Verso, 2003), xiii, 15.

final report indicated that the Zionists were talking about the massive resettlement of Arabs who constituted over nine-tenths of the Palestinian population.[15] In the opinion of the Commission, the plan was against the national self-determination right of Arabs,[16] and in general expressed pessimism about the future of Arab-Jewish coexistence.

From the very beginning, the Zionist leaders as the architects of the plan were concerned over the Arabs' reaction. Ahad Ha'am was probably the first Zionist leader who expressed his concern over this subject when he wrote, "We abroad are accustomed to believe that *Eretz Israel* is almost totally desolate at present. . . but in reality it is not so. . . . Arabs, especially those in towns, see and understand our activities and aims in the country but keep quiet and pretend as if they did not know, and that is because they don't see any danger to their future in our activities at present, and they try to exploit us, too, and profit from the new guests while laughing at us in their hearts. But if the time comes and our people make such progress as to displace the people of the country. . . they will not lightly surrender the place."[17] David Ben-Gurion, who later served as the first prime minister of Israel, had a similar impression when he spoke to the Jewish settlers: "Everybody sees a difficulty in the question of relations between Arabs and Jews. . . but not everybody sees that there is no solution to this question. No solution! There is a gulf, and nothing can bridge it. . . .We, as a nation, want this country to be ours; the Arabs, as a nation, want this country to be theirs."[18] Indeed, the question of relations with the Arabs, which was a sore spot before the establishment of the state of Israel, remained as a viable issue to haunt the Zionist movement for the next three-quarters of a century.

The very early clashes between the Arab inhabitants of Palestine and the Jews surfaced in two separate incidents in 1929 in Hebron, where over two hundred Jews were massacred.[19] It is noteworthy that most of the victims were neither new settler to

---

[15] Ibid., xii.

[16] N. Chomsky, *The Fateful Triangle: The United States, Israel and the Palestinians* (Boston: South End Press, 1983), 91.

[17] A. Eban, *Heritage: Civilization and the Jews* (New York: Summit Books, 1984), 249.

[18] D. Schafer, "The Seeds of Enmity," *The Humanist*, September/October (2002): 10.

[19] A. Dershowitz, *The Case for Israel* (Hoboken, NJ: John Wiley, 2003), 42.

Palestine nor were they necessarily pleased with the Zionist activities.[20]

The mass migration of sixty-five thousand Jews to Palestine in the period from 1933 (when the Nazis came to power in Germany) until 1939 (coinciding with the beginning of World War II) irritated the Arabs and prompted the British government to issue the White Paper on May 17, 1939, restricting the immigration of Jews to Palestine and also prohibiting the sale of land to them. By now the Jewish population of Palestine had grown to four hundred and fifty thousand from seventy-eight thousand in 1900. It was not surprising that Zionists viewed the White Paper as a "black document" for world Jewry,[21] and the extremist leaders of the movement, among them Vladimir Jabotinsky and Menachem Begin, seceded from the main organization and established the World Union of Zionist Revisionists[22] and a coalition of "the movement of Hebrew resistance or *Tenu`at ha-Meri-ha-Ivri*," respectively, both utilizing violent strategies against British interests in Palestine.[23, 24]

The migration of Jews mostly from Eastern Europe, the Middle East, and Northern Africa to Palestine continued during the years of World War II. On November 29, 1947, the United Nations passed Resolution 181 of the partition of Palestine, according to which two separate states for Jews and Palestinian Arabs were to be established. The proposed plan called for a Palestinian state of forty-five hundred square miles next to the state of Israel of fifty-five hundred square miles.[25] At this juncture, 600,000 Jews and 1.3 million Arabs were the inhabitants of Palestine.[26, 27] Zionists, except for the extremist group of Irgun under the leadership of Menachem

---

[20] Ibid.

[21] A. Eban, *Heritage: Civilization and the Jews* (New York: Summit Books, 1984), 321.

[22] A. Shlaim, *The Iron Wall: Israel and the Arab World* (New York: W. W. Norton, 2001), 11.

[23] E. Barnavi, *A Historical Atlas of the Jewish People* (New York: Schocken Books, 1992), 242.

[24] B. Avishai, *The Tragedy of Zionism: How its Revolutionary Past Haunts Israel Democracy* (New York, Helios Press, 2002), 170.

[25] D. Schafer, "The Seeds of Enmity," *The Humanist* September/October (2002): 14.

[26] A. Dershowitz, *The Case for Israel* (Hoboken, NJ: John Wiley, 2003), 67.

[27] N. G. Finkelstein, *Image and Reality of the Israel-Palestine Conflict* (London: Verso, 2003), 37.

Begin, accepted the resolution, whereas the Palestinians and Arab countries categorically rejected it.[28] The Irgun viewed the partition of Palestine as an illegal act that could never be recognized, and proclaimed Jerusalem as the permanent capital of Israel, "All of it. And for ever."[29] On the other hand, the lack of leadership and social disintegration of Palestinians at this historic juncture prevented them from taking this opportunity in their own hands and establishing a Palestinian state side by side with Israel.[30]

The establishment of the state of Israel in May 1948 added a new dimension to the hostilities between the Arabs and Israel. In the aftermath of this joyful event for Jews in general and for Zionists in particular, Arab countries, under the banner of the destruction of Israel, mobilized their forces against the new state. The first Arab-Israeli war—what Jews called the War of Independence and the Arabs viewed as a war of expansion[31]—lasted until January 1949 and produced over 600,000 Palestinian refugees.[32, 33] Half of the refugees were the Arabs who had left their homes principally because of fear,[34] while the other half were forced out to create space for the migration of Jews from Europe and other Arab countries.[35, 36] From this point on, the two issues of the refugees and the borders turned out to be the centerpiece of the conflict between Israel and the Arabs.[37]

The military victory of 1948 instilled a new psychology into the minds of Israeli administration, and according to Nahum

---

[28] P. Johnson, *A History of the Jews* (New York: HarperPerennial, 1987), 532.

[29] A. Shlaim, *The Iron Wall: Israel and the Arab World* (New York: W. W. Norton, 2001), 25.

[30] D. Schafer, "The Seeds of Enmity," *The Humanist* September/October (2002): 12.

[31] H. Draper, *Zionism, Israel and the Arabs* (Berkeley, CA: Center for Socialist History, 1997), 1.

[32] A. Shlaim, *The Iron Wall: Israel and the Arab World* (New York: W. W. Norton, 2001), 31.

[33] N. G. Finkelstein, *Image and Reality of the Israel-Palestine Conflict* (London: Verso, 2003), 52.

[34] *Institute for Palestine Studies Report*, quoted in A. Dershowitz, *The Case for Israel* (Hoboken, NJ: John Wiley, 2003), 84.

[35] *Encyclopedia Encarta*, "Palestine," CD-ROM edition, 2000, Microsoft Corporation.

[36] N. G. Finkelstein, *Image and Reality of the Israel-Palestine Conflict* (London: Verso, 2003), 53, 60.

[37] A. Shlaim, *The Iron Wall: Israel and the Arab World* (New York: W. W. Norton, 2001), 49.

Goldmann, the American Zionist leader, it showed "the advantage of direct action over negotiation and diplomacy," an outlook that shaped the Israeli policy line toward the Arab world.[38] In a way, this line of policy was also a reaction to the lack of interest expressed by the Arab leaders in negotiating.[39]

The attitude of the Arab countries toward their Jewish citizens also changed concomitant with the extension of hostilities between the Arabs of Palestine and Israel. Islamic militancy, along with extreme nationalism, created an atmosphere of unrest in these countries and eventually forced the Jewish population to migrate, mostly to Israel.[40] Under these circumstances, the rights of Jewish citizens in Arab countries were often subjugated to anti-Israel sentiments. In a matter of eight years, from 1948 to 1956, over half a million Jews left Arab countries, and the ancient Jewish communities in those regions came to an end.[41] The Jewish community of Morocco, because of the migration of about a quarter of a million Jews, ended in 1955. In Iraq, the Jewish community ceased to exist in 1951 after one hundred and twenty-five thousand Jews left the country. The migration of thirty-four thousand Jews from Libya, forty-eight thousand from Yemen, thirty-six thousand from Tunisia, and thirteen thousand from Algeria signaled the end of the Jewish communities in those countries.[42] The Jewish community of Egypt was expelled in 1956 in the aftermath of Egyptian defeat in the war against Israel, also known as the Sinai Campaign.

The second Arab-Israeli war was preceded by the escalation of tensions between Israel and the Arabs over the border skirmishes that were triggered by the closure of the Straits of Suez to Israeli shipping.[43] There are, however, bodies of evidence suggesting that Nasser was neither planning nor could afford a new war against Israel

---

[38] Ibid., 40.

[39] Ibid., 49.

[40] E. Barnavi, *A Historical Atlas of the Jewish People* (New York: Schocken Books, 1992), 258.

[41] A. Dershowitz, *The Case for Israel* (Hoboken, NJ: John Wiley, 2003), 59.

[42] B. Avishai, *The Tragedy of Zionism: How its Revolutionary Past Haunts Israel Democracy* (New York, Helios Press, 2002), 207.

[43] G. Wigoder, *The New Standard Jewish Encyclopedia* (New York: Facts on File, 1992), 692.

at this juncture.[44, 45] Indeed, the intervention by the two superpowers, Soviet Union and United States, saved Egypt in Suez war.[46] The war did not produce any territorial changes between Israel and the Arab countries, but it preceded the fall of the premiership of Moshe Sharret, who represented the moderate school of thought on Arab-Israeli relations[47] and could no longer stand the adventures of the army generals.[48] By his departure, indeed the moderate faction relinquished power back to Ben-Gurion, who believed in an iron fist policy toward the Arabs.[49]

In 1958, two years after the Suez war, with the commendation of Gamal Abdul Nasser, who had aspirations to lead the pan-Arab movement against Israel, the Palestine Liberation Organization (PLO) was founded. Under his leadership, the Palestinian struggle against Israel was proclaimed to be the concern of the entire Arab world.[50] The next three decades witnessed the PLO engaging in a number of terrorist activities against Israel and the United States.[51] Concurrently, these terrorist endeavors fed Western media the substrate they required to mobilize world public opinion around the axiom of "Arabs against peace."[52]

In the spring of 1967, another clash between Arabs and Israel occurred. Nasser succeeded in putting together a coalition of six Arab countries: Egypt, Syria, Iraq, Sudan, Yemen, and Algeria. Proclaiming the imminent annihilation of Israel, Egyptian forces occupied Sharm el-Sheikh on May 20, 1967. On June 4, Israel responded and in a surprise attack defeated the Arab armies for the

---

[44] N. G. Finkelstein, *Image and Reality of the Israel-Palestine Conflict* (London: Verso, 2003), 134–139.

[45] I. Deutscher, "The Israeli-Arab War. June 1967," in A. Shatz, *Prophets Outcast* (New York: Nation Books, 2004), 179.

[46] M. Rodinson, Marxism and the Muslim World (New York, Monthly Review Press, 1981), 282

[47] A. Shlaim, *The Iron Wall: Israel and the Arab World* (New York: W. W. Norton, 2001), 162.

[48] Ibid., 113, 115.

[49] Ibid., 125.

[50] Ibid., 187.

[51] A. Dershowitz, *The Case for Israel* (Hoboken, NJ: John Wiley, 2003), 105.

[52] N. Chomsky, *The Fateful Triangle: The United States, Israel and the Palestinians* (Boston: South End Press, 1983), 164–167.

third time in what is known as the Six-Day war.[53] Israel captured Sinai, the Gaza Strip, the West Bank, and Golan Heights, and integrated East Jerusalem. As a result of this war, another 430,000 Arabs were added to the pile of refugees,[54] Israel began the construction of Jewish settlements in the captured territories, and Secretary of Defense Moshe Dayan declared that the settlements in the territories would stay forever.[55] It has been argued that concern over the emerging Arab nationalism under the leadership of Nasser played a crucial role in the Six-Day war.[56]

On November 22, 1967, the United Nations Security Council passed Resolution 242 calling upon Israel to pull back to its borders prior to the Six-Day war. The language of this resolution was intentionally left vague so it would not obstruct the future negotiations between all parties.[57] Nonetheless, hard-line Arab countries and the PLO rejected the resolution because it meant peaceful coexistence with Israel, and Israel also was not keen about it because the resolution did not address the Arab-Israeli conflict in whole.[58] After the Israeli victory in the 1967 war, maintaining control over the captured territories west of the Jordan River, without incorporating these areas into the Jewish state, became the main theme of Israeli policy.[59]

Under the premiership of Golda Meir, from 1968 to 1974, relations between Israel and its Arab neighbors were in a stalemate. In general, the Arabs were more interested in recovering the lost territories than maintaining peace, and Israel was only prepared for peace under its own terms. In 1972, Jordan offered a federation plan to be named the United Arab Kingdom, comprising a Jordanian

---

[53] E. Barnavi, *A Historical Atlas of the Jewish People* (New York: Schocken Books, 1992), 260.
[54] N. Chomsky, *The Fateful Triangle: The United States, Israel and the Palestinians* (Boston: South End Press, 1983), 97.
[55] Ibid., 104.
[56] N. G. Finkelstein, *Image and Reality of the Israel-Palestine Conflict* (London: Verso, 2003), 142, 193–196.
[57] Ibid., 41.
[58] *Encyclopedia Judaica*, "Arab World," CD-ROM edition, 1997, Judaica Multimedia.
[59] A. Shlaim, *The Iron Wall: Israel and the Arab World* (New York: W. W. Norton, 2001), 255.

region in the East Bank and a Palestinian region in the West Bank and Gaza Strip. The PLO, Egypt, and Israel, each for different considerations, rejected the plan.[60]

On October 4, 1973, Egyptian and Syrian armies surprised Israel in what is known as the Yom Kippur war. The Arabs' motivation in waging the war was merely to end the political deadlock and to entice the world's superpowers into pressuring Israel to withdraw from the captured territories.[61] Israel was not prepared for the war, and in the early stages Egypt and Syria made remarkable progress. Israel later barely managed to hold on to the captured territories. On October 22, 1973, the United Nations Security Council Resolution 338 called for a ceasefire. Both sides abided two days later.[62]

In January 1976, the United States vetoed a United Nations Security Council resolution calling for a settlement along the 1967 borders and the establishment of a Palestinian state next to Israel.[63] The daring move of Egyptian President Anwar Sadat to declare Egypt's willingness to recognize the state of Israel unilaterally, and in spite of opposition from other Arab countries, resolved into an agreement between the two countries. Eventually, in 1979, Israel released the Sinai Peninsula back to Egypt. Hertzberg argues that Prime Minister Begin returned Sinai to Egypt with less reluctance because the peninsula was not part of the sacred and untouchable biblical Israel. Those who come to power after Begin, he projected, would take a different position on the remaining captured territories.[64, 65]

It has been argued that what was signed between Israel and Egypt was not a peace agreement, since the source of a future war (namely the Palestinian issue) was never addressed. Rather, it was

---

[60] Ibid., 313.

[61] Ibid., 319.

[62] E. Barnavi, *A Historical Atlas of the Jewish People* (New York: Schocken Books, 1992), 264.

[63] N. Chomsky, *The Fateful Triangle: The United States, Israel and the Palestinians* (Boston: South End Press, 1983), 67.

[64] A. Hertzberg, *The Zionist Idea* (Philadelphia: Jewish Publication Society, 1997), 627.

[65] A. Shlaim, *The Iron Wall: Israel and the Arab World* (New York: W. W. Norton, 2001), 353 .

essentially a ceasefire agreement.[66] Nonetheless, over the next two decades, the Jewish settlements, under the name of security, increased remarkably in the West Bank, which now was called by their biblical names of Judea and Samaria, with the expectation that they would never separate from Israel.[67, 68]

Israel completed withdrawal from the Sinai Peninsula by April 1982, as it had agreed in the Camp David Accord. The increased presence of the PLO in southern Lebanon, their violent activities against Jewish settlements, and the assassination of the Israel ambassador to England on June 3, 1982, provided excuses for Israel to invade Lebanon on June 6 to suppress the Palestinian activities and punish Lebanon for hosting them. It is said that the invasion of Lebanon was indeed part of a larger plan to support the Maronite Christians in forming a government friendly to Israel, to oust the Syrian forces, to destroy the infrastructure of the PLO in southern Lebanon (resulting in the migration of Palestinians to Jordan), and to transform Jordan into a Palestinian state.[69] Nonetheless, what Israel called a war against terrorism and the Arabs called an Israeli occupation of southern Lebanon produced about eighteen thousand Lebanese dead in addition to many Palestinians and Syrians.[70]

Two weeks after the end of the war, on the eve of Rosh-Ha-Shana, the massacre of seven hundred to eight hundred Palestinian refugees in the Sabra and Shatilla camps[71] outside Beirut by Christian Phalange forces outraged the world and mobilized public opinion against the Jewish state. Public opinion in the United States, Israel's friendliest constituency, found Israel at least partially responsible for the massacre of civilians in the Palestinian camps. Six out of ten

[66] Y. Leibowitz, *Judaism, Human Values, and the Jewish State* (Cambridge, MA: Harvard University Press, 1992), 234.

[67] A. Hertzberg, *The Zionist Idea* (Philadelphia: Jewish Publication Society, 1997), 628.

[68] A. Shlaim, *The Iron Wall: Israel and the Arab World* (New York: W. W. Norton, 2001), 316.

[69] Ibid., 396.

[70] *Encyclopedia Encarta*, "Lebanon (Country)," CD-ROM edition, 2000, Microsoft Corporation.

[71] A. Shlaim, *The Iron Wall: Israel and the Arab World* (New York: W. W. Norton, 2001), 416.

Americans felt that Israel had used more force in southern Lebanon than was necessary.[72]

Even American Jews, who historically identified with the state of Israel, sensed that Begin's policies were harming the support of Israel in the United States. More than half of those polled thought Israel must bear partial responsibility for the massacre since it occurred in the area under the control of Israeli forces.

Jewish intellectuals in America were even more vocal. Professors Nathan Glazer and Seymour Martin Lipset called the operation in southern Lebanon "ill-advised." They argued that in contrast to 1967 and 1973, Israel's survival in 1982 was not at stake and the ceasefire across the Israel-Lebanese border was still effective.[73]

Inside Israel, the reaction was not any different. On the evening of September 25, 1982, over four hundred thousand Israelis demonstrated in Tel-Aviv demanding a formal judicial investigation of the massacre and calling for the resignation of Prime Minister Begin and Defense Minister Ariel Sharon.[74] The Lebanon war was indeed the first Israeli-Arab war where public opinion was not behind the government.[75]

Israel's invasion of southern Lebanon and its aftermath strengthened the antiwar movement inside Israel, on the one hand, and burdened Israel-Diaspora relations, on the other hand.[76] It was after the invasion of Lebanon that many Jews for the first time questioned the wisdom of indisputable support for the state of Israel.[77] Indeed, some Jews of the Diaspora viewed the behavior of the Jewish state to be against the values upon which the state was founded.

[72] *Encyclopedia Judaica*, "War in Lebanon: Public Opinion," CD-ROM edition, 1997, Judaica Multimedia.

[73] *New York Times*, June 30, 1982.

[74] *Encyclopedia Judaica*, "War in Lebanon: Dissent in Israel," CD-ROM edition, 1997, Judaica Multimedia.

[75] J. Revel, *How Democracies Perish* (New York: Doubleday, 1984), 113.

[76] *Encyclopedia Judaica*, "War in Lebanon: Dissent in Israel," CD-ROM edition, 1997, Judaica Multimedia.

[77] T. L. Friedman, *From Beirut to Jerusalem* (New York: Farrar, Straus, Giroux, 1989), 478.

Overall, the voice of dissatisfaction was considerably louder in Europe than in the United States.[78]

The Intifada, or "uprising," was a spontaneous popular movement that initially began in the Gaza Strip in December 1987 and spread to the West Bank. The movement commenced as an act of social disobedience to Israeli rule in the occupied territories and presented as a series of demonstrations, strikes, riots, and acts of violence. The movement overall had a tremendous impact on Israeli-Palestinian relationships. First, the Intifada was a complete surprise to Israel and resulted in a major division in the Israeli political arena. While the Left sensed the necessity for a political solution, the Right saw the remedy in the implementation of more force.[79] Second, the Intifada movement brought the Palestinian issue once again into the spotlight, and the PLO was recognized as the sole representative of the Palestinian people. Consequently, the Jordanians, who had negotiated on behalf of the Palestinians with Israel on several occasions up to this point, left the scene permanently.[80] As another repercussion of Intifada, Israel came to the understanding that it had to talk to the Palestinians directly, instead of negotiating through world powers like the Ottoman Empire, the British government, and the United States, as the Zionist leaders and later Israel had done in the past.[81] Third, in the background of the movement, radical organizations like the Islamic resistance movement of Hamas and the Islamic Jihad were born.[82] Fourth, the Intifada received wide media coverage in the world, and for the first time, Israel, under the pressure of public opinion, realized there was a limit to what force could achieve in the territories. Influenced by the Islamic revolution in Iran, the original aspiration of the Intifada movement was to establish an Islamic state in all of Palestine, but in 1988, the PLO changed its position and adopted a resolution for the establishment of a Palestinian state neighboring Israel.[83]

---

[78] *Encyclopedia Judaica*, "War in Lebanon: The Media," CD-ROM edition, 1997, Judaica Multimedia.

[79] A. Shlaim, *The Iron Wall: Israel and the Arab World* (New York: W. W. Norton, 2001), 452.

[80] Ibid., 458.

[81] Ibid., 467.

[82] Ibid., 454.

[83] *Encyclopedia Encarta*, "Intifada," CD-ROM edition, 2000, Microsoft Corporation.

Once it had lost its Soviet backing, Syria demonstrated an enthusiasm to deal with the United States; so did Lebanon and Jordan. Israel, Syria, Lebanon, Jordan, Egypt, and for the first time the Palestinian delegate participated in the Madrid Peace Conference in October 1991.[84] The Palestinian delegate performed extremely well by showing a great deal of moderation. The Conference indeed encouraged U.S. policymakers to change their position more favorably toward the Palestinians. Under pressure exercised by the United States and partly influenced by the Intifada movement,[85] Israel adopted a policy of direct talks with Palestinians that eventually brought Yitzhak Rabin and Yasser Arafat to sign a peace treaty, the Oslo Accord, on September 13, 1993. According to the treaty, a limited Palestinian self-rule in the Israeli-occupied territories—in the Gaza Strip and the West Bank—became a reality.[86] The second accord in September 1995 expanded the limited Palestinian self-rule to the West Bank and gave the Israelis the right to send armed forces into the Palestinian areas if necessary.

Binyamin Netanyahu, the leader of the Likud party, categorically rejected the Oslo Accord as a surrender agreement and threatened to cancel it once he came into power.[87] Indeed, his premiership was distinguished by the expansion of settlements, the delayed pull-back of Israeli forces from Palestinian territories, and his refusal to open the pathway between the Gaza Strip and the West Bank, as had been contemplated in the Oslo Accord.[88] The archaeological digging under the Dome of Rock, the holy Muslim site, which incited a Palestinian violent uprising, was indeed the last nail he hammered into the coffin of the Oslo Peace Accord.

The election of Ehud Barak in 1999 as the prime minister once again raised hope for peace. He pledged to follow the Oslo path, but he reiterated that Israel would never pull back to 1967 borders and

---

[84] A. Shlaim, *The Iron Wall: Israel and the Arab World* (New York: W. W. Norton, 2001), 487.
[85] *Encyclopedia Encarta*, "Intifada," CD-ROM edition, 2000, Microsoft Corporation.
[86] *Encyclopedia Encarta*, "Palestine," CD-ROM edition, 2000, Microsoft Corporation.
[87] A. Shlaim, *The Iron Wall: Israel and the Arab World* (New York: W. W. Norton, 2001), 521.
[88] Ibid., 576.

would not give up the control of Jerusalem.[89] On the other hand, through the Camp David peace process of July 2000, Arafat continued to insist upon a Palestinian state based upon 1967 borders, with minor modifications.[90] When peace talks between the Israelis and Palestinians failed and the violence intensified, the Israelis elected Ariel Sharon, a right-wing hard-liner, in February 2001. Under Sharon's premiership, the region experienced the worst violence in decades. Palestinian suicide bombers managed to kill and wound scores of Israeli soldiers and civilians. Israeli forces occupied the West Bank and engaged in all-out military incursions aimed at crippling the Palestinian infrastructure and killing the militants as well as many civilians. The casualties of the Palestinians and Israelis between September 2000 and January 2004 have been estimated at 2,573 and 888, respectively.[91] Finally, the terrorist attack to the World Trade Center in New York on September 11, 2001, did not help the Palestinian cause. At the core of the neoconservative policies that were implemented by the United States after 2000, Israel was embraced on principle.[92] The new relationship between the United States and Israel left more room for the Jewish state's undertakings in the occupied territories, and shifted the Israeli security issue ahead of peace negotiations.[93] Indeed, Israel, under the banner of rooting out Palestinian terror,[94] justified an intense response to the anti-Israeli violence by ignoring the principle of proportionality[95] and implementing collective punishment in the territories;[96] what in turn not only provoked the international community against Israel's foreign policy[97] but also revived a new wave of anti-Semitism. Regretfully, the anti-Semitism that was marginalized in shame in many communities around the world, by riding on the tide of

---

[89] Ibid., 608.

[90] N. G. Finkelstein, *Image and Reality of the Israel-Palestine Conflict* (London: Verso, 2003), xxi.

[91] *Intifada in Numbers,* quoted at amicidisraele.org.

[92] E. Shorris, "Ignoble Liars," *Harper's* June 2004: 70.

[93] E. Kaplan, "The Jewish Divide on Israel," *The Nation* July 12, 2004.

[94] N. G. Finkelstein, *Image and Reality of the Israel-Palestine Conflict* (London: Verso, 2003), xxiii.

[95] M. Warschawski, *Toward an Open Tomb: The Crisis of Israeli Society* (New York: Monthly Review Press, 2004), 25.

[96] E. W. Said, *Orientalism* (New York: Vintage Press, 1994), xvii.

[97] A. Dershowitz, *The Case for Israel* (Hoboken, NJ: John Wiley, 2003), 171.

opposition to Israel's undertakings in the occupied territories, gained a new momentum.[98]

On November 11, 2004, Yasser Arafat, president of the Palestinian Authority, died. Only history will judge whether he was "a terrorist who failed his people" or he was "a man capable to keep Palestinian hope and aspiration alive." Moreover, it remains to be seen whether the demise of a man who was the symbol of Palestinian nationalism for over fifty years paved the road to the embattled peace or if the struggle among the fighting factions in Palestine would only promise a new wave of violence.

In summary, for more than half a century, both sides have engaged in violence while concurrently their propaganda machines have tried hard to mobilize the public opinion of Palestinians and Israelis against each other. Hence, many Israeli Jews stereotyped Arabs in general and Palestinians in particular as primitive people who only understand the language of force.[99] Many Arabs, on the other hand, pictured Israelis and Jews as immoral, corrupt, and selfish, who were only eager to control the world.[100] In the forefront of this hatred there have been five wars, a pile of refugees, the killing of thousands of Arabs and Israelis, and the assassinations of those moderate leaders who dared to propose a peaceful solution to the conflict, among them King Abdullah of Jordan in 1951, President Anwar Sadat of Egypt in 1981, and Prime Minister Yitzhak Rabin of Israel in 1995. Today, the issue is passionate, since both Palestinian Arabs and Israeli Jews like to identify themselves as strong and independent nation-states, and tragically both want to have their state in the same place.[101, 102] This intricate peculiarity has indeed enticed some to advocate the single-state solution[103] and others a confederate state[104] of Jews and Arabs in Palestine as the only viable solutions to

---

[98] A. Cockburn and J. St. Clair, *The Politics of Anti-Semitism* (Petrolia, CA: CounterPunch Press, 2003), 44.

[99] D. K. Shipler,. *Arab and Jew* (New York: Times Books, 1986), 222.

[100] Ibid., 314.

[101] Ibid., 77.

[102] N. G. Finkelstein, *Image and Reality of the Israel-Palestine Conflict* (London, Verso, 2003), 99.

[103] Ibid., 183.

[104] H. Arendt, "'The Jew as Pariah': Peace or Armistice in the Near East?" in A. Shatz, *Prophets Outcast* (New York, Nation Books, 2004), 95.

the conflict. It has been argued that the present Balkanization of the region, where each small area expresses an extreme nationalism, would serve as a battleground where only great powers can take advantage.[105]

The intricacy of the Arab-Israel conflict can only be understood once the roles of the key interactive players of the conflict have been carefully assessed. The triumph of the Six-Day war and the historic claim on Jerusalem by both sides, the policy of United States toward Israel, the lack of cohesiveness in the Arab world, and the utilization of the Arab-Israel conflict as an instrument of a power struggle by the Arab states are among the issues that are herein carefully addressed.

The astounding victory of Israel in the Six-Day war in 1967 placed the Arab-Israel conflict in a new perspective.

On the one hand, the PLO and Arab states somehow softened their previous position toward Israel after the Six-Day war.[106] Those Arab countries that had maintained a radical, hard-line position, and were principally rejecting Israel's right of existence up to this point, for the first time were prepared to accept the right of existence for Israel under certain conditions. Indeed, it was in February 1970 that Nasser for the first time declared that a durable peace between Israel and the Arab states was possible if Israel left the captured territories and accepted a form of settlement for the Palestinian refugees.[107] Israel, however, did not take that idea seriously and did not respond to this declaration at the time.[108] Israel's position has been criticized even by political commentators who had justified Israeli cause until 1967 on the ground of softening the Arabs stubborn attitude toward Israel's right to exist.[109]

---

[105] Ibid., 93

[106] E. Barnavi, *A Historical Atlas of the Jewish People* (New York: Schocken Books, 1992), 264.

[107] N. Chomsky, *The Fateful Triangle: The United States, Israel and the Palestinians* (Boston: South End Press, 1983), 64.

[108] A. Shlaim, *The Iron Wall: Israel and the Arab World* (New York: W. W. Norton, 2001), 299.

[109] J. Daniel, *The Jewish Prison: A Rebellious Meditation on the State of Judaism* cited by A. Shatz, *The Jewish Question* (New York Review of Books, 52:14, September 2005)

On the other hand, the 1967 victory changed the meaning of the Jewish state. Prior to the Six-Day war, the state of Israel was viewed as a homeland for the Jews, originally proposed as a remedy to anti-Semitism in Europe and elsewhere. However, after the victory, a messianic desire, long dormant in Israeli society and the Diaspora, emerged. At this historic juncture, the religious Zionists, influenced by the teachings of Rabbi Abraham Isaac Kook (1865–1935), a rabbinical and Zionist thinker, grasped the opportunity to point out the "biblical borders" of the state of Israel and vigorously argued that no Jewish state had the legitimate right to exchange "land for peace," since that kind of effort would obstruct the messianic process.[110] On the subjects of redemption and the Land of Israel, Rabbi Kook wrote, "All of our people believe that we are in the first stage of the Final Redemption. . . . This ancient tradition about the Redemption bears witness to the spiritual light by which the Jew understands himself and all the events of his history to the last generation, the one that is awaiting the Redemption that is near at hand.[111] . . . Eretz Israel is not something apart from the soul of the Jewish people; it is no mere national possession, serving as a means of unifying our people and buttressing its material, or even its spiritual survival."[112]

Religious Zionists and the followers of Rabbi Kook viewed the victory in the Six-Day war, having been preceded by the Holocaust for twenty-some years, as a sign of the coming of the Messiah. According to Talmudic teachings, the son of Satan shall rule the world before the coming of the Messiah. Therefore, they interpreted the Holocaust and the terrible suffering during the Nazi regime as the rule of the son of Satan, and the establishment of the state of Israel and the victory in the Six-Day war as the first stage of the final Redemption. It is noteworthy that even many authorities in Orthodox Judaism do not support this interpretation.[113] In this regard, Arthur Hertzberg, a prominent figure supporting peace with the Palestinians, believes we can only build the future of Jewish people through wisdom, understanding, and modesty, but not through

---

[110] A. Hertzberg, *The Zionist Idea* (Philadelphia: Jewish Publication Society, 1997), 626.
[111] Ibid., 430–431.
[112] Ibid., 419.
[113] E. Barnavi, *A Historical Atlas of the Jewish People* (New York: Schocken Books, 1992), 203.

fundamentalism. Those who view the establishment of the state of Israel as the first stage of the final Redemption are not thinking sound. The state of Israel, in their opinion, was not a remedy to anti-Semitism but a prerequisite to the coming of the Messiah. It is such thinking that made it possible for Dr. Baruch Goldstein to feel justified in committing the mass murder of Muslim worshippers in Hebron on February 25, 1994. It was the same thinking that influenced Yigal Amir to assassinate Prime Minister Yitzhak Rabin on November 4, 1995. Both Goldstein and Amir had no doubt that they were committing these killings in good conscience, in obedience to a higher law than the legalities of the state of Israel.[114]

It was in this manner that the Israeli community was divided into two camps. On one side were those who believed in the exchange of land for peace with the Palestinians. The other camp maintained a fundamentalist position, insisting on the "undivided land of Israel" with its biblical definition,[115] hence opposing any negotiations with the Palestinians over land. Moreover, the supporters of the "undivided land of Israel" have often argued that the exchange of "land for peace" could compromise the future security of the state of Israel. On the subject of security, however, Professor Leibowitz wrote: "There is no assurance of survival in the world. Perhaps there is assurance for the Chinese, because it is almost impossible to wipe them out. But do the Poles have any assurance? . . . Zionism's demand for a guaranteed security arises from the 19th century outlook, which considered security one of the normal characteristics of human life. But in our day we can see—even on the level of science fiction—that the human race feels its life to be hanging by a thread."[116] In his opinion, "No conditions, no strategic boundaries, could assure Israel's security with absolute certainty. When we established our State in this country, we undertook to pay a price for our national independence. We shall always have to exert considerable effort to survive. The dangers can only be minimized through our political sagacity. Without it, our power alone will not suffice."[117] The supporters of the "undivided

---

[114] A. Hertzberg, *The Zionist Idea* (Philadelphia: Jewish Publication Society, 1997), 626.
[115] Ezekiel 47:13–20.
[116] Y. Leibowitz, *Judaism, Human Values and the Jewish State* (Cambridge, MA: Harvard University Press, 1992), 196.
[117] Ibid., 246.

land of Israel" have also argued that the annexation of the West Bank, by incorporating a large number of Palestinians with a higher birth rate, would undermine the Jewish character of the state of Israel,[118] a concern that has preoccupied the mind of Zionists from the outset.[119]

The historical claim on Jerusalem, by both Palestinian Arabs and Israeli Jews, is yet another thorn in the eye of the Middle East conflict that\, does not justify the claims of either side on this land.[120,121] The place has been fought over and over again for almost four thousand years, and the fact that one people lived in this land sometime in the past does not necessarily entitled them to own the land today.[122] Leibowitz further argues that should the scheme of an

---

[118] A. Shlaim, *The Iron Wall: Israel and the Arab World* (New York: W. W. Norton, 2001), 430.

[119] I. Deutscher, "The Israeli-Arab War, June 1967," in A. Shatz, *Prophets Outcast* (New York: Nation Books, 2004), 176.

[120] Y. Leibowitz, *Judaism, Human Values, and the Jewish State* (Cambridge, MA: Harvard University Press, 1992), 236.

[121] N. G. Finkelstein, *Image and Reality of the Israel-Palestine Conflict* (London: Verso, 2003), 101.

[122] Throughout history, Jerusalem has been handed around among various powers at different times:

- In the fourth millennium BCE, Jerusalem was inhabited by Canaanites who were under Egyptian hegemony.
- Around the first millennium BCE, David conquered Jerusalem, and his successor, Solomon, built the First Temple of Jerusalem.
- Babylonians destroyed Jerusalem in 586 BCE
- Persian Empire defeated the Babylonians in 539 BCE, incorporated Jerusalem into their empire, and built the Second Temple of Jerusalem.
- Alexander the Great conquered Jerusalem in 333 BCE and brought in the Greek influence.
- Antiochus IV destroyed part of Jerusalem in 168 BCE
- Maccabees revolted against the Seleucids in 165 BCE and established the Hasmonaean dynasty.
- Pompeii, the Roman commander, conquered Jerusalem in 63 BCE and incorporated it into the Roman Empire.
- During the Zealot uprising from 66 to 70 CE, the Jews tried hard to regain control of Jerusalem from the Romans and failed.
- Titus, the son of Emperor Vespasian, ruined the Second Temple of Jerusalem in 70 CE.
- Jews, under the leadership of Simon Bar Kokhba, revolted against the Romans in 132–135 CE to control Jerusalem and failed again. From this point on, Jerusalem as a capital city was no more relevant.

"undivided land of Israel" have succeeded and even if the Arabs did not become the majority, the state would no longer be a Jewish state and could not meet the religious needs of the supporters of the plan, and indeed might endanger the security. Certainly, there would be problems of ruling over two peoples that do not cohere together as a single nation.[123]

The second issue that makes the Arab-Israeli conflict so complicated is the United States's policy toward Israel. Historically, the United States has vacillated between two policies toward the Arab-Israeli conflict: it either endorsed the international consensus, including U.N. Resolution 242 or it rejected the peace negotiation with the Palestinians altogether. The latter policy originates from the notions that since the Arabs deny the right of self-determination for Jews in Palestine, therefore they are not prepared for a peaceful settlement with Israel.[124] Within the context of the Rejectionism policy, the United States has categorically refused to communicate directly with the Palestinians until recently.

The adoption of the Rejectionism policy by the United States originates from two major dynamics. First, the United States views Israel as a strategic asset for itself. Israel is strategically valuable to the United States for the purpose of controlling Middle East oil, deterring the indigenous threats to the United States elsewhere,[125] and

---

- Roman Emperor Constantine I undertook the building of a church in Jerusalem from 303 to 337 CE.
- From 611 to 622 CE, Jerusalem was incorporated into the Sassanid Empire.
- Muslims conquered Jerusalem in 637 CE and built the Dome of Rock and the Mosque of Omar.
- Crusaders regained Jerusalem from the Seljuks in 1099 CE.
- Saladin recaptured Jerusalem from the Christians in 1187 CE.
- Jerusalem was an integrated territory of the Ottoman Empire by 1517 CE.
- With the defeat of the Ottoman Empire in 1917, Jerusalem was part of British Mandate.
- United Nations resolution of partition of Palestine into two separate states was signed in 1947. According to this resolution, Jerusalem would become an international city.

[123] Y. Leibowitz, *Judaism, Human Values, and the Jewish State* (Cambridge, MA: Harvard University Press, 1992), 234.

[124] N. Chomsky, *The Fateful Triangle: The United States, Israel and Palestinians* (Boston: South End Press, 1983), 39–40.

[125] Ibid., 17–20.

the historic role Israel played along with the United States during the years of the Cold War.[126] This close relationship between the two countries, it has been argued, grew after the Six-Day war in 1967 and was further nurtured after the 1973 war.[127] Today, Israel stands as a solid partner of United States, saving billions of research dollars in weapon systems and technology research for America. Above all, there is no concern that Israel may be absorbed by a rival country or may have to face up an internal opposition toward the special relation between the two countries.[128]

The second dynamic originates from the cultural similarities between the United States and Israel and the value system that is shared by both of its peoples.[129] This aspect, no matter how trivial it may sound, has an enormous impact on how the political system and the media in America may react to the Arab-Israeli conflict. Among these cultural issues one cannot ignore the fact that Israel is the only Western-style democracy in the Middle East and thus far has maintained this system of government despite ongoing conflicts in the region.[130]

In the same way, the average American can identify with the Israeli value system more comfortably than with that of Arabs, which is a value system that categorically differs from the American system on issues such as individual freedom, women's rights, political pluralism, and separation of church and state. Accordingly, the American media and members of the U.S. Congress view and analyze the Arab-Israeli conflict within the context of this value system.

Within the context of the cultural dynamic, there is the political and financial support of Christian evangelical groups for

[126] J. J. Goldberg, *Jewish Power: Inside the Jewish Establishment* (Reading, MA: Addison-Wesley, 1996), 199.
[127] A. F. K. Organski, *$36 Billion Bargain*, reviewed by D. Pipes@danielpipes.org/article/604.
[128] M. Plitnick, *Myth and Reality: Jewish Influence on US Middle East*, Jewish Voice for Peace Newsletter, June 2005
[129] S. P. Huntington, *The Clash of Civilizations: Remaking of World Order* (New York: Simon & Schuster, 1996), 254.
[130] J. J. Goldberg, *Jewish Power: Inside the Jewish Establishment* (Reading, MA: Addison-Wesley, 1996), 265.

Israel.[131] These groups, which enjoy a wide political base in the United States, have access to vast financial resources, and support Israel much more generously than the American Jews can afford.[132] They are deeply religious, interpret the Bible literally, and support Israel against any land compromise with the Palestinians that might jeopardize the biblical prophecies on *millenarian* or the second coming of Christ.[133] It is within the same context that the role of these "Christian Zionist" groups, with their lobbyist machine far stronger than the American-Israel Public Affairs Committee (AIPAC) [134] and the Presidents Conference,[135] the two pro-Israel lobbies, can be understood. In fact, there are a considerable number of devoted Christians among the members of Congress who support Israel merely because of the holy land[136] and other religious considerations.[137] Indeed, it has been argued that this Christian ideology has a stronger influence on pro-Israel voting in the U.S. Congress than Jewish campaign money. The democratic image of Israel, the history of Orientalism and Arab unpopularity,[138] the Christian sympathy for the holy land, and the memories of the Holocaust marked with sympathy for the Jews are instrumental in

---

[131] M. Plitnick, "Reclaiming the Struggle Against Anti-Semitism" in *Reframing Anti-Semitism: Alternative Jewish Perspectives* (Oakland, CA: Jewish Voice for Peace, 2004), 8.

[132] B. Broadway, "The Evangelical-Israel Connection," *Washington Post*, March 27, 2004.

[133] E. Abrams, *Faith or Fear* (New York: Free Press, 1997), 63.

[134] AIPAC was established in 1954 and is principally involved in shaping Congressional opinion. With an annual revenue of over $15 million in 1990, outstanding campaign skills, and a network of contacts, AIPAC is as influential as the tobacco and gun lobbies and has succeeded in influencing the American political system through lawful mechanisms. Some, however, have argued that AIPAC is nothing more than a paper tiger that may collapse at the raise of an eyebrow by the U.S. Congress. (See A. Cockburn and J. St. Clair, *The Politics of Anti-Semitism* [Petrolia, CA: CounterPunch, 2003], 104.)

[135] The Presidents Conference was created in the mid-1950s to express American Jewry's consensus support for Israel. This political body generally addresses the executive branch of the U.S. government. In fact, the White House and the State Department have recognized the Presidents Conference as the voice of the American Jewish community.

[136] J. J. Goldberg, *Jewish Power: Inside the Jewish Establishment* (Reading, PA: Addison-Wesley, 1996), 266–267.

[137] N. G. Finkelstein, *Image and Reality of the Israel-Palestine Conflict* (London: Verso, 2003), xxxi.

[138] E. S. Said, *Orientalism* (New York: Vintage Books, 1994), 26.

solidly lining up the legislators behind Israel.[139] The legislative support for Israel was furthered when the neoconservative ideology of the recent U.S. administration squarely linked the Palestinian struggle with that of terrorism following the September 11, 2001, event.[140] In essence, cultural differences between Palestinian Arabs and Israeli Jews, religion being an important element among many of the population, have made the matters significantly worse. Should the conflict with the same characteristics and intensity have happened between two peoples within the same civilization, its resolution would have been probably more likely.[141]

For most American Jews, Israel is survival—not only survival of a Zionist dream but also survival of Jews and Judaism.[142, 143] Because of this special emotional attachment, watching an Israeli soldier get killed by the hands of a few Arabs reminds average Jews of the nineteen centuries of oppression when they were helpless.[144] Consequently, American Jewry has an exceptionally positive attitude toward the state of Israel and behaves in a quite focused manner when it comes to its moral or financial support.[145]

This special feeling for Israel has been further enforced by a number of Zionist assumptions, such as (1) when Israel is threatened, then the entire world Jewry is endangered; (2) Israel's security can only be guaranteed through force; and (3) those who criticize Israel's foreign policy do not care about its security and, for that matter, the future of Judaism.[146]

---

[139] J. J. Goldberg, *Jewish Power: Inside the Jewish Establishment* (Reading, MA: Addison-Wesley, 1996), 266.

[140] M. Warschawski, *Toward an Open Tomb: The Crisis of Israeli Society* (New York: Monthly Review Press, 2004), 13.

[141] S. P. Huntington, *The Clash of Civilizations: Remarking of World Order* (New York: Simon & Schuster, 1996), 256.

[142] P. Findley, *They Dare to Speak Out* (Chicago: Lawrence Hill Books, 1989), 265.

[143] J. J. Goldberg, *Jewish Power: Inside the Jewish Establishment* (Reading, MA: Addison-Wesley, 1996), 148.

[144] I. Chernus, *American Jews and Israel* (Boulder, CO: Rocky Mountain Peace and Justice Center, 1997).

[145] P. Findley, *They Dare to Speak Out* (Chicago: Lawrence Hill Books, 1985), 26.

[146] H. Draper, *Zionism, Israel and the Arabs* (Berkeley, CA: Center for Socialist History, 1997), 161.

Along these lines of rationalization, the criticism of Israel's foreign policy has been often interpreted as an anti-Semitic sentiment,[147] an opinion that has never been documented as the official position of the state of Israel.[148] This outlook, however, has been often used to silence Israel's critics,[149] a practice that has been viewed as utter censorship.[150] Contrarily, we must not also ignore the anti-Semites who hide their hatred for Jews behind the Palestinian cause.[151]

Nonetheless, the Jewish opinion is not monolithic, and Jews remain divided on the Arab-Israeli peace process. There have been moderate elements, even among the leadership of the Zionist movement, such as Nahum Goldmann. He served as the president of the World Zionist Organization from 1956 to 1968 and was one of those unique personalities who dared to express his dissatisfaction with the Israeli policy toward Arabs. He was not only unhappy with some of the harsh Israeli policies but equally with the overzealous applause of American Jewry for these policies. In October 1981, Goldmann wrote, "We will have to understand that Jewish suffering during the Holocaust no longer will serve as a protection, and we certainly must refrain from using the argument of the Holocaust to justify whatever we may do. To use the Holocaust as an excuse for the bombing of Lebanon, for instance, as Menachem Begin does, is a kind of 'Hillul Hashem' [sacrilege], a banalization of the sacred tragedy of the Shoah [Holocaust], which must not be misused to justify politically doubtful and morally indefensible policies."[152] Nonetheless, the followers of the peaceful solution of the Arab-Israeli conflict are in a weaker position today.

---

[147] B. Klug, "The Myth of the New Anti-Semitism," *The Nation*, February 2, 2004.

[148] A. Dershowitz, *The Case for Israel* (Hoboken, NJ: John Wiley, 2003), 209.

[149] A. Cockburn and J. Saint Clair, *The Politics of Anti-Semitism* (Petrolia, CA: CounterPunch, 2003), 13.

[150] J. Butler, "No, It Is Not Anti-Semitism," in H. Picciotto & M. Plitnick, *Reframing Anti-Semitism: Alternative Jewish Perspectives* (Oakland, CA: Jewish Voice for Peace, 2004), 26.

[151] H. Picciotto and M. Plitnick, *Reframing Anti-Semitism: Alternative Jewish Perspectives* (Oakland, CA: Jewish Voice for Peace, 2004), ii.

[152] *Shalom Network Newsletter*, October/November 1981, reprinted from the *London Jewish Chronicle*, quoted in N. Chomsky, *The Fateful Triangle: The United States, Israel and the Palestinians* (Boston: South End Press, 1983), 98.

On the Arab side, the subject is equally complicated. Historically, the antagonism between twenty-one Arab countries has been stronger than their desire for the unity required addressing the Arab-Israeli conflict. Although a number of assemblies, summit meetings, and short-lived federations and confederations, under the banner of the Arab League, Federation of Arab Republics, Arab Monetary Fund, and Organization of Arab Oil Exporting Countries, convened in the past, none of them were fruitful or accomplished anything meaningful. Throughout these years, the Arab-Israeli conflict only served as a catalyst for the inter-Arab relations.[153] Generally, following each Israeli military victory, Arab leaders came close to each other temporarily, passed a number of proposals and resolutions, but soon, over different issues, separated and went their own way. Indeed, the Arab leaders often got into a polemic among themselves on different issues, using the Arab-Israeli conflict as an instrument of a power struggle. In some instances, the Arab leaders even established their own paramilitary groups in Palestine, and the rival fighting among these groups hampered peaceful resolution of the conflict. Nonetheless, the attitude of the Arab countries toward the Arab-Israeli conflict has not been homogeneous. Syria, Iraq, Libya, Yemen, and Algeria belong to the "rejection front" and have essentially maintained a position against Israel's right of existence. Moderate Arab countries like Egypt, Jordan, Tunisia, Sudan, and Morocco, on the other hand, accept the right of existence for Israel under certain provisions. The position of Saudi Arabia and Kuwait on this matter has been historically vague and unclear. In essence, for a number of economic and political reasons, Palestinians in general and the PLO in particular never enjoyed political independence. Moreover, lack of cohesiveness in the Arab world has hampered timely decision making whenever opportunities have revealed themselves. Not having a political strategy, excessively depending on nationalist demagogy,[154] indulging in illusionary behavior,[155] and ignoring the far-reaching consequences of their enemy's rapid

---

[153] *Encyclopedia Judaica*, "Inter-Arab Affairs; Arab Unity," CD-ROM edition, 1997, Judaica Multimedia.
[154] I. Deuscher, "The Israeli-Arab War, June 1967," in A. Shatz, *Prophets Outcast* (New York: Nation Books, 2004), 177.
[155] H. Arendt, "'The Jew as Pariah': Peace or Armistice in the Near East," in A. Shatz, *Prophets Outcast* (New York: Nation Books, 2004), 71.

economic development,[156] the Palestinians[157] have failed to grasp the historic opportunities of the settlement of the conflict if they arose.

In addition, the type of struggle that the Palestinians have waged against the occupation has brought them unfavorable publicity in the West and particularly in the United States. In other words, their struggle against occupation has often been interpreted as mere animosity of the Islamic people against non-Muslims.[158] The use of violence as an instrument of struggle,[159] inappropriate and often uncalculated gestures of the Palestinian authorities,[160] their indulgence in threatening Israel's existence,[161] along with the enthusiasm of the Western media for taking advantage of the conflict, has pushed the issue of occupation into oblivion and instead has brought the subject of terrorism into the spotlight. Consequently, the public support for the Palestinian cause has been significantly eroded. Furthermore, in contrast to American Jews, who are usually assertive in their demands, Arab-Americans with their substantial resources have failed to show enthusiasm, energy, organization, and a sense of political philanthropy in order to offset the pro-Israeli lobby in the United States.[162]

Today, at the commencement of the twenty-first century, the real players in the conflict are the following:

1.   The hard-line Israelis, who, in their assessments, have fought four victorious wars against the Arabs and do not believe they should give the captured territories back without a substantial concession by the Arab countries in the form of guaranteed national security and provisions for their spiritual needs. Some elements within this camp certainly hope their hard-line approach would

---

[156] Ibid., 76.

[157] Palestinian population in millions in 2003:

Israel	West Bank	Gaza	Jordan	Lebanon	Syria	Others
1.2	2.3	1.4	2.8	0.5	0.5	0.5

[158] E. W. Said, *Orientalism* (New York: Vintage Books, 1994), 107.

[159] J. J. Goldberg, *Jewish Power: Inside the American Jewish Establishment* (Reading, MA: Addison-Wesley, 1996), 203.

[160] A. Dershowitz, *The Case for Israel* (Hoboken, NJ: John Wiley, 2003), 186, 199.

[161] I. Deuscher, "The Israeli-Arab War, June 1967" in A. Shatz, *Prophets Outcast* (New York: Nation Books, 2004), 177.

[162] P. Findley, *They Dare to Speak Out* (Chicago: Lawrence Hill Books, 1985), 324.

eventually liberate the entire "Land of Israel," and the sacrifice of Jews is a nominal price to pay for this gain.[163] They fail, however, to realize that the continued occupation only increases hatred and tension, with outcomes that could be self-destructive for the Jewish state.[164, 165] Indeed, consequent to this apprehension, newer generation of Israelis seem to be less apt to sharing with Palestinians and overall they care less for democracy.[166] The present state of affairs has indeed enticed Israel to follow a policy of "unilateral separation"[167] that has made a dialogue between Israel and international public opinion quite awkward.[168]

Moreover, the permanent state of war has a serious impact on people's norms of conduct and in turn tarnishes the democratic attributes of the state.[169] Dragging of the status quo will be harder for the Israelis who have a progressive social life and a flourishing economy.[170]

2.   Militant hard-line Palestinians, who have not genuinely accepted Israel's right of existence and whose main focus of attention is the issue of occupation.[171] In their calculations, Israel only withdraws from the territories when the cost of occupation, human and economic, rises.[172] These forces are generally sponsored and financially supported by the Arab states and often view the Middle East peace as an end to their very existence; hence, they are hardly taking a compromising posture.

---

[163] I. Zertal, *Israel's Holocaust and the Politics of Nationhood* (London: Cambridge University Press, 2005).

[164] Y. Leibowitz, "Occupation and Terror," in A. Shatz, *Prophets Outcast* (New York: Nation Books, 2004), 268.

[165] M. Ellis, "The Palestinian Uprising and the Future of the Jewish People," in A. Shatz, *Prophets Outcast* (New York: Nation Books, 2004), 337.

[166] B. Avishai, *The Tragedy of Zionism: How its Revolutionary Past Haunts Israel Democracy* (New York, Helios Press, 2002), 348.

[167] M. Warschawski, *Toward an Open Tomb: The Crisis of Israeli Society* (New York,: Monthly Review Press, 2004), 49.

[168] Ibid., 47.

[169] Ibid., 62, 64.

[170] H. Arendt, "'The Jew as Pariah': Peace or Armistice in the Near East," in A. Shatz, *Prophets Outcast* (New York: Nation Books, 2004), 73.

[171] A. Dershowitz, *The Case for Israel* (Hoboken, NJ: John Wiley, 2003), 65.

[172] N. G. Finkelstein, *Image and Reality of the Israel-Palestine Conflict* (London: Verso, 2003), xxxiv.

3.   The United States, as the superpower, is the only force capable of mediating the conflict and yet is not willing or perhaps cannot offer an even-handed mediation.[173] Critics argue that as long as the vital interests of the United States are not at stake and the public pressure has not seriously risen, the United States will not force Israel to make major concessions.[174] Others, however, have argued that after September 11, 2001, the United States is no longer satisfied with stability alone,[175] and has an ambitious geopolitical reconfiguration plan of the Middle East in mind.[176]

4.   The Arab states that have utilized the conflict as an instrument of power struggle among themselves in the past and have tried to get the most out of the situation to their advantage. These governments categorically lack a base support among their people and have to give in to the great powers' interest in the region for their survival. In this scenario, as long as the players follow their own lines, expectation for a meaningful and lasting peace would be unrealistic.

In spite of the violence exercised by both Palestinians and Israelis to achieve their goals, the bulk of Israeli Jews and Palestinian Arabs demand a genuine peace. Let us hope that one day all sides of the conflict will realize that their stubborn attachment to the disserviceable goal is nothing more than foolishness.[177]

Along this line of analysis, Abba Eban, the late foreign minister of Israel, suggested that "wars, sieges, blockades, cease-fires, armistices, terrorism, oil embargoes, Great Power pressures, and UN resolutions have been all tried. Peace is the only thing that has not been tried."[178]

---

[173] T. Judt, "Israel: An Alternative Future," in A. Shatz, *Prophets Outcast* (New York: Nation Books, 2004), 399.

[174] N. G. Finkelstein, *Image and Reality of the Israel-Palestine Conflict* (London: Verso, 2003), xxxvii.

[175] M. Warschawski, *Toward an Open Tomb: The Crisis of Israeli Society* (New York: Monthly Review Press, 2004), 101.

[176] A. Cockburn and J. St. Clair, *The Politics of Anti-Semitism* (Petrolia: CA: CounterPunch, 2003), 142.

[177] B. W. Tuchman, *The March of Folly: From Troy to Vietnam* (New York: Ballantine Books, 1984), 96.

[178] A. Eban, *Heritage: Civilization and the Jews* (New York: Summit Books, 1984), 332.

Contrary to this optimism, there is also a notion that without implementing an international force to separate the two warring parties, the necessary trust between Palestinians and Israelis cannot be built, without which the peace loving people on both sides shall be captives to terrorism.[179]

The State of Israel and the Diaspora

At the turn of the century, the Zionist founders envisioned that Jewish life in exile would end once Jewish nationalism in the form of a Jewish state was established. They believed that when the Jews were offered a free life in their own land, they would resettle naturally. Indeed, some in Zionist circles assumed that Jewish life in exile was not only doomed, but it also deserved to be so. Nevertheless, contrary to their expectations, the establishment of the state of Israel did not end the Diaspora, and in fact reinforced it.

The relation of Israel and the Diaspora is an issue of great interest. With the establishment of Israel in 1948, the World Zionist Organization was incorporated into an arm of the government and soon realized that settlement in Israel meant little to the Jewish Diaspora, particularly in the areas with social and economic stability such as Western Europe and North America. Indeed, certain elements of Jewish leadership in these communities wrote it off as dangerous nationalism.[180] In time, the Israel's expectations of the Diaspora changed. All Israel then expected from the Diaspora was support rather than resettlement, as it had been envisioned half a century ago.[181] It is within the context of this discussion that after the establishment of Israel, Abba Eban acknowledged two groups of Jews and valued the role of Jewish communities outside the ancient homeland when he wrote,

From this point onward, there are two impulses at work. There is a longing of Jews to live within their own context, their own land, their own tongue, their own faith, their own particularity, and ultimately to renew the conditions of their original independence. This theme came to

---

[179] B. Avishai, *The Tragedy of Zionism: How its Revolutionary Past Haunts Israel Democracy* (New York, Helios Press, 2002), 366.
[180] Ibid., 151
[181] Ibid., 152.

fulfillment and expression in Israel's rebirth. But for most of history and in most places, the Jews have not been content to be as the ancient prophet described them, a people that dwell alone and is not reckoned among nations. On the contrary, they have been a people that have insisted on sending the repercussions of its history far and wide, into the ocean of universal culture. Thus, there is virtually no civilization that does not have a Jewish component, just as there is no Jewish civilization that does not bear the mark of another culture.[182]

Even though Jewish communities of the Diaspora chose against resettlement in Israel, they advanced their support for Israel generously. In order to understand the depth of the feelings among Jews, we can look at a survey of a Jewish community in Chicago as a representative of American Jewish life. Marshall Sklare of Yeshiva University, who conducted this study in 1965, found that 65 percent of the responders viewed the destruction of Israel as a "deep sense of loss," while another 25 percent considered it as a "sense of loss," but not a deep sense. In another survey in 1989, 65 percent of American Jews viewed the destruction of Israel as "one of the greatest personal tragedies in their lives."[183]

In the eyes of the Diaspora, this deep feeling toward Israel is a reflection of the Holocaust. Israel and its security are viewed as a symbol of Jewish survival and a safeguard against another Holocaust. Accordingly, any suffering inflicted upon Israel is a reminder of nineteen centuries of persecution, alienation, and oppression for the average Jews of the Diaspora.[184]

Finally, it is within the context of this kind of analysis that criticism of Israel's foreign policy is often viewed and discredited as an anti-Semitic sentiment.[185]

The intimate relationship between Israel and the Diaspora is not as sacred as it has been pictured by the media, and at times in the past has gone through rough periods. The reaction of the Diaspora

---

[182] A. Eban, *Heritage: Civilization and the Jews* (New York: Summit Books, 1984), 335–339.

[183] J. J. Goldberg, *Jewish Power: Inside the American Jewish Establishment* (Reading, MA: Addison-Wesley, 1996), 148.

[184] I. Chernus, *American Jews and Israel* (Boulder, CO: Rocky Mountain Peace and Justice Center, 1997).

[185] A. Cockburn and J. St. Clair, *The Politics of Anti-Semitism* (Petrolia, CA: CounterPunch, 2003), 6.

toward Israeli policies is diverse.[186] Although it has been argued
effectively that the Jews of the Diaspora are obligated to support
Israel at any cost and the relations between the two have been
historically viewed in this manner, the Diaspora has not expressed a
homogenous sentiment on a number of subjects.[187] From time to time,
certain segments of the Diaspora have expressed their displeasure on
issues such as Israeli human rights violations, expansion of
settlements in the Palestinian territories, weapons sales to the
apartheid government of South Africa, Israel's secret engagement in
nuclear testing, the indirect role of Israel in the Sabra and Shatilla
refugee camp massacres in 1982, and Israel's role in the Iran-Contra
affair.[188]

On the issue of the expansion of settlements, the Jews of the
Diaspora were split. While Americans for Peace Now and the Jewish
peace lobby condemned "the settlements" and publicly endorsed a
two-state solution to the Israeli-Palestinian conflict, other Jewish
organizations such as the Zionist Organization of America and
National Council of Jewish Women stood solidly behind Israeli
government policies.

However, the most painful period in the relationship between
the Diaspora and Israel that confronted the American Jewish
community against the state of Israel was the issue of conversion to
Judaism and the revival of the controversy over who is a Jew.

According to the Law of Return that was enacted in July
1950, every Jew in the Diaspora has the right to settle in Israel and
immediately become an Israeli citizen. Within the context of this law,
a Jew has been defined as any individual who was born of a Jewish
mother or converted to Judaism. The fact of the matter is that
American Reform rabbis have been involved with the process of
converting the gentile spouses of American Jews for decades. In
Israel, however, Orthodox Judaism does not honor the process of
conversion performed by Reform rabbis and still consider these
spouses gentiles.[189] Indeed, the Orthodox parties in Israel have been

---

[186] Ibid., 53.
[187] T. Judt, "Israel: An Alternative Future," in A. Shatz, *Prophets Outcast* (New
York: Nation Books, 2004), 402.
[188] *Encyclopedia Judaica*, "United States of America," CD-ROM edition, 1997,
Judaica Multimedia.
[189] J. J. Goldberg, *Jewish Power: Inside the American Jewish Establishment*
(Reading, MA: Addison-Wesley, 1996), 338.

challenging the 'who is a Jew?' issue for the past three decades and are keen to redefine it exclusively according to Halakhah or rabbinical law. In spite of the fact that over 80 percent of the Israeli population considers themselves nonreligious and progressive, their reform congregations have no power to force their constituents' views on this matter.[190]

The conflict between American Reform Judaism and Israeli Orthodox Judaism over the "who is a Jew?" issue reached its peak in 1987, when non-Orthodox Jewish organizations united and voiced their displeasure. In the words of Shoshanna Cardin, the past president of the Council of Jewish Federation, "It was the first time American Jewry had publicly challenged the Israeli government."[191] In the aftermath of this event, the government of Yitzhak Shamir broke with religious parties and joined the national coalition. Reform Jews of the Diaspora considered the event of 1987 as a victory, but the "who is a Jew?" issue was not resolved; it just became dormant. Indeed, the Jewish leadership on both sides of the issue preferred to set aside the conflict for the time being.[192]

It was not only American Jews who were unhappy about certain Israel policies here and there; Israelis were also disappointed in the behavior of American Jews from time to time. For instance, during the Gulf War, Israel lost over half a million American Jewish tourists from August 1990 to March 1991, while in the same period no significant drop in tourism from Europeans and Christian Americans was noted.[193]

The attitude and the position of the Diaspora toward Israeli policies and other related matters have been criticized on the grounds that Jewish leadership has not enforced an equal Israel-Diaspora partnership policy.[194] Along the same line of thinking further argument has been advanced that Israel must be freed of any

---

[190] *Encyclopedia Judaica*, "Jewish Identity," CD-ROM edition, 1997, Judaica Multimedia.
[191] J. J. Goldberg, *Jewish Power: Inside the American Jewish Establishment* (Reading, MA: Addison-Wesley, 1996), 340.
[192] Ibid., 346.
[193] *Encyclopedia Judaica*, "America," CD-ROM edition, 1997, Judaica Multimedia.
[194] J. J. Goldberg, *Jewish Power: Inside the American Jewish Establishment* (Reading, MA: Addison-Wesley, 1996), 365.

obligation toward the Diaspora so it may be a state of its own, focusing on its vital interest in the region.[195]

The State of Israel and Jewish Fundamentalism

Into the third millennium, in addition to Israel's conflict with Palestinian Arabs and its disconcerted relationship with the Diaspora, Israel is facing a major internal issue. The topic has attracted the attention of many social scientists and people of opinion of the past decade and has enticed some to express their concern. In 1984, Abba Eban wrote on the subject, "The paradox of the future is that Israel's most intricate and sensitive relationship may come to be not with the Arab world or the international community, but with the Jews—that is, in a deeper sense, with the own self."[196] What is this paradox and where does this contradiction within Israeli society originate?

The establishment of the state of Israel in 1948 was predominantly due to the efforts of the Ashkenazi Jews. The founders of the state were mostly European Jews who had migrated to Palestine after 1932 and particularly during the reign of the Nazis in Germany. Therefore, at the outset of the establishment of the state of Israel, the non-Ashkenazi population of the state was relatively small. By 1965, in light of the migration of Jews from the Middle East and North Africa, the Ashkenazi population declined and stabilized around 40 percent. The non-Ashkenazi population that migrated to Israel was more traditional; they had a strong messianic conviction and hence were often skeptical about Zionism, and above all, a majority of them believed in the total authority of the clergy and viewed rabbis as "holy men" the way they had subordinated to them up to the seventeenth century.[197] Nonetheless, the state of Israel adopted a policy to promote secular education among the Oriental immigrants throughout these years. However, in the mid-1970s, and particularly after the mass migration of Jews from the Soviet Union in the early 1990s, the fundamentalist elements of both Ashkenazi and

---

[195] B. Klug, "A Time to Speak Out," in A. Shatz, *Prophets Outcast* (New York: Nation Books, 2004), 391.

[196] A. Eban, *Heritage: Civilization and the Jews* (New York: Summit Books, 1984), 318.

[197] I. Shahak and N. Mezvinsky, *Jewish Fundamentalism in Israel* (London: Pluto Press, 1999), 48.

Oriental Jews exploited the issue of "education" as an instrument to mobilize the more traditional Jewish masses around their cause.[198] In essence, they rejected the non-Talmudic educational value systems not established by Halakhah. Their opposition to secular education has succeeded in attracting a large number of Oriental and traditional Jews in recent years.

In the present-day Israeli political arena, the fundamentalist activities have been crystallized in the Haredim, or "God-fearing" movement. On the basis of the 1996 elections, Haredim represents about 11 percent of Israeli society and has been organized mainly into three parties:[199] (1) Yahadut Ha'Torah, or "Judaism of the Law," the party of Ashkenazi Haredim; (2) Shas, an acronym for Sephardi List for Tradition, the party of Oriental Haredim; and (3) the National Religious Party, which embraces a more moderate element of fundamentalism. Although Haredim represents a distinct minority of the Israeli population, they carry a prominent political clout. The political power of Haredim stems from the fact that many secular Jews in power, because of political gain, either support the Haredim policies or do not take a strong stand against them. Nevertheless, the relation between the parties of the right and Haredim is stronger.[200]

The tenets of the Haredim movement are based upon an ultra orthodox interpretation of the Talmudic narratives. Haredim is, in essence, an extension of the messianic movement of the pre-Enlightenment period; they view the state of Israel as another Diaspora and try not to be identified with Zionism as much as possible. Moreover, they strongly believe in the uniqueness and particularity of the Jews. More moderate elements of the movement subscribe to the notion that Jews are destined to be unique because of their past history, and this is not a matter of choice.[201] Concepts such as separation of powers, civil liberties, and the rule of civil law mean little to them.[202]

---

[198] M. Warschawski, *Toward an Open Tomb: The Crisis of Israeli Society* (New York: Monthly Review Press, 2004), 59.

[199] I. Shahak and N. Mezvinsky, *Jewish Fundamentalism in Israel* (London: Pluto Press, 1999), 8.

[200] Ibid., 10, 16.

[201] Ibid., 14.

[202] M. Warschawski, *Toward an Open Tomb: The Crisis of Israeli Society* (New York: Monthly Review Press, 2004), 92.

The Haredim movement and its social stance is strongly gender oriented. They have generally followed the Talmudic guidelines where women do not need education, and in fact certain forms of study are forbidden to them. They even impose restrictions on women engaging in certain religious rituals. For instance, the Haredim community prohibits women from praying in groups, wearing *tallit*, or reading from a Torah scroll at the Western Wall.[203] Haredim frequently have referred to women of social and professional status as witches and demons, embracing the old dictum of "women's place is in the home." They condemn women engaging in public activities where they might attain a position of leading men. Like Islamic fundamentalists, Haredim implements a strict separation of girls and boys in schools and men and women in workplaces and make every effort to enforce the women's dress code in their neighborhood.[204]

Because of its messianic viewpoint, the Haredim movement is categorically against the spirit of a "land for peace" exchange. Naturally, their followers vigorously promote the Jewish settlements within the Palestinian territories and are against the government making any territorial concessions. Indeed, soon after the Yom Kippur war in 1973, the National Religious Party founded the Bloc of the Faithful, or Gush Emunim, a coalition of religious fundamentalists and those with ambitious territorial expansion,[205] to promote the establishment of new settlements and expansion of the existing ones.[206] Gush Emunim is committed to preserving the Greater Land of Israel, including the West Bank and Gaza Strip captured in the 1967 war.[207] They are loud and clear in proclaiming that Jews came to Israel not because of political and security considerations but rather because this land was promised to them.[208]According to Israel Shahak, Gush Emunim views the expansion of settlements as a divine

---

[203] R. Haut, "Woman and Judaism: Some Important Issues," *Congress Monthly*, March/April 2001: 12.
[204] I. Shahak and N. Mezvinsky, *Jewish Fundamentalism in Israel* (London: Pluto Press, 1999), 38–39.
[205] A. Eban, *Personal Witness: Israel through My Eyes* (New York: G. P. Putnam's, 1992), 462.
[206] S. G. Freedman, *Jew vs. Jew* (New York: Touchstone, 2000), 166.
[207] G. Wigoder, *The New Standard Jewish Encyclopedia* (New York: Facts on File, 1992), 392.
[208] D. K. Shipler, *Arab and Jew* (New York: Times Books, 1986), 146.

command ordered by God.[209] Therefore, it is not surprising to discover an overrepresentation of Haredim and Gush Emunim followers in the settlements where average Israelis usually do not show an interest to live.[210] In contrast to the state of Israel that is utilizing the settlements as a strategic device to control the territories, the Gush Emunim and Haredim movements view them as a model of a new society, a model that in their assessment would expand and eventually encompass the entire Israeli society.[211] In other words, they envision an Israeli society where the rabbinical authority on social and political matters remains unchallenged. Furthermore, they are hardly concerned about the isolation of the state of Israel in public opinion, and indeed they see it as a safeguard against the assimilation and secularization of Jews.[212]

In the eyes of Jewish fundamentalists, Arthur Hertzberg points out, the state of Israel was neither established as a measure to rescue Jews from anti-Semitism, nor was it founded to create a new culture for Jews who were not comfortable within the tenets of inherited tradition. In contrast, the Jewish state exists to serve God. Hence, in their opinion, the Jewish state has no right to arrive at decisions through a democratic process; on the contrary, any decision made by the state must go through a divine judgment.[213] He further says that it was on the basis of this scheme of thinking that Dr. Baruch Goldstein justified the mass murder of Muslim worshippers in Hebron on February 25, 1994, and Yigal Amir assassinated Prime Minister Yitzhak Rabin on November 4, 1995. Hertzberg concludes, "Both Goldstein and Amir had no doubt that they were committing these killings in good conscience, in obedience to a higher law than the legalities of the State of Israel." [214] By the same token, others have proclaimed that the Jewish fundamentalist circle viewed Prime Minister Rabin and his cabinet as an obstacle to their messianic

---

[209] I. Shahak and N. Mezvinsky, *Jewish Fundamentalism in Israel* (London: Pluto Press, 1999), 86.

[210] S. G. Freedman, *Jew vs. Jew* (New York: Touchstone, 2000), 166.

[211] I. Shahak and N. Mezvinsky, *Jewish Fundamentalism in Israel* (London: Pluto Press, 1999), 83.

[212] A. Eban, *Personal Witness: Israel through My Eyes* (New York: G. P. Putnam's, 1992), 468.

[213] A. Hertzberg, *The Zionist Idea* (Philadelphia: Jewish Publication Society, 1997), 626.

[214] Ibid.

movement,[215] and they argued that the state of Israel, by accepting the Oslo Accord, had betrayed its sacred mission in the process of redemption.[216] However, there is little doubt that numerous religious institutions, among them the International Rabbinical Coalition for Israel, with over three thousand members, were adamantly against the Oslo Accord.[217]

The militancy of some of these messianic movements and their inclination to convey the kingdom of God through armed violence,[218] as were exercised in the case of the Baruch Goldstein massacre and the assassination of Prime Minister Yitzhak Rabin, are quite bothersome. Critics have expressed the opinion that the assassination of Rabin signifies the end of an era of tolerance in Israeli society.[219] Nonetheless, the adoption of violence as a means of struggle is not confined to the Haredim movement, and in fact originates from the fundamental belief systems of all major religions.[220] This violent global religious resurgence is not only a reaction to the inevitability of science and technology and the lifestyle that they produce[221] but is also a reaction against secularism, moral relativism, self-reliance, and an insistence upon the values of order and discipline, and human solidarity.[222]

The Haredim and Gush Emunim movements of the National Religious Party represent a distinct minority, but in contrast to the rest of Israeli society, they are well organized and focused and their leaders are dedicated to their cause. It is because of their dedication and honesty in handling financial matters that they have managed to attract some of the mainstream Israeli Jews in recent years.[223]

Moreover, the ambiguous attitude of the Israeli government and the main political parties toward the fundamentalist movements

---

[215] M. Warschawski, *Toward an Open Tomb: The Crisis of Israeli Society* (New York: Monthly Review Press, 2004), 79.

[216] I. Shahak and N. Mezvinsky, *Jewish Fundamentalism in Israel* (London: Pluto Press, 1999), 87.

[217] S. G. Freedman, *Jew vs. Jew* (New York: Touchstone, 2000), 203.

[218] P. Jenkins, "The Next Christianity," *Atlantic Monthly*, October (2002): 62.

[219] M. Warschawski, *Toward an Open Tomb: The Crisis of Israeli Society* (New York: Monthly Review Press, 2004), 84.

[220] M. Juergensmeyer, *Terror in the Mind of God: The Global Rise of Religious Violence* (Berkeley: University of California Press, 2000), 6.

[221] S. P. Huntington, *The Clash of Civilizations* (New York: Touchstone, 1996), 100.

[222] Ibid., 98.

[223] Ibid.

and their unwillingness to implement discipline, merely because of negative publicity, has been instrumental in the growth of these groups in recent years.[224] In the final analysis, while Israeli policies are generally assessed and planned by the secular Jews, they are often influenced by the Jewish religious past, where the Haredim movement leaves its trail.[225] What the fundamentalist and ultra orthodox groups envision for Israeli society might be far fetched, but they can exercise a stiff resistance against the future dismantling of the Jewish settlements in the territories and the resolution of the Palestinian-Israeli conflict.

On the basis of what has been presented on this topic and in contrast to what it may seem on the surface, the Jewish community of Israel does not enjoy homogeneity. Even though the framework of the state is based upon a secular government, more or less according to the nation-state models that appeared in Europe after the French Revolution, certain religious attributes are most visible in the fabric of the state of Israel. For instance, the judiciary is comprised of two secular and rabbinical court systems. The Knesset officially granted the jurisdiction over marriage and divorce to the rabbinical courts in 1953. Marriage, divorce, alimony, child support, conversion to Judaism, and burial are exclusively under rabbinical jurisdiction. Jews may marry only by a traditional *huppah ve-kiddushin* ceremony, and the procedure must be handled by those rabbis approved by the Chief Rabbinate.[226] These courts exercise their duties according to Halakhah, the legal portion of the Talmud.[227] In spite of a nonobservant majority in Israel who view religion as a matter of individual conscience and reject the entire concept of legislative restrictions on religious grounds, the progressive religious movement has no official standing. They cannot perform the marriage ceremony, grant divorces, or convert gentiles to Judaism. Indeed, the mandatory Ordinance of 1927, which required the consent of the Chief Rabbinate in these matters, is still held as the law of the land.[228] In addition to marriage and related matters, rabbinical courts have also sole

---

[224] I. Shahak and N. Mezvinsky, *Jewish Fundamentalism in Israel* (London: Pluto Press, 1999), 112.

[225] Ibid., 22.

[226] *Encyclopedia Judaica*, "Marriage," CD-ROM edition, 1997, Judaica Multimedia.

[227] G. Wigoder, *The New Standard Jewish Encyclopedia* (New York: Facts on File, 1992), 403.

[228] *Encyclopedia Judaica*, "Marriage," CD-ROM edition, 1997, Judaica Multimedia.

jurisdiction over burial. Moreover, the state provides support for religious school and yeshiva students who are exempt from military service.[229] It has long been argued that Israel can maintain a functional democracy only through one of the two mechanisms: either by curbing the Jewishness of the state to a mere symbolic attribute or by securing a purely Jewish citizenship within the country.[230]

Nonetheless, the combination of the aforementioned factors could conceivably abate the secularism within the Israeli society of the future and in turn deteriorate the state of Israel as an institution of democracy.[231] Jewish fundamentalism, similar to its Islamic and Christian counterparts, attributes the declining moral quality to secularization, rather than growing economic inequalities,[232] and hence has a very low leniency for pluralism and cannot tolerate the divergence of opinions on social and political issues. Concern has been expressed that a future fundamentalist government in Israel would not treat the rest of the Israeli Jews as equal citizens, as their Islamic counterparts in Iran did not either.[233]

Finally, should there be a peace between the Israelis and Palestinians in the future, it is anticipated that the tension and friction between the secular and the fundamentalist elements within Israeli society would intensify. Therefore, it is quite conceivable that Israel would be one of the future battlefields for the struggle between modernity and tradition in the world.

Changing Patterns of Jewish Demography in America

Marrano refugees were indeed the pioneers who escaped the Spanish Inquisition, joined expeditions, crossed the Atlantic Ocean, and created the Jewish communities of the modern world.[234] Most of the Marranos initially settled on the eastern coast of Brazil, a

---

[229] S. G. Freedman, *Jew vs. Jew* (New York: Touchstone, 2000), 75.

[230] N. Chomsky, "Israel and the Palestinians," in A. Shatz, *Prophets Outcast* (New York: Nation Books, 2004), 227.

[231] M. Warschawski, *Toward an Open Tomb: The Crisis of Israeli Society* (New York: Monthly Review Press, 2004), 87.

[232] J. J. Goldberg, *Jewish Power: Inside the American Jewish Establishment* (Reading, MA: Addison-Wesley, 1996), 44 .

[233] I. Shahak and N. Mezvinsky, *Jewish Fundamentalism in Israel* (London: Pluto Press, 1999), 149.

[234] J. J. Goldberg, *Jewish Power: Inside the American Jewish Establishment* (Reading, MA: Addison-Wesley, 1996), 90.

Portuguese colony, and actively participated in sugar plantations and the timber industry. From Brazil, the Marranos migrated to Guyana, a Dutch colony, and later to the British colonies of Barbados and Jamaica. In 1654, a group of twenty-three Brazilian Marranos joined Jacob Bar Simpson, a Jew from Holland, and established the first Jewish community in New Amsterdam (New York).[235] The sporadic migration of Sephardic Jews from Brazil, other South American countries, and Europe continued until the early nineteenth century.

The Jewish population of the United States grew sharply during two distinct periods. From 1800 to 1860, Ashkenazi Jews of mainly German origin migrated to the United States, not because of anti-Semitism but in search of better living conditions. The second phase belongs to a large-scale migration that occurred in the aftermath of the massacre of Eastern European Jews in the 1880s. Hence, the Jewish population of the United States grew to three million in less than forty years. Within the same period, the Jewish population of New York City, that was at eighty thousand, increased to 1.2 million. Accordingly, the ratio of Eastern Europeans to the total Jewish population that was 1:6 in 1880 drastically changed to 5:6 in 1920.

Ashkenazi Jews, when compared to their Eastern European coreligionists, were educated, less traditional, and more receptive to Reform Judaism. They were well acquainted with urban living. The community of Ashkenazi Jews grew rapidly and accumulated wealth and prosperity to secure a strong Jewish establishment. This marked contrast between the German Ashkenazi Jews and the Sephardic Jews of Eastern Europe initially created a significant conflict between the two,[236] but eventually the former learned to participate in the social rehabilitation of the latter.

The very first effort of this type was the establishment of the Hebrew Immigrant Aid Society (HIAS) in 1884. HIAS was instrumental in supporting the Jewish immigrants in the areas of entry process, home finding, and job seeking. In addition to building schools and synagogues, the German Jews founded numerous training professional institutions to teach them the English language,

---

[235] E. Barnavi, *A Historical Atlas of Jewish People* (New York: Schocken Books, 1992), 216.
[236] J. J. Goldberg, *Jewish Power: Inside the American Jewish Establishment* (Reading, MA: Addison-Wesley, 1996), 101 .

accounting, trades, and skills in order to raise their living standards. Textile and clothing industries were exclusively in the hands of German Jews, and therefore they committed themselves to recruit Eastern European Jews into these industries.

Today, North America has the largest Jewish community in the world. Since the U.S. Census prohibits any reference to the religion of citizens, other approaches have been undertaken to assess the American Jewish demography. The National Jewish Population Survey of 1970/71 is an approach that was carried out under the auspices of the Council of Jewish Federation and was based upon a national sample of 7,179 Jewish households. In this study, families were identified as Jewish if any of the occupants either had been born Jewish or had a Jewish-born parent or regarded themselves as being Jewish.[237] A survey of this kind has been undertaken a number of times since 1971. The following is a comparison of the Jewish population in the United States from samples collected in 1970 and twenty years later in 1990.[238]

Population	1970	1990
Total population in Jewish households	5,850,000	8,200,000
Jewish and Jewish background	5,480,000	6,840,000
Core Jewish religion	5,420,000	5,515,000
U.S. population	203,211,000	248,710,000
Total Jews as percentage of U.S. population	2.7	2.7
Core Jews as percentage of U.S. population	2.7	2.2

Jews are the most successful minority in the United States. They owe their outstanding achievements to a number of communal characteristics:

Jews and Episcopalians, more than any other religious groups, pursue education. A higher proportion of Jews pursue education, and on average they spend more years in learning. One out of six Jews and one out of ten Episcopalians have postgraduate

---

[237] D. Singer and R. R. Seldin, *American Jewish Yearbook* (New York: American Jewish Committee, 1992), 80.
[238] Ibid., 144.

degrees.[239] An interest in learning is probably the only stereotypical character of the Jews.[240] In support of this statement, we might review the U.S. government statistics comparing educational achievements of the Jews with those of white Americans, published in 1988.[241]

Education	Jews (%)	White Americans (%)
High school or lower	28.5	62.2
College	18.7	17.3
College completed	26.8	8.11
Graduate studies	25.9	8.7

Jews are attracted to certain lines of occupations. In order to understand this characteristic of Jewish communities, we might first look at the statistics of the Jewish occupations of the Diaspora prepared in the 1930s.[242]

Country	Trade/ Comme rce (%)	Private Sector (%)	Crafts/ Industry (%)	Agricul ture (%)	Clerical (%)
Argentina	55.0	7.0			
Brazil	66.0	6.0			
Germany	49.8	9.4	18.7		
Mexico	68.3	2.5			
Morocco	46.5	7.6	36.1	4.1	
Poland	38.2		45.4		
U.S.A.	50.0	10.0	28.0		
U.S.S.R.		12.8	35.8	7.1	37.2

The proportion of Jews in trade and commerce, particularly after World War II, increased strikingly.[243] However, only a small

---

[239] D. J. Bogue, *The Population of the United States: Historical Trends and Future Projections* (New York: Free Press, 1985), 656.

[240] I. Chernus, Pacifica Radio Archive.

[241] D. Singer and R. R. Seldin, *American Jewish Yearbook* (New York: American Jewish Committee,1992), 159.

[242] G. Wigoder, *The New Standard Jewish Encyclopedia* (New York: Facts on File, 1992), 719.

[243] E. Barnavi, *A Historical Atlas of the Jewish People* (New York: Schocken Books, 1992), 218.

percentage of Jews have been attracted to agriculture.[244] These data indeed are a reflection of the above-average educational achievements of the Jews.[245]

Occupation	Jewish Population (%)	U.S. White Population (%)
Agriculture	—	4.2
Clerical/sales	24.4	17.5
Crafts	8.5	19.8
Managers	16.7	14.3
Operatives	6.4	19.6
Professionals	39.0	15.8
Services	5.0	8.9

Interestingly, this pattern of occupation has not changed significantly over the past forty years in the United States, and the inconsistent efforts to persuade Jews to other occupations have been unsuccessful.

American Jews characteristically have settled in large metropolitan centers. In an estimate prepared in 1991, more than half of the American Jews were living in the six large metropolitan cities:

City	Jewish population
New York	1,671,000
Los Angeles	501,000
Philadelphia	250,000
Miami	250,000
Chicago	248,000
Washington	165,000

American Jews do not have a homogeneous attitude and practice of religion. The classic Jewish communities of the past, with their homogenous attachment to religion, have been replaced by the communities with a marked religious heterogeneity. The National

---

[244] D. Singer and R. R. Seldin, *American Jewish Year Book* (New York: American Jewish Committee, 1992), 162.
[245] D. J. Bogue, *The Population of the United State: Historical Trends and Future Projections* (New York: Free Press, 1985), 658.

Jewish Population Survey of 1990 revealed that the largest single Jewish denomination in America was Reform, followed by Conservatives, nondenominational, and Orthodox Jews.

Denomination	Core Jewish adult responders (%)	Born Jewish Responders (%)
Orthodox	6.1	7.0
Conservative	35.1	39.6
Reform	38.0	42.7
Reconstructionist	1.3	1.5
Just Jewish	10.1	8.0
Something else	9.4	1.1
Total	100.0	100.0

Moreover, the Jewish population of America enjoys dynamism of shifting from one denomination to another. A comparison of the present denominations with those under which Jews were raised strongly supports this notion:

Denomination Raised	Still Orthodox (%)	Still Conservative (%)	Still Reform (%)	Still Recons. (%)	Still Just Jewish (%)
Orthodox	89.1	32.4	11.7	17.1	15.5
Conservative	4.8	60.1	25.9	44.4	18.4
Reform	0.4	4.2	58.6	13.9	14.5
Reconstructionist	—	—	0.3	17.2	—
Just Jewish	5.0	1.5	2.4	5.5	46.7
Non-Jewish	0.7	1.7	1.0	1.9	5.0
Total percentage	100.0	100.0	100.0	100.0	100.0

Adapted from *American Jewish Yearbook 1992.*

For instance, only 60 percent of those who were raised as conservatives are still conservatives. In fact, 32.4 percent of the conservatives were raised Orthodox.

The survey also looked at the pattern of ritual practices among American Jews involving the lighting of Sabbath candles, observing the dietary laws, fasting on Yom Kippur, attending Seder on Passover, and lighting Hanukkah candles as parameters of the assessment.

Practices	Core Jewish Adult Responders (%)
Sabbath candle lighting	16.9
Separate dishes	13.0
Fasting on Yom Kippur	48.5
Attending Seder	61.7
Lighting Hanukkah candles	59.7

Adapted from *American Jewish Yearbook 1992.*

In essence, while the majority of American Jews proclaim that being Jewish is "very" or "fairly" important to them, their Jewishness is merely confined to five rituals of Passover, Yom Kippur, Bar Mitzvah or Bat Mitzvah, and Hanukkah.[246] On the basis of present data, it has been concluded that those who still consider themselves "Jewish" have been shifting away from Orthodoxy toward Reform and a secular Jewish identity.[247] Indeed, this form of religious pluralism has been instrumental in enabling Jews to flourish in America today.[248] The Jewish community in America did not flourish until it was fully integrated into the American social fabric of the postmodern era.

Acceptance of the Jews into mainstream America did not come easily;[249] it was only achieved through the active participation of Jews in a number of social activities. Within a few months after the end of World War II, Jewish organizations launched a broad campaign to eliminate discrimination and prejudice in America against Jews and other minorities.[250] Discrimination and prejudice in housing, immigration, workplace, and employment were legally challenged in every court of the land. Later, the meddling of the state into religion came under legal scrutiny, and efforts were made to force the government to abide by the principle of the separation of

---

[246] J. J. Goldberg, *Jewish Power: Inside the American Jewish Establishment* (Reading, MA: Addison-Wesley, 1996), 72.

[247] Ibid., 132.

[248] A. M. Dershowitz, *The Vanishing American Jew* (New York: Touchstone Book, 1998), 15.

[249] J. J. Goldberg, *Jewish Power: Inside the American Jewish Establishment* (Reading, MA: Addison-Wesley, 1996), 117.

[250] Ibid., 119.

church and state. Finally, the Reform Jewish organizations vigorously campaigned on behalf of a Unitarian family, which resulted in the Supreme Court ruling against Bible reading and prayer in public schools in 1963.[251] Leaving the tragedy of the Holocaust behind, American Jewry in general was now struggling on many fronts for the civil rights of minorities and against discrimination.

The Jewish crusade against discrimination initially started within a few organizations and shortly thereafter spread to black communities, labor unions, and liberal institutions. Indeed, this grassroots movement of the postwar years complemented the work that the American Civil Liberties Union (ACLU) had begun in the 1920s and the National Association for the Advancement of Colored People (NAACP) had engaged in during the 1930s.[252] Strong Jewish representation in these social activities, along with public sympathy for the Jews in the decade that followed World War II, integrated Jews into American life[253] and earned them public acceptance. A survey in 1962 found that only 1 percent of Americans were seeing Jews as a menace, down from 24 percent in 1944; 17 percent perceived Jews as having too much power, down from 67 percent in 1945; and 6 percent said they would think twice before hiring a Jewish person, down from 43 percent in 1940.[254]

The prosperity of the Jewish community in America coincided with a change in demography. In 1937, Jews constituted 4 percent of the American population,[255] a figure that declined to 2.2 percent in 1990.[256] This sharp decline in the Jewish population of America has been attributed to factors such as lower fertility rate,[257] rising age at first marriage,[258] intermarriage,[259] and assimilation into Western culture.

---

[251] Ibid., 124.

[252] Ibid., 121.

[253] Ibid., 132.

[254] Ibid., 117.

[255] N. Glazer, "New Perspective in American Jewish Sociology," in *American Jewish Yearbook* (New York: American Jewish Committee, 1987), 8.

[256] D. Singer and R. R. Seldin, *American Jewish Yearbook* (New York: American Jewish Committee, 1992), 144.

[257] D. Singer and R. R. Seldin, *American Jewish Yearbook* (New York: American Jewish Committee, 1998), 487.

[258] R. M. Geffen, "Intermarriage and the Premise of American Jewish Life," *American Jewish Congress Monthly*, March/April (2001): 6.

[259] National Jewish Population Survey 2000–2001.

Jewish fertility rates, as revealed in the National Jewish Population Survey of 1970[260] and again in 1990,[261] are substantially lower than the general population. In the age bracket of forty to forty-four, Jewish women had an average of 1.6 children, significantly less than the 2.1 for the general white population. These figures for the age bracket of forty-five to forty-nine were 1.9 and 2.3 children for Jewish women and white women, respectively. On the basis of these surveys, the fertility rate of American Jews is indeed slightly below the replacement level,[262] and should this pattern continue, a significant growth in the Jewish population cannot be expected. The following table clearly portrays that the post-World War II decline in the growth of the Jewish population is not confined to the United States and is indeed a global phenomenon:

Period	World Jewish Population Growth
1945–1955	800,000
1955–1965	700,000
1965–1975	242,000
1975–1985	129,000
1985–1995	117,000

Adapted from D. Singer and R. R. Seldin, *American Jewish Yearbook* (New York: American Jewish Committee, 1998), 483.

The impact of intermarriage on the future size of the Jewish population has been a subject of interest and concern. The greater freedom of moving, choice of residence, and type and place of education and employment are among the factors that have significantly contributed to the higher rate of intermarriage in the Jewish communities.

Since 1925, there has been a consistent increase in the proportion of Jews who have married with non-Jews. While prior to 1925 only 2 percent of Jews married non-Jews, the figure increased to 6 percent between 1940 and 1960, to 12 percent between 1961 and 1964, and to 29 percent in the interval between 1985 and 1990.[263]

---

[260] *Encyclopedia Judaica*, "Population," CD-ROM edition, 1997, Judaica Multimedia.
[261] D. Singer and R. R. Seldin, *American Jewish Yearbook* (New York: American Jewish Committee, 1998), 22.
[262] Ibid., 487.
[263] Ibid., 126–128.

Whereas 89 percent of born Jews married another born Jew prior to 1965, this figure declined to 68 percent in the period between 1969 and 1974, to 49 percent between 1975 and 1984, and reached 43 percent in 1985 to 1990, five years preceding the National Jewish Population Survey. Interestingly, half of the participants in another recent Jewish opinion survey believed that opposition to the Jewish-gentile marriage was un-American behavior.[264]

Egon Mayer, who has studied the subject of intermarriage in more detail, concluded that intermarriage did not induce a decline in religiosity.[265] In contrast, he observed that three-quarters of the Jews who intermarried were either agnostic, atheist, or believed in some sort of God, without involving themselves in organized worship to begin with. The decline in religious practice and traditional belief among the mixed marriages, in his opinion, was the cause of intermarriage rather than its effect. In Mayer's study, the majority of intermarriage subjects were college educated, and they had either lost faith after the death or divorce of their parents or were turned off by the regimented or hypocritical aspects of institutional religion.[266]

Religious denomination highly affects both the fertility rate and the intermarriage rate among American Jews. The following table has been adapted from the National Jewish Population Survey of 1990:[267]

	Secular (%)	Reform (%)	Conservative (%)	Hasid/ Orthodox (%)
Intermarriage Rate	72	53	37	3
Fertility Rate	1.62	1.79	1.82	6.4

---

[264] R. M. Geffen, "Intermarriage and the Premise of American Jewish Life," *American Jewish Congress Monthly*, March/April (2001): 8.

[265] In Jewish history, there have been many prominent figures who have intermarried. Among biblical legends, Joseph married an Egyptian; Moses married Zippo rah, a Medianite; David married a Philistine and his mother was a Moabite; King Solomon married women of different ethnicity; and Judah married a Canaanite.

[266] R. D. Feldman, "Who's Afraid of Intermarriage?" *Humanistic Judaism* 27(3) (1999): 29.

[267] A. M. Dershowitz, *The Vanishing American Jew* (New York: Touchstone, 1996), 26.

Should this trend continue, it is projected that by the end of the twenty-first century, not only the Jewish population as a whole will significantly decline, but Hasidic/Orthodox Jews will constitute a larger proportion of the Jewish population.[268,269] Considering that secular and Reform Jews have historically made the greatest contribution of the past two centuries to science, art, and the humanities, the new profile of the American Jewish community shall be devoid of their influence and social clout of the past. In other words, "The Jewish community of 2076 will bear little resemblance to the vibrant, influential, mainstream one of today."[270]

Nonetheless, the anxiety over the shrinking American Jewish community has been a subject of intense discussion. Similarly, a dramatic change in the ratio of reform and secular Jews over conservative and orthodox members have been interpreted as a future drawback in the social, cultural, and political influence of the Jews as a minority in this country. In turn, apprehension over these issues has moved the leadership of American Jewry closer to the Christian Right movement,[271, 272] away from their traditional liberal allies such as labor coalitions, liberal intellectuals, and blacks, partly because of malaise and disintegration of the latter groups during the past two decades.[273] Consequently, the closeness between the two conservative Jewish and Christian establishments seems to be troubling in several respects.

First, the Christian Right movement is categorically against the principle of separation of church and state. In their judgment, America was founded by Christians upon Christian values; hence, they are trying hard to restore Christian values into the institutions of the government, the values that liberal forces, in their opinion, have taken away from them. In the words of the leaders of the movement,

---

[268] Ibid., 24.

[269] E. Abrams, *Faith or Fear: How Jews Can Survive in a Christian America* (New York: Free Press, 1997), 177.

[270] A. M. Dershowitz, *The Vanishing American Jew* (New York: Touchstone, 1996), 25.

[271] J. J. Goldberg, *Jewish Power: Inside the American Jewish Establishment* (Reading, MA: Addison-Wesley, 1996), 110.

[272] A. M. Dershowitz, *The Vanishing American Jew* (New York: Touchstone, 1996), 157.

[273] J. J. Goldberg, *Jewish Power: Inside the American Jewish Establishment* (Reading, MA: Addison-Wesley, 1996), 365.

"If the Christian people work together, they can succeed during this decade in winning back control of the institutions that have been taken from them over the past 70 years. Expect confrontations that will be not only unpleasant but at times physically bloody."[274] Indeed, historically many elements within the conservative camp view liberalism a force undermining state and church.[275] Rightfully, certain elements among the leaders of American Reform Judaism have expressed their concern that the Christian Coalition's "real priorities remain changing the Constitution to tear down the wall separating church and state."[276] In essence, the doctrine of the Christian Coalition movement calls for a "Christian America" and a "Christian Nation,"[277] hence undermining the very basic principle of secular democracy.

Second, the Christian Right is strong-minded enough to dismantle the social and political pluralism that has played an essential role in promoting the civic rights of minorities. In this setting, the Jews, instead of having an equal status with Christians in society, will only be tolerated. The final act in the scenario of evangelical theocracy calls for the conversion of Jews to Christianity,[278] a practice that is already in progress in the form of institutions like Jews for Jesus and has been quite disturbing to most Jews.[279] Indeed, as far as evangelical theologians are concerned Judaism as a religion ended after the destruction of the Second Temple in 70 CE.[280]

In other words, those social attributes of America that made it possible for Jews to enter the mainstream of society post–World War II are the ones that have been targeted by the Christian Right movement. It is within the context of this discussion that the Christian

---

[274] R. Boston, *The Most Dangerous Man in America?* (New York: Prometheus Books, 1996), 63.

[275] B. Englemann, *Germany without Jews* (New York, Bantam Books, 1984), 24.

[276] D. Singer and R. R. Seldin, *American Jewish Yearbook* (New York: American Jewish Committee, 1998), 80.

[277] R. Boston, *The Most Dangerous Man in America?* (New York: Prometheus Books, 1996), 155.

[278] A. M. Dershowitz, *The Vanishing American Jew* (New York: Touchstone, 1996), 143.

[279] E. Abrams, *Faith or Fear: How Jews Can Survive in a Christian America* (New York: Free Press, 1997), 80.

[280] Ibid., 86.

Right movement is viewed by many as the most serious external adversary to Jewish equal rights of the postmodern era.[281]

The Crisis of the Jewish Identity: The Future Perspective

As late as the seventeenth century, it was clear who was a Jew. Within the Jewish circles, everyone was a Jew, and outside these communities, everyone was a gentile. Both in Europe and elsewhere by far, Jews were living in separate quarters, and every one of them knew who was a Jew. In order to control the life in these quarters, the Christian states of Europe had relinquished part of their power to the religious leaders who had every authority to mold the Jewishness in these communities.

In the aftermath of the Jewish emancipation of the eighteenth century and later, the new circumstances encouraged Jewish communities to tear down the walls that had separated them from the outside world. Steadily, Jews left ghettoes, often against rabbinical advice, and joined the rest of the world. Soon the Jewish reformation of the nineteenth and early twentieth centuries brought on a variety of denominations: ultra-Orthodox, Orthodox, Conservative, Reform, and secular Judaism.[282] Therefore, the religion and ethnicity of Jews that for centuries was a single entity moved apart. Hence, a spectrum of Jews emerged, and the Jewish communities diversified and lost their traditional unity. At one end of the spectrum are the Orthodox and ultra-Orthodox Jews who do not distinguish Jewish ethnicity from the Jewish religion, are not prepared to compromise Halakhah with modernity, and simply do not see non-Orthodox Jews as authentic.[283] At the other end of the spectrum are secular Jews, who strongly believe in Jewishness, or Jewish peoplehood, apart from the Jewish religion. And in between there are myriad combinations of the two extremes.

Today, the struggle between the two extremes within the spectrum—what has been called a "civil war"—has torn apart the

---

[281] A. M. Dershowitz, *The Vanishing American Jew* (New York: Touchstone, 1996), 149.

[282] A. Eban, *Heritage: Civilization and the Jews* (New York: Summit Books, 1984), 334.

[283] E. Abrams, *Faith or Fear: How Jews Can Survive in a Christian America* (New York: Free Press, 1997), 183.

Jewish communities, congregations, and families.[284] This civil war has been waged on different fronts such as the role of women in worship, the relation of the Diaspora to the state of Israel, the Middle East peace process, the conversion of gentiles to Judaism, and the role of Orthodox authority in civil life. Indeed, this is a struggle between liberal and conservative, between tradition and modernity, between individual rights and communal priorities, and above all, between unity and pluralism.

It has been argued that after almost half a century, because secular forces have relinquished their responsibility in this debate to the Orthodox elements, the latter have been exclusively charged to define the Jewish identity. In the meantime, the Jewish orthodoxy also has not shied away in asserting their authority in this matter, in spite of the fact that they only represent a minority of the world Jewry.

At the core of this civil war that has afflicted the Jewish communities of the postmodern era is the issue of Jewish identity and the ongoing controversy over "who defines that identity?" and on what basis we decide "who is a Jew?"

Orthodox and ultra-Orthodox Jews altogether make up about 7 percent of the Jews in the United States and about 11 percent in Israel. About one-third of these groups are ultra-Orthodox Jews who have been shaped by the Haredim movement in both countries.[285] In the opinion of Orthodox Jews, the fundamental culture of the past is simply more convincing and is a more genuine guide for the future. They believe that the modern world and its accomplishments may only be utilized at God's service. They argue that modernity and its achievements in science, medicine, and technology are worthy as long as they are used to serve God and promote the Jewish tradition. Men, in their view, must engage in studying the Torah, and women are expected to give birth and raise children, who will in turn serve God. The Haredims, in contrast to Reform and secular Judaism, are vocal, assertive, and committed to their cause and maintain an uncompromising position on present-day secular issues such as social pluralism, women's rights, conversion to Judaism, exclusivity of the

---

[284] S. G. Freedman, *Jew vs. Jew* (New York: Touchstone, 2000), 23.
[285] National Jewish Population Survey 1990.

Jews,[286] and exchange of land for peace with Palestine.[287] While in the past they were in seclusion, in more recent years, and particularly after the triumph of the Six-Day war, they are actively pursuing bringing back Jews into their stringent and orthodox circle. Contrary to the silent majority of Jews, the Orthodox Jews and ultra-Orthodox Haredim are always present in the social arena. The Haredims use education as their stronghold. They provide teachers for the bulk of day schools, where mainstream Jews either are not interested in participating or have no resources. While the average Jews have enthusiastically encouraged their children to get into secular professions such as medicine and law, the children of Orthodox families fill yeshiva schools.[288] The graduates of these religious schools eagerly accept teaching positions in day schools and naturally present their own version of Judaism to Jewish children—the stringent teachings that sometimes may shock their parents. Consequently, Jewish education has been entirely left in the hands of Orthodox religious elements.[289] In contrast, secular Jews were active and resourceful in Jewish literature only in the period between the Jewish Enlightenment, Haskalah, and World War II. Today, very few of them can effectively participate in a meaningful dialogue on the subject of Jewish education.[290]

In the United States, Haredims have their own rabbinical union, *Agudas Ha-Rabonnim*, which is comprised of Orthodox rabbis who are not affiliated with the mainstream Orthodox Rabbinical Council of America and who refuse to join other Jewish organizations.[291] At the climax of their clash with the rest of American Jewry, the Agudas Ha-Rabonnim denounced Reform and conservative Judaism, the movements that represent more than two-thirds of the Jewish population in America, as "not Judaism at all."[292] In exchange, the chancellor of the Theological Seminary, a Jewish conservative institution, called the Orthodox Chief Rabbinate of Israel

---

[286] A. Hertzberg and A. Hirt-Manheimer, *Jews: The Essence and Character of a People* (New York: HarperSanFrancisco, 1998), 139.

[287] *Encyclopedia Judaica*, "Haredim," CD-ROM edition, 1997, Judaica Multimedia.

[288] S. G. Freedman, *Jew vs. Jew* (New York: Touchstone, 2000), 224.

[289] A. M. Dershowitz, *The Vanishing American Jew* (New York: Touchstone, 1996), 18.

[290] Ibid., 293.

[291] *Encyclopedia Judaica*, "Haredim," CD-ROM edition, 1997, Judaica Multimedia.

[292] S. G. Freedman, *Jew vs. Jew* (New York: Touchstone, 2000), 24.

"dysfunctional" and "without a scintilla of moral worth."[293] Nonetheless, this kind of frenzied rhetoric among different denominations continues.

In Israel, Haredim parties are often invited to participate in coalition governments with both major parties, and in exchange they receive concessions, particularly in the area of education. Here again, Jewish education in its scope goes far beyond religion and rituals and more and more comes under the influence of orthodoxy.

On the other extreme, secular Jews argue that within the last two centuries, the West has genuinely accepted the Jews, and institutional anti-Semitism, for all practical purposes, is nonexistent. Although there are still anti-Semitic sentiments here and there, these sentiments are not endorsed or supported by the state or church institutions. When a gentile engages in anti-Semitic behavior, it is actually the gentile world that condemns that behavior. Today, an anti-Semitic sentiment is a stigma by which no decent gentile would like to be identified. We have been indisputably accepted into the mainstream of Western life, where opportunities are no longer restricted to a few of us as court physicians or state financiers like we used to be in the Middle Ages. Our rights as citizens are no longer questioned, and we can grasp and enjoy opportunities as they arise before us. Under these circumstances, many leave Judaism, through secularization and intermarriage, because they do not see a strong justification in remaining traditional Jews.[294] In contrast to lay opinion, the bulk of the Jews who leave Judaism do not assimilate; instead, they secularize. In other words, they do not depart from Judaism to become Christians or Muslims; they leave traditional Judaism merely to embrace social pluralism.

Keeping the attributes of both extremes in mind, one could only envision that secularization, intermarriage, and the low fertility rate of the Jews are closer to the secular end of the Jewish continuum, and combined with the higher fertility rate of the Jews closer to the religious core of Judaism, would drastically change the profile of the Jewish communities of the future. To our surprise, those communities would lose their present-day creativity, resourcefulness, and

---

[293] Ibid.

[294] A. M. Dershowitz, *The Vanishing American Jew* (New York: Touchstone, 1997), 45.

inspiration,[295] the attributes that by and large have been carried on the shoulders of Reform and secular Jews through the past two centuries.

Indeed, the Jews closer to the secular extreme not only have contributed vastly to world science, art, music, and literature, but the grand vision of the Zionists to establish the state of Israel came through the hard work of more secular Jews.[296] In essence, those closer to the secular extreme of the Jewish continuum remind us that individualism and the move toward the privatization of religious beliefs are crucial in protecting social pluralism and tolerance.

Hence, we must embrace a spirit of the Reformation and include all denominations of Judaism under a common canopy, rather than excluding those of us who may show little interest in stringent religious rules and the meaningless rituals.[297] At the turn of the millennium, the ever-increasing diversity within the Jewish communities has created a great dilemma.

These communities may either write off those members who do not meet the stringent traditional definition of a "Jew" and call them "non-Jews," or alternatively they can respond to the interests and the needs of these communities and revisit their definition of who is a Jew.[298]

There is no indisputable answer to the question of "who is a Jew?" The definition of "who is a Jew?" has changed according to circumstances throughout Jewish history and therefore can be changed again to accommodate the requirements of modern communities. In the biblical period, all of those who belonged to the Jewish community were Jews. In this phase of Jewish history, a patrilineal descent was strongly recognized, and a Jew was defined as an individual whose father was a Jew.[299] The strangers who joined the Jewish communities were considered Jews once they had undergone

---

[295] Ibid., 55.

[296] D. Liberman, "Can There Be a Judaism Without Jewish Ethnicity?" *Humanistic Judaism* 25:3 (1997): 22.

[297] E. J. Klien, "Dershowitz's Wake-up Call for Secular Jews," *Humanistic Judaism* 25:3 (1997): 50.

[298] B. Reisman, "Are American Jews Assimilating or Acculturating?" *Humanistic Judaism* 25:3 (1997): 19.

[299] A. M. Dershowitz, *The Vanishing American Jew* (New York: Touchstone, 1998), 204.

circumcision, although there are indications in the Bible that they were not fully accepted as Jews.[300]

During the rabbinical period, this principle was changed, and by the second century CE, a Jew was defined as someone who was born to a Jewish mother. It is not well understood why rabbis changed the biblical patrilineal to the rabbinical matrilineal principle. While the role of mother in the education of children and the denial of paternity rights in cases of "sinful union"[301] have often been cited as explanations, it is quite conceivable that the new principle has been adopted from Roman law.[302]

Another definition of Jewish identity was offered by Maimonides, a representative of the orthodoxy of the twelfth century, in his famous "articles of faith."[303] In his opinion, he who believed with perfect faith in the following "thirteen principles of Judaism" was considered a Jew:

1. The existence of God, which is perfect and sufficient unto itself and which is the cause of the existence of all other beings.

2. God's unity, which is unlike all other kinds of unity.

3. God must not be conceived in bodily terms, and the anthropomorphic expressions applied to God in Scripture have to be understood in a metaphorical sense.

4. God is eternal.

5. God alone is to be worshiped and obeyed. There are no mediating powers able freely to grant men's petitions, and intermediaries must not be invoked.

6. Prophecy.

---

[300] Deuteronomy 14:21.

[301] The union of a Jewish woman and a gentile husband was a rare event in the traditional Jewish communities up to the turn of the century. Historically, rabbis considered the marriage between a Jewish girl and her gentile husband a "sinful union." In these circumstances, the parents often regarded their daughter as dead and mourned her. The children of these marriages were considered Jews, but their gentile father, in the eyes of rabbis, had no paternal rights. Similar treatment was exercised in cases of rape of Jewish women by gentile men.

[302] A. M. Dershowitz, *The Vanishing American Jew* (New York: Touchstone, 1998), 366.

[303] *Encyclopedia Judaica*, "Articles of Faith," CD-ROM edition, 1997, Judaica Multimedia.

7. Moses is unsurpassed by any other prophet.

8. The entire Torah was given to Moses.

9. Moses's Torah will not be abrogated or superseded by another divine law, nor will anything be added to or taken away from it.

10. God knows the actions of men.

11. God rewards those who fulfill the commandments of the Torah and punishes those who transgress them.

12. The coming of the Messiah.

13. The resurrection of the dead.

According to this rigid definition, one may be born to a Jewish mother yet not be considered a Jew. Indeed, it has been proclaimed that such an intransigent definition only considers a small number of never-doubting fundamentalists as real Jews today.[304]

Moses Mendelssohn, in the period immediately before emancipation, defined the Jewish identity in a manner that was partly compatible with the spirit of the Age of Enlightenment and yet justified the Jewish particularity. In his opinion, three articles constituted the Jewish identity:

1. Eternal truths or verities, what has been more or less crystallized within the Mosaic Ten Commandments, generally based upon reason, is common to many religions and is compatible with the universal concept of religion expressed by Spinoza.

2. Acceptance of the Bible as a historical fact

3. Practice of ceremonial laws or rituals that were bringing about morality and religiosity, referring to the Jewish chosenness.

In the process of Jewish emancipation and afterward, the last article was widely challenged by many rational thinkers on different grounds. For example, how ceremonial practice such as separating meat and dairy in kitchens and on the table would affect our morality; why Jewish ceremonial law has such an impact; and why other forms of rituals would not make us better people.

---

[304] A. M. Dershowitz, *The Vanishing American Jew* (New York: Touchstone, 1998), 208.

What Moses Mendelssohn had composed as articles of Jewish identity did not convince many and failed to persuade even the generation that followed him, including most of his children.[305]

The emancipation of Jews in Europe and the foundation of Reform Judaism in Germany and the United States advanced a more liberal definition of "who is a Jew?" A Jew was then defined as someone who adopted primarily the moral values and the cultural contents of Judaism.[306] Therefore, at the climax of nineteenth-century liberalism, one could maintain his or her Jewish identity despite minimal or no association with Jewish communities.

Political Zionism of the twentieth century attached a national and territorial attribute to the definition of "who is a Jew?" In the opinion of the pioneers of political Zionism, once Jews of the Diaspora settled in their homeland Israel, they are all considered Jews, regardless of their religious denomination.[307] By the same token, Zionists argued that secular Judaism is only possible when Jews enjoy their own territorial concentration in the form of a nation. However, this definition becomes blurred and less convincing when we realize that Orthodox Israelis consider themselves primarily Jews, while the secular segments of the society call themselves above all Israelis.[308] In other words, mere territorial and national identity does not provide the same level of Jewishness.

Another depiction of Jewish identity defines the Jews as historical ethnic people "into which a person is born and to which he belongs, whether he lives up in his linguistic, cultural and religious habits or not."[309] According to this definition, then, everyone born to Jewish parents is considered a Jew even if he or she converted to another religion or decided to abandon Jewish religious practice altogether.

Others have argued that Jewish identity is based upon Jewish suffering, meaning that Jews are those who suffer as Jews, regardless

---

[305] D. B. Ruderman, *Jewish Intellectual History: 16th to 20th Century* (Chantilly, VA: Teaching Company, 2002), Part II (CD-ROM).
[306] Ibid.
[307] E. J. Klien, "Dershowitz's Wake-up Call for Secular Jews," *Humanistic Judaism* 25:3 (1997): 50.
[308] *Encyclopedia Judaica*, "Jewish Identity," CD-ROM edition, 1997, Judaica Multimedia.
[309] Ibid.

of their own perception of suffering and the intensity of their religious practice.[310] Along this line of thinking came the notion that we have to find out how our adversaries identify us.[311] For instance, in order to spot a Jew, the Nazis did not go through the trouble of determining whether a Jew kept Sabbath or how often he or she attended synagogue. On the other hand, they simply considered all who claimed to be Jew and those who were born to Jewish parents as Jews. In essence, it is the conscience of the individual that defines the Jewish identity.

Finally, there is the opinion that the Jewish identity is not exclusively abstracted in Jewish religion; rather, Jewishness is indeed identified by many parameters like Jewish literature, art, music, ethics, culture, as well as religion.[312] In fact, there is no single common characteristic that defines Jewishness. These attributes are dynamic and ever-changing features molded and modified in time according to circumstances. Throughout history, many Jewish features, characters, and attributes have disappeared and have given their place to new and different ones. Even if we insist that religion is the single common characteristic upon which Jews and non-Jews may be distinguished from each other, then we have to define which version of religion or denomination we must consider as Judaism. The more Orthodox version of religion we select as our standard, the larger segment of our Jewish population will be lost to non-Jewish circles.

Consequently, Orthodox Jews will grow out of proportion and other denominations shrink, and it is quite likely that we give up many of our vital attributes as a civilization.[313] *In other words, the orthodoxy by overindulgence in rituals rejects more of our community toward assimilation and secularization.* Along these lines, Hertzberg asserts that the orthodoxy could not keep most of its children within its ranks through the nineteenth and twentieth centuries, and it was indeed for that reason that modern Jewish denominations flourished. How can they then claim that their version of Judaism is the only

---

[310] Ibid.

[311] S. G. Freedman, *Jew vs. Jew* (New York: Touchstone, 2000), 344.

[312] Ibid., 350.

[313] B. Avishai, *The Tragedy of Zionism: How its Revolutionary Past Haunts Israel Democracy* (New York, Helios Press, 2002), 361.

effective remedy to assimilation today?[314] There are so many decent Jews who contribute enormously to the Jewish civilization, and yet they do not necessarily follow the Jewish rituals. By the same token, some have gone so far as to suggest that even atheism does not conflict with Judaism, since there are so many good Jews who may have serious doubts about God.[315]

The majority of world Jewry in modern times, however, has defined the Jewish identity *as a community of history and destiny of those who still feel their concern and interest in this community.*[316] Since first century C.E. Jews lost their sovereign boundaries and Hebrew was replaced initially by Aramaic and later Jews spoke and wrote in Arabic and Spanish, and then in German, English and French. Some communities adopted dialects such as Yiddish and Ladino. However, none of these were recognized as the national language of Jewish people. Today, Jews also do not enjoy a common cultural tradition. All they have in common is a pattern of social behaviors and a religion— albeit practiced variably that have provided them a false national status.[317]

As we glance through these pages, we realize there is no single and universally acceptable definition of "who is a Jew?" Therefore, there are two choices before us. Either, like the Christians of post-Protestant Reformation, we are prepared to set aside our differences and focus on our common characteristics, or we come to a bitter realization that our unity throughout history was all because of our external enemies, without which we shall be hopelessly divided.[318]

Jews enter into the third millennium with a conviction that the forces of modernity are exceedingly strong,[319] and in order to thrive in this environment, they must adapt to the new circumstances. In essence, the controversy over "who is a Jew?" or the Jewish

---

[314] A. Hertzberg and A. Hirt-Manheimer, *Jews: The Essence and Character of a People* (New York: HarperSanFrancisco, 1998), 283.

[315] A. M. Dershowitz, *The Vanishing American Jew* (New York: Touchstone, 1998), 187.

[316] *Encyclopedia Judaica*, "Jewish Identity," CD-ROM edition, 1997, Judaica Multimedia.

[317] A. Koestler, *The Thirteenth Tribe* (New York, Random House, 1976), 225

[318] S. G. Freedman, *Jew vs. Jew* (New York: Touchstone, 2000), 347.

[319] S. P. Huntington, *The Clash of Civilizations* (New York: Touchstone, 1997), 78.

identity formulates the ways Jews are going to face up to the social
challenges of the postmodern era. It is up to us how to grasp this issue
and from which angle to look upon it. Are we going to shape our
future by becoming less tribal and build less on a perception of us and
them?[320] How are we going to look at the Jewish mysteries of
preservation, resonance, and *suffering*? In other words, how did we
manage to survive and have such an immense impact on religion,
philosophy, art, science, and literature of other peoples, and why did
we go through so much suffering throughout history? Are we going to
attribute them to our "chosenness," or, in contrast, do we see them as
reflections of two millennia of persecution, intimidation, and coercion
we have been through? Do we arrive at the understanding that what
really matters is not what we think, but how we behave?[321] Are we
going to take a realistic approach to intermarriage? Are we going to
accept those who intermarried and embrace them among ourselves, or
will we reject them as non-Jews? Would the progressive elements of
world Jewry recognize their responsibility in the Jewish education
and willingly collaborate with Orthodox elements to fight against
Jewish ignorance and illiteracy, or will they continue to relinquish
this great task exclusively to the orthodoxy, as they have done in the
past? Would a new Jewish leadership surface and lead us to a
compromise where individuals would do what promotes the
communal interests and the community would respect Jewish
multiplicity? Do we succeed in establishing a social pluralism in our
communities and bridge the gaps between secularism and orthodoxy?
Conversely, are we going to insist upon the unity under one's
terms,[322] expecting every Jew to think and act like us? Would our
Jewish leadership continue to fasten exclusively to the Holocaust and
anti-Semitism or would they address issues such as pluralism and
continuity in our communities?[323] Are we going to show sensitivity to
women's needs and address their rights as we enter into the third
millennium, or we are going to be adamant about our traditional
gender differences? Are we going to support only those social forces

---

[320] J. Chuman, "Religion and Ethnicity: Which Has More Saying Power?"
Humanistic Judaism 25(3) (1997): 24.
[321] A. Hertzberg and A. Hirt-Manheimer, *Jews: The Essence and Character of a
People* (New York: HarperSanFrancisco, 1998), 141.
[322] E. Abrams, *Faith or Fear: How Jews Can Survive in a Christian America* (New
York: Free Press, 1997), 184.
[323] S. G. Freedman, *Jew vs. Jew* (New York: Touchstone, 2000), 343.

that justify political authority by constantly invoking God and religion,[324] or are we going to support those social elements enthusiastic about the principles of the separation of church and state, a lack of which would bring more suffering to our people?[325] Only the future carries the answers to these questions, which might resolve our prospect at this historic juncture. In the words of Abba Eban, we are a small people with a large experience,[326] and then it is up to us how to utilize that skill toward building the future as a people.

Chronology:

1929	Over 200 Jews were massacred in clashes with Palestinian Arabs
1947	U.N. Resolution 181 on partition of Palestine
1948	British mandate on Palestine ended and state of Israel was established
1948	Israel's military victory in first war
1951	Assassination of King Abdullah of Jordan
1956	The Suez War
1958	Palestine Liberation Organization was founded
1967	The Six-Day war
1967	U.N. passed Resolution 242 calling upon Israel to pull back to borders prior to Six-Day war
1970	Gamal Abdul Nasser declared that a durable peace with Israel was possible
1972	Jordan offered the Federation plan of United Arab Kingdom
1973	Yom Kippur war
1976	United States vetoed the U.N. Security Council resolution calling for a settlement along 1967 borders
1979	Israel returned Sinai Peninsula to Egypt
1981	Assassination of President Anwar Sadat of Egypt
1982	Israel invaded Southern Lebanon; massacre of Palestinians in Sabra and Shatilla camps

---

[324] P. Jenkins, "The Next Christianity", *Atlantic Monthly*, October 2002: 55.
[325] A. M. Dershowitz, *The Vanishing American Jew* (New York: Touchstone, 1998), 157.
[326] A. Eban, *Heritage: Civilization and the Jews* (New York: Summit, 1984), 335.

1987	Intifada began in Gaza Strip
1993	Yasser Arafat and Yitzhak Rabin signed the Oslo Accord
1995	Assassination of Prime Minister Yitzhak Rabin
1999	Ehud Barak was elected as prime minister and pledged to follow Oslo Accord, but he reiterated that Israel would never pull back to 1967 borders
2001	Ariel Sharon was elected as prime minister of Israel, implementing a tougher policy toward the Arabs
2004	Yasser Arafat, president of Palestinian authority, dies

T

U

V

W